A History of the British Isles

Third Edition

Jeremy Black

No portion of this publication may be reproduced, copied or
transmitted save with written permission or in accordance with
the provisions of the Copyright, Designs and Patents Act 1988,
or under the terms of any licence permitting limited copying
issued by the Copyright Licensing Agency, Saffron House,
6–10 Kirby Street, London EC1N 8TS.

Any person who does any unauthorized act in relation to this
publication may be liable to criminal prosecution and civil claims
for damages.

The author has asserted his right to be identified as the author
of this work in accordance with the Copyright,
Designs and Patents Act 1988.

First edition 1996, published in hardback only
First time in paperback 1997
Second edition 2003
Third edition 2012

Published by
PALGRAVE MACMILLAN

Palgrave Macmillan in the UK is an imprint of Macmillan Publishers
Limited, registered in England, company number 785998, of
Houndmills, Basingstoke, Hampshire RG21 6XS.

Palgrave Macmillan in the US is a division of St Martin's Press LLC,
175 Fifth Avenue, New York, NY 10010.

Palgrave Macmillan is the global academic imprint of the above
companies and has companies and representatives throughout
the world.

Palgrave® and Macmillan® are registered trademarks in the
United States, the United Kingdom, Europe and other countries.

ISBN 978–0–230–36205–5   hardback
ISBN 978–0–230–36206–2   paperback

This book is printed on paper suitable for recycling and made from
fully managed and sustained forest sources. Logging, pulping and
manufacturing processes are expected to conform to the
environmental regulations of the country of origin.

A catalogue record for this book is available from the British Library.

A catalog record for this book is available from the Library of Congress.

10   9   8   7   6   5   4   3   2   1
21 20 19 18 17 16 15 14 13 12

Printed in China

For Jonathan Barry

Contents

List of Maps

Preface

In some respects this has been the most interesting and most difficult book that I have attempted. Most interesting because I have had to read so widely, most difficult because of the discipline of writing in accordance with particular guidelines and to a tight word-limit. What has been discarded in endless redrafting could have made several books, which shows not only the richness and variety of the history of the British Isles, but also the different ways in which it could be approached. Any history inevitably invites suggestions about different approaches, contrasting arguments, divergent conclusions. The history of the British Isles is the history of the English, Irish, Scots and Welsh. Britain itself has a shorter history as a united state and it is important to place due weight on separate and diverse national traditions.

At the risk of anachronism, terms such as England, Wales, Scotland, Ireland, France and East Anglia are used throughout so that modern readers can better understand which areas are being referred to. The Act of Union of 1800 with Ireland created from 1801 the state termed the United Kingdom of Great Britain and Ireland. After southern Ireland became the Irish Free State (from 1937, Eire), following the Anglo-Irish treaty of 1921, the United Kingdom became the United Kingdom of Great Britain and Northern Ireland. Great Britain therefore refers to England, Scotland and Wales. However, neither United Kingdom nor Great Britain lend themselves to use as adjectives, and the term Britain is frequently applied to both. As employed in this book, it does not imply the existence of a state nor any teleological development towards such a power, but rather, like Italy for most of its history, a geographical entity. The British Isles is the term used for Britain and Ireland.

There is no obvious way to tackle this subject. It is clear that there is much to be gained from asking questions about the relationship between the constituent parts of Britain and, indeed, the British Isles. These reveal the contingent nature of relations and undermine any teleology of the emergence of Britain. They also place the history of the parts of the British Isles in a more meaningful setting than that implied by such a teleology, namely in a narrative and analytical context set in part by relations and comparisons with other parts of the world. It is also important, however, to underline the extent to which the history of the British Isles is one of separate peoples and polities who only comparatively recently were brought together in a British state. There is therefore a separateness to much of this book that is deliberate, and an attempt to avoid a suggestion that a history of Britain involves downplaying this separateness. There is also a determined effort to give due weight to England, the most powerful and populous of the British entities and the one that usually receives insufficient attention when the British perspective is emphasised. It is particularly important not to downplay the regionalism of much English history.

There is no point pretending some Olympian detachment or Delphic omniscience. The emphasis between the sections, geographical, thematic and chronological, reflects personal choice. They reflect my views as a historian faced with the difficult tasks of trying to cover such a vast subject. It is important for the reader to be aware that what is here, how it is treated and organised, and what is omitted, reflects a process of choice. The past is viewed very differently by commentators, and these differences should lead us to more searching questions about what is being discussed and about the process of writing history. Readers should consider how *they* would organise the book.

This point is stressed because this book is written in a conviction that a 'trade' or 'text' book should not talk down to the readers nor treat them as a passive body that is there to be entertained. I work on the basis that my readers are intelligent people who may not have the time to study the subject but who do not need to be restricted to the comforting pattern of a conventional approach and narrative; which, in the case of this topic, generally means a book devoted to political history. I hope my decisions on what to include and how best to cover it prove as stimulating for the readers as they have done for the writer.

This edition is timely and necessary both because of the wealth of scholarship that has appeared since the last one was written and because the content and teaching of national history are currently highly contentious. Moreover, there is the question of how best to understand recent trends. This edition benefits from a complete rewriting of the early and concluding sections as well as from greater attention to social developments. More generally, the entire text has been revised and new material has been incorporated throughout.

It is a great pleasure to dedicate this edition to Jonathan Barry, a good friend of many years' standing and fellow member of the Exeter community. I have always greatly admired his grasp of the complexities of social and cultural history. In preparing this edition, I have benefited from the opportunity to visit historical sites that were new to me, culminating with a visit to the Outer Hebrides in July 2011. British history feels very different viewed from within standing stone circles at Callanish on Lewis or clambering up nearby drystone towers.

History is a cumulative process and I am very conscious of the debt I owe others. I am most grateful to Jocelyn Stockley for meticulous help with the copy-editing. I would particularly like to thank Jonathan Barry, Michael Bennett, Bill Gibson, David Griffiths, Bob Higham, Keith Laybourn, Murray Pittock, Michael Prestwich, Bill Purdue, Nigel Saul and an anonymous reader for commenting on all or part of an earlier draft. In doing so, I wish to underline the extent to which the work of all historians rests on a discussion with that of their predecessors and colleagues.

JEREMY BLACK

Introduction

That the past, our past, can be seen in so many different lights adds to its fascination. There is not only the question of what to discuss, but the problem of how best to do so. If it is difficult enough for us to establish the course of history, it is even harder to assess causes and to explain the complexity of some. These are especially acute problems with a book of this scale. There is a powerful tendency, when writing a history that stretches over more than two millennia but relatively few pages, to shape the past into patterns and to stress the beneficial nature of the changes that have occurred. This Whiggish approach to British history was particularly dominant in the nineteenth and early twentieth centuries; it emphasised a Protestant identity for the nation, the growth of respect for property, the rule of law and parliamentary democracy as a means to secure liberty and order, and a nationalistic self-confidence that combined a patriotic sense of national uniqueness with a xenophobic contempt for foreigners, especially Catholics. The positive contribution of Protestantism and liberty to prosperity and social development was stressed, but a very partial account of the latter was offered, concentrating on the growth of a strong middle class.

In modern academic circles Whig history is apparently dead, displaced by the scholarly developments of the last sixty years. At the popular level, however, traditional history and historical images are still well-liked, generally reflect Whiggish notions and often have little to do with the academic developments that have enriched our understanding of British history and the diversity of people in the British Isles. Biographies and narratives are at a premium. Narrative history is especially popular. This can be seen in child, adolescent, and adult reading patterns, and there is a parallel in literature. The persistent popularity of the detective novel, with its stress on the role of the individual and chance, and with a strong narrative structure, and, in most cases, its strong moral element, is especially noteworthy. The genre provides exciting, often exemplary, stories, which are precisely what are sought by most readers of history. In combination, narrative and the Whig approach offer a readily accessible means to produce a clear account of a highly complex subject: human history.

The combination of narrative and the Whig approach, however, is misleading not least because the latter tended to make outcomes appear necessary and inevitable. This book, in contrast, seeks to avoid an emphasis on inevitability. It is important to appreciate that choices have always existed, that policy was not pre-ordained by the 'structures' of economic or other circumstances, that contingencies and the views of individuals were of consequence. It is necessary to grasp the uncertainties of the past, the roles of chance and perception; to restore a human perspective to an historical imagination too often dominated by impersonal forces. If this approach can lead to greater difficulties in posing and answering questions of the relationships between change and continuity, the short term and the long, it is appropriate to point out that history is not an unbroken mirror reflecting our views, but a fractured glass turning in the wind, with pieces missing or opaque, and a general pattern that is difficult to distinguish and impossible to do so to general satisfaction.

The selection of central themes is therefore in large part a personal response to the multifaceted nature of the past. Two emerge clearly: first the political relations both between the constituent parts of Britain and between them and the rest of Europe; and secondly the impact of technology. The latter is particularly important and becoming more so. The impact of man on his environment has been far more insistent in the age of industrialisation and urbanisation than hitherto. A population of unprecedented size poses serious problems for the country. Meanwhile, the nature of life has changed. Most people no longer have to live by the sweat of their brow; they are more likely to sit in an office, manipulating electronic machinery, whether manufacturing goods or working in the financial or service industries. They do not face starvation if they fall ill. They take longevity, perhaps even prosperity or a supposed right to affluence beyond the dreams of their ancestors, for granted.

People themselves have changed. Inoculations to prevent serious diseases are now universal. Mechanical and chemical contraception has led to the replacement of earlier patterns of sexual activity and procreation. Technical and medical advances have led to the ability effectively to replace parts of the body, such as hips and knees. People look different: they are taller and fatter than in the past; teeth have been filled or crowned or replaced by dentures; the water is fluoridated. Clothes are made from man-made or enhanced fibres. Food is processed, coloured and preserved as a result of the combination of modern science and mass-production techniques. Obesity has become a serious problem.

These changes are emphasised in the chapter on the twentieth century, but elements are of longer standing, as have been shifts towards a more immediate 'mass culture'. Widespread literacy in the nineteenth century, followed by the spread of new media in the twentieth, led to a dynamic, constantly renewed relationship between the producers and consumers of information and images. This was subversive of earlier means of disseminating and inculcating ideas. As aspects of a changing material history, a vastly expanded press, and new media, notably radio, television and later electronic media, did not necessarily lead to the spread of radical ideas, for they could equally serve to reiterate conservative views. However, by regularly providing information and stimuli, successive new media played a major role in a democratisation of society that has been a predominant theme over the last century and a half. In the nineteenth century the newspaper became an accepted means for the pursuance of disputes, contributing to a more peaceful and public means of conducting political, social, economic and religious disagreements.

Democratisation was not the same as democracy, publicity did not entail the public nature of all politics, but, in the twentieth century, the information presented to the public became more extensive and its impact more insistent. Whereas Edward VIII's relationship with Mrs Simpson (later the Duchess of Windsor) in the 1930s was known only to a restricted circle, the same was not true of the activities of his grand-nephew, Prince Charles. Politicians today press avidly for equal exposure on television, although there are also grave worries about privacy.

This book itself is a testimony to changing circumstances. Technology is all-pervasive: the use of a word processor permitted frequent redrafting. There is also the clear sense that it is necessary to produce a work that is accessible to a wide audience. Consumer choice is crucial, and censorship, or the need to follow a 'party line', is not a factor. Indeed, it is the freedom with which the book has been written that is the most encouraging feature of this work. In Britain it is possible to write a book of this type without the problems and fears that an author would experience in much of the world. There is no room for triumphalism: the position may not last. Nevertheless, it is part of the strength of much of British society that, in a troubling present, it can look at itself and its past without complacency or the need to reiterate national myths. Would that that were true more widely.

Maps

PRE-ROMAN AND ROMAN BRITAIN

- Places

1 London	6 York	11 Inchtuthil
2 Chester	7 Lincoln	12 Bath
3 St Albans	8 Wroxeter	13 Halkyn
4 Gloucester	9 Colchester	14 Dolaucothi
5 Caerleon	10 Exeter	15 Stonehenge
		16 Avebury

Areas

A Suffolk	E Wales	I Shropshire
B Kent	F Anglesey	J Hereford
C Cumbria	G Glamorgan	K East Anglia
D Yorkshire	H Clwyd	

☐ Legionary fortresses
not all occupied at once

+HHH+ Antonine Wall

+++++ Hadrian's wall

⟶ Caesar's invasion route in 55 and 54 BC

--➤ Claudius's invasion route in 43 AD

▨ Over 200 m

▰ Over 500 m

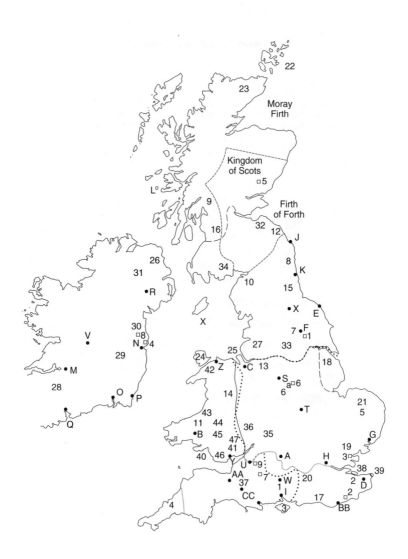

Moray
Firth

Kingdom
of Scots

Firth
of Forth

ANGLO-SAXON BRITAIN

- Places

A Dorchester-on-Thames	H London	P Wexford	X Catterick
B Carmarthen	I Southampton	Q Cork	Y Caerleon
C Chester	J Lindisfarne	R Armagh	Z Degannwy
D Canterbury	K Jarrow	S Derby	AA Athelney
E Whitby	L Iona	T Leicester	BB Pevensey
F York	M Limerick	U Bath	CC South Cadbury
G Ipswich	N Dublin	V Clonmacois	
	O Waterford	W Winchester	

Areas

1 Hampshire	13 Cheshire	25 Wirral	37 Wessex
2 Kent	14 Powys	26 Antrim	38 Sheppey
3 Isle of Wight	15 Northumbria	27 Lancashire	39 Thanet
4 Cornwall	16 Strathclyde	28 Munster	40 Gower
5 East Anglia	17 Sussex	29 Leinster	41 Gwent
6 Mercia	18 Lindsey	30 Meath	42 Gwynedd
7 Deira	19 Essex	31 Ulster	43 Ceredigion
8 Bernicia	20 Surrey	32 Lothian	44 Builth
9 Argyll	21 Norfolk	33 Elmet	45 Brycheiniog
10 Cumbria	22 Orkney	34 Rheged	46 Glywysing
11 Dyfed	23 Caithness	35 Hwicce	47 Ergyng
12 Gododdin	24 Anglesey	36 Magonsaetan	

- Battles

1 Stamford Bridge	6 Repton
2 Hastings	7 Edington
3 Maldon	8 Tara
4 Clontarf	9 Wroughton
5 Nechtansmere	

······ Boundary of Mercia in 800   — — Boundary of Northumbria in 650

——— Boundary of Wessex in 830   ----- Kingdom of Scots in 1018

—— Offa's Dyke

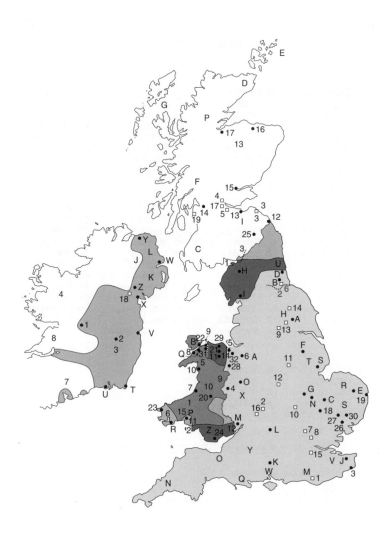

MEDIEVAL BRITISH ISLES

- Places

A	York	P	Camarthen	6	Chester	21	St Asaph
B	Durham	Q	Bangor	7	Aberystwyth	22	Beaumaris
C	Ely	R	Tenby	8	Caernarfon	23	St Davids
D	Newcastle	S	Boston	9	Conwy	24	Llandaff
E	Norwich	T	Wexford	10	Harlech	25	Roxburgh
F	Lincoln	U	Waterford	11	Denbigh	26	Hadleigh
G	Stamford	V	Dublin	12	Berwick	27	Long Melford
H	Carlisle	W	Carrickfergus	13	Edinburgh	28	Holt
I	Kendal	X	Dundalk	14	Glasgow	29	Rhuddlan
J	Canterbury	Y	Coleraine	15	Perth	30	Lavenham
K	Winchester	Z	Newry	16	Elgin	31	Degannwy
L	Dorchester-on-Thames	1	Athlone	17	Inverness	32	Hawarden
M	Tintern	2	Kildare	18	Cambridge		
N	Peterborough	3	Dover	19	Great Yarmouth		
O	Shrewsbury	4	Montgomery				
		5	Flint	20	Builth		

Regions

A	Cheshire	L	Antrim	W	Hampshire	8	Thomond
B	Anglesey	M	Sussex	X	Herefordshire	9	Powys
C	Galloway	N	Cornwall	Y	Wiltshire	10	Deheubarth
D	Caithness	O	Somerset	Z	Glamorgan	11	Kidwelly
E	Orkney	P	Ross	1	Ceredigion	12	Gwent
F	Argyll	Q	Dorset	2	Gower	13	Moray
G	Western Isles	R	Norfolk	3	Leinster	14	Clwyd
H	Yorkshire	S	Suffolk	4	Connacht	15	Dyfed
I	Lothian	T	Lincolnshire	5	Gwynedd		
J	Ulster	U	Northumbria	6	Pembrokeshire		
K	Down	V	Kent	7	Desmond		

□ Battles

Rivers ······

1	Lewes	8	Barnet	15	Sevenoaks	1	Solway Firth (bay)
2	Evesham	9	Wakefield	16	Tewkesbury	2	Tees
3	Dunbar	10	Northampton	17	Bannockburn	3	Liddel
4	Stirling	11	Stoke	18	Faughart	4	Conway
5	Falkirk	12	Bosworth	19	Largs		
6	Neville's Cross	13	Towton				
7	St Albans	14	Boroughbridge				

Areas under effective control of the English crown and its subjects at the death of William I, 1087

Additions to this area by 1100

Additions to this area by 1189

Additions to this area by 1290

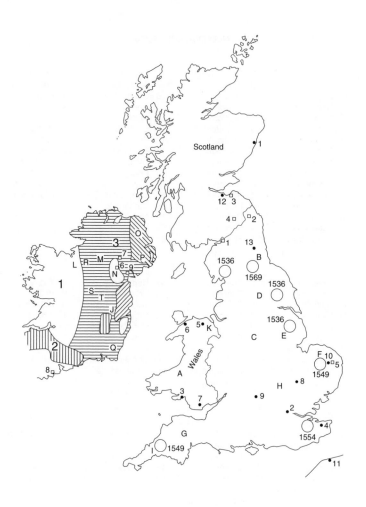

Scotland

Wales

THE SIXTEENTH CENTURY

- Places

1	Aberdeen	6	Bangor	11	Calais
2	London	7	Llandaff	12	Edinburgh
3	Swansea	8	Cambridge	13	Durham
4	Canterbury	9	Oxford		
5	St Asaph	10	Norwich		

Counties

A	Cardiganshire	H	Bedfordshire	O	Antrim
B	Durham	I	Cornwall	P	Down
C	Derbyshire	J	Kildare	Q	Wexford
D	Yorkshire	K	Flintshire	R	Leitrim
E	Lincolnshire	L	Sligo	S	Longford
F	Norfolk	M	Fermanagh	T	Westmeath
G	Devon	N	Monaghan		

□ Battles

1	Solway Moss	6	Clontibret
2	Flodden	7	Yellow Ford
3	Pinkie	8	Kinsale
4	Ancrum Moor	9	Moyry Pass
5	Dussindale		

Regions (larger than counties)

1 Connacht

2 Munster

3 Ulster

○ Centres of Rebellion in England

///// The Pale c. 1550

||||| Plantations established before 1603

\\\\\ Scottish settlements

≡ Plantations established 1603–49

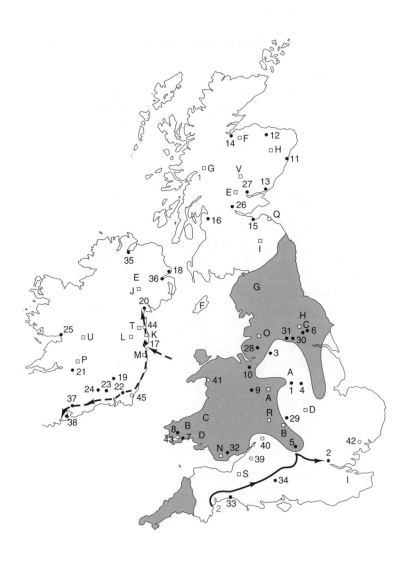

THE CIVIL WARS 1638–1691

• Towns

1 Derby	11 Aberdeen	21 Limerick	31 Bradford
2 London	12 Elgin	22 Ross	32 Llandaff
3 Manchester	13 Dundee	23 Carrick	33 Lyme Regis
4 Nottingham	14 Inverness	24 Clonmel	34 Salisbury
5 Oxford	15 Edinburgh	25 Galway	35 Derry
6 York	16 Glasgow	26 Stirling	36 Belfast
7 Tenby	17 Dublin	27 Perth	37 Cork
8 Haverfordwest	18 Carrickfergus	28 Wigan	38 Kinsale
9 Shrewsbury	19 Kilkenny	29 Warwick	
10 Chester	20 Dundalk	30 Leeds	

□ Battles

A Hopton Heath 1643	I Philiphaugh 1645	Q Dunbar 1650
B Edgehill 1642	J Benburb 1646	R Worcester 1651
C Marston Moor 1644	K Julianstown 1641	S Sedgemoor 1685
D Naseby 1645	L Dungan Hill 1647	T Boyne 1690
E Tippermuir 1644	M Baggot-rath 1649	U Aughrim 1691
F Auldearn 1645	N St Fagan's 1648	V Killiecrankie 1689
G Inverlochy 1645	O Preston 1648	
H Alford 1645	P Scarrifhollis 1650	

○ Besieged Towns   Areas

39 Bristol 1643	A Derbyshire	H Yorkshire
40 Gloucester 1643	B Pembrokeshire	I Kent
41 Harlech 1647	C Cardiganshire	
42 Colchester 1648	D Carmarthenshire	Places
43 Pembroke 1648	E Ulster	
44 Drogheda 1649	F Isle of Man	1 Glencoe
45 Wexford 1649	G Cumberland	2 Torbay

▨ Areas of Royalist support in England
and Wales, 1 May 1643

Campaigns

– → Cromwell's route in 1649

——→ William of Orange's route in 1688

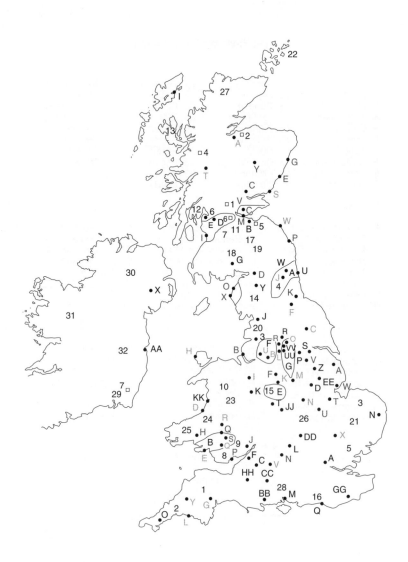

BRITAIN 1750–1900

- Places

A	London	O	Truro	I	Troon	F	Darlington
AA	Dublin	P	Doncaster	J	Tintern	G	Exeter
B	Edinburgh	Q	Brighton	K	Stockton	H	Holyhead
BB	Wimborne	R	Bradford	L	Plymouth	I	Crewe
C	Bath	S	Scunthorpe	M	Forth Bridge	J	Gateshead
CC	Wilton	T	Birmingham	N	Swindon	K	Burton-on-Trent
D	Grantham	U	Sunderland	O	Workington	L	Huddersfield
DD	Wolverton	UU	Dewsbury	P	Bambrugh	M	Nottingham
E	Glasgow	V	Dunfermline	Q	Merthyr Tydfil	N	Leicester
EE	Sleaford	VV	Batley	R	Halifax	O	Leeds
F	Bristol	W	Newcastle	S	Ebbw Vale	P	Cardiff
G	Dumfries	X	Carrickfergus	T	Spalding	Q	Rhondda
GG	Battle	Y	Penrith	U	Stamford	R	Brecon
H	Bruton	Z	Lincoln	V	Gainsborough	S	Dundee
I	Stornoway	A	Louth	W	Boston	T	Fort William
J	Lancaster	B	Liverpool	X	Whitehaven	U	Bolton
JJ	Stoneleigh	C	Perth	Y	Braemar	V	Devizes
K	Shrewsbury	D	Carlisle	A	Inverness	W	Berwick
KK	Aberdovey	E	Montrose	B	Manchester	X	Cambridge
L	Oxford	F	Derby	C	York	Y	Launceston
M	Southampton	G	Aberdeen	D	Aberystwyth		
N	Norwich	H	Carmarthen	E	Swansea		

Regions

1	Devon	12	Renfrew	23	Montgomeryshire
2	Cornwall	13	Skye	24	Cardiganshire
3	Norfolk	14	Lake District	25	Pembrokeshire
4	Durham	15	Black Country	26	Northamptonshire
5	Essex	16	Sussex	27	Sutherland
6	Strathclyde	17	Selkirk	28	Hampshire
7	Lanarkshire	18	Dumfries	29	Wexford
8	Glamorgan	19	Roxburghshire	30	Ulster
9	Monmouthshire	20	Lancashire	31	Connacht
10	Merioneth	21	East Anglia	32	Leinster
11	Midlothian	22	Orkney Islands		

□ Battles

1 Sheriffmuir 1715
2 Culloden 1746
3 Preston 1716
4 Glenshiel 1719
5 Prestonpans 1745
6 Falkirk 1746
7 Vinegar Hill 1798

Major Coalfields

A North-East
B South Wales
C Fife
D Strathclyde
E Midlands
F Lancashire
G Nottinghamshire/Yorkshire

THE BRITISH EMPIRE 1914

Major naval stations

1 Falkland Islands
2 St Helena
3 Ascension
4 Cape Town
5 Mauritius
6 Trincomalee
7 Singapore
8 Hong Kong
9 Alexandria
10 Labuan
11 Fiji
12 Esquimalt
13 Halifax
14 Bombay
15 Calcutta
16 Lagos
17 Gibraltar
18 Malta
19 Aden
20 Sydney
21 Bahamas
22 Bermuda
23 Adelaide
24 Seychelles

A Australia	I India	Q Nigeria
B New Zealand	J Cyprus	R Gold Coast
C Tasmania	K Sudan	S Sierra Leone
D Malaya	L Egypt	T Gambia
E New Guinea	M Uganda	U Canada
F Kenya	N S. Africa	V Newfoundland
G Ceylon	O N. Rhodesia	W British West Indies
H Burma	P S. Rhodesia	X British Guiana

1

Pre-Roman and Roman Britain

Among the stalactites and stalagmites of Kent's Cavern, the impressive cave system at Torbay in Devon, early hominids, Neanderthals and Stone Age men successively lived. The caves gave them shelter from south-west winds and opened to the light from the east. Earlier, bears had hibernated in the darker recesses of the caves. Now the caves are an inspiring visit for tourists and a challenge for artists; but, for most of their long human history, they reflected the struggle of man, like other creatures, to adapt successfully to the land. Moreover, the long and complex history of the British Isles in part represents the interaction of man and a very varied natural environment.

This environment is the proper focus at the outset because it greatly helped shape life in Britain, and is still very important today. The British Isles are both part of Europe and yet, from the Mesolithic period in about 6500 BCE,[1] separated from it by the sea. They have a very varied geology, topography, climate and natural vegetation. We should be careful about projecting the modern environment onto the past: climate and drainage, even the coastline and water levels, were different. Yet, in simple terms, the bulk of the west and north of Britain is higher and wetter, its soils poorer, and its agriculture pastoral rather than arable: centred on animals, not crops. Much of Ireland is like west and north Britain, although there is less high land. However, there are many exceptions to this description of the British Isles as a result of a highly complex geological history and of great climatic variations.

---

[1] BCE (Before Common Era) is the equivalent to BC (Before Christ), and CE to AD (Anno Domini).

Thus, the north and west contain fertile lowlands, such as the central lowlands of Scotland, the Vale of York in Yorkshire, and the Vale of Eden in Cumbria; while the south and east contain areas of poor fertility, such as the sandy wastes of the Breckland in Suffolk or the hilly greensand of the Weald in Kent.

Despite this, the essential contrast in England is between the colder, hillier north and the warmer, lower south, the wetter west and the drier east, and, despite the effects of climate change in the past, these contrasts have been consistent. And there are political consequences. Upland areas such as the Pennines, a range of hills that forms the backbone of northern England, have not generally served as centres of power. Instead, prior to the Roman invasion, hill forts were more numerous in the south and west of England. There were relatively few in the north and east. Some were in the Cheviots and Lothians of southern Scotland, but there were very few indeed in the Pennines proper. For much of English and Scottish history, wealth and influence have been disproportionately present in the south of each country, with the east also being generally more significant than the west. Wales clearly shows the consequences of terrain and climate. It is largely mountainous: 60 per cent of the surface area is above the 200-metre line. Until nineteenth-century bridge-building and tunnelling, such terrain acted as an effective brake on communications: the natural links in Wales run east–west, not north–south, and this situation has had historical and political implications over the centuries. Exposed to prevalent westerly winds that are forced to rise to cross its mountains, Wales, like Ireland, west Scotland, and north-west and south-west England, receives a heavy rainfall. This plays a major role in washing the soil from its uplands. Thus, aside from the difficulty of cultivating mountainous terrain, much of upland Britain has relatively poor, often acidic, soil and is unsuitable for continuous or intensive cultivation. This situation encourages a dependence on the rearing of animals, a form of agriculture that cannot support the higher population levels of arable regions.

Within Europe, early man lived first in the warmer areas of the south, but, when the climate permitted between the advance of the glaciers, spread from there into northern Europe. Human remains of early hominids and finds of tool assemblages have been found in many sites in southern England. Neanderthal hunters also left sites there, but these are far fewer than in France, especially south-west France, and Germany. The Neanderthals were replaced by anatomically modern humans during the Upper Palaeolithic period (*c.* 40,000 to *c.* 10,000 years ago). This lengthy period saw a development of social structures and stone-blade technology, although subsequent weathering, ploughing and other activity have greatly limited the surviving evidence. People retained useful objects for future use, had craftsmen with ideas of symmetry, and performed tasks entailing a division of labour. However, settlement was episodic, with the advance of the glaciers during the Ice Ages leading to periods without occupation, notably the Anglian glaciation.

After the last Ice Age came to an end, in around 10,000 BCE, there was a northward movement of forest and wildlife zones across the North European Plain, which then included Britain. Subsequently, in now warmer England, the trees of a cold climate – birch, pine and hazel – were replaced by oak, elm, ash and lime between 7500 and 5000 BCE. These deciduous forests were rich in plant and animal life. The warmer climate led to the arrival of red and roe deer and wild pig from further south, which encouraged a rise in the number of hunter-gatherers in the Mesolithic period (*c.* 8300 BCE to *c.* 4500 BCE). For example, the woodlands of the Thames valley provided shelter for animals, such as deer, which, in turn, attracted hunters. They were equipped with microlithic flints mounted in wood or bone hafts, which provided effective tools for use, for example, as knives or as arrowheads. Sites in which human remains of early hominids and finds of tool assembly have been discovered include Stoke Newington in London.

Settlements spread considerably and became more fixed, notably in the river valleys, and trade developed. Evidence for tool manufacture increased. As the ice melted, the sea level rose, and, in about 6500 BCE, the land-bridge that joined England to the Continent across the southern North Sea was cut. More than half the human history of Britain had already passed by then.

This break did not prevent a transfer of agricultural development from the Continent. Domestic crops and agriculture spread into England in the fifth millennium BCE, although hunting, fishing and gathering wild plants continued. The first signs of farming occurred in Scotland in about 4500 BCE. The plough was in use in southern England in about 3500 BCE, which helped increase crop yields, and encouraged the clearing of forest, leading to a drop in surviving tree pollen. The spread of domestic animals, cattle, pigs, sheep, and goats, from the early Neolithic, brought milk, wool and an ability to pull ploughs, and was followed by wheeled vehicles. Animals played a major role in the economy, culture and religion. Animal motifs were incorporated in art, and animals had religious symbolism, being linked with particular deities. There is surviving archaeological evidence of farmsteads; and then villages, for example Skara Brae in the Orkneys, which dates from about 3000 BCE.

As the population rose and became settled rather than semi-nomadic, surviving evidence of permanent human presence in the landscape increases. This evidence takes the form, during the Neolithic period (*c*. 4000 to *c*. 2000 BCE), of 'causewayed' camps, ritual monuments, and burial chambers, notably long and round barrows. Stone alignments and circles were created in England, Ireland, Scotland and Wales. Dating from about 3200 to 1500 BCE, they became progressively more complex, suggesting a tendency towards ritual and maybe political centralisation. The religious practices of the people are obscure, although astronomical knowledge clearly played a major role; the midsummer sun rises along the axis of Stonehenge. Ritual centres such as Avebury and Stonehenge in southern England or the vast and complex tombs of the Boyne Valley in Ireland would have each required at least hundreds of thousands of man-hours to construct and were evidence of large-scale communal activity.

Trade developed as the flint necessary for agricultural tools and axes was mined and exchanged. Moreover, commerce along the coasts and across seas was a crucial development. By the third millennium BCE, copper metallurgy had spread into southern Britain. This increase in the material culture was followed in about 2000 BCE by the dissemination of a new burial pattern, known as 'Beaker', from the distinctive pottery in graves: these were individual burials with rich grave-goods, suggesting a more stratified society. There are also more known Late than Early Neolithic sites.

The Copper Age was followed, from about 2200 BCE to about 800 BCE, by that of bronze, a harder alloy of copper that was more effective in tools and weapons. Bronze replaced not only copper but also hard stone and flint. Social stratification appears to have become more pronounced. Numerous and large surviving burial mounds or barrows have been linked to areas likely to have benefited from trade, suggesting the existence of an elite. Aside from trade, agriculture increased in response to the rising population, and land boundaries and, later, fields were laid out, notably from about 1500–1000 BCE on. Pollen and sediment studies suggest that the shift from nomadism to settlement and farming occurred especially in the Bronze Age, around 2000 BCE. This shift probably led to the widespread clearing of woodland in the second millennium BCE, although woodland remained a major economic resource, notably for timber and hunting.

Settlement became more permanent, and was linked to the development of trading routes, for example the middle Thames, and related commercial networks. Moreover, marginal areas were increasingly cleared of trees and cultivated. It has been suggested that Bronze Age society was more bellicose. There is increased evidence of fortifications, notably of defended hill-top settlements, of land divisions, suggesting that ownership of land was becoming more contested, and of weapons; and it has been argued that society was dominated by warriors.

They were to be challenged by the use of a new metal, in the Iron Age, which lasted from about 800 BCE to CE 43. The smelting and forging of iron spread from West Asia and arrived in England by 700 BCE. By 500 BCE iron tools were being used to clear trees. The use of iron hoes and nails brought a new flexibility to agriculture and construction. Iron also made better weapons, particularly when carbon was added to make steel.

England was exposed to pressure from the Celts, a culture that appeared in South Germany in about 800 BCE and then spread over much of France. The extent of Celtic influence in Britain is controversial. Features of Celtic settlement, culture and civilisation have been found in southern England, but it is unclear how much was due to a widespread population movement, to more limited immigration, or to trade. It is likely that all three played a role and by the first century CE Celts were also dominant as far as Ireland.

In the first millennium BCE the population of Britain rose and agriculture improved. For most of their history, the map of power in the British Isles was one that was heavily influenced by the geography of agriculture and agrarian systems, and this was particularly true of the pre-Roman period. Coins (with the first written words), proto-towns (larger and more complex settlements), and tribal 'states' with chieftain patterns of tribal organisation and populations of tens of thousands, existed in southern England, while much of the woodland had been cleared, especially in areas of light soil, and agriculture was both varied and extensive.

The situation was different in the north, Wales, Scotland and Ireland, although population estimates for Iron Age Scotland belie this to a degree. Relatively low population levels and a poorly-developed agricultural base ensured that there was only a small surplus of wealth for taxation in these areas and thus only a limited ability to support political and governmental activity. Most of late Iron Age Wales, for example, left no trace of pottery, although some fine metalwork has been left. In contrast, southern England was linked in this period to nearby areas of the Continent: to northern Gaul (France) and the Low Countries.

In conclusion, Britain was far from stagnant on the eve of the Roman conquest. It supported a growing population, a settled society and an aristocratic elite, although the tribal states did not amount to a sophisticated governmental system. The population may have been about two million and there is much evidence for the manufacture of iron. Population pressure in both England and Scotland is indicated by the settlement of relatively undesirable areas. Moreover, archaeological work has led to a significant increase in the number of known sites.

ROMAN CONQUEST

Having conquered Gaul (France), the Roman military leader Julius Caesar claimed that it was necessary to stop British support for the Celts still resisting there; there may indeed have been British assistance for the Veneti of Brittany. Caesar was also probably motivated by a desire for glory and plunder, and by the need to employ his troops. In 55 and 54 BCE, he launched expeditions against southern England, but met unexpectedly strong resistance and storms. As a result, Caesar was happy to return to Gaul.

Under his successors trade links developed with Britain and there were diplomatic contacts, but there was no military action until 43 CE when the Emperor Claudius invaded. He sought to gain a military reputation to strengthen his position in Rome and invaded because Rome's protégés in southern Britain had lost control. It is unclear what would have happened but for Roman conquest. Whereas a unified Pictavia in the area of Scotland not conquered by Rome is uncertain but has more advocates than in the past, the part of Germany that was not conquered by Rome was essentially to develop into a number of small kingdoms that focused on farming but also took part in trade, as did Ireland. Urban development was limited outside the Roman world, although the later histories of Glasgow and Hamburg scarcely suggest that Roman conquest was necessary for subsequent prominence.

The Romans rapidly conquered lowland Britain in the 40s and 50s CE. There was considerable resistance, led initially by the Catuvellani and, in particular, their leader Caratacus, to give them the Roman spelling of their names – inevitably, since almost all our knowledge of this period comes from Roman written sources. Having been victorious in South-East England, the Romans invaded Wales in pursuit of Caratacus. They also advanced simultaneously along a number of routes across southern England.

Initially, client rulers were left in place in a number of areas, notably Surrey, Sussex and Hampshire under the Atrebates tribe and East Anglia under the Iceni. In 60 CE the Governor, Gaius Suetonius Paulinus, was campaigning in north Wales against the Druids, anti-Roman priests and their supporters, when a major rising was staged by the Iceni tribe under their female leader Boudicca (Boadicea is a later corruption of the name). They were enraged by callous Roman rule and by the Romans' treatment of the royal family, including the flogging of Boudicca and the rape of her daughters. The major Roman settlements, then Colchester, St Albans and London, were destroyed, but Paulinus crushed the Iceni in battle and they were then brutally 'pacified'. Boudicca died, probably by suicide.

In the seventies, the Romans pressed forward again. The Brigantes of northern England were subjugated in 71–4, Wales following. By 78 CE all of England and Wales was under Roman control, and this remained the case until links with Rome collapsed in 409. However, Britain was not conquered in its entirety, and the continued presence of a frontier zone ensured that Britain absorbed a relatively high percentage of Roman military expenditure, and had a comparatively large number of troops. As a result of these troops, Britain played an important role during struggles for control in the Roman empire and also had a series of forts which became the basis for towns.

Highland Scotland was never conquered by the Romans: the terrain was far more difficult for an invading power than lowland Britain and it was well defended. Agricola, governor from 77 to 83, invaded Scotland, winning a notable victory at Mons Graupius, but only the Scottish lowlands south of the Forth–Clyde line were conquered. The Romans could win victories in Aberdeenshire as Agricola and Severus did, but retention proved a different matter. The Romans had to advance on the east coast route, which was always vulnerable to attack from the Angus glens, and did not master the penetration of the Carse of Stirling as Edward I was eventually to do. Although Agricola considered its conquest, Ireland was not attacked by the Romans. It nevertheless received a small but steady flow of Roman coins and other imported materials. They were in all likelihood the result of mercenary activity and trade coming from Irish Sea garrison ports in western Britain such as Chester.

The Roman conquest thus, even as it united southern Britain for the first time in its history, also demonstrated a central feature of British history: a lack of political uniformity. In part, this lack of uniformity reflected a variety of local socio-environmental systems stemming from the physical variety of the island. Furthermore, in both Ireland and across much of Scotland, it is possible to point to continuities with the Iron Age, as much as to change, whether resulting from contact with the Romans or not. There was certainly Roman influence in both areas.

The frontier zone was most clearly marked by Hadrian's Wall, built by the Emperor Hadrian, who visited Britain in 122. The wall was constructed from about 122 along the Tyne–Solway line, across the narrowest part of the island, to protect England from invasion from the north and as a means to control the upland zone by preventing free movement. To the south, the generally peaceful nature of Roman society encouraged a process of Romanisation. Roman citizenship was restricted neither to Romans nor to Italians. The Emperor Caracalla was the first to universalise it formally, although ninety years after Hadrian. Non-Romans could rise to the heights of power. Similarly, Roman conquest did not mean expropriation of all power.

Roman religious cults spread, although assimilation with native Celtic beliefs was important. When Christianity became the state religion in the fourth century CE, this brought more systematic cultural links between England and the Continent, links not shared by non-Roman Scotland. In contrast to Christianity, the pre-Roman druids, whom the Romans stamped out, and the cults of the Olympian gods which they introduced, had both lacked diocesan structure and doctrinal regulation. The Olympian cults, however, prefigured Christianity in linking England to the Continent. So also did the cult of Mithras which was of Persian origin and closely connected with the Roman army. Mithras was seen as an agent of good or light endlessly fighting evil or darkness. Mithraic congregations normally met in underground or partly underground buildings. Women were excluded, as from much else of Roman life.

In addition, pre-Roman pagan practices still continued, an aspect of the limited impact of Roman culture. Outside the towns, England was not as thoroughly Romanised as other provinces. Roman Britain, nevertheless, acquired an urban system linked and structured by roads, such as Ermine, Stane and Watling Streets and the Fosse Way. Reflecting the quality of Roman engineering, these roads were built to a high standard, with stone foundations and gravel surfaces. Towns such as Londinium (London), Verulamium (St Albans), Lindum (Lincoln), and Eboracum (York) were centres of authority, consumption and Roman culture, including, eventually, Christianity. Some towns, usually with chester in their name, emerged alongside Roman fortresses, but others developed as a result of initiatives by the native elites keen to adopt Roman culture and material life.

Links with the Continent increased and fostered economic development, while urbanisation brought out the possibilities for economic specialisation offered by developing networks of exchange. Britain was valuable as a source of mineral exports, especially silver, lead, gold and iron. Thus, Britain made a major contribution to the economics and finances of the empire. Mining was of particular importance in Wales. Although there was pre-Roman mining, there was a tremendous expansion under the Romans, of gold at Dolaucothi, lead at Halkyn and copper in Anglesey. Other exports included grain, woollen goods and hunting dogs, while imports focused on consumer goods, notably wine, glass, pottery, marble, olive oil, and the preserved fish sauce called garum that was important to the Roman diet.

Agriculture, much of which centred on Romanised farms or villas, was important and the bulk of the population lived in the countryside. Farming also improved. In the late third and fourth centuries, larger ploughs were introduced and coulters were added, leading to the cutting of deeper furrows, which permitted the working of heavier soils. The introduction of two-handed scythes enabled hay to be cut faster and thus larger quantities to be stored for winter forage. Corn-drying kilns were constructed, and crop rotations were introduced, while animals were overwintered in hay meadows. Animal- or water-powered mills were significant.

The greater quantity of archaeological material surviving from the Roman period suggests a society producing and trading far more goods than its Iron Age predecessors. The prosperity of the rural economy underwrote the cost of building numerous villas: large

noble houses in the country constructed in a Roman style and
heated from under the floor by a hypocaust system. Another testimony of the human imprint was the wiping out of the bear in
England by the end of the Roman period. Humans were the dominant species. Meanwhile, the clearing of virgin woodland in lowland
England continued.

THE END OF ROMAN BRITAIN

Like other parts of the Roman empire, Britain suffered not only
rebellions, for example in 286 or 287 to 296, but also increasing attack
from 'barbarians': Picts from Scotland, and Angles, Jutes and Saxons
from northern Germany and Denmark. By 270 the Saxon Shore, a chain
of ten forts, stretched from Brancaster in Norfolk to Portchester in
Hampshire. Attacks became serious in the 340s, and a successful invasion in 367 led to widespread devastation. New forts were also built on
the west coast, from Cardiff to Lancaster, to counter the threat of Irish
Sea raiders. Order was restored by Theodosius in 368–9. However,
'barbarian' assaults played a major role in the decline of trade and urban
stagnation that affected Britain in the fourth century. At Verulamium
(St Albans), for example, urban decay led to the use of the theatre as a
rubbish dump.

The ability of the empire to resist these attacks was eroded, and
links with Rome were further weakened by Roman usurpers based
in Britain, such as Magnus Maximus in 383–8 and Constantine III
in 406–9. In 406, when Gaul (France) was invaded by 'barbarians'
from across the Rhine, Britain created its own emperor, Constantine
III. He took a significant part of the island's military forces to Gaul
and they did not return. The Romano-Britons, disillusioned with the
rebel Constantine's activities, expelled his administrators in 409 and
appealed to the true Emperor, Honorius, for the restoration of legitimate rule. Hard-pressed in Italy by Alaric, the Visigothic leader, who
indeed captured Rome in 410, Honorius could do no more than tell
them to look to their own defence.

This was the end of the Roman empire in Britain, although not
of Roman Britain. Nevertheless, the subsequent break-up of Roman
Britain into a number of kingdoms suggests that its internal unity
should not be exaggerated. Moreover, the Romans relied fairly heavily
in the fourth century on German troops brought in as mercenaries.

St Germanus, Bishop of Auxerre, who visited Britain in 429 to combat the Pelagian heresy, which denied the doctrine of original sin, noted the survival of cities, but that their defence was in local hands, rather than those of Roman troops. From mid-century, the situation appears to have deteriorated as a result of 'barbarian' invasion. In about 446, an appeal for help was sent to Rome, but, again, it was in no position to send assistance.

2

British, English and Scandinavians, AD 400–1066

THE ANGLO-SAXON INVASIONS

The fifth century is an especially obscure period. The early Germanic population, mostly invaders but some descendants of people brought in as mercenaries and settlers in the late Roman period, left no written record. Bede (672/3–735), the first English historian, and other later written sources provide a different account from the archaeological evidence. The latter, anyway, has to be used with care because of the difficulty of interpreting evidence and its uneven spread, reflecting, in part, the varied pattern of excavation and fieldwork activity. It is far from clear how far continuity or discontinuity should be stressed between Roman and post-Roman Britain, and difficult to distinguish between the consequences of the end to imperial Roman rule and that of the invaders who brought Germanisation. In particular, it is unclear how far there were large-scale movements of people or invasions by smaller warrior groups; there is an active debate on this. It was traditionally thought, on the basis of language and place-names, that there had been a mass migration. In the 1970s and 1980s, in contrast, it was fashionable to argue for a small elite invasion. Now DNA analysis is leading to a revival of the hypothesis of a mass-migration.

The invaders, part of the 'barbarian' invasions of the Roman world, attacked eastern and southern England. The Jutes established themselves in Kent, the Isle of Wight and parts of Hampshire, the Saxons elsewhere in southern England (Sussex: South Saxons; Essex: East Saxons; Middlesex: Middle Saxons), the Angles further north. However, the English tribal names and their distribution was largely the product of Bede's analysis in his *Ecclesiastical History of the English People* (*c.* 731) and what this information tells us about the fifth century is more problematic.

The progress of these invading groups was resisted, for longer and more successfully than in France, Spain or Italy, although resistance was gravely handicapped by internal divisions. Resistance may have been greater because there was more at stake for the Romano-British elite: the assimilation with invaders that characterised France, for example, was absent. In about 500 the Britons, maybe under Artorius (Arthur), possibly won a major battle against the Saxons at Mons Badonicus, and it is possible that a large hall at the hill fort at South Cadbury was the feasting hall of a warrior of the period, the basis of the legend of Arthur's Camelot. Hill forts such as South Cadbury, which has defences and a hall of the post-Roman period, may have been the bases of British power in some western and northern areas.

England, nevertheless, was gradually conquered, and much of Roman Britain was destroyed or fell into decay. However, Romanised town and villa life and Christianity did not cease abruptly. Continuity of site use (though probably not of urban institutions) at some of the major towns, for example Canterbury, has now been suggested by archaeological work. Urban building forms continued into the sixth century at Wroxeter, and some of the barrack houses at Birdoswald were rebuilt after the end of Roman rule. Moreover, in conquered areas, many Romano-Britons survived as slaves and peasants. The high levels of population that had characterised Roman Britain appear to have persisted until the mid-sixth-century outbreak of the bubonic plague that devastated much of the ancient world.

It has also been argued that the great majority of the population remained British, but acculturated to a militarily dominant invading elite. Archaeological evidence suggests that, alongside the abandonment of many Roman sites on clay soils, the new settlers continued the Romano-British pattern of generally neglecting clay lands, in favour of lighter, and more easily cultivated, soils on gravel, sand and chalk. As a consequence, the Anglo-Saxons occupied an already managed landscape. The trend of archaeological argument has been to emphasise that the Romano-British countryside was well-occupied and that early English settlers had to fit into it and around it. Most place-names do not occur in written form until later land-charters or even *Domesday Book* (1086), so knowing what the naming situation was, and how it came about, in the early period is very difficult. However, the common place-name 'ley' (from Old English *lēah*), meaning woodland clearing or clearing where there is a settlement, suggests a process of expansion into woodland. Another key name was *tūn*, meaning enclosure or settlement.

Yet, alongside elements of continuity, the languages and culture of Roman Britain were largely lost in England, and, as trade declined, the former Roman province became a subsistence economy and a violent society with relatively few ceramics or coins in the archaeological record. There are few fifth- and sixth-century settlement sites, although there are many more burial sites. The Anglo-Saxon settlers not only concentrated on agriculture, but were largely self-sufficient. Settlement was less dense than under the Romans. Trade was of limited importance to the Anglo-Saxon economy. Roman Londinium was abandoned, but, during the early Saxon period, the centre of settlement shifted to the west of the city, along the banks of the Thames, and Saxon archaeological finds for this town of Ludenwic dated to 550–700 were found in the 1990s.

The invaders were all pagans and, in the eastern areas first taken over by the English, Christianity withered, although it continued in the western areas. However, under the Romans, the religion had not been widespread in Britain, and the extent to which Christianity was part of the Roman legacy, at least at the upper levels of society, is controversial. Some scholars have argued that the Romano-British elite was pagan.

In the sixth century the Angles and Saxons advanced considerably. One of the most important Saxon kingdoms, Wessex, that of the West Saxons, based around Dorchester-on-Thames and in Hampshire, advanced west, although it was not to conquer Dorset until the late sixth or seventh centuries and Cornwall until 838. The Angles established kingdoms in East Anglia, the Midlands (Mercia), Yorkshire (Deira), and north of the Tees (Bernicia). The latter two joined to become Northumbria, which conquered the British kingdoms of Elmet and Rheged so as to dominate the north of England.

It would be misleading to see these centuries simply as the Dark Ages, and solely as centuries of violence, discontinuity and plague. There is potential in a long-term approach for understanding the Dark Ages in pre-Roman terms, viewing Romanisation as something which overlay deeper 'rhythms' of continuity in settlement, land use and trade. Britain indeed remained a society largely true to its agrarian roots and less Romanised than other provinces such as France and Spain. Outside the towns, the British influence on Roman Britain had been considerable.

It is also possible to offer a positive assessment of aspects of early Anglo-Saxon society. Cemeteries have yielded some important early Anglo-Saxon pottery and metalwork. The rich and ornate goods, many from the Continent and Byzantium (the Eastern Roman Empire), found in the ship burials at Sutton Hoo and, to a lesser extent, at Snape and in Kentish cemeteries, testified to the wealth of the East-Anglian and Kentish dynasties, and the importance of links with the Continent. The Sutton Hoo burial (*c.* 630) near Woodbridge, Suffolk, probably contained the tomb of King Raedwald of East Anglia. The exceptional quality of the ornamental work found with the burial is evidence of the wealth and splendour of some elements of seventh-century society. The richness of high status material culture has also emerged from a more recent hoard found in 2009 near Hammerwich, Staffordshire. These finds prompt speculation about the riches of Anglo-Saxon civilisation that have been lost. In part, this wealth was a case of regrowth, as the Sutton Hoo burial would probably have been inconceivable a century earlier. It reflected a new political complexity and also stronger contacts with the Continent.

SCOTLAND AND IRELAND

Between Hadrian's Wall and the Antonine Wall, the central and western parts of southern Scotland were occupied by British tribes which formed the kingdoms of Rheged in the south-west, and slightly later, Cumbria/Strathclyde which straddled the modern Anglo-Scottish border. Anglian settlers occupied the eastern coastal districts as far north as the Firth of Forth. Picts, who occupied the lands north of the Firth of Forth, left art of a high order, particularly carved stones that were presumably commissioned by their nobility. Pictish kings displayed their prowess in warfare and hunting. They also kept sacral figures – wizards or shamans – who underlined the status of the kings within the community.

The Scots were subsequently presented by chroniclers as Irish-speakers who settled in Argyll, from perhaps as early as the fourth century, but it is possible that this account exaggerates the impact of Ireland: instead of a wholesale migration, there may have been a much more small-scale one, possibly involving a change in political control. Moreover, as nineteenth-century invasion theses retreat, the view that there were always, or at least long before 500, Scots in western Scotland

and the islands is gaining ground. In the event, the Scottish kingdom of Dal Riata, with its major seat of power at Dunadd, and which benefited from its association with Christianity, absorbed the Pictish kingship and created the new kingdom of Alba (a Gaelic word for Britain) in the ninth century.

As in Scotland north of the Forth, there was no continuity from Roman rule in Ireland. It is clear that Christianity spread in Ireland in the fifth century. It may have reached southern Ireland from parts of western Britain the previous century. St Patrick came from Britain, possibly from one of the settlements along Hadrian's Wall, in the fifth century and there were some Christian influences even before his arrival. Ireland also had cultural links with Spain and western France. Ireland was thus affected by Christianity, but not, directly, by Roman cultural influence. Its culture was a complex mix of influences: pagan and Christian, oral and literate, native and imported.

More generally, Celtic Christianity was a dynamic element of a spreading cultural world. Traders brought Celtic Christianity to an area possibly extending as far north as the Faeroes and Scotland as well as to Ireland and Cornwall, and the great Celtic saints, notably Patrick, David, Columba, Brendan, and Columbanus, were active from the fifth century. The earliest layer of Irish Christianity was episcopal, but this soon became overshadowed by the influential monasteries. Celtic Christianity was dominated by monasticism, mysticism, and elements of syncretism from paganism. Celtic art interacted with Christianity: crosses were highly decorated, stone carvings were abundant, and there is evidence of Celtic hymnody.

WALES

Town life in fifth-century Wales continued in the Roman settlement in Caerleon and, possibly, Carmarthen, and Roman estate units may have continued to function in south-east Wales. Although Wales was less 'Romanised' than England, Rome continued to cast a shadow over it, both politically and culturally, but the Roman system collapsed. Wales ceased to be part of a major empire and, instead, became an assortment of political units focusing on the largely tribal leadership of locally powerful warlords, and resisting English conquest. Trade links by sea remained important in post-Roman Wales, and the same routes served both for the expansion of Christianity there, and for settlement from

Ireland. Roads remained vital land trade routes. Missionary activity from Gaul began in the fifth century.

If reliable information on the history of Wales for the rest of the first millennium CE is sparse, a product of its relative lack of political and cultural development compared with much of England, a number of themes nevertheless emerge. Christianity was clearly a major and growing force. There is evidence of ecclesiastical sites from all over Wales – monasteries, churches and hermitages – and it is clear that the church played an important role in cultural matters. Nevertheless, although Latin was used for liturgical (religious) purposes and for post-Roman gravestones and other inscriptions, and there was a significant element of Latin in its vocabulary, the Celtic language of the pre-Roman and Roman periods survived as an active vernacular and began its development into Welsh. It was at this stage that the 'P' branch of the Celtic languages rapidly evolved into Breton (in Brittany), Cornish, Welsh and Strathclyde/Cumbrian, while the other 'Q' branch became the Gaelic of Ireland, the Isle of Man and Scotland.

Wales had a 'Celtic culture' in common with other areas of Britain not conquered by the Anglo-Saxons. An older culture, or at least language, had survived both Rome and the Anglo-Saxon invaders. From the early/mid-first millennium CE in Wales there are quite a few inscriptions and from the later first millennium there is a good deal of Christian stone sculpture. However, no one, not the people who lived in what is now Wales, not the Angles, nor the Saxons, nor the Romans, had any consciousness of Wales or for that matter of England as such until the sixth century or later. There were separate kingdoms within Wales.

Wales, although it is a geographical expression, is culturally far more problematic, being as much as anything a survivor from an older civilisation which the Anglo-Saxons mainly supplanted. The struggles with the invaders lasted a long time; ultimately, the building of Offa's Dyke by King Offa of Mercia (r. 757–96) was to mark the definition of a boundary between Mercia and the Welsh kingdom of Powys. The sections to the north and south of that were probably not Offa's work and are of various dates. Nowhere else in the British Isles was a frontier quite so crucial, as the advance of the Anglo-Saxons, and later the Normans, was to help condition Welsh history. Indeed Wales was given its name by the English in terms of otherness: the Saxons used *Walas* or *Wealas* to describe the Britons and it meant both serfs and foreigners; the Welsh term for Wales, which probably arose in this period, was *Cymru*, meaning 'fellow countrymen' in English.

As the Anglo-Saxons advanced westwards, the land links between the surviving Romano-British communities were severed: Cumbria/ Strathclyde, Wales and Cornwall could not unite to any purpose. In particular, the struggle for control of northern England helped to define the future political shape of Britain. In 616, Ethelfrith of Northumbria conquered Cheshire, killing the king of Powys in a battle at Chester, and separated Wales from Cumbria. His successor, Edwin, continued Northumbrian pressure on the Welsh, defeating Cadwallon of Gwynedd in 629. Cadwallon, a Christian, then formed an alliance with the pagan Penda of Mercia (r. 632–54), and, in 633, invaded Northumbria, defeating and killing Edwin at Heathfield. Cadwallon was, however, in turn defeated and killed by Edwin's nephew, Oswald, the following year, and the Welsh lost their land links with the Cumbrians. Land links with the Celts of the south-west had been lost when Gloucestershire was conquered in the 570s. Wales became the most important area of surviving Romano-British civilisation.

THE SPREAD OF CHRISTIANITY

The replacement of the religious pluralism of Roman and post-Roman Britain by Christianity was to align the British Isles culturally far more closely with the Continent. A mission from Pope Gregory the Great, under Augustine, came in 597 to Canterbury, the capital of Kent, and had some success in the south-east. However, it was the Irish Church that was the base for the conversion of much of Britain. Christian missionaries came to Scotland from Ireland with the Scots. Although the Irish Church had a system of bishoprics, the numerous monasteries, such as Armagh and Clonmacnois, were more important. They were centres of devotional, missionary and cultural activity, including writing.

The church of Iona, off the west coast of modern Scotland, was founded by Columba, an Irish monk, in 563, and the Picts were converted by the early eighth century. A mission from Iona, under Aidan, founded Lindisfarne in Northumbria in 635. From that monastery, Mercia was converted. The Irish Church also had a major cultural influence in Anglo-Saxon England. There was tension, however, over the authority of the Papacy and the exact calculation of the date of Easter. As a result of the support of King Oswy of Northumbria at the Synod (Church meeting) of Whitby in 664, Roman customs prevailed, the authority of Iona over the Northumbrian Church was broken, and the path cleared for the organisation of the English Church by Theodore of Tarsus, whom the Pope appointed Archbishop of Canterbury. Irish monks played a major role throughout western Europe in both scholarship and missionary activity. They were particularly important at Charlemagne's court and in spreading Christianity in Germany. This flourishing Irish cultural and intellectual life was shattered by the Viking occupation. Ireland produced Europe's first post-Roman vernacular literature.

England, in turn, now became a major base for missionary activity, spreading Christianity in the Low Countries, Germany and, later, Scandinavia. Within the British Isles, pagan cults and practices were gradually destroyed or worn down by the Church, now sure of secular support. From the late seventh century, monastic churches or minsters were constructed at important centres. They provided pastoral care to sizeable areas but these were split up into small local parishes focused on parish churches. In England, most local parish churches were probably not founded until the tenth and eleventh centuries, and their foundation went on into the twelfth century. Many of them had started life as the private churches of secular landlords. In Wales, the 'Llan' probably emerged as an enclosure with a site for worship before the tenth century.

Christianity meant a spread of education and literacy, and the beginnings of written law, not least to protect churchmen and their property. Written instruments might serve to convey rights in land. Society was becoming at least partly institutionalised. The Church was a means of reintroducing Roman technologies and practices, including reading and writing, to the parts of early medieval Europe that had lost them, as well as introducing them elsewhere. The Church as the only institution that spanned the British Isles was also a major agent encouraging the flourishing of trade and the reintroduction and spread of coinage. Although, initially, a king's baptism was sufficient to 'convert' a whole tribe or kingdom, the baptism of all believers ensured that Christianity also became part of the personal and collective identity of everyone.

Christianity provided new media for the Anglo-Saxon artist in the form of stone sculpture and manuscript illumination. The 'Lindisfarne Gospels', probably the greatest of the great works of Northumbrian monasticism, illuminated between 689 and 721, revealed Irish influence in its script and ornamentation. Many of the decorative motifs used had their roots in pagan Saxon art, but others in the art of the Christian Mediterranean. One legacy of the culture was the Anglo-Saxon crosses, such as the Bewcastle and Ruthwell crosses. They probably served as funerary monuments or sanctuary markers. The principal carved decoration presented a series of sophisticated and literate scenes. The Ruthwell Cross bears, in runic lettering, a version of the Anglo-Saxon poem *The Dream of the Rood*, a powerful account of the crucifixion as told by the cross.

THE RISE OF LARGE KINGDOMS

The most important political development from the sixth and seventh centuries in England was the coalescence of the numerous small kingdoms into three major kingdoms, Northumbria, Mercia and Wessex. The process can be seen in cellular terms, with small units, probably based on successful warbands, amalgamating into larger units. Chance, especially the personalities of rulers and the results of warfare, helps to explain why some areas ceased to be independent kingdoms, while others flourished. Initially, Kent and East Anglia were important, but neither was able to benefit from the advance of the Anglo-Saxon frontier which, instead, helped the kingdoms of the frontier. The west Midland kingdoms of the Hwicce and the Magonsaetan were absorbed by Mercia, which from 654, and possibly the 630s, also dominated East Anglia: the king was killed in battle by Penda of Mercia in the 630s. Moreover, Oxfordshire, which had been a Saxon region, also became part of Mercia. With time, and particularly after *c.* 700, ruling houses were increasingly differentiated from those of landowners, and royal justice was to be differentiated from that of kin, feud and surety. A comparable process occurred in Wales.

Ireland was divided into about 100, mostly small kingdoms, each occupied by a tribe. Ties of dependence linked lesser kings to their more powerful counterparts, and by the eighth century certain kings had thus considerably extended their area of authority. The notion of the 'high king' developed in Ireland and, to some extent, elsewhere in the British Isles.

The relationship between kingdoms was very volatile. It was difficult to perpetuate any hegemony. In England, Aethelbert of Kent was able to act as a *bretwalda* (overking) in the 590s, which helps explain the importance of Augustine's success in Canterbury. Kent's influence helped ensure the establishment of a bishopric in London in 604. However, for most of the following century, the position of *bretwalda* belonged to Oswald (r. 634–41), Oswy (r. 641–70) and Egfrith (r. 670–85) of

Northumbria. They ruled between the Humber and the Forth in eastern Britain and the Mersey and the Ayr in the west, and were at times treated as overlords by the rulers of Mercia, Wessex, Strathclyde and the Pict and Scottish territories, but Northumbrian power was contested by Penda of Mercia (r. 632–54).

Defeat at the hands of Mercia (678) and the Picts (685) brought Northumbrian hegemony to an end. In 685, Bridei, king of the Picts, defeated and killed Egfrith at Nechtansmere near Forfar. Helped by the subsequent absence of a Northumbrian revival, this battle was crucial to the establishment of the geographical and political relationship of what, considerably later, were to be England and Scotland.

Northumbrian hegemony was replaced by that of Mercia, especially under Offa (r. 757–96). An effective ruler, he controlled such formerly independent kingdoms as Essex, Lindsey, East Anglia, Kent and Sussex, as well as London. As a result, Offa ruled a wealthy area with much money, whereas the Mercian heartland in the north-west Midlands was not monetarised. Wessex recognised Mercian protection in 786 and Offa's charters (formal documents) used the term 'King of the English' at least once. Offa is most famous for the earth dyke, a frontier line with the Welsh kingdom of Powys that may well have been a defensive work. The building of it must have entailed considerable organisation, a testimony to the administrative capability of Mercian England, as were the reforms to the coinage. Offa was responsible for a more standardised silver penny, bearing the king's head, which became the basis of English currency. Many earlier kings had issued coins, and their law codes made regular reference to coin use, but from Offa's time the quantity in circulation increased.

Offa's Dyke reflected the degree to which pressure from the English east shaped the extent of Wales, a process unmatched in this period for Scotland and Ireland, although the dyke was not the end of Mercian expansion. Durable and effective control of much of Britain was, however, beyond the capability of any one of the kingdoms. Cenwulf of Mercia (r. 796–821) harshly suppressed a rebellion in Kent in 798, but Wessex rejected Mercian protection in 802. Moreover, Mercia was weakened in the 820s by conflict in Wales and dynastic feuds; and in 825, after defeating the Mercians at Ellandun, Egbert of Wessex conquered Kent, Essex, Surrey and Sussex. Mercia followed in 829 but was soon independent again. Thus, there was little sign of political unification.

There were faint indications of a sense of national identity: the canons of the Synod of Hertford (672) were issued for, and applied to, the whole English Church, and Bede, a Northumbrian monk, wrote his *Ecclesiastical History of the English People* in 731. His purpose was ecclesiastical, not political, although his view of the English kingdoms at work ensured that he became a 'founder' of English history. In 829, Northumbria also acknowledged Egbert's overlordship, but, as yet, there was scant sense that Wessex would emerge as the centre of an English state.

Attempts to spread power brought a tentative measure of cohesion over much of what was to become Scotland. In the mid-eighth century, Angus mac Fergus (d. 761), King of the Picts, was able to make the Scottish kingdom of Dal Riata accept his overlordship, although he was unsuccessful with the British kingdom of Strathclyde. The practice of overlordship and 'high kings' was almost predicated on the assumption that large areas would be difficult to govern. After Angus died, Pictland was affected by serious strains, Dal Riata regained autonomy, and in 789 both Dal Riata and Pictland were brought under the control of a prominent Dal Riatan figure, Constantine. This new polity was from about 900 to be termed Alba, and eventually, Scot-land, a name demonstrating the seniority of the Scotti, or the Dal Riatan branch. Historians still debate how far Pictish identity was peacefully transmitted into the new polity, and how far violence was involved.

SOCIETY

The nature of the sources ensures that any account of society in the British Isles is necessarily tentative. Archaeological research can only reveal so much, particularly for the life of the bulk of the population, and written sources are very limited. Nevertheless, new archaeological methodologies offer many insights. For example, work on fossilised human stool has indicated the unhealthy nature of life in York in about 950.

Several themes emerge. The rationale and conduct of power were both violent. Feuds within and between royal families and between tribes ensured that society remained violent, the ethos of heroism revealed in the epic poem *Beowulf* being one of glory won through fighting. Society was also clearly unequal. Within each kingdom, below the ruling group, society was divided on both sides of the Irish Sea between free and unfree men; the latter worked the land. In modern society, there is a clear distinction between the sovereign power (the state/government) and a citizenry enjoying equal rights and status; but pre-modern society was characterised by the pervasive impact of different privileges and, within the elite, of relationships joining ruler and ruled which were deliberately personal, rather than distant and impersonal; the ethos of the warband. Status was measured by *wergild*: the different sums payable in disparate social groups as compensation for killing a man. The law code of Ine, King of Wessex, drafted between 688 and 694, distinguished the *wergilds* of the British elements in society from those of the English (Anglo-Saxon) elements: the former were second-class citizens. More generally, unfree men included both slaves and serfs, but the status of the two groups was different.

Society was not only hierarchical, but also male-dominated, deferential and patriarchal, while respect for age and authority, religious and secular, legal and law-enforcing, was crucial. The basic distinction was between the sexes. Women were subordinated to men and expected to defer to them, and wives were represented by their husbands in law. Gender roles were embodied in religious models such as the Virgin Mary and the saints. Women nevertheless played a vital role in the economy. Households were economic units to which women contributed greatly; not least by making clothes and processing food. Women, moreover, were not without rights. In the later Anglo-Saxon period there is evidence of their inheriting, holding and bequeathing lands, while married women could control separate property. Aside from the 'enclave' world of the nunnery, individual women also could gain prominence, most obviously as members of royal families, as with Aethelflaed, who ruled English Mercia in 911–18, or Emma, successively influential wife of Aethelred the Unready and Cnut. The Pictish royal succession was matrilineal. Furthermore, whatever the superior status and rights of men, relationships within marriage reflected both strength of personality and affection, a pattern that was also true of parent–child relations.

And yet personality and affection operated within a context of differential power and authority. A society of inherited status ensured that many women were treated like chattels or political counters. The centrality of military activity and ethos left scant independent role for women. Furthermore, female behaviour was classified and stereotyped by reference to religion. Alongside positive images of the woman as bride, wife and mother, there was a strong negative tradition of the woman as whore or harlot.

The roles of the environment and the human ecosystem were only slightly affected by technology. Indeed, patterns of life and death reflected the dominant role of the seasons. Moreover, physical strength and stature were of considerable importance, and wisdom was attached to age. There was no cult of youth or value attached to novelty: these are essentially developments of the last 250 years, and more particularly the last 90. Instead, society was reverential of and referential to the past. Inegalitarian social practices and institutions were taken for granted, and were also central to 'politics', an activity restricted to the social elite. Although tempered by the rise of lordship and kingship, kinship groups were of considerable importance and had defined legal roles in inheritance and in taking vengeance for hurts to kin members. Kin links were central to the practice of blood feuds.

People mostly lived in farmsteads and small hamlets. However, the open-field system and nucleated villages that were to be associated with the high-medieval period developed widely from the eighth century and were a major feature of later Anglo-Saxon social development. As farming systems became more settled, local manorial lordship developed. Hereditary tenure of land became more important and there was a closer definition of the status, rights and duties of *thegns* (nobles). Inheritance was important to social and political relationships, because of the nature of the economic system. Land, and labour on it, were central, and its ownership was markedly inegalitarian.

The British Isles were predominantly rural, in location, economy, politics and ethos; more so than during the Roman period. A small number of major ports – Ipswich, London, Sandwich, Southampton and York – developed spectacularly in the eighth century, as overseas and coastal trade became more regular. In the 730s, Bede described London as 'a mart of many peoples'. The Roman bridge at London was possibly rebuilt in the mid-ninth century. Southampton, which may have been planned by King Ine of Wessex (r. 688–726; he also built Taunton), is estimated to have covered 111 acres and was a major centre of trade and minting, although the site moved from the eighth to tenth centuries. Coinage developed in England in the late seventh and eighth centuries and, thanks to extensive metal-detector finds in recent years, it is now clear that the volume of coinage in the early eighth century was very high in eastern and southern England. This wealth reflected the scale and importance of England's major export, wool. By the tenth century, a more extensive urban network was in place in England, with numerous *burhs* (fortified proto-towns) founded by Alfred and his successors.

Some of the Alfredian and later *burhs* were re-foundations of Roman towns; whereas others were newly-created places.

Yet, although domestic and foreign trade became more important, agriculture remained central. It suffered from limited knowledge and technology in, for example, power sources and transmission, and in the selective breeding of crops and animals. There was a serious shortage of fertiliser, and fields therefore had to be left fallow (uncultivated) to restore their fertility. Livestock may have been smaller than their Roman predecessors and far smaller than their modern descendants; and meat and milk yields were much lower than today. Most labour was manual, repetitive, often arduous and usually monotonous.

Communications were relatively primitive, both for goods and for people. Long-distance bulk transport was only economic by water. Initially, the two major water systems centred on the Wash/Humber and Severn/Avon respectively, but the latter declined from the late sixth century as the related trade from the Mediterranean via Atlantic Spain and France to Cornwall declined. Instead, the Thames system centred on London grew in significance. However, rivers were affected by freezing, drought, silting and weirs, while sea travel was at the mercy of wind, waves and tides. On land, ridge routes were important as valleys were prone to flooding while their soil was often heavy and difficult to traverse. Bridging and ferry points that could be reached by ridge-routes were the central points in the communication system, linking in with the key water-routes. The greater role of bridges is suggested by the extent to which, from the 740s, labour service for bridge-building and repair became an important provision in charters. Horses were used for power and as pack animals for transport, as well as for military service and pleasure. Despite these limitations, settlement spread during the period. In Norfolk, for example, the seventh and eighth centuries saw a fleshing out of the earlier settlement pattern. It was to be a relatively prosperous society that attracted the attention of the Vikings.

VIKING ATTACKS

Much of Europe suffered a second wave of 'barbarian' attacks in the eighth, ninth and tenth centuries: Magyars from the east, Arabs from the south, and Vikings (Danes, Norwegians and Swedes) from Scandinavia. The Vikings, traders, colonisers and fighters, spread east to Russia, and west to Iceland, Greenland and the coast of North America. The main burden of Viking attack was on the British Isles, northern France and the Low Countries in the ninth century, with a fresh wave of attacks on Britain between 980 and 1075. The Vikings, possibly with limited land available for colonisation in Scandinavia, were motivated by opportunities for raiding and settlement in more prosperous and fertile lands, such as much of the British Isles, which were vulnerable to the amphibious operations that the Scandinavians could mount so well. Viking longboats, with their sails, stepped masts, true keels, and steering rudders, were effective ocean-going ships capable of taking to the Atlantic; but also able, thanks to their shallow draught, to be rowed in coastal waters and up rivers, even if there was only three feet of water.

Britain had been free from attack from the Continent for two centuries, but in 789 Danish ships were first recorded in English waters, and in 793–4 the pagan Norwegians brutally sacked the monastery of Lindisfarne, a major Northumbrian cultural and religious centre. Viking pressure increased in the 830s and 840s and the coastal regions of the British Isles were all affected. The Norse (Norwegians) overran and settled the Orkneys, the Shetlands, the far north of Scotland, and much of its west coast, as well as coastal regions of Ireland. In the Northern Isles and north-east Caithness the settlement was so extensive that the local language became a Norse dialect until replaced by Scots in the sixteenth to eighteenth centuries. The monastery of Iona was attacked in 795 and sacked in 802.

The Norse also made a major impact on Ireland. They were first recorded in 794 when they sacked *rechru* – probably Rathlin Island. The wealthy Irish monasteries attracted attack, and the numerous rivers and lakes facilitated Viking movement. From the 840s their military presence became stronger, with larger forces that overwintered in Ireland and developed permanent coastal bases. The first, Dublin, established in 841, was followed by Limerick, Wexford, Waterford and Cork: the early bases were destroyed in 902, but were re-created: the 'five towns' date to after 917. From such bases, the Norse dominated the Irish Sea and its trade and intervened in Wales, the Isle of Man, which they settled in the last quarter of the ninth century, and on the west coast of England. Viking pressure on Ireland increased from the early tenth century.

Moreover, the Norse from the 850s began pressing on the north Welsh coast, especially Anglesey, and plundered the royal seat of the major Welsh kingdom of Gwynedd in 968. In addition, in 870, Olaf, Norse king of Dublin, captured Dumbarton Rock, the leading position of the kingdom of Strathclyde. In the first two decades of the tenth century, the Norse colonised the coastline of north-west England, invading the Wirral from Dublin in 902. The place-names of Scandinavian settlements, with their typical endings of *–by*, *–scale* and *–thwaite*, are quite extensive in Cumbria and coastal Lancashire. Other Scandinavian place-names occur in parts of Ireland, such as east Antrim.

Danish pressure also increased on southern and eastern England. From the mid-ninth century the Vikings came not to plunder, but to conquer and stay. Danish invaders took up winter quarters in south-eastern England: in Thanet in 850 and Sheppey in 854. The Danish 'Great Army' abandoned operations in northern France and overran East Anglia (865) and Yorkshire (866–7): York was stormed in 866. Wessex had defeated attacks in 838 and 851, but in 871 King Alfred (r. 871–99) was nearly crushed and had to agree to pay tribute.

The Danes then turned on Mercia, which was conquered: King Burgred was defeated at Repton and fled to Rome. His successor, Ceowulf, paid tribute for western Mercia, while Mercia east and north of Watling Street – which became known as the Danelaw – became Danish. In 877 the Danes launched a sudden attack on Alfred, leading him to flee to the Somerset marshes at Athelney. He successfully reorganised his forces and defeated the Danes at Edington (878). The victory was followed by the Treaty of Wedmore in 879, leaving the Danes with the Danelaw. The Danish advance had been stopped.

There was considerable Danish settlement in the Danelaw. This is indicated by place-names, especially the endings of *–by* and *–thorp*, as well as the names of individuals noted in documents and material remains, although there is no agreement on the proportion of the population of the Danelaw that was Danish. As earlier with the Anglo-Saxon invasions, some interpretations stress major immigration, others a transfer of political control. The concentration of Danish place-names in particular parts of the Danelaw suggests extensive but patchy immigration as the background to a general process of hybridisation.

THE GROWTH OF WESSEX

Having stopped the Danes, Alfred went onto the offensive, capturing London in 886, and sought to strengthen Wessex. He built a fleet, created a more effective system of military recruitment and constructed a system of *burhs* (fortified proto-towns). These policies helped Alfred to defeat further Danish attacks in 892–6. At the same time, there was more resistance to the Norwegians in Ireland. They were increasingly confined to their bases and were driven from Dublin in 902 although they regained control in 917.

Alfred also aimed at stabilising society and creating a more effective Christian polity. He issued a code of existing law, began minting sound pennies (a clear sign of a well-established kingdom), fostered an image of Christian kingship, patronised learning, and established schools in order to produce priests and laity who would be wise and just leaders and administrators; as well as settling his kingdom to enable him to defeat the Danes and expand. Seeking to sustain his image, Alfred commissioned a biography, *The Life of King Alfred* (893), from Bishop Asser. This stressed his suffering and endurance, presenting effective royal leadership in a markedly Christian light.

Alfred's policies were continued by his successors. Conflict with the Vikings played a crucial role in the development of the English state, just as the Viking invasions of Scotland played a part in the growing power of the kingdom of the Scots. The earlier destruction of the other Anglo-Saxon ruling houses allowed Alfred and his successors to be portrayed as 'English', rather than merely 'West Saxon', kings. He presented himself as the champion of Christianity and all Anglo-Saxons against the pagan Danes, and was the crucial figure in the shift towards a new politics and a new country. However, although the process of advance under Alfred's heirs could be and has been presented as one of reconquest, the driving back of the Danes and the Norwegians, it was also one of conquest, in which the rulers of Wessex brought modern England under their authority.

A succession of able rulers was crucial. Edward the Elder (r. 899–924) and his sister Aethelflaed, Lady of the Mercians (r. 911–18), Athelstan (r. 924–39), and Edmund (r. 939–46) conquered East Anglia, and Danish Mercia and Northumbria, and English (western) Mercia was absorbed by Wessex in 918, the end of what had been a major independent power. Aethelflaed took Derby and obtained control of Leicester, exploits which the (West Saxon) *Anglo-Saxon Chronicle* appropriated to her brother, King Edward. The defeated Danes were allowed to keep their lands and the Danelaw retained distinctive features, including its own legal system. The Danes, however, converted to Christianity, apparently offering no significant resistance to adopting the Christianity of those amongst whom they settled.

The conquest of the north was a more protracted affair than that of the Midlands, and the Viking kingdom of York received important support from the Vikings in Dublin in resisting the advance of Wessex. The West Saxon rulers also laid claim to the overlordship of all Britain.

In 920 the rulers of Scotland, York, English Northumbria (the area north of the Tees that had successfully resisted the Vikings), and the Strathclyde Britons are said, by West Saxon sources, to have accepted Edward's lordship. His successor, Athelstan, captured York (927), invaded Scotland (934), defeated a united force of Scots, Strathclyde Britons and Norse from Ireland at Brunanburh (937), and formed alliances with leading Continental rulers. Athelstan saw himself as a king or overking or even emperor of Britain and this came out in his charters and coins to reflect a new conception of monarch and realm. Early on, he used the title of his father, Edward, and grandfather, Alfred, 'King of the Anglo-Saxons', but, following his conquest of Northumbria in 927, he started to call himself *rex Anglorum*, King of the English. For his coins, Athelstan chose a new image, becoming the first Anglo-Saxon king to be shown wearing a crown and described as *rex totius Britanniae*, King of all the British. The long witness lists to his charters provide evidence of significant national assemblies that look toward later parliament.

After Athelstan's death, however, Olaf II Guthfrithson, king of Dublin, gained York and the north Midlands with the support of the local population. York did not finally succumb to West Saxon control until 954 when Eric Bloodaxe, its last Norwegian king, was killed in an ambush. This left the West Saxon dynasty under Eadred (r. 946–55) dominant in England. In 973, Edgar (r. 959–75) was able to stage an elaborate coronation at Bath in which he was the first ruler to be *crowned* as King of the English; the title itself had been used by Offa and Athelstan. This crowning was crucial in the formation of the unified English nation. Probably as a consequence of the influence of Carolingian (the Frankish dynasty of Charlemagne) ideology, specifically the idea of a Christian empire, expressed by Jonas of Orleans and Hincmar of Rheims, which influenced Athelstan and Edgar, tenth-century Wessex moved towards a notion of kingship different from that of the amalgam of kingdoms epitomised by Offa's Mercia. The period from Alfred to Edgar was that of the definition of an English state, one that did not require, nor was constrained by, precise ethnic, tribal or geographical borders.

The expanding West Saxon state also developed internally. A county or shire system was consolidated and extended. The shires were in turn divided into hundreds or *wapentakes*, which were responsible for maintaining law and order. This was a priority for rulers such as Aethelstan concerned to end the lawlessness associated with the Danish conquest. The public courts were a link between rulers and free men; while a system of officials – *ealdormen*, sheriffs, port-reeves and hundredmen – linked the ruler and the localities. The county system offered decentralisation, but was also controlled with sophistication through writs. Service to the king led to gains of land and status: what had been the personal loyalties of the warband were increasingly given territorial form, regularity and aristocratic status and continuity.

There was also a system of assessment for taxation and military service. The coinage was improved and under Edgar it was re-minted on average every six years, a major administrative achievement that would not have been possible a century earlier. The state of the coinage indicated the development both of a cash economy and of an administrative system in which taxation and expenditure played major roles. Under Athelstan, Canterbury, London and Winchester were allocated eight moneyers each, while most towns only had one. Under Edward the Confessor (r. 1042–66), the coinage was re-minted every two or three years, with the coins struck at more than fifty mints. Re-coinages were a demonstration of national authority and power. Monetarisation also spread elsewhere in the British Isles, for example in the Isle of Man in the eleventh century.

The development in England of a sophisticated and spatially defined governmental system was matched by a revival of the Church, which had been greatly disrupted by Viking invasion and settlement. New monasteries were founded and monastic life was revived. This process began with the initiatives of Alfred, but continued under his successors. New dioceses were created at Crediton, Wells and Ramsbury in 909. Athelstan was particularly associated with the Church and proved a devout supporter. The process of revival culminated in a period of impressive activity in the late tenth century. Under Dunstan, Archbishop of Canterbury 960–88, there was a reform of the monasteries, in reaction to the ninth-century decline. Canterbury, Sherborne, Winchester and Worcester all became monastic cathedrals. As in Alba (in Scotland), the Church lent ideological and administrative support to the monarchy and also provided the context for cultural activity, including manuscript illumination (illustrations) and stone carving.

By c. 1000, England was an unusually developed state by European standards – in its royal and local government network, its shire framework, its shire towns, its centrally controlled, but regionally-produced coinage, its legal system, its close links between Crown and Church, and the absence of a strong separatist politics. Combined with the wealth of its economy, it is easy to appreciate the appeal of England to later Danish and Norman conquerors. Nor is it a surprise that the Normans left much of the system in place and developed it.

IRELAND

Resistance to Viking invasion also served to bring a measure of political consolidation in the Celtic lands: the history of the British Isles became very much a matter of the survival of the fittest or at least most fortunate. Máel Sechnaill I (d. 862) was the first ruler to wield authority over most of Ireland. At the battle of Tara (980), Máel Sechnaill II, high king of Ireland, defeated the Dublin forces and seriously weakened the Vikings. Brian Bórama (c. 926–1014), the son of a minor Irish king, defeated the Norse of Limerick at the battle of Sulcoit in about 968, gained control of Munster, captured Dublin in 1000, deposed Máel Sechnaill II, and was recognised as high king in 1002. His defeat of his Irish rival Máel Mórda, king of Leinster, and of the latter's Viking allies from Dublin, Orkney and Scandinavia, at Clontarf (1014) decisively weakened the Vikings in Ireland, although Brian was killed in the battle and did not face a challenge comparable to that faced by Aethelred 'the Unready' in England. Brian was replaced by Máel Sechnaill II, but, after his death, no high king ruled without significant opposition.

Indeed, Ireland did not see the development of a strong state comparable to England. The crucial political level became that of the sub- or provincial kingdoms: Connacht, Leinster, Meath, Munster and Ulster. Each, especially the last, was in turn divided into independent lordships based essentially on tribal domains. Powerful sub-kings, such as Turloch O'Brien of Munster (d. 1086) and his son Muircertach (r. 1086–1119), and Turloch O'Connor of Connacht (r. 1119–56) and his son Rory (r. 1166–83), won and maintained the high kingship in bitter struggles. Norse influence continued, and many leading figures were bilingual in Irish and Norse.

SCOTLAND

Viking attack weakened the Dal Riatan dynasty that had gained control of Pictland and in about 843 it was replaced by Kenneth MacAlpin (d. 858) who became ruler of the Scots and Picts. He and his descendants did not, however, control all of the area of modern Scotland. The area centred on the Moray Firth resisted control until the early twelfth century. The Western Isles and seaboard were also independent, while, to the south, there was Strathclyde and also Northumbria, which ruled Lothian. Kenneth MacAlpin's descendants were more interested in expanding south than north, overrunning Strathclyde early in the tenth century and Lothian later that century. Victory at Carham in 1018 cemented the latter achievement. The River Tweed, Cheviot Hills and Solway Firth provided a geographical boundary between Scotland and England, but the frontier between them was not fixed and there was no ethnic unity to either. What eventually became Scotland was ethnically, geographically, economically and culturally diverse, and included Scots, Picts, the Britons of Strathclyde and the Angles of Lothian. Until the mid-twelfth century it was unclear whether much of what is now northern England, and especially Cumbria and Northumberland, would be part of England or of Scotland. Moreover, the Hebrides and the Isle of Man remained a separate lordship under Norway until 1266 and Orkney and Shetland until 1468.

The same processes of development seen in Wessex were also influential in Scotland. The Church and association with particular churches, saints, relics and clerics brought ideological sanction, propaganda strength, administrative support and backing in particular localities. Nobility developed as an inherited characteristic and this growing stability helped provide administrative strength alongside military reach, enhancing the power of the monarch. Although Scotland was far less monetised an economy, society and political system than England, and did not mint its own coinage, its administration developed, with mormaers holding regional power and thanes being responsible for tax collection and local control.

WALES

Wales was the least affected of the four 'countries' by the Vikings, although the most affected by pressure from within the British Isles. Important as English pressure was, however, it would be wrong to juxtapose overly coherent realities of Welshness and Englishness, or to argue that the English set the terms for Welsh political development, and to neglect the role of internecine, particularly dynastic, struggles. Thus, the failure of the kingdoms of Deheubarth and Gwrtheyrnion in central Wales to survive was due in part to the greater strength of Gwynedd and Dyfed.

Welsh inheritance customs – the division of property among sons – may have made it difficult to translate territorial gains into more cohesive statehood, although kingship was, at least in theory, indivisible. What probably happened in the case of such rulers as Rhodri Mawr of Gwynedd (d. 878) was that they might accumulate several kingships and, on their deaths, individual kingships would be inherited by different sons. Nevertheless, Rhodri's grandson, Hywel Dda, Howel the Good (d. 950), eventually came to rule over most of Wales. Hywel was a major figure, the first Welsh king who certainly issued his own coinage, and in about 928 he went on pilgrimage to Rome. By later tradition, Hywel is also held to have been the codifier of Welsh law (though this may be a twelfth-century appeal to history). The laws attributed to him were the basis of an ordered kindred society, until 1284 in some respects and until 1536 in others.

Hywel's death was followed by internecine conflict and more anti-English activity, and the English state, with its growing pretensions to overlordship in Britain, came to intervene with increasing frequency. The South Welsh in 886 made some kind of submission to Alfred, to whom they turned for help against the Vikings, and this may have lasted into the early tenth century. Welsh rulers attended Athelstan's court and were regarded by him as subordinates. Under Edward the Confessor (r. 1042–66), the royal titles of King of the English and of the British were used indifferently and, although Ireland was completely independent, Wales and Scotland were in part dependent.

The political geography of Wales may be compared with that of England; kingship was inherent in the individual kingdoms and there was no kingship of Wales. But, whereas in England unity was created by the Viking destruction of all kingships bar one (Wessex), this did not happen in Wales, and a similar process of consolidation in the face of foreign attack was delayed until the Anglo-Normans conquered much of Wales.

The Welsh rulers of the period spent much of their time in fighting. The rise of Gwynedd under Llywelyn ap Seisyll (d. *c.* 1023) and his son Gruffudd ap Llywelyn (d. 1063) formed the most important development in the pre-Norman period. Territorial consolidation was complicated by foreign intervention: the Dublin Norse assisted Gruffudd's opponents. Welsh rulers, including Gruffudd, were willing to seek such support. Gruffudd, however, had serious clashes with the English, particularly with Harold Godwineson of Wessex. In 1063 Harold, campaigning by land and sea, harried Wales until Gruffudd was killed by some of his men and his head delivered to Harold, who also took his wife. Gruffudd's half-brothers were allowed to inherit Gwynedd and Powys on condition that they swore allegiance.

It is unclear whether Gwynedd could have developed as Wessex did in the tenth and eleventh centuries, serving as the basis for a Welsh state. Unlike England, there is little sign of governmental sophistication in Wales, and less than there was in Scotland. The 'conquest' of one part of Wales, Scotland or Ireland by the ruler of another amounted to a personal submission and the giving of hostages rather than the loss of administrative control and consolidation. What is clear is that the power of the rulers of Gwynedd and Scotland and the high kings of Ireland rested on military success. After the Norman conquest of England, the military pressure on these rulers was to increase appreciably.

A CENTURY OF INVASION

In the eleventh century, the largest British state, the English kingdom created by the rulers of Wessex, was overthrown twice by foreign invasion. In each case, England became a subject – part of a polity (political organisation) based on the Continent. The second conquest, that by the Normans, was followed by a social recasting of England; but not the first.

The first invasion arose from the revival of Danish vitality; although now the Danes came not as independent warbands but as the forces of another well-developed kingdom. Economic growth, a monetary economy and wealth in silver made England a tempting target. Danish raids on coastal regions of England resumed in 980 and were followed by major attacks from 991, the year in which the Danes defeated the Essex militia at Maldon. English resistance was organised by Edgar's younger son, Aethelred 'the Unready' (r. 978–1016), who came to the throne after his supporters murdered his elder brother. Like King John, Aethelred, who ruled for nearly forty years, has been underrated. He made major efforts to organise an effective response to the Danes, but, like John, and later Charles I, he appears to have lacked the ability to command or elicit trust, both vital facets of kingship in an aristocratic society.

Aethelred may have faced Danish armies that at times were larger than those that had attacked Alfred's Wessex. He attempted to buy the

Danes off with Danegeld (protection money). At least £240,000 was paid, and much has been discovered in coin hoards in Scandinavia. The money was a testimony to the wealth and organisation of the English state, although the figures given in the *Anglo-Saxon Chronicle* may be exaggerated and anyway the policy was unsuccessful in the long term. Although resistance continued for many years, King Swein of Denmark led major attacks in 1003–6 and 1013. The last led Aethelred to flee to Normandy. By the Peace of Alney (1016), England was divided between Swein's son, Cnut, and Aethelred's eldest son, the vigorous Edmund Ironside, and, when Edmund soon died, Cnut, under the terms of the earlier peace accord, became king of all England (r. 1016–35), being 'elected' or recognised as king by the Witan, the great council of the kingdom.

After Cnut inherited Denmark from his elder brother in 1019, England became part of a multiple kingdom. He executed or exiled his opponents, introduced a number of Danes into the aristocracy and divided the kingdom into a small number of earldoms. Yet Cnut sought to rule not as a conqueror, but as a lord of both Danes and non-Danes. He was the king of a number of kingdoms, not a monarch seeking to enlarge one kingdom. Cnut took over an effective governmental system, did what an English monarch was supposed to do as head of state and, unlike the Norman William the Conqueror, did not have to face rebellions. In 1018, he reiterated the legislation of his predecessors. Cnut did not purge the Church, was the benefactor of a number of prominent English monasteries and was not culturally alienated from the Anglo-Saxon world. He made London his military and governmental centre in England.

Cnut's empire fell apart after his death. His son Harthacnut, who succeeded to Denmark and had a claim to England, was challenged for the latter by his half-brother, Harold Harefoot. Powerful support from the earls of Mercia and Wessex led Harold to gain control of the entire kingdom in 1037. Harthacnut replaced him when Harold died in 1039, and had his half-brother's body exhumed and thrown into the River Thames. Harthacnut, however, died without children in 1042. The willingness, in 1016 and 1035, to agree to partition is noteworthy, but so also is the short-lived nature of both these agreements.

Although the Norwegians continued to be important around the Irish Sea and in northern and western Scotland, the Viking age was over in England. There were to be later attacks – Harald Hardrada of Norway invaded in 1066, the Danes in 1069–70 and 1075 – but they were unsuccessful. England was no longer to look to Scandinavia, but, instead, was soon to be immersed in the politics of France.

Under Edward 'the Confessor' (r. 1042–66), Aethelred's surviving son, the house of Wessex was restored. His reign shared in the demographic growth, agrarian expansion and commercial growth of the tenth and eleventh centuries. As an instance of growing profitability, property boundaries became increasingly demarcated. Trade routes such as the Thames were developed. Wool exports to Flanders were of growing value, as the arts of sheep and corn husbandry were mastered using the sheepfold. Breeds of sheep with good wool were developed. There was also considerable trade with the Rhineland, from which millstones and pottery were imported. Long-distance trade with Italy and Spain also grew, with the export of wool and probably slaves in return for spices and wax.

However, the reign was dominated by the question of the succession. The childless Edward favoured the ducal house of Normandy, the family of his mother Emma which had sheltered him for many years. Norman influence was resisted by Edward's father-in-law, Earl Godwine of Wessex. In 1051–2, Godwine rebelled and was exiled, only to return and oblige Edward to reinstate him and expel his Norman friends. After Godwine died in 1052, his eldest son, Harold, succeeded him and dominated England for the rest of Edward's reign. Edward focused on Westminster where he both rebuilt the monastery and also constructed a royal palace. The monastery with its abbey church became part of a large palace complex, the church becoming the first large Romanesque building in England.

After Edward died on 5 January 1066, Harold was elected or recognised as king by the Witan, the great council of the kingdom. Harold stated that Edward had granted him the kingdom on his deathbed; but Duke William of Normandy claimed that Edward had promised him the succession when he visited England in 1051 and that Harold had acknowledged this claim in 1064.

Fearing Norman invasion, Harold concentrated his forces on the south coast, but William was delayed by contrary winds and Harold therefore marched north in September 1066 to confront a Norwegian invasion under Harald Hardrada that was supported by Harold's exiled brother, Tostig. The invaders defeated the local forces and seized York on 20 September, only to be surprised and crushed by Harold in their camp at Stamford Bridge (25 September). Harald and Tostig were both killed.

Three days later, William landed at Pevensey on the south coast. Harold rushed south to attack William before the Normans established themselves. The English army, however, was weakened by casualties at Stamford Bridge and by fatigue from its long marches, and was outnumbered near Hastings on 14 October by about 7,000 troops to 5,000. Harold chose a strong defensive position on the slopes of a hill, thus offering protection against the Norman cavalry. The battle was hard-fought, its outcome far from certain, but the shieldwall of the English housecarls was disrupted by advances designed to exploit real or feigned retreats by the Normans and at last the English position was broken, Harold falling, apparently with an arrow in his eye; although he may have been hacked down by horsemen.

William then moved rapidly to exploit his victory. His demoralised opponents lacked determined leadership: many of the natural leaders had died at Hastings, and Edgar Atheling, grandson of Edmund Ironside, the Anglo-Saxon claimant to the throne, was weak and a mere totem figure. Unable to storm London Bridge, William crossed the Thames to the west of London where morale crumbled. At Berkhamsted his opponents submitted. On Christmas Day 1066, William was acclaimed king in Westminster Abbey. A high level of tension was indicated when the acclamation of William as king by the English in the church led Norman troops outside to fear opposition. They reacted by setting fire to several buildings and killing some of the bystanders.

The most powerful of the states in the British Isles had fallen with unprecedented speed, in part due to the unification of England by the house of Wessex. England was now to be exposed to the full force of new political, social and cultural impulses, and, largely through Anglo-Norman, or, as they became, English intermediaries, these impulses were to affect or influence the subsequent history of the rest of the British Isles.

In Scotland, there was also a violent discontinuity in the eleventh century, although this was not due to Viking or Norman conquest. Instead, the complex interrelationship of a lack of a settled succession law and the role of powerful regional potentates, led Macbeth, a member of the royal family who dominated Moray, to challenge Duncan who had inherited the throne from Malcolm in 1034 through his mother, Malcolm's daughter: matrilineal descent lacked the prestige of its patrilineal counterpart. In 1040, with the help of Earl Torfinn of Orkney, Macbeth defeated and overthrew Duncan. He ruled until defeated by Duncan's son Malcolm, in 1057. Malcolm was helped by Earl Sigurd of Northumberland, but this intervention, which could now be seen as foreign, in no way compared to the changes that were to be wrought by William I in England. Instead, Malcolm III had to consolidate the position of his dynasty. Thus, very different political inheritances characterised England and Scotland after 1066, although both were to be affected by some common trends, not least feudalism.

3

The Middle Ages

INTRODUCTION

The two dates most commonly associated with the Middle Ages in England are 1066 and 1485. William the Conqueror's victory at Hastings in 1066 brought the Normans to the throne of England, and was ultimately responsible for shifting the British Isles from the Scandinavian world to one centred on France. Richard III's defeat by Henry Tudor at the battle of Bosworth in 1485 is popularly seen to mark the close of the Middle Ages. There are dangers in endowing either of these dates, particularly 1485, with undue significance, but both are in a way appropriate. Both relate to England and each centres on a change in the ruling dynasty. Although there are no reliable population figures – the first national census was not until 1801 – medieval England contained more people, was wealthier, and featured more in European politics than Ireland, Scotland or Wales.

The politics of England, as of Scotland, centred on the ruler, on his views and entourage, whereas for Ireland and Wales it was the case of the rulers. The character of a reign depended on the personality of the monarch and this was of great importance for the stability of the country, for the personal relationship between the monarch and the great nobles (aristocrats) was crucial to political order. It is therefore possible to write a history of the Middle Ages that centres on the rulers and is merely an account of their reigns in chronological order. Such an approach captures much of the reality of the high politics of the period, but it would also omit much that was of consequence to developments. Two crucial aspects that would be omitted are social history and the regional dimension. Both must therefore be addressed in addition to the high political history of the period.

Information on England at the outset is provided by the *Domesday Book* (1086), a land survey ordered by William the Conqueror so that he could ascertain his own resources and those of his tenants, although what *Domesday* was for is still highly controversial. There is nothing comparable for Ireland, Wales or Scotland. *Domesday*'s contents provide a guide to the extent to which English landowners had been replaced by Normans. Both as a result of the 1066 campaign and as a consequence of the suppression of subsequent rebellions, there had been a social revolution at the level of the elite.

This had had far less effect at the level of the bulk of the population. Their life continued to be dominated by the pressures of agricultural life and the rhythms of a harsh demographic regime, notably low life expectancy. *Domesday* revealed the extent to which the detailed nature of local environments influenced settlement patterns and economic activities. Thus, the silts and peat fens in the south-east of Lincolnshire were little settled: the marshland attracted few, bar salt-makers. In Norfolk, the fertile, well-drained river valleys were far more heavily populated than the high, dry interfluves; and readily-worked lighter soils were easier to plough than poorly-drained heavy soils.

Under the Normans, the crucial economic unit was the manor, the jurisdictional unit consisting of a demesne (home farm) directly under the lord, and the rest of the estate from which the lord was entitled to day labour, rent and the profits of justice. Whereas justice is taken for granted today as a public system, the Middle Ages was a period in which there was much private justice. Food-rents and labour services had existed under the Anglo-Saxons, but the Normans brought heavier tenurial burdens as a consequence of their social system of feudalism, under which manors were granted to vassals in return for military service. Peasants became subject to closer control and some free men had their status and rights lessened by the new lords. The Norman conquest thus changed more than simply the world of high politics.

NORMANISATION

Unlike the Danish seizure of the throne by Cnut in 1016, that by William was followed by a social revolution. William, who claimed to be the nominated successor of Edward the Confessor, may not have intended this, for Englishmen who submitted at the beginning of his reign were allowed to keep their lands and William appointed two in succession as Earl of Northumbria, but the scale of the popular resistance to the spread and consolidation of Norman rule led to the adoption of a harsher attitude. Like the Anglo-Saxon resistance to the Danes in the late ninth and early eleventh centuries, resistance was considerable, and there was an additional factor in the shape of supportive foreign intervention from Denmark (1069–70) and Scotland (1070). Risings in Herefordshire, Kent, the north, and the south-west (1067–8), were followed by a major crisis in 1069 involving risings in the north, the West Country, and the west Midlands, as well as Danish and Scottish invasions. Under Hereward the Wake, the Isle of Ely resisted. In 1068, both Edgar, Edward the Confessor's grand-nephew who had submitted to William in late 1066, and Earl Gospatric of Northumbria, rebelled, leading William to establish garrisons at York and Durham. The latter garrison was, however, massacred in 1069, and when the revolt spread William responded with the brutalisation of the population in the 'harrying of the north' in the winter of 1069–70.

Lack of coordination among the rebellions and the failure of sustained Scandinavian assistance were crucial to the consolidation of the new regime, but the length of time that this process took means that it is inappropriate to think of the Norman conquest as being completed in 1066. Norman authority north of the River Tees did not become a reality until 1072 when William led an army north, forced Malcolm III of Scotland to do homage for Lothian, installed Waltheof, a member of the native ruling house whom he had married to a niece, as Earl of Northumbria, and built a castle at Durham. In 1075, a rebellion by disaffected Normans was combined with English and Danish action, but the rebels were unsuccessful. Waltheof, one of their number, was executed, and the new Bishop of Durham, a Lorrainer, was made Earl, but he was killed in a fresh rebellion in 1080, and William had again to send forces to restore order. A castle was erected at what was to become Newcastle, and effective Norman power thus reached the River Tyne. A Norman was appointed Bishop of Durham. Northumberland was not Normanised until the reign of Henry I (1100–35).

The devastation and dislocation that these conflicts brought helped to ensure that the new order created by the Normans, a warrior people, had a military logic and structure. This structure was demonstrated most clearly by the construction of numerous castles, as much signs of Norman power as the roads and forts of Roman Britain and the fortified towns of late Saxon England. The location of castles reflected a number of factors, not only military imperatives but also local resources and politics. Early Norman castles were generally earth-and-timber constructions, for these could be built quickly, and were thus a flexible means of defence. Such castles as Norwich, built by 1075, were 'motte and bailey' structures: wooden stockades atop earth mounds. As with the Romans, a process of consolidation led to more imposing and permanent structures. By 1125 Norwich's mound was crowned by a strong square stone keep.

It is entirely appropriate that the most prominent surviving remains from Norman England should be stone castles, such as the White Tower at the centre of the Tower of London, and stone cathedrals, such as Durham. They were expressions of power and control, centres for government, political and religious. The first castles constructed in Lincolnshire were those of Lincoln and Stamford. They were probably built to control both towns and routes, although the reasons why individual castles were built are often unclear.

Power is an appropriate theme: the expropriations of the early Norman period constituted and reflected a change that was more sweeping than anything subsequent in English history: the only comparison is with the destruction of Catholic power and expropriation of Catholic lands in late seventeenth-century Ireland. Many castles, for example Cambridge, Chester and Wallingford, were built over existing towns, devastating their townscapes. The destruction associated with the Norman conquest hit the economy hard.

The rebellion of 1069 encouraged a Normanisation of both Church and land, the latter largely to the benefit of those who had helped most in the conquest. Senior clerical appointments (and thus the control over Church lands) largely went to foreigners while the majority of English landlords were dispossessed. Most of the new rulers of the localities were Normans, though others from northern France also benefited. Alongside a ruling dynasty that linked England and Normandy, a single aristocracy was created, while the foundation of 'daughter' houses of Norman monasteries created new links in the Church, as did the appointment of foreign clerics such as the Italian archbishops of Canterbury, Lanfranc 1070–89 and Anselm 1093–1109. The Pope had supported the Norman invasion. Latin replaced Anglo-Saxon in official documents in the 1070s: William was not simply acting as the Confessor's heir.

Castles were royal or private. They were the centres of power, of royal government and of what has been termed the feudal system.

Though feudalism is generally attributed to the Norman conquest, aspects of it existed in Anglo-Saxon England and might have become stronger even without the conquest. The essential characteristics of the system were the personal relationship, cemented in an act of homage, between lord and vassal. In this relationship the lord promised support and protection in return for service, principally military, and the grant-ing of lands, or fiefs, to vassals, again in return for service, principally military. The usefulness of the term 'feudalism' as a description of this system is controversial, in part because a familiar definition and use of the term, that derived from Karl Marx, does not centre on military service but on a much broader economic concept focused on control over land and labour. It is important, however, to focus attention on the contractual tie between lord and vassal, which was central to the development of a system of political relations which invested the vassal/subject with rights. A feudal tenant could break his obligation to his overlord if the latter broke his to him, whereas in a sacral monarchy a tenant in his capacity as a subject could not break his obligation to obey. The obligations implicit in feudalism, therefore, ultimately made Magna Carta (see p. 61) possible.

Norman lords held their estates by a military tenancy obliging them to provide a number of knights for service roughly proportionate to the size of the estate, an obligation that was usually discharged by enfeoffing the required number with lands of their own in return for service. However, the *familia regis*, the king's military household, was a permanent and professional military body that was therefore more important than the feudal host. The first three Norman monarchs were capable military leaders and this was important to the consolidation of their position.

THE POLITICS OF NORMAN ENGLAND

Initially designed to assist in the consolidation of Norman rule, castles rapidly lost the function of holding down the English, for the latter were turned into a conquered people remarkably quickly. Though there was considerable assimilation, there was no comparison with the Roman attempt to co-opt and Romanise local elites: the Normans were too land-hungry, and they had a different ethos from that of the Romans. In addition, the energy and strength of Norman England were expressed in a determination to push the frontiers back, and castles played a crucial role in this process. They, however, were also swiftly required for another function: dealing with disputes within the Norman elite.

Rivalry within the Norman elite reflected competition between nobles, disputes between them and monarchs and, most seriously, succession problems in the Norman dynasty. Impartibility (undivided inheritance) vied with the practice of all members of a family having a claim; and while male primogeniture (succession by the eldest male child) became the rule very quickly, it was resisted by other claimants. William I (r. 1066–87) died as a result of injuries sustained when thrown by his horse in the French town of Mantes, which he had burnt as a result of a border conflict. William was succeeded in Normandy by his oldest son Robert, who was in rebellion against him when William died, but he bequeathed England to the second son, William II 'Rufus' (r. 1087–1100). The latter tried to reunite the inheritance and, after some fighting, Robert pawned Normandy to William in 1096 in order to raise funds to go on the First Crusade. Politically and militarily successful, Rufus became unpopular with the Church because of his treatment of it. By leaving bishoprics vacant, Rufus was able to enjoy their revenues, while a dispute with Archbishop Anselm of Canterbury, over Rufus's lack of support for ecclesiastical reform and his hostility to papal authority, led Anselm to leave the country in 1097.

However, Rufus had a very high reputation in lay knightly circles. In 1092 he entered Cumbria with an army. The area had been disputed between the kings of the Scots and the Earls of Northumbria, but Malcolm III of Scotland had been acknowledged as overlord in 1058. Rufus created a town and built a castle at Carlisle, established a Norman ally at Kendal and made the Solway and the Liddel the northern border of the kingdom. He was also successful against Norman rebels and the French. Rufus's death in the New Forest in 1100 was probably a hunting accident, though there have been claims that he was murdered.

Rufus was succeeded in England by his younger brother, Henry I (r. 1100–35). Robert, who had taken part in the capture of Jerusalem (1099), returned to Normandy in 1100 and in 1101 invaded England, but Henry persuaded him to renounce his claim to the throne. Relations between the two brothers remained poor, however, and in 1105 Henry invaded Normandy. In 1106 he defeated Robert at Tinchebrai and conquered Normandy, imprisoning his brother until his death in 1134. It was important to keep England and Normandy together, because so many barons had lands on both sides of the Channel. With a single Anglo-Norman aristocracy, if England and Normandy were separated between two competing rulers, then the hapless members of the aristocracy would be forced to choose between them. To address this fundamental tension within the Anglo-Norman state, stability could only be regained through reunification.

The duchy, however, had a long land frontier and, in the kings of France and counts of Anjou, aggressive neighbours. Furthermore, the creation of the Anglo-Norman polity upset the political situation in northern France. Just as Cnut had concentrated on Scandinavia, so the often brutal Henry devoted most of his energies to consolidating his position in northern France, by war and diplomacy. Norman power was extended by bringing the neighbouring principalities of Maine and Brittany under control, and Louis VI of France was defeated at Brémule (1119). Henry was an effective military leader.

The costs of Henry's protracted conflicts were in large part met by England, the administration being conducted by the Exchequer, which was able to provide a regular and methodical collection of royal revenues and control of expenditure. The precocious administrative development of England was in part a result of Henry I's concentration on Normandy. Means had to be found of ruling England efficiently in the absence of the king. In part it resulted from the application of new ideas and methods, notably the abacus, used as the basis of Exchequer methods of calculation, though much of the governmental machinery of the Anglo-Saxon monarchy was maintained. Old institutions were used for the benefit of new rulers with particular concepts of justice and government, and novel problems, especially those arising from the Norman link. Both royal and ecclesiastical government therefore changed appreciably. The expansion of royal judicial activity under Henry I and the appointment by the Crown of local and itinerant justices, were signs of a more sophisticated and settled administration which extended across the whole kingdom. Thanks to an adroit mixture of ruthlessness, patronage and consultation with the magnates, and his effective administration, Henry kept England stable, though the *Anglo-Saxon Chronicle* presents a picture of an oppressively predatory government.

Stability was jeopardised by the succession. Henry I failed in the most crucial obligation of a monarch, that of leaving an uncontested succession. He was very fertile, siring over twenty illegitimate children, but his only legitimate son, William, died, when the *White Ship* was wrecked during a Channel crossing in 1120. Despite Henry's remarriage, there was to be no other son. Henry's hopes therefore rested on his daughter, Matilda, who in 1128 was married to Geoffrey Plantagenet, heir to the county of Anjou.

When Henry died in 1135, the throne, however, was seized by the initially popular Stephen of Blois (r. 1135–54), son of William I's daughter Adela. Matilda invaded in 1139 and captured her cousin Stephen at the battle of Lincoln (1141). The turn of fate was then rapid. Matilda's haughty behaviour soon lost her London, while, also in 1141, she was defeated at Winchester by Stephen's wife, also Matilda. As a result, Henry's daughter Matilda had to exchange Stephen for her captured half-brother Robert of Gloucester. The crisis of Stephen's reign reflected and in turn exacerbated problems arising from the uncertainties of succession in the new feudal order. Prominent nobles, such as John the Marshal in Wiltshire and Hampshire, used the civil war to consolidate their own positions and pursue their own interests. Local authority was seized by such nobles and much of Henry I's system of government collapsed. Stephen's reign acquired a reputation as a period of anarchy, when, in the words of the *Anglo-Saxon Chronicle*, 'Christ and his saints slept'. David I of Scotland took over Cumbria and Northumberland. In 1144 Geoffrey Plantagenet completed the conquest of Normandy and in 1152 his heir, Henry, invaded England. The nobility on both sides wanted peace and their lands on both sides of the Channel, and in 1153 they obtained the Treaty of Westminster. Stephen was to remain king, but agreed to adopt Henry as his heir. Stephen died within a year and Henry II (r. 1154–89) came to the throne as the first of the Angevin (Plantagenet) dynasty.

The world of Norman England thus ended, as it had begun, in war. Indeed, conflict had been the dominant theme of the period: the conquest of England, campaigns against Welsh and Scots, frequent hostilities with other rulers in France, and, most seriously, after the death of William the Conqueror, civil war within the Norman elite, most crucially the ruling dynasty. It was scarcely surprising that military obligation should have played such a prominent role in the social structure, that fealty, loyalty and protection should have been so crucial to political links, nor that so much should have been expended on constructing and maintaining castles. Not all castles had massive stone keeps: those have survived better than the initially far more numerous mottes and ringworks, which relied on earthworks; but they exemplify the resources, not least of money, skill and labour, taken from a relatively poor, low-productivity agrarian economy and devoted to war and military matters; while the cathedrals and churches of the period demonstrate that the same was true of expenditure on the Church. In 1138, for example, Stephen's influential brother, Henry of Blois, Bishop of Winchester, is reported to have begun six castles. In some respects, this consistent expenditure had a more serious impact on the lives of the people of Norman England than the individual wars of the period. The most serious, the civil wars of Stephen's reign, were traditionally regarded as devastating, though more recently, as with the Wars of the Roses, historians have tended to reduce earlier assessments of their destructiveness. Nevertheless, it is worth considering the psychological costs of a lengthy civil war, and the impact of an abrupt change on people who had known over three decades of civil peace under Henry I. More significantly, the wars of the period placed greater weight on the already-strong military values of society. England was scarcely unique in this emphasis, but it was an essential feature of her society.

The other essential characteristics of society were determined by environment, technological level and socio-cultural inheritance. The Judeao-Christian inheritance, clearly enunciated in the teachings and laws of the Church, decreed monogamy and forbade polygamy, marriage with close kin, incest, homosexuality, abortion, infanticide, adultery, pederasty and bestiality. Birth was stipulated as the purpose of matrimony, and condemned outside it. Divorce was very difficult and annulment the preserve of nobles and royalty. This moral 'agenda' was decreed and enforced with greater vigour after the disruption of the ninth- and early eleventh-century Viking invasions, and even more so after the Norman conquest, though the effectiveness of its enforcement was probably limited until the bureaucratic developments of the twelfth century. The Norman conquest led to a reassertion of episcopal authority, to a further expansion of the parochial (parish) system at the expense of the older network of minster churches, to monastic revival, and to the creation of a new monastic structure firmly linked to developments in northern France.

New institutional developments were related to the imposition of a 'foreign' emphasis, but they also reflected a widespread movement for Church reform that characterised the late eleventh century, and was supported by archbishops Lanfranc and Anselm of Canterbury (1070–1109). Lanfranc established the primacy of Canterbury over York and the authority of the archbishops over the bishops. The diocesan system was reorganised with some sees transferred to more major centres, for example from Dorchester-on-Thames to Lincoln, and new bishoprics were founded at Ely and Carlisle. New monastic orders spread, especially the Cistercians, who by 1154 had established about forty monasteries, including Rievaulx, Fountains and Rufford.

The reform impulse led to attempts to enforce clerical celibacy and to end the clerical dynasties that had been important among the parochial clergy. Foreign prelates sought to discipline the mainly English lesser clergy. Lay ownership of tithes was condemned. By 1200 the parish system as it was substantially to continue in rural England into the modern period had been created through a vast increase in the numbers of local churches. Most surviving medieval parish churches have an eleventh- or twelfth-century core.

The Romanesque style of architecture also spread across England, bringing large churches characterised by thick walls, long, relatively narrow naves, and massive columns and arches, as, for example, at Durham, Ely and Peterborough; although few large-scale Norman interiors were stone-vaulted. Large-scale Romanesque architecture was first developed in England in the late tenth century, and Edward the Confessor followed Norman models for his new Westminster Abbey built in the 1050s. However, the Romanesque style was developed more forcefully after the conquest. Cultural links after 1066 were very much with northern France. The conquest brought in a French-speaking elite and Old English was submerged. Anglo-Saxon personal names were displaced by a new set of Norman and general Christian names: William, Robert, Richard, John and Thomas. It was not until the late fourteenth century that English became an acceptable language in upper-class circles.

THE NORMANS AND WALES

The Norman conquest of England was in time to have a major impact on Ireland, Scotland and Wales. The last was affected most immediately, though in the eleventh and twelfth centuries Wales did not follow England in being rapidly overrun by the Normans. Instead, its position was more like that of Scotland under the Romans: conquered only in part. William the Conqueror was not interested in the conquest of Wales, which, unlike Scotland, did not exist as a single political entity. He saw himself as the legitimate heir of the West Saxon dynasty and therefore as the inheritor of that dynasty's relationship with its Welsh and Scottish neighbours. What William and his successors probably sought in Wales was stability. Such royal campaigns as there were in Wales were not aimed at conquest; there was always a specific and more limited objective.

Conquest in Wales was of individual kingdoms or political units by individual Norman adventurers: this was a land of opportunity for land-hungry younger sons, although some of the most significant early Normans, such as Roger de Montgomery and William fitz Osbern, were leading court magnates. In one case, that of Glamorgan, a whole overkingdom was conquered. These Normans were operating outside the kingdom of England; they were not under the direct auspices of the king. However, they would not touch a ruler who had a formal agreement with the king; they tended to move in when there was a vacancy or a disputed succession. Norman attitudes towards the Welsh reflected a more general contempt for Celtic society, which was seen as barbarian and immoral, a view in which ignorance combined with prejudice.

Initially, the Normans advanced with great momentum, along the lowlands near the south and north coasts, and up the river valleys. The Welsh, however, benefited not only from their terrain, much of which offered little advantage to the cavalry of the Normans, but also from the military skills and determination honed by conflict within their own ranks, conflict that continued throughout the period, and was particularly acute in the 1070s and 1080s.

The Normans sought to anchor their advance with castles and settlements, but the latter were restricted to lowland areas, especially in coastal south Wales. The 'march' created by Norman conquest remained part of Wales, not a kind of no-man's-land between Wales and England. Marcher lordship has generally been seen essentially as Welsh political authority exercised by Anglo-Norman lords by right of conquest, placing Welsh royal rights in baronial hands. More recently, however, it has been presented as compact feudal lordships, with much in common with lordships in northern France (whose lords made war and peace and exercised 'high justice'), and with the 'castleries' of early Norman England. Marcher lordships, however, came to look increasingly odd as the march stayed outside the orbit of the developing common law and centralised government in England.

The authority of the archbishopric of Canterbury was extended over the sees of St David's and Llandaff. Roman usage had spread in the Celtic Church prior to the Norman conquest, Bangor in 768 being the first to conform; but, as in England, the role of clerical dynasties remained important until after the conquest. It was then that a diocesan and parochial structure was introduced: Llandaff was established as a bishopric in 1107, St David's in 1115, Bangor in 1120 and St Asaph in 1143. As in England, the Cistercian monastic order brought new energy.

Cistercian abbeys were founded both by Norman – Neath (*c.* 1129), Tintern (1131) and Margam (1147) – and by Welsh lords: Whitland (1143), Strata Florida (1164).

SCOTLAND

While neither Wales nor Ireland made significant moves towards political unification and governmental development in the century following the Norman conquest of England, the Scottish kingdom became more powerful. The authority of the kings over much of their kingdom, especially Galloway and the Highlands, was limited. Norwegian control of the Western Isles acted as a challenge to Scottish control of nearby areas of the mainland. In 1164, Somerled, Ri of the Isles, attacked Renfrew, the principal seat of the Stewarts, a family loyal to the kings of the Scots, only to be killed in the subsequent battle.

The fertile central belt was under the control of the Scottish Crown, and, although ethnically diverse, Scotland was given political direction by its capable rulers. As a consequence, the movement of Norman nobles, mostly from England, into Scotland in the twelfth century, families that were to play a major role in Scottish history, such as Barclay, Bruce, Hay, Menzies, Lindsay, Montgomery and Wallace, was not a matter of the piecemeal conquest of the more vulnerable lands, as initially in Wales and Ireland, but an immigration reflecting the sponsorship of the kings. This was related to the introduction of Norman administrative methods and French secular culture by Malcolm III's youngest son, David I (r. 1124–53). David was educated at the court of his brother-in-law, Henry I, and held the Earldom of Huntingdon in England. This was an instance of the interconnection of fealties. In the same way that the king of the Scots owed feudal fealty to the king of England for the earldom, so the king of England owed it to the king of France for Normandy and, later, the Angevin (Anjou) lands.

As king, David minted the first Scottish coins, and introduced feudal tenures and organised the central government on the Anglo-Norman pattern, although the older-style Celtic social organisation also continued and it is important not to overlook the extent to which Normanisation was frequently simply a stage in a longer-term process of social stratification and administrative development. The latter led to the production of documents that throw much light on economic, social and political processes, but that can create a misleading impression of new beginnings.

Normanisation also affected the Scottish Church, leading to new monastic foundations and stronger continental links. David was a very generous benefactor, introducing the reformed monastic orders; his extensive monastic foundations also extended royal influence. Yet Normanisation was not accompanied by the massive expropriation and disruption that had affected England after 1066. Furthermore, both in Church and state (in so far as the two can be separated), it is necessary to move beyond a debate about the strength of Normanisation in order to see a more general process of Europeanisation, with Continental patterns becoming more insistent. It is necessary that British history should not suffer from the insularity for which it condemns English history.

The Scottish kingdom of the twelfth and thirteenth centuries was strong. The Norman spread of the ethos and procedures of feudalism, as well as the military machine of knights and castles, the improved administrative mechanisms, especially the establishment of sheriffdoms in the early twelfth century, the skill of the rulers, and the economic expansion of the period, served as the basis for an extension of royal authority. English and Flemish immigrants played a major role in a growth of urban activity that was very important for economic development. So also was the export via Berwick of wool and hides from the lands developed by the monastic orders, particularly in the Borders. Throughout Europe, these centuries were a period of substantial demographic and economic growth as recovery from the early medieval decline gathered pace. This recovery fuelled the development of states and the pursuit of their wars, as well as the cultural expansion that focused on the Gothic style, the expansion of education and the growing density of Christian institutions. Within the British Isles, these processes were most pronounced in England.

THE ECONOMY 1100–1350

Greater activity led to the establishment of more settlements in lowland England and Scotland by the eleventh century, and was particularly important for the expansion of the open-field system, in which large unhedged arable fields were divided into narrow strips cultivated by individual peasants under a system of communal supervision. Though sometimes seen as the standard form of medieval English and Scottish agriculture, it was in fact typical, in England, of the Midlands, and in Scotland of lowland regions, but was largely absent from the upland areas of Scotland and of north and west England, as well as from Kent. In these regions, pasture was predominant, though there was also some arable farming.

Hard work was involved throughout, but the technological basis of medieval agricultural life was not unvarying. Implements, machines and sources of power all played a role. The introduction of the mouldboard plough in Scotland in the ninth century permitted the cultivation of heavier soils. There was also a switch from oxen to the faster and more adaptable, but costlier, horses for ploughing, though this change was not completed until the fifteenth century.

Changes in crops were also important. Large-scale field cultivation of legumes, which enriched the soil and provided fodder, began in the early thirteenth century in England, vetches being first recorded in 1268: natural fodder thus gave way to cultivated. Norfolk crop yields rose to levels that were not to be surpassed until the eighteenth century, in large part because the development of integrated mixed-farming systems offered the benefit of both arable and pastoral husbandry.

Moreover, the use of power sources increased efficiency. Windmills were introduced in England in the second quarter of the twelfth century and spread particularly fast in eastern England in the 1180s. The spread of water-powered mills helped both corn milling and the fulling that was important to the cloth industry. An increase in the cultivated area and in agricultural productivity permitted a fairly steady growth in the English population in the centuries between the Anglo-Saxon settlement and the eleventh century, and then rapid growth from the late twelfth century to around 1300. There was possibly a doubling of the English population between 1180 and 1330 to perhaps six million, and a dramatic increase in the number involved in non-agricultural pursuits, although a sharp increase in the percentage of the population involved in non-agricultural occupations would seem to be a late medieval phenomenon. According to the tax valuations required for the lay subsidy of 1334, the five wealthiest counties per square mile were, in order, Middlesex, Oxfordshire, Norfolk, Bedfordshire, and Berkshire.

The nature of the working population changed. Chattel slavery (the form of Anglo-Saxon slavery) became extinct in the early twelfth century as a result of the ready availability of labour and Church pressure, as well as of the power of lords over their serfs or villeins. These were peasants who owed their lords often heavy labour services, as well as other obligations, such as having to use the lord's mill, which was a source of both power and profit to lords. The power of lords helped to enforce their rights over tenants. Given the limited scope for increasing the productivity of cultivated land, rising population entailed an expansion in the acreage of cultivated land, much woodland being cleared in, for example, the Lake District, but also soil deterioration, falling yields, and pressure on the living standards of the agricultural labour force, especially if they had little, if any, land. Lowland England showed signs of overcrowding in the early fourteenth century. Work on skeletal remains certainly suggests a decline in living standards. There was also a rise in the age of marriage as people deferred marriage until they had land or the means to support a family. This rise was not deliberately done to reduce the number of children.

The twelfth and thirteenth centuries also saw significant increases in town foundation, both planned and unplanned. In already existing towns, growth within town defences led to denser occupation, while, from the twelfth century, suburbs developed outside the walls. Society became more complex, with broadened distribution of wealth, as well as increases in monetary transactions, the volume of the currency, economic diversification and trade, both domestic and foreign. There was greater specialisation in occupations, increased social mobility and literacy, and the spread of industry into some rural areas. By the thirteenth century, for example, there were few places in Lincolnshire which were further than five miles from a market: seven markets in the county were mentioned in *Domesday Book* in 1086; fifty-five licensed from 1250 to 1299 alone.

These markets linked the localities into wider commercial networks, transmitting goods, demands, information and innovation. The Gough Map of about 1375 shows nearly 3,000 miles of road in England, while, funded by tolls, bridges replaced fords. From the late eleventh century, a large stone bridge and causeway at Oxford crossed both the Thames and its flood-plain. This route was to help move goods, notably wool, to the port at Southampton. Water routes, both sea and river, such as the Thames, were particularly important for the movement of bulky goods. Grain was moved down the Thames to London from the busy entrepot of Henley. The River Lea was used to move food from East Anglia to London. Through rapidly growing ports, such as Boston in Lincolnshire, the leading wool exporter in England, the localities were linked to European markets. By the early fourteenth century, possibly a fifth of the English population may have depended on trade and services. Economic sophistication increased. The value of coin circulating in England may have risen from about one shilling per head in 1180 to six in 1467.

The increasing role of money in the economy throughout the British Isles, and thus in revenue and taxation, helped to ensure that socio-economic shifts had direct governmental and political consequences. The feudal structures established by William I were based on land, but the burdens of vassals were very speedily commuted into cash. This development reflected a number of factors including the need for money and flexibility, and the subdivision of knights' fees, so that, by the early twelfth century, fractions of knights were owed as military service, fractions that were fulfilled by cash payments. In addition, some lords preferred to fulfil their military obligations by employing household knights and expecting their tenants to provide money, not military service.

The initial relationship created by the allocation of land slackened with time and with the impact of hereditary property rights. This relationship altered from that of lord and man, to landlord and tenant and lord and client, and the change was a cause of growing tension that probably helped to increase litigation during the reign of Henry II (1154–89). More specifically, the increase in litigation arose from a lack of clarity in relation to succession in feudal tenures, compounded by the disorder, land seizures and confiscations of Stephen's reign. More generally, aristocratic society was never static. By 1200 what has been termed bastard feudalism, and more commonly associated with the later medieval period, was already in evidence in magnate retinues: instead of all dependants being landed tenants, many of the members of the retinues received rewards in cash. This cash came from the tenants as well as from benefits derived from the Crown.

Far from being static, or changing only slowly and with reluctance, medieval society had a dynamic response to altering economic and political circumstances. By 1130, money rents were very common on royal manors and other large estates in England. Over the following 150 years, the amount and proportion of governmental revenues coming from taxation increased substantially. This was to help in a political transformation in which the essentially personal links between monarch and greater nobles, and the associated politics of patronage and protection, of the eleventh century, both Anglo-Saxon and Norman, were joined by a more coherent sense of national political identity, in which issues related to taxation played a major role. Thus the men who represented the regional community or community of the realm, principally the greater nobles, were by the late thirteenth century also to express their views in Parliament, a new sphere of political pretension and activity, and one that reflected the stress on national financial demands and national grievances that were so important in the thirteenth century. Yet, as will be discussed (p. 62), more than one strand can be traced.

Economic and institutional changes were vital to the development of a regional community, but so also was a crucial legacy of the Norman conquest: war stemming from continuous confrontation with a neighbouring Crown. The Welsh and the Scots were only able to press on frontier areas. But, after 1066, England was part of a state that spanned the Channel, one that found itself obliged to ward off the ambitions of other expanding states, most significantly the kingdom of France. The continuous military effort that this entailed was to be a central theme in the three centuries following the death of Stephen in 1154. Indeed, from the Roman conquest onwards, a united England was often to be politically associated with part of the Continent: as under the Romans (78–409), Cnut and his sons (1016–42), the medieval rulers (1066–1453) and the Hanoverians (1714–1837). The nature of this relationship was far from constant, but the resultant political strains were most apparent in the medieval period.

ANGEVIN KINGSHIP

Between 1154 and 1453 the rulers of England and much of the aristocracy were involved in a quest for territory and control, both in the British Isles and in France; although 'empire' was not a term that contemporaries used, as to them the empire was the German or Holy Roman empire. Henry II (r. 1154–89) did not try to develop a single cohesive system; instead, he expected to divide the large group of lordships he had accumulated among his sons. His successors were less interested in such a division. The quest for territory was due largely to the ambitions of England's rulers, who saw themselves not simply as kings of England, but as rulers of, or claimants to, the wider inheritance of Henry II, and, in time, to the French throne. Under the Angevins, the Norman practice of viewing Britain from the perspective of European rulers was continued.

Unlike his Norman predecessors, Henry's succession in England was not a signal for conspiracy and conflict: the war for succession had already been fought during Stephen's reign. Henry's most important step was his retrieval of Cumbria and Northumbria from Malcolm IV of Scotland, for the fluid Anglo-Scottish frontier reflected the respective strength of those in power and it had been pushed south during Stephen's reign, despite the English victory at the Battle of the Standard (1138): David I had taken control of Carlisle and Cumbria. Until the mid-twelfth century, it had been unclear whether what is now northern England would be part of England or of Scotland. Henry II ensured the former in 1157, although it was only finally settled at the Quitclaim of York in 1237.

The situation in France was less happy. In 1152, Henry had married Eleanor of Aquitaine, the imperious divorced wife of Louis VII of France, who brought control of the Duchy of Aquitaine (most of south-west France). Combined with the Norman and Angevin (Anjou) inheritances which he had gained in 1151, this made him the most powerful ruler in France. Henry had more land and power than the king of France, his suzerain (feudal lord for his French territories). Moreover, in his first twelve years, Henry used this power to resolve inheritance disputes in his favour, gaining control of Brittany and more of southern France. He received the homage of the Count of Toulouse and affirmed his hegemony over Auvergne. The enmity of the kings of France, however, ensured that when Henry's family divided over the inheritance (for like William the Conqueror, Henry II had several sons) and Henry was faced by a general rebellion in 1173–4, Louis VII was willing to intervene. Such foreign intervention was a problem in Henry II's continental empire, but not for him in the British Isles. There, it was Henry's power that was dynamic. The campaigns of 1157, 1163 and 1165 made little impact on Wales, but were a sign that the situation had changed since Stephen's reign.

INVASION OF IRELAND

Anglo-Norman colonisation was not confined within and near England's far-from-fixed borders. On 1–2 May 1169, a 600-strong force landed at Bannow Bay between Wexford and Waterford. With some Irish and Norse support, the Anglo-Normans seized Wexford and its neighbourhood: their skilful combination of cavalry and archers gave them a military advantage over the Irish. Further Anglo-Norman forces arrived in 1169 and 1170, including Richard of Clare, 'Strongbow', a prominent Anglo-Norman from Wales. In 1170, Strongbow seized Waterford and, in alliance with the king of Leinster, Dermot MacMurrough, Dublin. The following year, Strongbow defeated the displaced Norse

king of Dublin, Asgall, and the Irish high king, Rory O'Connor. Henry
II arrived in late 1171 in order to establish his rights in accordance
with the papal bull of 1155 from the only English pope, Adrian IV. The
Pope approved the invasion on the grounds of advancing ecclesiastical
reform in Ireland, although the authenticity of the bull is open to question. Henry II imposed his authority on his barons, granting Strongbow
Leinster, but taking control of Dublin, Waterford and Wexford himself.
Henry also obtained the submission of many of the Irish kings and of
the Irish Church, which also promised to adhere to English practices.
The Treaty of Windsor of 1175 recognised Henry as lord of Ireland,
a title implying overlordship over the petty kings. O'Connor was left
only as king of Connacht and overlord of the as yet unconquered parts
of the country. The kings of England only became kings of Ireland in
the sixteenth century.

Lacking a strong state to organise resistance, much of Ireland was rapidly captured. Anglo-Norman progress was marked by the construction
of castles, such as Carrickfergus, Dundalk, Coleraine, Trim, and Kildare.
Like Wales, and in contrast to Scotland and England, Ireland was far from
unified, which provided opportunities for aristocratic and royal Anglo-
Norman ambitions. A new order was established in Ireland, with a lordship,
based on Dublin, under royal control, and the introduction there of English
administrative practices. Dublin's connection with Canterbury led it to
emerge as a metropolitan see: its archbishops were English-born.

The extent to which royal control was to be disrupted by Scottish
invasion in 1315 was an indication of the value to earlier English
rulers of Ireland of an absence of foreign intervention. It was far more
important, practicable and profitable for the ruthless Philip Augustus,
king of France 1180–1223, to undermine the Angevin empire in France,
especially to end John's control of Normandy, than in the British Isles.
However, later French kings were to find the latter policy a way to
weaken first the English effort in France and finally English foreign
policy more generally.

Anglo-Norman control was extended in the thirteenth century,
including a gradual expansion across the River Shannon into Connacht.
In *c.* 1210 the Irish Justiciar, Bishop John de Grey, led a force to Athlone
and built a stone bridge over the Shannon and a stone castle. This
replaced earlier wooden works and provided the security that allowed
the town to develop as a centre of English influence. From the 1280s,
however, resistance mounted, reflecting the extent to which the Irish had
not become English, while the English settlers had not become Irish.

Like Wales, Anglo-Norman Ireland was divided into the area where the king's writ ran effectively, by the fifteenth century called, in Ireland, the Pale, and regions under feudal lords, who held their own courts and ran their own administrations. The more fertile areas of Ireland, for example the plains of the east-centre, acquired a network of towns, while numerous nucleated villages developed.

HENRY II AND HIS SONS

Henry II, both talented and difficult, is best remembered for his quarrel with Thomas Becket, Archbishop of Canterbury, which led to Becket's murder in 1170. Like a later Chancellor, Sir Thomas More, who fell out with a powerful and demanding king, in his case Henry VIII, with fatal results, Becket was initially a friend of the monarch's, but, after being made archbishop, he defended the right of clergy not to be tried by lay-men, but, instead, in Church courts. Also at stake was freedom of appeal and access to the Pope, at a time when the papal Curia (government), under a succession of lawyer popes, was becoming effectively the legal centre of Christendom and thus a prime source of authority and money. Freedom of appeal to Rome defined ecclesiastical jurisdictions and almost Church life as such.

Becket fled the country in 1164 when Henry turned the resources of royal judicial power against him. Nevertheless, as with the rifts in his own family, Henry had to consider the views of a foreign power, in this case the Papacy, and they helped to lead him towards compromise. Returning in 1170, Becket was unwilling, however, to abide by the spirit of compromise that was necessary both if his return was to be a success, and, more generally, for workable royal–papal and church–state relations. Henry's outraged explosion, 'Will no one rid me of this turbulent priest?', was taken at face value by four of his knights, who killed the archbishop in his cathedral. Becket was to be canonised, and his shrine at Canterbury to become a major centre of pilgrimage until the reign of Henry VIII, but his death changed little: the balance of compromise had not shifted greatly, though restrictions on appeals to Rome were lifted and the basic immunity of criminous clerics from lay jurisdiction was confirmed.

No such upsets affected the processes of administrative development that were so important in Henry's reign, both in finance and in justice. The standardised common law gained in strength. Apart from some special privileges for the Danelaw, pre-conquest kings had issued laws for all their subjects and Henry II therefore built on well-laid foundations. English common law helped to consolidate England as a remarkably homogeneous state by European standards, and in the thirteenth century played a role in fostering a sense of common Englishness. The growth of the common law, the penetration of royal justice, and the sense of the 'crown' as distinct from the person of the king (who was often out of the kingdom) all encouraged a sense of regnal community.

The expansion of government activity required increasing numbers of professional administrators, a group that had first emerged clearly in the reign of Henry I. These *curiales* were mostly 'new men' who were resented by longer-established nobles. Thanks in part to the *curiales*, the enforcement of justice and the collection of royal revenues improved and the processes of government became more effective and regular. This was shown by the introduction of regular record-keeping: the Exchequer pipe rolls, continually from early in Henry II's reign, and the close and patent rolls of the Chancery from just after 1200. The development of justice was a royal initiative, land actions were begun by royal writs, law and order enforced by royal justices itinerant. Procedure was regularised through the king's actions. The processes of government were less dependent on the personal intervention of the monarch than had been the case under the Normans, which was just as well as Henry II spent most of his reign on the Continent, although continuity was provided by the office of Justiciar.

On the other hand, the Crown became more dependent on financial windfalls as its landed income declined, while improvements in the administration of justice were balanced by a striking arbitrariness on the part of the Crown. This arbitrariness extended across society and tenants-in-chief were very much at the king's will. Moreover, the area designated as royal forest and its law were both extended as far as possible in order to make people pay for exemptions from them. Forest law was not affected by the forms and standards of the common law, but instead by royal will. The Angevins' exploitation of their feudal rights and the justice system led to the barons and others making common cause against them.

The greater coercive power of government made it a formidable instrument of tyranny. This was one reason for the popularity, in some quarters, of Becket, who had stood up to royal power, and for the immense resentment royal government aroused under King John. Bureaucratic principles of impartial government were slow to develop.

In 1207–8 John wrote, 'it is no more than just that we should do better by those who are with us than by those who are against us'.

The views and interests of the monarch were also crucial to government procedure. The medieval period was to witness changing patterns of royal administration, with the emphasis either on royal Household government or on government through Exchequer and Chancery. Under John, Henry III and Edward I, the Household, initially the Chamber and then the Wardrobe, was very dominant; whereas under Edward III there was far greater Exchequer control. Such variations remained the pattern during the Tudor period, and indeed medieval English monarchy prefigured Tudor government in many respects, including the scale of royal patronage and of office-holding under the Crown.

Three of Henry's five legitimate sons predeceased him, and he was succeeded by his third son, Richard I (r. 1189–99). Richard had joined his brothers in 1173–4 in their French-supported rebellion against Henry II, and thereafter had acquired considerable military experience in suppressing rebellions in Aquitaine, the duchy which he had inherited from his mother. As king, he spent an even greater proportion of his reign abroad than Henry had done. A key participant in the Third Crusade against the Muslims in the Middle East, he captured the major fortress of Acre and defeated the Muslim ruler Saladin at the battle of Arsuf (1191), but he narrowly failed to reach Jerusalem. When Richard was imprisoned in Germany on his way back (1192–4), his absence was exploited by his younger brother John and, more seriously, by Philip Augustus. Richard was ransomed for 150,000 marks, a huge sum (a mark was two-thirds of a pound), and it was a considerable tribute to English wealth and government that the money was raised.

Richard spent most of the rest of his reign in his Continental lands recovering what had been lost during his absence, a process that led to his death in a siege. He passed debt, conflict with France and baronial anger with royal government on to his successor. Alongside this negative assessment, it is noteworthy that Richard was hugely influential in reshaping Angevin and English kingship in his chivalric image. Richard was held up as a role model for later kings, as well as being seen as a hero in the Robin Hood legends.

Without legitimate children, Richard was succeeded by his brother John (r. 1199–1216). John's position was weakened by the tactless handling of his French vassals, which was exacerbated by accurate rumours that he had been responsible for the death in 1203 of his nephew Arthur, Duke of Brittany, the son of his older brother Geoffrey, who had predeceased Henry II. The determination and military success of Philip Augustus led to John losing much of his father's vast continental possessions, including Normandy and Anjou, in 1203–4. Naturally avaricious and suspicious, John was not improved by adversity. He was tough and nasty, lacked the skills of man-management, and could not soften the impact of intrusive and aggressive government. John's efforts to raise funds to help in the reconquest of lost lands, and his determined exploitation of the royal position, aroused opposition, while a dispute over an election to the archbishopric of Canterbury led to a quarrel with a very determined adversary, Pope Innocent III. In 1208 Innocent laid England under an interdict, suspending all church services, and in 1209 excommunicated John.

MAGNA CARTA, 1215

John was able to buy his peace with Innocent by making England a fief of the papacy (1213), but his other enemies were harder to deal with. John's attempt to recover his continental inheritance ended in failure when his allies, supported by an English expeditionary force, were defeated by the French at Bouvines (1214). This defeat helped to encourage John's domestic opponents to rise in rebellion, with support from Alexander II, whose Scottish army marched the length of England to Dover. In 1215, John was forced by the rebellious barons to accept the terms of what was to be later called Magna Carta in order to ensure a political settlement for what was for him an unsuccessful conflict. This charter of liberties was a condemnation of John's use of feudal, judicial and other governmental powers, for it defined and limited royal rights. Magna Carta was in effect an enormous list of everything that was wrong with government as John applied it. It covered practically everything, hence later calls for its confirmation. Baronial liberties were protected and freemen were provided with some guarantees against arbitrary royal actions. The Crown was not to be able to determine its rights alone. Instead, Magna Carta asserted the importance of the principle of placing royal power under the law, a principle followed up in 1258 in opposition to Henry III in the Provisions of Oxford.

Constraining monarchs to accept limitations was always, however, a problematic course of action, for the effectiveness of such a settlement depended on royal willingness to change attitudes and policy or on the creation of a body able to force the monarch to do so. John's unwillingness to implement the agreement, which he rapidly repudiated, led his opponents to offer the throne to Philip Augustus's son, Louis. England drifted into a serious civil war and John died in 1216, shortly after the quicksands and tide of the Wash had claimed a valuable part of his baggage train.

John's son, Henry III (r. 1216–72), was a more acceptable monarch to both supporters and opponents: as a child of 9 he was no threat. Helped by victory in war, especially the battle of Lincoln and Hubert de Burgh's naval victory off Dover, both in 1217, Henry's supporters drove Louis to abandon the struggle by the Treaty of Lambeth of 1217. Henry did not gain effective power until 1232, but neither during his minority nor subsequently was it possible to defeat the French on the Continent and regain the lands lost by John. The disastrous 1242 Poitevin campaign damaged the king's reputation and finances, and in the Treaty of Paris of 1259 Henry finally accepted the losses that left him only Gascony, part of Aquitaine with its principal centre at Bordeaux.

During Henry's minority the idea of restricting a ruler through written regulations and insisting that he seek the advice of the nobility developed. 'Great Councils' were summoned to win baronial consent, and thus cooperation. The emphasis on consultation looked toward the development of Parliament. Magna Carta was frequently reissued. In confirming it, John's successors agreed to rule according to its terms.

However, Henry became unpopular due to his granting favour to foreign-born friends, relations and advisors, rather than only members of the English elite, and to the fact that his government entailed as much financial pressure as the king could exert, and that there was much misrule and corruption by both royal and baronial officials. Like his father, Henry proved unable to sustain acceptable relations with his leading subjects, and, by the Provisions of Oxford (1258) and of Westminster (1259), they sought to take power out of his hands, to enforce what they regarded as good kingship. Politics was about principles as well as personalities.

War broke out in 1264 and that year many of the barons, under the king's brother-in-law, the French-born Simon de Montfort, Earl of Leicester, defeated Henry at Lewes. Simon's victory left de Montfort in control of king and government, but Henry's son Edward escaped from custody in 1265, raised an army and defeated de Montfort decisively at Evesham in 1265. The royal cause was helped because quite a number of the barons had stayed loyal, while others had been alienated by de Montfort. Royal authority was restored, though Henry took pains to adopt a more careful attitude in his remaining years.

THE END OF WELSH INDEPENDENCE

Gerald of Wales (*c.* 1145–1223), the Norman-Welsh Archdeacon of Brecon, accompanied the Archbishop of Canterbury on his preaching tour of 1188 to gain support for the Third Crusade and described it in *The Journey Through Wales*; he also wrote a *Description of Wales*. Gerald is not a particularly reliable source, and, as in other such works of travel, there are numerous generalisations: 'the Welsh are the most particular in shaving the lower parts of the body . . . the Welsh sing their traditional songs, not in unison . . . but in parts, in many modes and modulations . . . Both sexes take great care of their teeth . . . for the Welsh generosity and hospitality are the greatest of all virtues.' Nevertheless, Gerald had a clear sense of Welshness: he was not writing of Gwynedd and Deheubarth as if their people were different. This reflected the idea of the Welsh as *Cymry*, 'compatriots', a community united by a shared and mutually supporting culture, mythology, language, customs and laws. Despite their fissiparous politics, the Welsh saw themselves as one people occupying one country, although the language was highly dialectic and differed a great deal in the north and south. However, the fragmentation of power and the practice of partible inheritance were fundamental weaknesses in a political structure confronted with a powerful external threat.

Cymru was taken closest to political fulfilment by Llywelyn the Great (d. 1240) and his grandson, Llywelyn ap Gruffudd, 'the Last' (d. 1282), of Gwynedd. They united native Wales (*pura Wallia*). The thirteenth century was the period when Gwynedd finally emerged as the dominant power and the two Llywelyns sought to create a Welsh political unit and single political authority where none had existed before. It is not known who thought of this in the first place, but the new development was associated with the general growth of jurisdictional definition and written government in the thirteenth century, together with the growth in moveable wealth, which gave a sharper focus to princely claims everywhere. In Wales, traditions of 'national' history and identity, which had been invented and propagated by the native poets and scholars, were given more political reality by 'modernising' princes, who built castles, developed rights and resources, founded monasteries and granted borough charters, and were served by a small circle of administrators, including churchmen educated outside Wales. Thus, in order to resist English claims, the princes had to copy their methods. The object of the two Llywelyns was to extend overlordship over the other native rulers and at the same time to persuade the English Crown to accept the homage of the prince of Gwynedd for the whole of native Wales, the other rulers having done homage to the prince. What was needed to confirm this was a treaty with the Crown.

Between 1272 and 1277 there was a sequence of crises in Anglo-Welsh relations, although it is unlikely that either side wanted war. Llywelyn failed to do homage to Edward I and lacked the ability to define a compromise. In 1277, Edward set out to settle relations. He invaded with massive force and the support of the other Welsh rulers and Welsh exiles. While secondary forces advanced in central and south Wales, Edward attacked Gwynedd, using his navy to cut off Anglesey, Gwynedd's major source of food. Bottling up Llywelyn in Snowdonia, Edward kept him short of supplies until he accepted terms at the Treaty of Aberconwy (1277). Llywelyn was made to do homage to Edward and to surrender the lands east of the River Conwy. His Welsh opponents were granted territories, and the homage of most of the Welsh leaders was transferred to the king: Welsh Wales was not to be united by Gwynedd. The principality was now restricted to Snowdonia and Anglesey.

The peace was followed by a degree of anglicisation of government and church that created problems. Archbishop Peckham of Canterbury told Llywelyn that Welsh customs were only to be observed if reasonable. In 1282, Llywelyn's brother Dafydd rebelled and Llywelyn became involved. Edward repeated his strategy of 1277; Llywelyn, fearing winter starvation, broke out of Snowdonia, but was killed near Builth on 11 December. Dafydd, who was largely responsible for the rebellion, became a fugitive in Snowdonia. In 1283 he was captured and executed at Shrewsbury: hanged, his entrails torn out, beheaded and quartered.

The contrasting military fate of Wales and Scotland cannot be attributed to divisions among the Welsh or to the extent to which the English received Welsh support; the same was true of Scotland. The failures of earlier English expeditions indicated that there was no inevitability in Welsh defeat, but the English undoubtedly were helped by the relatively compact nature of Gwynedd, by the proximity of bases, especially Chester and Shrewsbury, by their far superior resources in terms of men, money and supplies, by naval power, and by the absence of foreign assistance for Llywelyn: there was no help from France or Scotland and the only intervention from Ireland was of troops sent to help the English.

POST-CONQUEST WALES

The conquest was secured by a new military order and followed by a political settlement. The Anglo-Norman presence in Wales had for long been based on castles, and the campaigns of 1277 and 1282 were each followed by extensive construction. After 1277 there was work at Aberystwyth, Builth, Flint and Rhuddlan castles, but after 1282 there were new sites for fortification and a new strategic task because Gwynedd was now Crown property. Caernarfon, the intended centre of royal power, Conwy, Harlech and Beaumaris were all coastal castles that could be supplied by sea. The construction of these massive works, stone-built unlike the early earth and wood castles, was a formidable undertaking, costing at least £93,000, an immense sum, and using thousands of workers. Lordship castles were also constructed at Chirk, Denbigh and Holt. Thirteenth-century native Welsh rulers had previously built castles, such as Dolbadarn and Bere, but now castle-building was to be under English royal control. The latter was also the case in England as from Stephen's reign all castles had required the king's permission.

The new political settlement ended Welsh independence, although the political and constitutional achievements of the rulers of Gwynedd served as a basis for rule by Edward I and his successors. The principality recognised in 1277 did survive, but it formed a dependency of England from 1284 and was granted in 1301 to Edward I's eldest son, who was created Prince of Wales. The principality would not be annexed to England until 1536 – but it was no longer independent. Edward I applied feudal law and saw himself as the heir to Llywelyn's forfeited estate, and the Crown thus obtained much of Wales, including all of Gwynedd. In effect the 'frontier' had been closed and it was therefore necessary and possible to create a new administrative and judicial structure for the Crown lands. The Statute of Wales (1284) added an extra tier of government to the principality, extending the English system of shire administration to Anglesey, Caernarfon, Flint and Merioneth, in addition to Cardigan and Carmarthen, which had emerged as counties earlier in the thirteenth century. English criminal law was introduced, although civil law remained largely Welsh. Caernarfon and Carmarthen became centres of royal administration, while the new castles of Aberystwyth, Beaumaris, Caernarfon, Conwy, Denbigh, Flint and Rhuddlan were associated with new or transformed towns that were created for settlement by English craftsmen and merchants and that were clearly seen as centres of English influence and culture – although by 1305 the richest burgess in Beaumaris was a Welshman.

The conquest of Gwynedd was a major achievement for Edward I. Although Cornwall was the first 'frontier' to be closed, it had never posed a military challenge comparable to Wales. Edward's conquest made larger defensive works in Cheshire and Shropshire relatively valueless and the castles there fell into ruin. The very failures of Edward's father and grandfather (Henry III and John) had encouraged him to act, as did the extent to which the Welsh problem was interwoven with English domestic politics: Llywelyn had indeed married a daughter of Simon de Montfort.

There was further resistance after 1283, including revolts in 1287 and, more seriously, 1294–5, but it is unclear how far the Welsh saw themselves as a conquered people. There was resentment at the domination of administration and Church by Englishmen and also at the commercial privileges granted to the inhabitants of the new towns. The conquest of Gwynedd was not followed by a wholesale expropriation of property comparable to that after the Norman conquest of England and, although the Church was brought more into line with English practice, there was again nothing to compare with the situation in England under William I. At the local level, there was little change: the same families, the traditional leaders of the community, remained in charge.

Much of Wales, especially south Wales, was still under the control of the Anglo-Norman Marcher families that had conquered it. Known collectively as the Welsh March, these lordships were not integrated into shires and were autonomous: their lords had effective administrative and legal control. Most Marcher lordships gradually came, by marriage or inheritance, into the possession of magnate families. Prominent lordships included Glamorgan (which belonged to the Clare family), Maelienydd and Radnor (Mortimer), Brecon (Bohun), Abergavenny (Hastings), Ruthin (Grey) and Pembroke (Valence). Edward I thus made no attempt to create an integrated state in Wales: instead he dealt with the immediate problem of Gwynedd. Yet the great power of the Marcher lords was a potential threat to the stability of the Crown, and Edward tried to assert his powers as sovereign over them too. So long as this contrast in government remained, royal authority was fragmented and there was no government agency that could lend bureaucratic shape to the notion of Wales. As in so much of the pre-modern British Isles, diversity was the keynote.

Alongside any emphasis on conquest, it is important to note the degree to which English ascendancy in the non-English parts of the British Isles was established in the twelfth and thirteenth centuries by peaceful means, including settlement and the stimulus to economic activity through access to English markets, notably with the cattle trade.

THIRTEENTH-CENTURY SCOTLAND

In the thirteenth century, the British Isles had two strong states, England and Scotland. They drew on similar administrative and military legacies. Each faced internal challenges, but in many respects the English monarchy was less successful in charting an internal political course without civil war and constitutional struggle. The Scottish kings spread their power out from the central lowlands. Thus, for example, William the Lion (r. 1165–1214), the grandson of David I, both sought to increase his authority in Galloway and, in 1187, at the battle of the Muir of Mamgarvy, defeated a powerful dynastic rebellion in Moray. William was also able to defeat an invasion of Moray by Harald, Earl of Orkney, a product of the Viking diaspora, and to invade Caithness, which was part of Harald's earldom, and nominally subject to the king of the Scots. William's son, Alexander II (r. 1214–49), extended royal control in Argyll and Caithness and repelled a Norse invasion in 1230. Alexander died while attempting to gain the Hebrides from Norway. His son, Alexander III (r. 1249–86), maintained the pressure to create a stronger and more centralised state. This was resisted by Hakon IV of Norway, but, at the battle of Largs (1263), in some respects a skirmish, Hakon's amphibious force was checked before being badly damaged by a storm on the way home. The more general failure of the entire Norwegian axis led to Scotland gaining the Western Isles by the Treaty of Perth (1266).

The kings had encountered resistance in extending their authority over the ethnic hybrid that was Scotland. Galloway, for example, for long felt little affinity with the Scottish Crown: in the anti-foreign revolt of Uhtred and Gilbert of Galloway, in 1174, the Gallovodians slew the officials placed over them and attacked Anglo-Norman lords. Yet the monarchs were generally successful. For example, the position of the Scottish Crown in Caithness improved considerably in 1150–1266.

Furthermore, the formation of a distinctively Scottish Church contributed to a developing sense of national identity that led to

'Scotland' being used to refer to all the territories that owed allegiance to the king of Scots. In 1192 Pope Celestine II issued, at William the Lion's request, a bull, *Cum Universi*, placing the nine Scottish bishoprics directly under the see of Rome and, by implication, denying the metropolitan claims of jurisdiction of the English archbishoprics of York and Canterbury (although Galloway remained under the authority of York), bringing to an end a long controversy. The papal bull halted what was essentially a matter of jurisdictional dispute and pride, but which could have developed eventually into a form of English ecclesiastical imperialism, and it thus strengthened the authority of the Scottish monarchy. While an emphasis on the imposition of authority, royal and ecclesiastical, is useful, it is also appropriate to emphasise the extent to which broader social, economic and cultural developments contributed to a measure of cohesion. The notion of Scotland became stronger as patterns of behaviour associated with the royal heartland spread into other areas.

THE ANGLO-SCOTTISH STRUGGLE

Under Alexander III, the power of the Canmore dynasty of Scottish rulers reached its zenith. English claims to overlordship prevented the Papacy from granting the right to crowning and anointing, but it granted the status of special daughter of the Church, ensuring ecclesiastical independence. As so often, dynastic chance was to bring weakness and strife. Alexander died in 1286, to be succeeded by a young granddaughter, Margaret, the three-year-old Maid of Norway. Edward I saw this as an opportunity to increase his family's power and in 1289 secured the Treaty of Salisbury by which the marriage of Margaret and the future Edward II was agreed. The rights and laws of Scotland were to be preserved, but, in essence, the union of the Crowns that was eventually to happen in 1603 seemed likely in 1289. Had it done so, it is interesting to consider how far the two countries could have remained united, and, if so, how far a process of convergence, political, administrative and cultural, would have occurred.

Margaret, however, died *en route* for Scotland in 1290, leaving a number of claimants to the throne. Edward I was asked to adjudicate and pressurised the claimants into recognising his overlordship over the Crown of Scotland, before declaring John Balliol king in 1292. Balliol swore fealty and did homage to Edward. English hegemony in the

British Isles seemed established. Edward's subsequent interventionism, not least his encouragement of appeals by Scots to English courts, was, however, unacceptable to many Scots and, with tension rising due to Scottish links with Philip IV of France, who had seized Gascony in 1294, Edward invaded Scotland in 1296. Berwick, the assault on which Edward led in person, fell, several thousand Scots being put to the sword. After a successful campaign, in which the Scots were defeated at Dunbar, Balliol surrendered the kingdom to Edward, who marched as far north as Banff. Edward termed himself Lord of Scotland, putting the kingdom in abeyance.

Edward's triumph was short-lived, as in 1297 William Wallace rebelled and defeated the English at Stirling, while Andrew de Moray raised the standard at Avoch on the Black Isle near Inverness. Indeed, the pronounced support from the Highlands for the War of Independence was an important sign of growing Scottish unity. Wallace then revealed the danger of a hostile Scotland by ravaging Northumbria. Edward I was in Flanders, opposing the French and their allies: yet again continental commitments were weakening the position of the English Crown within Britain.

A truce with France enabled Edward I to march north in 1298. Attacking Wallace at Falkirk, he found the Scottish pikemen massed in tightly packed *schiltroms*, able to defy the English cavalry, but they were broken by Edward's archers and cavalry. Further campaigns brought territorial gains, but Edward's forces were overstretched and resistance was not crushed, though Wallace was captured and executed in 1305. The following year, Robert Bruce rebelled and had himself crowned Robert I, and in 1307 Edward I died at Burgh-on-Sands on his way to campaign in Scotland.

Edward II (1307–27) had inherited none of his father's military ability or ambition, and the less intense pace of English military pressure helped Bruce to consolidate his position in Scotland. He defeated his Scottish rivals and in 1309 called his first parliament. In 1314, Edinburgh fell to Bruce, and the garrison in Stirling promised to surrender if not relieved. Poorly led by Edward, the English relieving force was defeated at Bannockburn by the Scottish army, pikemen on well-chosen ground routing cavalry, while the English handled their archers very badly. Edward fled and, after the surrender of Stirling, the English position was challenged in Ireland, which was invaded by Bruce's brother, Edward Bruce, in 1315, and in northern England. In 1318 Berwick fell and in 1319 and 1322 the Scots ravaged Yorkshire.

Independence was asserted anew by the Declaration of Arbroath of 1320 which offered a precarious affirmation of a sense of nationhood. English counter-attacks were unsuccessful and in 1328, by the Treaty of Northampton-Edinburgh, Scottish independence and Bruce's kingship were recognised. The resulting focus on Scottish identity challenged not only cultural relations with England but also the sense of linkage with Ireland, not least the belief in an Irish homeland for the Scots.

This was not the end of the Scottish wars of independence. The treaty was highly unpopular in England, even in the northern shires which had suffered most from Scottish attacks. It was always likely that the war would resume. In 1332 Edward Balliol claimed the throne and declared himself Edward III's liegeman. He was driven out by the adherents of Bruce's infant son, David II (1329–71), but, the following year, English archers under Edward III defeated the Scots at Halidon Hill and captured Berwick; and in 1334 Edward III restored Balliol and received Lothian from him. The weak Balliol was, however, again driven out, and the English invaded Scotland again in 1335, 1336 and 1341, holding, for a while, much of the country, but Edward III had to divert most of his resources to war with France. David, urged on by his French allies, was able to invade England in 1346, though he was defeated at Neville's Cross, Durham, taken prisoner and held captive until 1357. Edward III invaded Scotland again in 1356, but peace was made in 1357.

England was far stronger than Scotland, and it is worth considering whether conquest was possible but for the diversion of English strength to war with France, a conflict whose scale is suggested by the term 'The Hundred Years War'. Hostilities arose with Scotland in 1296 largely because of the quarrel from 1293 between Edward I and Philip IV of France, in which the Scots became involved. Had there not been that additional complication, Edward might have run Balliol on a looser rein, and the Scots might have acted more cautiously. Again in the 1330s Scotland mattered largely because, like the Low Countries, it was an area in which Edward III and Philip VI of France were competing. David II was an exile under Philip's protection in 1334–41. War with France did not preclude, as in 1346 and 1356, English attacks on Scotland, and the vulnerability of the centres of Scottish power and economy to English invasion is notable in any account of these attacks. In 1335 Edward III found no difficulty in occupying Glasgow and Perth, and in 1336 north-east Scotland; in 1356 Henry of Lancaster occupied Perth, Elgin and Inverness.

Had the English been able to maintain and support a permanent military presence in lowland Scotland, the Scottish kingdom might have been so weakened and divided as to cease to be a powerful challenge. Divisions among the Scottish nobility, which greatly helped the English, might have been exploited to spread the power of the king of England, who would have been able to mount a more effective claim to the Crown of Scotland, either for himself or for a protégé. However, the episodic military commitment dictated by Scotland's secondary role in English military policy from the late 1330s exacerbated the natural logistical problems of campaigning there and ensured that fixed positions were given insufficient support. This left the Scots with the military initiative, which was fatal to the English cause. When the English invaded, the Scots could avoid battle and concentrate on harrying the English force and denying them supplies, a policy that thwarted Edward's invasion of Lothian in 1356. In addition, it would have been staggeringly expensive to maintain a large number of English garrisons, and, as Scotland itself would not have been rich enough to be made to fund its own occupation, the cost would have fallen on England. Successful war in France, by contrast, was partially self-financing.

LATE MEDIEVAL IRELAND

Defeat for the English in Scotland was matched by failure in Ireland. Edward Bruce invaded Ireland in May 1315 and it has been argued that Robert I wished it conquered as a prelude, with the hope of a Welsh alliance, to a pan-Celtic invasion of England. The Anglo-Irish were defeated by the Scots, who campaigned with great savagery, until Edward Bruce was crushed and killed at Fochart on 14 October 1318, one of the more important battles of the Middle Ages. The possibility of a Scottish conquest of Ireland had been wrecked. Nevertheless, English lordship in Ireland had been gravely weakened, and the Bruce invasion encouraged the Gaelic resurgence that ended both English hopes of conquest and the surplus contributed by the Irish Exchequer to its English counterpart. Despite major expeditions from England in the 1360s, 1370s and 1390s, the situation continued to deteriorate.

Warfare hit Irish society. For example, Athlone was burnt on several occasions in 1218–1315, its bridge broken down in an attack of *c.* 1272, and after the burning of 1315 there was no further mention of the medieval town. The Dublin administration retained only nominal control by allowing the Anglo-Irish Dillons to act as hereditary constables of the castle and, even so, they were often driven out by the Gaelic O'Kellys of Ui Maine.

By the following century, direct English control was limited to the Pale, the area around Dublin, while the semi-autonomous Anglo-Irish lords and the independent Gaelic chieftains controlled most of the island. The Anglo-Irish Earldom of Ulster contracted markedly from 1333 in the face of a Gaelic resurgence. A branch of the Tyrone O'Neills overran the southern half of Antrim and the northern half of County Down and by 1460 the Ulster centre of Carrickfergus was paying them protection. More generally, English rulers feared that the Anglo-Irish were going native, and they made efforts to prop up the English lordship. However, the expedition by Richard II in 1399 was the last by an English king until William III invaded in 1690, although there were important English expeditions in the late sixteenth and mid-seventeenth centuries. The fifteenth century was a lowpoint of English interest in Ireland.

THE DIVIDED ISLES

Political division was to be one of the most important political legacies of the Middle Ages. The British Isles were not united politically before the religious divisions stemming from the Reformation in the sixteenth century, and the subsequent strengthening of national consciousness made any such process far less easy. In hindsight, it is possible to emphasise the difficulty of the task. The English relied in Scotland not on colonisation but on collaboration, but it proved impossible to sustain the necessary level. The centre of English power was in the south of England, far distant from Scotland and Ireland. War in both countries posed formidable logistical difficulties for any invader. The Romans had not managed to conquer Scotland. By 1290, Scotland had already developed an effective monarchy and acquired 'modern' military techniques. And yet the extraordinary vitality of the Normans, who, through conquest, created a kingdom in southern Italy as well as England, and the fluidity of boundaries on the Continent, are reminders of the possibilities that existed. There were definite opportunities in the medieval period for enlarging, through marriage or conquest, the kingdom of England, and thus creating the basis of a British state, a British aristocratic elite and a British consciousness. However, the very fluidity of political circumstances and chance that characterised the international politics of the period, a situation exacerbated by the central role of the vagaries of dynastic chance, the births, marriages, skill and deaths of monarchs, would necessarily have challenged any such achievement. It is unclear that any British unity could have survived the conspiracies and civil conflict of the fifteenth century. The break-up of the Union of Kalmar, by which Sweden, Norway and Denmark had been jointly ruled (1397–1523), is instructive; but so also is the unification of Spain, at least at the dynastic level, a process in which war as well as marriage played a role.

If the division of the British Isles was one of the crucial political legacies of the medieval period, another was the loss, with the exception of Calais, of the continental territories of the kings of England. After the reigns of John and Henry III, relatively little remained of the legacy of Henry II, but Edward I was determined to protect Gascony from the consequences of French overlordship. His ability to do so was lessened by the domestic strains produced by his policies, especially his heavy financial demands. These affected the response to the extensive reform of law and administration that he carried through by a series of statutes in 1275–90. Financial factors also played a role in Edward's expulsion of the Jews in 1290. Edward's relations with the nobility were very tense in the 1290s, and the issues of taxation and grievances came to play a major role. The clergy and the merchants were also alienated. Unrest culminated in a political crisis in 1297, in which many nobles resisted demands for high war taxation. The situation was to deteriorate seriously in the following century.

EDWARD II, 1307–27

Edward II inherited serious problems, including war in Scotland, but he exacerbated them by his character and political incompetence. Edward's inability to deal with the Scots owed much to his quarrels with his leading barons, especially over Piers Gaveston, his arrogant Gascon favourite. Edward I, who regarded him as a sinister influence, had banished Gaveston, but he was recalled by Edward II, made Earl of Cornwall and given much wealth and influence. This led to a political crisis. In 1311, Edward was forced to accept Ordinances restricting his power and in 1312 Gaveston was murdered by hostile nobles. The king's cousin, Thomas, Earl of Lancaster, a supporter of the Ordinances, then controlled the government, until Edward was able to defeat him at Boroughbridge (1322) and have him executed. The Ordinances were then repealed, but Edward remained unpopular, not least because of his new favourites, the Despensers, father and son. Their regime was very rapacious and ignored inheritance rights.

Edward II was not a martial ruler. Furthermore, he failed to conform to contemporary notions of kingship: he lacked dignity and had unroyal hobbies, such as boating and ditching. His relationship with Gaveston and Despenser led to rumours of homosexuality, but he had four legitimate children and at least one illegitimate one and it is unlikely that his relationship with his favourites was sexual.

However, Edward's focusing of patronage on and via his favourites led to discontent which was exploited by his wife Isabella, daughter of Philip IV of France. With her lover, Roger Mortimer, she captured Edward in 1326. He was then deposed in favour of his son and disposed of in Berkeley Castle, probably by a red-hot poker inserted through his anus, a means of death that left few incriminating signs (1327). This first murder of a king since 978 (assuming that William II was shot accidentally), was to be followed by the murders of Richard II (1400), Henry VI (1471) and Edward V (1483), evidence both of the instability of the period and of the continued importance of the monarchy.

EDWARD III, 1327–77

Isabella and Mortimer controlled the first years of Edward III's reign, but in 1330 Edward and his friends seized Mortimer and had him hanged and Isabella imprisoned. Edward restored royal authority and prestige after the chaos of his father's reign and was particularly successful in winning the support of the barons: he avoided favourites and brought many barons into his circle as knights of the Order of the Garter, which he established in 1348.

Edward's reign was dominated by the beginning of the Hundred Years War with France. The origins of the war lay primarily in Gascony and, secondarily, in Anglo-French rivalry in the Low Countries. The French fleet was smashed at Sluys (1340), a battle dominated by the boarding of ships. France was invaded and, at Crecy (1346) and Poitiers (1356), longbowmen decimated the attacking French. This led to the Treaty of Brétigny (1360), in which Edward promised to renounce his claim to the French throne, to Normandy and to Anjou, but was recognised as

Duke (with full sovereignty) of the whole of Aquitaine, as well as ruler of Calais, which had been gained in 1347. John II of France, who had been captured at Poitiers by Edward's eldest son, Edward, the 'Black Prince', promised to renounce his claim to sovereignty over Edward's continental dominions, but the treaty was never ratified.

Had the treaty held it would have been the high-water mark of the medieval English monarchy: they would have been the most powerful rulers in western Europe. However, the triumph proved illusory and the attempt to preserve it led to heavy political costs. War resumed in 1369 because the French encouraged opposition to the Black Prince's governorship of Aquitaine. Edward III reasserted his claim to the French throne, but the war went badly for him both in Aquitaine and at sea. Poitou was lost in 1369–73. By the time of the Truce of Bruges (1375), Edward retained little more than the coastal bases of Calais, Bordeaux and Bayonne.

Even the early decades of success had not prevented bitter criticism of the cost of conflict and the conduct of government, with a serious crisis in 1339–41 and renewed criticism of tax requests in the Parliaments of 1343, 1344, 1346, 1348 and 1352. In the second half of Edward's long reign criticism mounted. The war was no longer successful and Edward lost his political grip. His costly and unpopular mistress, Alice Perrers, served as a focus for tension. The government was criticised for failing to protect the country from papal demands. Tax requests caused problems at the Parliaments of 1372 and 1373, and in 1376 the so-called Good Parliament saw a major attack on the government. The Commons took the initiative, electing their first speaker to represent them, impeaching (prosecuting) two senior officials for corruption, and rejecting tax demands. The new process of impeachment made the king's ministers accountable to Parliament.

DEVELOPMENT OF PARLIAMENTS

From the early thirteenth century there was an increasing sense in both England and Scotland of the need for and importance of a political body that would serve, however episodically, as a national political focus. In England, this led to a broadening out of a body that had essentially originated as a baronial council but whose origins can be traced back to the tenth-century national councils of the Anglo-Saxon rulers. Under Henry III shire knights began to be elected to Parliament; they were a development from the lesser tenants-in-chief summoned to earlier councils and, from 1215, parliaments. Parliament was first and foremost the highest court in the land and, more than anything, this was what gave it some institutional continuity. However, the demands for war taxation helped to entrench its political role. The name *parliamentum* or *parlement* was first applied in the thirteenth century. The new concept of representation was outlined in the writs summoning representatives of the clergy, counties and boroughs to the 1295 Parliament. They were instructed to appear, with authority to give advice and consent on behalf of the communities they represented; the nobles appeared on their own behalf.

During the fourteenth century the institutional practices and pretensions of Parliament were established and elaborated. Under Edward III the representatives of the counties and boroughs became a fixed part of Parliament and began to meet as a separate assembly, the origins of the House of Commons. In its early stages, Parliament was no different, to any great extent, from its Continental counterparts, but the frequent need to raise taxation to pay for warfare led to Parliament becoming more important. War could not pay for itself, not least because the government relied on paid troops rather than a feudal host. Instead, as it became clear that parliamentary consent to taxation was necessary, the representatives of the counties and boroughs were given a key role in consenting to taxation.

Similarly in Scotland, Parliament developed from the king's council of bishops and earls, becoming a body with both a political and a judicial role. In the early fourteenth century, this was supplemented by the presence of knights, freeholders and, from 1326, burgh commissioners. The need to pay taxes, not least the ransom for David II agreed in 1357, led the burgh (borough) representatives to gain regular access to Parliament. Unlike in England, there were no separate Houses of Lords and Commons, but, instead, one chamber.

In both England and Scotland, Parliament was a developing institution, the political consequences of which were far from clear. It could serve as a means for eliciting and expressing support and funds for royal policies, as in England in 1377 when the taxation refused the previous year by the Good Parliament was granted. Yet the use of parliamentary demands to influence the composition and intentions of government was another consequence, and the development of the corporate identity and continuity of Parliament constrained monarchical freedom of political manoeuvre. A statute (law passed by Parliament) of 1362 stated that Parliament must agree to all taxation of wool, England's crucial export. The growing role of taxation, as opposed to landed income, in royal revenues further increased Parliament's importance. It became an important focus for, and source of, political activity. Parliament also served to advance local interests, as with the River Lea Act of 1425, which was the first parliamentary legislation to improve a river for navigation.

FOURTEENTH-CENTURY CRISES IN ENGLAND

Most political systems with any degree of sophistication have periodic crises, and a period without crisis would require particular explanation. In the case of the fourteenth century, however, throughout the British Isles, and indeed Europe, there was the additional socio-economic crisis caused by the end of the long period of demographic and economic expansion that had underpinned social development since the tenth century. Population growth had led to demand-led economic activity and an expansion of the social fabric: new towns and villages, roads, and markets. Improved communications were important to a commercialisation that encouraged economic development.

This growth came to an end in the fourteenth century. The most decisive episode in this crisis was the Black Death, an epidemic, probably of bubonic plague, although this is contested. This epidemic killed a third or more of the English population between 1348 and 1351, seriously disrupted the economy and contributed to a loss of confidence. The Black Death originated in Central Asia, reached Italy in 1347 and spread thence through trading links, reaching England (first at Melcombe Regis) and Ireland in 1348, Wales in 1349 and Scotland in 1350; although Scotland probably suffered less severely than England, in part because it was less densely populated. With outbreaks in 1361, 1369, 1379–83, 1389–93, 1432–3, 1471 and 1479, plague now became endemic until the seventeenth century (the last major episode in Scotland was in 1649 and in England in 1665) and held the population down until about 1500. Birth rates did not rise to compensate. It has been estimated that the population of Hertfordshire fell by 47 per cent between 1307 and 1377. Between 1300 and 1500, the English population roughly halved.

Yet the Black Death was only the most spectacular instance of a more general crisis in the fourteenth century. Like the Great Famine of 1315–17 caused by harvest failure resulting from bad weather, the plague hit population levels that were anyway under pressure as a result of earlier expansion: population growth was not matched by a sufficient rise in food production, and progressive under-nourishment probably weakened resistance to disease, such as the major outbreak of dysentery in 1473. Soil exhaustion, caused by over-cultivation and an absence of sufficient fertiliser, was another serious aspect of the crisis. There was also a serious crisis in the textile industry in the early fourteenth century. Global cooling hit agricultural possibilities and productivity, and also led to more specific crises, notably the loss of cultivated land in the Orkneys to sand blown in from the more exposed foreshore.

The Black Death had minimal direct political repercussions, but a cumulative socio-economic crisis exploded in the Peasants' Revolt of 1381. This was more wide-ranging and reflected a longer tradition of dissidence than is generally appreciated. Strains in rural society had arisen from increased agricultural production for market and the determination of landlords to benefit fully from this, not least by using their feudal powers and by legislation in the shape of the Statute of Labourers. Landlords sought to prevent peasants exploiting the relative scarcity of labour arising from the Black Death by claiming higher wages or by moving to seek new opportunities.

Resistance to landlords became common and frequently violent. The situation was exacerbated by failure in the Hundred Years War with France, which led to raids on the coast; the problems of the important East Anglian cloth industry; and a pervasive anti-clericalism which sapped respect for authority. One indicator of the demographic and social crisis was the evidence of rural depopulation presented by deserted and shrunken villages, especially in the central Midlands and, less seriously, in the north-east of England and East Anglia. Over 2,000 English villages disappeared totally. As in Ireland, the fall in population led to a decline in cultivation and a rise in pastoralism, which contributed to the emphasis on wool production. There was also a decline in trade. About half of the fairs in Devon failed to survive after 1350.

A poll tax designed to fund the war with France pressed hard on the depressed rural economy, leading to high rates of evasion and to unrest that culminated in the Peasants' Revolt of 1381. This began in Essex and spread throughout southern England, being especially strong in Kent and East Anglia, but also leading to important disturbances in Sussex, Winchester, Somerset, Cambridge and Yorkshire. The destruction of manorial records reflected peasant hostility to baronial jurisdiction. The Chief Justice, Sir John Cavendish, who had enforced the attempt to fix low, pre-plague labour rates by the Statute of Labourers (1351), was killed in Suffolk. Led by Wat Tyler and a priest, John Ball, the rebels occupied London with the help of dissatisfied Londoners. The Tower of London was seized and prominent figures murdered, including Simon of Sudbury, who was both Archbishop of Canterbury and Chancellor (head of the legal system), and responsible for the poll tax. This was a crisis at the very centre of power.

The rebels did not, however, wish to create a new governmental system, but rather to pressurise the young king, Richard II, into changes of policy. On 15 June 1381, Richard met the main body of the rebels under Tyler at Smithfield near London. During the meeting, William Walworth, Mayor of London, believing that Tyler was threatening Richard, lunged forward and killed him. Astutely Richard averted further violence by promising to be the rebels' leader. The rebellion lost momentum with both the death of Tyler and Richard's grant of charters of freedom to the rebels. However, as soon as they had returned to their homes, Richard revoked the charters and punished their leaders.

The Peasants' Revolt was the most serious challenge to the established order in England until the crisis of the 1640s, because the Pilgrimage of Grace of 1536 did not take place at the centre of power. The Peasants' Revolt indicates the lack of social and ideological quiescence on the part of the bulk of the population, a group whose lives and views are obscured by their illiteracy and the emphasis on the elite in the surviving records. The nature of popular alienation can, however, be grasped by the events of 1381. Thus, in Norfolk, the rebels took control of all the major towns, attacked, plundered or killed prominent figures, particularly landlords who were also JPs (justices of the peace), burned manor court rolls and attacked foreign (Flemish) settlers. The rebellion there, however, was crushed within a month by the warlike Bishop Despenser of Norwich, who brought leadership and determination to the gentry. In Scotland, social relations were less extreme and there was no equivalent rising, but there was also no rising in Wales, while that in England was patchy and did not affect many regions.

RICHARD II, 1377–99

Because the Black Prince predeceased his father, Edward III was succeeded by his grandson, the young Richard II, born in 1367. Wilful and no warrior, Richard lacked personal prestige and fortitude, and as he grew older he found the lords who had dominated his minority unwilling to surrender power, not least because they saw his youth as qualifying his fitness to rule. At the 1386 'Wonderful Parliament', there was bitter criticism of Richard's favourites, especially Michael de la Pole, a merchant's son, whom he had made Chancellor and Earl of Suffolk. Pole was impeached and a great council appointed to oversee the royal Household. Richard had the judges declare Parliament's demands illegal (1387), but his leading supporter, Robert de Vere, Earl of Oxford, was routed at Radcot Bridge. A group of leading nobles then 'appealed' (accused) Richard's closest supporters of treason and the 'Merciless Parliament' of 1388 agreed the execution of these supporters.

Although the Appellants appointed pliable ministers, they were dismissed by Richard in 1389. In the early 1390s he ruled in a less provocative fashion, but tensions persisted. In 1394, one of the Appellants, the Earl of Arundel, turned up late for Queen Anne's funeral, and the angry Richard struck him unconscious with an usher's baton. In 1397, Richard turned on the former Appellants. A Parliament packed with his supporters annulled the acts of the Merciless Parliament. Arundel was beheaded for treason, and Thomas, Duke of Gloucester, one of Richard's uncles, was murdered. Richard followed this up by behaving in what was seen as a tyrannical fashion. People were intimidated into giving forced loans, and Richard used his retinue of Cheshire guards to terrorise his opponents. His actions made the absolutist and grandiose aspects of Richard's kingship far more menacing.

Richard's policies led to a reaction. In 1399, he deprived his cousin, the exiled Henry Bolingbroke, a former Appellant, of his inheritance, a step that dramatically underlined the insecurity of landed rights in the face of royal assertiveness; and then led a second expedition to restore royal power in Ireland. While he was away, Bolingbroke invaded England. Richard's unpopularity and incompetence left him with scant support, and when he returned from Ireland he was outmanoeuvred, seized, forced to abdicate and imprisoned. The following year, Richard was probably killed to prevent him from acting as a focus for opposition, although he may have chosen to refuse all food.

Richard's reign indicated the potential instability of the monarchical system, but he also faced the difficulties of an unstable situation. Each monarch reinterpreted the conventions of royal behaviour and readjusted the patronage system to reward his own supporters. This was difficult for magnates (great lords) who wished to be consulted, not least about the disposal of patronage. Economic difficulties and the role of money in social, economic, military and political relations ensured that this disposal was of ever greater importance. 'Bastard feudalism' was becoming more significant: a system in which lords rewarded and maintained their followers by annual payments of money, rather than land. This helped to make the political situation more volatile and made it easier for magnates who had access to wealth to maintain a substantial affinity (following), which could act on occasion as a small army. It also ensured that they had less of a cushion against the political consequences of financial difficulties. The removal of Richard II both reflected and facilitated a situation in which it was thus logical to try to coerce the monarch in order to ensure a favourable disposal of patronage. The significance of his overthrow was also increased by his absolutist aspirations.

Abler than Richard II, Robert Stewart, who succeeded his childless uncle David II in Scotland in 1371, was more astute in his dealings with the magnates, possibly because he was himself a magnate. He used his children to establish marital links, including with the MacDonald Lord of the Isles. Robert II's son, Robert III (1390–1406), was less fortunate, in large part because of divisions within the royal family, especially between his eldest son, David, and his brother Robert, Duke of Albany. David was seized in 1402 and died in captivity. However, these disputes did not lead to a civil war. Moreover, the Crown was less significant in Scotland than it was in England.

WALES IN THE LATER MIDDLE AGES

The Welsh played an important role in support of the English Crown in the fourteenth century. Many bowmen and spearmen from all over Wales served in the Hundred Years War. Nevertheless, between 1369 and 1378 Owain ap Thomas ap Rhodri, or, as the French called him, Yvain de Galles, the great-nephew of Llywelyn ap Gruffudd and the last heir of the Gwynedd dynasty, was active in French service. In 1369 and 1372 there were abortive expeditions to Wales and he was assassinated by an English agent in France in 1378. The rising of Owain Glyndŵr (known through Shakespeare as Owen Glendower) in 1400–8 was an indication of the extent of disaffection and the survival of separatist feeling in Wales. Yet Glyndŵr's earlier career testified to the process of accommodation. An important landowner, as a young man he was a squire to the Earl of Arundel and in 1385 he took part in Richard II's Scottish campaign.

Glyndŵr's revolt may be seen as part of a whole series of revolts which occurred in Europe between about 1350 and 1450. It was in some ways a reaction to the successive crises of the fourteenth century, including the Black Death, but it was also a protest by the leaders of the native community at their neglect by the authorities. Proclaiming himself Prince of Wales in 1400, Glyndŵr rose in north Wales, helped by dissatisfaction with the financial demands of English landowners. Carmarthen and most of south Wales were captured in 1403, Cardiff, Harlech and Aberystwyth in 1404. Glyndŵr sealed a treaty of alliance with the French who promised assistance, and sought to organise regular government, as well as an independent church and universities. A Welsh Parliament was summoned, while some of the English Marchers bought peace from Welsh raids by truces. In 1405 Glyndŵr agreed the Tripartite Indenture with Edmund Mortimer and Henry Percy, Earl of Northumberland, by which they were to depose Henry IV and divide England. Glyndŵr's share included, besides Wales, England west of a line from the Mersey to the source of the Trent and then to the Severn just north of Worcester.

In 1405 Glyndŵr, with French help, advanced as far as Worcester, but then withdrew. Henry IV's vigorous son Prince Hal, later Henry V, began to inflict serious defeats. Harlech and Aberystwyth were recaptured in 1408 and the south entirely reconquered. Support for the rebellion ebbed and the English were increasingly successful.

Glyndŵr disappeared in 1415. He has recently served as a potent symbol of Welsh nationalism, and is certainly more appropriate than the princely house of Gwynedd, whose members, albeit through necessity, spent much of their energy fighting each other and other Welsh rulers. There was, however, a strong opposition to Glyndŵr among some native gentry too; they saw alliance with the English Crown as the best way to maintain their privileges. Glyndŵr was a warrior of his times, who used devastation without remorse. The cathedrals of St Asaph and Bangor were burnt down, as were Cardiff and Carmarthen, but Prince Hal also brought widespread destruction, and the English had often used this technique. The destruction of homes and farm implements and the seizure of farm animals were the equivalent for many, especially the weak, of sentences of death or at least severe hardship and malnutrition. Glyndŵr, heavily outnumbered, prudently avoided battle on many occasions and his military career was not conventionally heroic.

More significantly, Glyndŵr was leading his followers towards a dead end. English power was such that it was only during periods of English civil conflict, such as the Percy rising of 1403, that it was possible for Welsh opponents to make much headway. At other times, the weight of English resources told. Had Glyndŵr been more successful, it would have exposed Wales to decades of incessant conflict and the Welsh to deep divisions. Like many leaders, he was more useful as a dead symbol for posterity.

From the fourteenth century, social changes were working to the emergence of a Welsh gentry class. The Black Death was instrumental in breaking down the old land-owning patterns. Kindred patrimonies (*gwelyau*) and the equality of status that was their central feature declined in favour of individual ownership. Inheritance and tenurial changes, especially the expansion of primogeniture and greater freedom in the disposal of land, facilitated the development of freehold estates, and landholders gained wealth through military or administrative service or marriage. They acquired Crown lands, built substantial dwellings and developed political pretensions within the framework of an English-governed Wales. The bards sustained a sense of Welsh identity, although not in anglicised regions such as South Pembrokeshire and Gower, but those who were politically significant did not see this identity in terms of independence. As the tribal clans broke up, patterns of identity altered. Within the principality royal authority had replaced that of the clan in the maintenance of law and order.

LATER MEDIEVAL SCOTLAND

The wars of independence (1296–1357) secured the independence and territorial integrity of Scotland, and this success helped develop a sense of national consciousness. A distinct Scottish ecclesiastical province was created by the Lateran Council of 1215. John Barbour's poem the *Brus*, composed in Scots in 1375, was an anti-English national epic centring on Robert the Bruce and the 'freedom' of Scotland. Other late medieval histories of Scotland – the *Chronicle of the Scottish People* by John Fordun (1380s), the *Orgynale Cronikil* by Andrew Wyntoun (1410s) and the *Scotichronicon* by Walter Bower (1440s) – were produced to show that Scotland was a distinct state with its own history. Its identity was defined by opposition to England.

It was also a relatively successful state, although, like England, Scotland faced serious problems of political stability. Albeit less so than was to be the case by 1600, as a result of climate change in the 'Little Ice Age', Scotland was poorer and less populous than England, its agriculture less developed and without an important export comparable to English wool or later cloth. Scottish government was less sophisticated than that of England, its armies were smaller, and there was little about Scottish governance that can be regarded as a developing state in the fourteenth century, although there were some important trends in the fifteenth.

Two rival factions within the royal family competed for control from 1384 when Robert II became too ill to reign. This led to much instability and violence. James I (r. 1406–37) was captured by the English while *en route* to France as a child, and was held for nineteen years before being returned in 1424. James only gained power in 1425 by bringing down the former regent, Murdac, 2nd Duke of Albany; son of the Duke who had dominated Robert III's last years. Albany and his relatives were seized and beheaded. James then re-imposed royal control in the Highlands, summoned a parliament in Inverness in 1427, executed recalcitrant chiefs and strengthened the royal power. In 1429 and 1431, however, James had to campaign against the Lord of the Isles in the Highlands. James was murdered in his bedchamber in an attempted coup in 1437.

James II (r. 1437–60) faced civil war between aristocratic factions during the 1440s. This was the politics of kidnappings and sudden executions, such as those of the members of the faction of Sir Alexander Livingstone in 1450. Like England, Scotland was a violent society in which blood feuds were important: Alexander Irvine, 5th Laird of Drum from 1457 to 1493, was dismissed as Sheriff of Aberdeen and sent to prison for waging a private war. Later, he got into trouble first for ambushing and killing two men and then for murdering and dismembering a chaplain, Sir Edward Macdowall, in Drum Castle. Local administration and justice were left to the nobility. Some powerful magnates, such as the Earls of Douglas in the Borders, had increased their possessions and power during the wars of independence, and this restricted royal authority. The MacDonalds, Lords of the Isles and Earls of Ross, were similarly strong in west-coast Scotland. Their title to the Earldom of Ross had been established by force: they lost the battle of Harlaw near Inverurie in 1411, to the Regent's ally, the Earl of Mar; but deployed 10,000 men that day and subsequently gained the earldom.

Yet, in 1452–5, James II was able to crush the main branch of the Douglases. He personally stabbed William, 8th Earl of Douglas, to death in 1452 while the Earl was under the king's safe-conduct. In 1455, the Douglas castle at Threave surrendered in the face of a 'great bombard [cannon]'. In 1476, James III (r. 1460–88) gained Ross, and in 1493, James IV (r. 1488–1513) destroyed the MacDonalds' position and extended his authority to the Hebrides. These gains were achieved with the help of most nobles, who did not see the kings as threats to their position.

England remained a problem for the Scottish monarchs, not least because their usual alliance with France, the Auld Alliance, brought them into conflict with her. James I was an English captive in 1406–24; while James II died when a wedge blew out of a cannon during the bombardment of English-held Roxburgh Castle in 1460. After Henry VI of England was given shelter in Scotland following his defeat at Towton in 1461, Edward IV encouraged the rebellion of John, 11th Earl of Ross, in 1462, while in 1482–3, Edward sought to replace James III with the latter's brother, Albany. James IV was killed at the battle of Flodden when he invaded England in 1513.

Conflict and confrontation with England were expensive, for example the naval race of the early sixteenth century. The *Great Michael*, an enormous warship built for James IV in 1511, cost £30,000 (Scots) to construct and had running costs of £668 monthly at a time when annual royal income was less than £4,000 per year. There were no other foreign commitments. The Viking presence finally disappeared: James III gained Orkney and the Shetlands by his 1469 marriage to Margaret of Denmark; the failure of her father to pay the agreed dowry led to their confiscation in 1472.

It would be mistaken to exaggerate Scotland's political success. Its monarchs confronted serious political challenges. James III faced aristocratic opposition from 1479 led by his royal brothers, as well as significant criticism from Parliament. Nevertheless, in 1479, his brother Alexander, Duke of Albany, was forced to flee to France, and his attempt to regain power, with English help, as Alexander IV in 1482, ultimately failed. James III, however, failed to build up support or to keep the magnates sweet. In 1488, unable to muster sufficient support, he was killed shortly after his defeat at Sauchieburn at the hands of a rebel force under the standard of his own son, then still a minor. The rebels took over the government, and, in turn, had to face rebellion in 1489. Given such problems at the centre, the stress on local control of much administration was prudent.

Yet in Scotland, as in England, the striking feature of most fifteenth-century violence was the attempt to seize control of the central government, generally in the person of the monarch. As in England, the calibre of the monarch and his ability to take command of a political situation made complex by competing factions was important. Political instability essentially arose not from challenges to the power of the state but rather from the emergence of two rival factions within the royal family. There was no doubt of the integrity of the state, and this national political consciousness was fortified by the frequency with which Parliament met in Scotland. James IV substantially increased the royal revenues, remained popular and brought considerable harmony to Scottish politics, although he used his position to follow an ultimately unsuccessful attempt to increase his international standing. There was also a renaissance of the Scottish court under James IV and James V. James IV spent heavily on beginning Holyrood Palace as a grand residence in Edinburgh.

ECONOMY AND SOCIETY IN FIFTEENTH-CENTURY ENGLAND

The difficulties of the agrarian economy following the Black Death created problems for most landlords until the 1470s, as did the serious climatic downturn. Rents fell, serfdom declined, villages were abandoned and the lynchets that permitted the cultivation of steep slopes were deserted. As subsistence farming came to the fore for a short while, the trade of most markets and fairs declined. Economic problems led to places being allowed a reduction of their tax assessments. However, the scarcity of labour resulting from endemic plague brought advantages to those of the peasantry that were able to exploit it, not least because of the decline of serfdom. The labour-rent of unfree peasants was generally commuted into money payments, and those were then integrated directly into the money economy. Several foreign visitors commented on the prosperity of England as a whole, not just of London. Labour shortages also encouraged a shift to pastoral farming, which needed fewer workers. Landlords enclosed their land for sheep farming, leading to rural depopulation in counties such as Lincolnshire. The severity of this situation was such that conversion of tilled land to pasture was made an offence by Parliament in 1489.

The spread of pasture led to a growth in wool and then in cloth exports. The English had developed breeds of sheep with particularly good wool, much sought after by the cloth-manufacturing centres of Flanders, and the wool trade had grown during the thirteenth century, bringing prosperity to towns such as Shrewsbury. From the fourteenth century, however, the wool was increasingly exported in the form of cloth as the impost on wool shifted some of the burden to Flanders (and thus France) and also provided a tax break for the development of the English cloth industry. East Anglia was the key centre of the industry. Great Yarmouth was responsible for three-quarters of the country's exports of worsted cloth, 12,000 worsteds passing through it in the tax year 1400–1. The growth in wool and cloth exports brought wealth to such East Anglian cloth centres as Hadleigh, Lavenham and Long Melford, and was reflected in their substantial churches. Economic developments also accentuated social differentiation: in Suffolk in 1327 there were only 28 parishes where one person contributed 30 per cent or more of the total tax paid; by 1524 there were more than 180. The West Country was another major centre of the cloth industry.

Wool and cloth exports also helped to keep England's trade in balance, were vital to governmental finances and helped to finance English participation in the Hundred Years War. In addition, the exports helped to accentuate the relative wealth of south-eastern England, increasingly the centre of power. They had a similar beneficial effect in Scotland. There also the major ports were those with access to the European mainland. By 1500, Edinburgh was responsible for about 60 per cent of Scotland's exports and was the leading city in the country; a central place with an important economic and political dynamic. Its significance represented the displacement of Berwick, increasingly under English control.

MEDIEVAL ENGLISH CULTURE

Cultural links after 1066 were very much with France. The conquest moved England from the Scandinavian to the western continental cultural sphere. Yet it would be wrong to neglect Norman adaptability. If buildings begun between 1066 and 1100 displayed distinctly Norman features, while few of the Anglo-Saxon decorative traditions were continued, the situation altered after 1100 with the revival of Anglo-Saxon styles of painting and the creation of a vibrant Anglo-Norman style.

It was not until the fourteenth century that English or Scots, not French or Latin literature developed, but this led to the writing of major works in English: the anonymous *Gawain and the Green Knight*, Geoffrey Chaucer's *Canterbury Tales* (*c.* 1387), William Langland's *Piers Plowman* (1362–92), and Thomas Malory's *Morte d'Arthur* (1469), as well as ballads, carols and mystery plays. The Scottish poet Robert Henryson wrote a number of fine works in the vernacular, including the *Testament of Cresseid*. Much literature, however, continued to be written in French or Latin, including most of the books owned by Richard II and his circle. Given that both English and French had multiple dialects it is more pertinent to note that England had two vernaculars: Middle English and Anglo-French. The latter continued important into the fifteenth century.

There were other aspects of vitality. Medieval English architecture was in many ways highly derivative of French models. Many quintessentially 'English' buildings such as Durham and Canterbury cathedrals were built by French architects working for Norman or Angevin masters. However, just as the rulers became in some measure anglicised, so an authentically English Gothic tradition grew up, most spectacularly in cathedrals such as Wells. The heyday of the Decorated style was in the early fourteenth century. Moreover, the Perpendicular, a native architectural style, was predominant from *c.* 1370 until the mid-1500s, and was seen in soaring works with large windows and fan vaulting, such as the chapel of King's College Cambridge. A distinctive style of English music, with composers such as William Cornish, John Dunstable and Walter Frye, attracted continental attention. Minstrel performances and itinerant troupes of players offered a secular counterpart to religious 'mystery plays'. The first known example of the latter occurred in Lancashire in 1352–3.

England was still very much part of an international cultural world, but it was playing a more active role within it, although English painting in the fifteenth century was of very poor quality, and English people who wanted their portraits painted went to Flanders and sat to artists such as Memling. The Eton College Chapel wall paintings, the most important English paintings of the late fifteenth century, are by painters who were Flemish or trained in Flanders.

RELIGION IN MEDIEVAL ENGLAND

The Norman conquest had brought England into the mainstream of western Christendom, exposing it to the new religious impulses of the eleventh and twelfth centuries, such as new monastic orders and the Crusades. The English Church was subject legally, and to a large extent in practice, to the Papacy. The clergy owed loyalty to two masters, the king and the Pope. International religious links led to clerics following careers abroad and their counterparts doing so in the British Isles. The spread of new monastic orders and of the friars affected the British Isles.

Britain shared in the revival of monasticism linked to the foundation of the (stricter) Cistercian Order in 1098. Rievaulx, the first English Cistercian abbey, was founded in 1132 and the Order spread rapidly over the following two decades, with notable foundations including Fountains and Buckfast; as well as Tintern in Wales and Melrose, Newbattle and Kinloss in Scotland. The Cistercians proved particularly adept at exploiting the profitability of wool production. The Dominican and Franciscan Orders of friars arrived in England in the 1220s.

A less attractive aspect of Britain's role in western Christendom was anti-semitism, which flourished on the Continent from the 1090s. The first reference to Jews in England is later, in the early twelfth century, but, thereafter, anti-semitism became a feature of English life, culminating in Edward I's expulsion of the Jews in 1290. William of Norwich in 1144 may be the first instance of a child whose murder was falsely blamed upon Jews. Anti-semitism reflected a hostility to aliens that became a readily apparent feature of medieval society. It was a counterpart to the Crusades.

There were also older and darker fears. The role of the dark – a world outside human understanding and control – in the life of the imagination was both aspect and product of a more generalised sense of fear. This was a world of malevolence, where the Devil and witches were real, part of the varied legions of evil. Many of these superstitions were fuelled by the Church. In 1479, James III of Scotland accused his brother, the Earl of Mar, of witchcraft. Several witches were accused of melting a wax image of James, and were burned, although there was nothing on the scale of the British witch craze of the late sixteenth and early seventeenth centuries.

More mundanely, many kings of England clashed with papal pretensions and ecclesiastical claims. John's refusal to accept the Pope's choice of Archbishop of Canterbury led to England being placed under an interdict, with all church services suspended in 1208. There was hostility to foreign ecclesiastical jurisdiction and to the movement of funds abroad, and legislation in the fourteenth century was designed to establish limits on papal rights: the Statutes of Provisors (1351) and *Praemunire* (1351, 1393). Anti-clericalism was exploited by the Lollard movement, which was inspired by John Wycliff (d. 1384), a radical Oxford theologian who denied the need for priestly intercession between God and man, the Pope's temporal authority and the doctrine of transubstantiation. Wycliff also translated the Bible into English, which the Church disapproved of. Wycliff emphasised the authority of scripture and criticised the wealth of the monastic orders. He was condemned by the Pope and the English Church. The Lollards were persecuted after Wycliff's death, especially after the failure of a Lollard conspiracy in 1414.

The popularity and vitality of the late medieval English Church are controversial issues. Some historians stress this popularity and vitality and argue that the Reformation was therefore widely unpopular; other scholars are not so sure. The liturgy of the faith can be seen as central to people's lives, giving them meaning and beauty, or anti-clericalism can be stressed. It is possible to emphasise the corporate nature of worship, especially the Mass, or to stress the argument that it was becoming more individual, with private prayers directing attention from the Latin liturgy enunciated by the priest. It is also possible to emphasise both approaches. Late medieval Catholicism can be seen as corrupt and anti-clericalism can be emphasised, while arguing that many people still found religion and the Church a source of inspiration and solace.

Whichever is the case, most priests were conscientious and relations with parishioners were generally good. The Church played a central role in society, not least as the crucial source of education, health and social welfare. Medieval hospitals were, for example, primarily religious institutions, offering warmth, food and shelter rather than clinical treatment. They provided shelter to lepers and others who would otherwise have been outcasts.

Traditional religious practices and beliefs were supported by a host of verbal and visual narratives, including carols, mystery plays, stained-glass windows, statues and wall paintings. That was why their subsequent abolition and destruction during the Reformation were so important. What is clear is that fifteenth-century English Christianity was still very much part of an international church, and that disquiet about some aspects of its position and about the existence of the Lollard heresy increased the sense of unease of the period.

HENRY IV, 1399–1413

Henry IV had moved boldly to seize the throne, but, once he had replaced and then murdered Richard II, he was confronted by a number of acute problems. The most serious at first was Owain Glyndŵr's rising in Wales (see p. 81–2), but Henry also faced the fragmentation of the English position in Ireland, French attacks on the English possessions in Aquitaine, difficulties with Scotland and serious opposition in England. Henry's seizure of the throne was helped by Richard II's childlessness, but his claim to the throne was questionable, certainly far worse than that of Edward III when Edward II was removed in 1327.

Henry was challenged within England by a mighty magnate family, the Percys, who wielded great power in the north. The Percys had backed Henry's seizure of the throne, but, angry with his refusal to do as they wanted, they rebelled in 1403 and allied with Glyndŵr. Henry IV responded vigorously, defeating and killing the Percy heir, 'Hotspur', Sir Henry Percy, at the battle of Shrewsbury and forcing his father, the Earl of Northumberland, to disband his forces. Royal patronage was now focused on Ralph Neville, Earl of Westmorland.

In 1405 Northumberland organised a new rebellion with Glyndŵr, Archbishop Scrope of York and Edmund Mortimer, Earl of March, who had a good hereditary claim to the throne as he was descended from Edward III's third son, compared with Henry's descent from the fourth. Scrope advanced ideas of the accountability of kingship, claiming that the senior clergy had a historical role as the monitor of kingship. Glyndŵr, Northumberland and March agreed to divide England in three, but the rebellion was defeated. Westmorland seized Scrope who was executed for treason. Subsequently a martyrdom cult commemorated 'York's own Becket'.

In 1408, there was another rebellion by the Earl of Northumberland, who was defeated and killed on Bramham Moor. These years of conspiracy and rebellion indicate the problems created by Henry's seizure of the throne: royal prestige had been greatly lessened; removing a king had become a dangerous precedent.

It is also clear that it is misleading to think of later medieval English politics in terms of the progressive extension of the role of Parliament. Indeed, in the fifteenth century, Parliament was far less important than aristocratic factionalism. Nevertheless, in 1407, Henry reaffirmed the established liberties of Lords and Commons to discuss, in the absence

of the king, the condition of the realm, while the Commons' right over
supply (voting taxation) was reaffirmed.

HENRY V, 1413–22

Henry IV's eldest son, the dynamic Prince Hal of Shakespeare's plays,
took a leading role in the fighting of his father's reign, in both England
and Wales. As ruler, Henry V was a warrior king. He easily crushed a
Lollard conspiracy organised by Sir John Oldcastle (1414) and an
attempt by the Earl of Cambridge to proclaim the Earl of March king
(1415). Rather than trying to advance English interests in Ireland or
Scotland, Henry then turned to the more glamorous goal of conquering
the parts of France recognised as Edward III's by the Treaty of Brétigny.
After careful preparations, he invaded Normandy in 1415, captured
the port of Harfleur and then set off to march overland to Calais. A far
larger French army sought to block him at Agincourt, but, as at Crecy
in 1346, the English archers smashed the successive advances of the
French, inflicting crippling losses.

As part of English history, the Battle of Agincourt always held an
important place, because it showed how a small army could defeat a
much larger one, and because it contributed to the national myth of a
feud between two countries (England and France). In the Second World
War, this was transposed onto the struggle against Germany. However,
the end of the Empire in the twentieth century and the martial attitudes
that surrounded it have left the battle with less contemporary resonance.
Agincourt was a crucial battle, both in traditionally marking the emergence under Henry V of a self-consciously *English* (rather than Norman
or Frenchified) court, and as a further stage in the unsuccessful quest
of the Hundred Years War to unite England and France under a single
monarch. This quest was ultimately a complete failure and the English
kings were ejected even from long-held possessions such as Bordeaux,
but the war was important in helping solidify English (and French)
senses of nationality, and its demands for money, men and supplies
were partly responsible for the precociously centralised and effective
government of England.

Agincourt helped to make Henry and the war popular in England,
and he followed it up by conquering Normandy in 1417–19. This
led Henry to renew the claim to the French throne. The French were
affected by civil war and in 1419 the powerful Duke of Burgundy

joined Henry. The following year, Henry's victories led to his betrothal to Catherine, the daughter of Charles VI of France. By the Treaty of Troyes (1420), Charles recognised Henry as his heir and as regent during his reign. Henry V wanted to be accepted by the French as their ruler, not as a conqueror. Charles's son, the Dauphin, continued, however, to resist and Henry died in 1422 on campaign near Paris, possibly of dysentery.

It is unclear what he might have achieved had Henry V lived, but his ambitions are a useful reminder of the danger of assuming that the future state structure of western Europe was clear, and of assuming the inevitability of developments. Indeed Parliament expressed anxiety about the relationship between the two Crowns and was keen to ensure that Henry never ruled in England in his capacity as King of France. Henry brought medieval English kingship to a peak of achievement and fame, successfully operating not only as a military leader, but also in relations with the nobility and clergy, in the restoration of public order, as a manager of Parliament and as an active administrator. Henry had far fewer problems with Parliament than his father. He was concerned to maintain justice and order, and was devoted to the Church: Henry viewed the Lollards as both heretical and seditious. The king's heroic image reflected not only his martial character and achievements, but also his promotion of English nationhood: Henry emphasised England's history and role, supported the cult of English saints and furthered the official use of the English language, all of which were inconsistent with his ambitions in France.

HENRY VI, 1422–61, 1470–1

Henry V's death left his son, Henry, king, though only nine months old. Later in 1422 he was also proclaimed King of France on the death of his grandfather, Charles VI. While one uncle, Humphrey, became Protector in England, another, John, Duke of Bedford, became Regent in France and sought to maintain Henry V's impetus and to defeat another uncle, Charles VI's son, now Charles VII. The English had much success by 1429, winning, for example, a major victory at Verneuil (1424). French resistance revived, however, when a charismatic peasant girl, Joan of Arc, inspired Charles VII. In 1429 an army led by Joan lifted the English siege of the strategic fortress of Orleans, and Charles was crowned at Rheims.

In response Henry was crowned at Paris in 1430, and the captured Joan was burned as a witch (1431). But it was by now too late. The balance of military success had moved. Once the English cause faltered, opposition to the war increased in England and allies wavered in France. The Burgundians had handed Joan over and had secured English control of Paris, but in 1435 they abandoned Henry VI. The English lost Paris the following year. After Bedford's death in 1435, the English suffered from poor leadership and were driven back by the French. Maine was lost in 1444. In 1449–51 Normandy and Gascony fell rapidly to Charles VII's stronger army, not least his impressive train of artillery. This brought victory in battle over English archers (Formigny, 1450) and the speedy fall of fortified positions. An English counteroffensive was crushed by the French at Castillon (1453).

France was lost. Calais was held until 1558 and the Channel Islands are British to this day. The claim to the French throne was only abandoned in the reign of George III (also, although more realistically, the last king in America), but these were faint echoes of a centuries-long link. A crucial precondition of the modern history of the British Isles was the more insular character of England after 1453. It was to be one of the keys to its subsequent domestic and international development.

WARS OF THE ROSES, 1450–87

The civil conflicts of late fifteenth-century England are given a misleading coherence by being called the Wars of the Roses. This is an unhelpful term, both because the 'Lancastrian red' rose and the 'Yorkist white' were not the sole identifications employed and also because the struggle between the families of Lancaster and York for the throne was but one theme in the conflict of the period. Violence began not on 22 May 1455 when Richard, Duke of York, attacked nobles close to Henry VI and his wife, Margaret of Anjou, at the battle of St Albans, but five years earlier when the chief minister, William, First Duke of Suffolk, was murdered on a boat in the English Channel, having been impeached in Parliament and banished, after a major uprising, Cade's Rebellion, in Kent. Suffolk was a court favourite, unpopular because he had monopolised patronage.

The two events reflected the political crisis of Henry VI's government, a political crisis related to failure in war at the hands of

France but also to the long-term economic crisis and to the bankruptcy of the Crown. Cade's Rebellion in 1450 reflected widespread discontent at a government seen as corrupt at home and unsuccessful abroad. Before being crushed, the rebels defeated a royal army at Sevenoaks, captured London and executed hated officials. There were also widespread disturbances in south and west England, including the killing of the bishop of Salisbury and attacks on Church property in Hampshire, Wiltshire and Dorset. The crisis helped undermine the position of Henry VI, making it easier for ambitious nobles to challenge him.

Henry VI was a poor leader; incompetent and ineffectual, he eventually went mad. He lacked the vigour and success that had enabled his two predecessors to overcome the weak Lancastrian claim, and in Richard, Duke of York, he faced a determined exponent of a rival and better dynastic claim to the succession of Edward III: York was descended from Edward's second son, Lionel of Clarence. Henry's partisanship in disputes between nobles compromised his royal status so that the royal government could not provide unity among the nobles, and thus stability and peace; and his wife, Margaret, was a determined supporter of faction.

Distrust within the elite was exacerbated by violence, creating blood feuds, notably between those on opposite sides at the battle of St Albans, for example between the houses of Beaufort and York. Regional and local struggles for dominance, particularly in the north between the Nevilles and the Percys, were also serious. The price of failure was often death. After the battle of Wakefield (1460) Richard of York's severed head, adorned with a paper crown, was publicly displayed on the gate of York. Henry VI's only child, Edward, Prince of Wales, was killed by the Yorkists at the battle of Tewkesbury (1471). As in Scotland with the fall of the Black Douglas clan before the power of James II in 1455, failure could also lead to loss of power, privilege, property and influence. It was not, therefore, surprising that there was a determination to win, a conviction of the importance of seizing power. This affected the claimants to the throne, as well as powerful nobles, such as Richard Neville, Earl of Warwick, the 'kingmaker', although it was also the case that some nobles did not take part in the wars, a group that was even larger in 1485 when Richard III and Henry Tudor fought for the throne.

The clashes of the 1450s became more serious in July 1460 when the Yorkist victory at the battle of Northampton led York to

claim the throne. Henry VI was captured, but Margaret and Prince
Edward were still at large. York set out to defeat them, but was killed
at Wakefield. His ambitious eldest son, Edward, realising that compromise with Margaret was impossible, then claimed the throne. Margaret
followed her victory at Wakefield by defeating Warwick, then a Yorkist,
at St Albans (1461), and releasing Henry VI; but London defied her,
and she then retreated north in the face of Edward's advance. The two
sides clashed at Towton (1461), the battle with the most combatants
and deaths yet fought on English soil. The Lancastrians were heavily
defeated and Edward IV (1461–83) then reigned with few problems
until he fell out with Warwick in 1469.

The two men differed over Edward's growing independence, both
in foreign policy and over his favour for his wife's relations, the
Woodvilles. The conventions of the 1450s and early 1460s that had
enabled opposition to Henry were now turned against Edward. Playing
a key role, Warwick defeated Edward at Edgecote (1469) and gained
power, only to lose it in 1470 and flee to France. He was there recon-
ciled with a fellow exile, Margaret, and committed himself to restoring
Henry VI.

With French help, Warwick and Edward IV's discontented brother,
George, Duke of Clarence, invaded in 1470. An outmanoeuvred Edward
fled into exile and Henry was restored. In 1471, however, Edward
invaded and, with adroit generalship and luck, defeated Warwick in
thick fog at the battle of Barnet, and Margaret at Tewkesbury. Warwick
was killed at Barnet. Edward's position was further secured when Henry
VI was killed while imprisoned in the Tower of London. Thereafter
England was more stable under Edward IV than it had been under
Henry VI. The finances were restored and the economy improved, but
the campaign in France in 1475 was unsuccessful, and Edward's popularity was limited.

Edward IV still faced problems, both from Lancastrian supporters
and within the royal family; Clarence had betrayed Warwick in 1471
but was killed in the Tower in 1478 for plotting against Edward:
according to contemporaries drowned in a butt (barrel) of malmsey
wine. Edward died at 40, too early to allow his young son, Edward V,
to establish himself on the throne. Edward IV's surviving brother,
Richard, Duke of Gloucester, had his nephews declared bastards,
became king as Richard III (r. 1483–5) and sent the young princes
to the Tower where they swiftly disappeared. They were probably

murdered. Richard III was very capable, but widely distrusted. He divided the Yorkist establishment by seizing the throne, had only a narrow base of support, and could not trust the uncommitted. Moreover, Henry, Duke of Buckingham, who had played a crucial role in Richard's seizure of the throne, rebelled in 1483, only to be captured and executed.

In 1485 the lottery of military fortune and dynastic extinction brought Henry Tudor to the throne of England. His father, Edmund, from the Tudors of Penmynydd, a leading Welsh family of officials and earlier the leading servants of the rulers of Gwynedd, had married Margaret Beaufort, the heiress of the cadet Lancastrian line. The main line had been cut short with the deaths of Henry VI and his son Edward, and Henry Tudor was thus the unlikely bearer of Lancastrian hopes against the house of York.

In 1485 Henry Tudor invaded with the help of French troops. The unpopular Richard III was only supported by a few nobles, and crucial betrayals at the battle of Bosworth gave Henry victory and the throne. Henry himself had even less aristocratic support than Richard; indifference and fear characterised a country exhausted by civil war and with little enthusiasm for either side. Had Richard triumphed he might have been able to consolidate his position: despite his unpopularity, he would have faced no strong Lancastrian claimant. However, the death of the childless Richard at Bosworth and the earlier deaths of the princes in the Tower and of Clarence gravely weakened the Yorkists and helped Henry to establish the new Tudor dynasty.

Nevertheless, Bosworth did not end the Wars of the Roses. Lambert Simnel and Perkin Warbeck claimed, respectively, to be Clarence's son, Edward, Earl of Warwick, then held in the Tower, and the younger of the sons of Edward IV, who had in fact died in the Tower. They were supported by domestic and foreign opponents of Henry, who had to fight to retain the throne. Simnel's army was defeated at Stoke (1487), the last battle of the Wars of the Roses, and Warbeck, a major nuisance around whom malcontents congregated, was captured (1497) and hanged (1499). Yorkist plots continued, centred on the de la Pole family, but the situation was more stable than it had been for decades. Henry's marriage in 1486 to Elizabeth of York, daughter of Edward IV, helped to unify the two factions, a process symbolised by the replacement of the roses of Lancaster and York by the Tudor rose.

HENRY VII, 1485–1509

Like Charles II in 1660–85, Henry's essential aim was to avoid having to go on his travels in exile again. He manoeuvred skilfully, both at home and abroad, and improved the effectiveness of the existing governmental machinery. Henry took an active role, personally supervising the administration and reasserting monarchical control over the nobility. As in Scotland under James IV (r. 1488–1513), the Crown's feudal rights and judicial authority were both reasserted, as was its position in the localities. Henry ruled with vigour: rebel estates were confiscated, he was unwilling to delegate his authority, and he placed people under bonds for good behaviour. As under James IV, governmental finances were dramatically improved, so that Henry VII left a modest fortune on his death, and law and order were enhanced. The private armed forces of nobles were limited. Henry was careful not to get involved in lengthy hostilities abroad. A short war with France was ended on satisfactory terms in 1492, and thereafter Henry negotiated to some effect, enabling England to become an important, albeit second-rank, power in European diplomacy.

NEW MONARCHY?

The England of the Yorkists and Henry VII is often seen as one of the 'new monarchies', experiencing a similar development to the France of Louis XI (r. 1461–83). It is, however, unclear how far new monarchy was really novel and based on a plan for establishing stronger royal authority and a more effective centrally-directed administrative system, and curbing the power of nobles, or whether it was substantially a matter of re-establishing royal power after a period of disruption; for France, Aragon, Castile and Scotland also experienced civil conflict at the same time as the Wars of the Roses. Certainly the process by which municipal, county and Crown officials gained authority, leading to more effective social control, was very long-term, dating back to the stabilisation of government from the reign of Henry II on. The situation was similar in Scotland. There, having succeeded his murdered father, James IV (r. 1488–1513) restored royal power and prestige. The 'new monarchs' in Britain needed their nobility: they might break individual nobles but there was no anti-aristocratic policy, although the later Stewarts (Stuarts) pursued a distinct policy of controlling the nobility as a whole through Crown institutions and other means. The same was true of Parliaments, although James IV called none after 1509. It is appropriate not to exaggerate change within the period 1460–1560 prior to the Reformation crisis, and instead to focus on the political problems and responses created by that crisis.

4

The Sixteenth Century

The particular importance of the period was that it witnessed a new emphasis on religious division, one that created serious problems at home and abroad, and that there was a related stress on relations between the parts of the British Isles. It is also significant in the long term that England developed trans-oceanic interests and ambitions, not least in the New World. At the same time, there were important continuities, including the dynastic need for heirs, which, in the sixteenth century, was a cause of religious strife focused on the new disruption presented by the break with the Papacy and the Protestant Reformation. First, however, it is appropriate to turn to pressures on society and the condition of the people.

SOCIAL AND ECONOMIC DEVELOPMENTS

The central fact affecting the lot of the British in the sixteenth and early seventeenth centuries was that there were more of them. The population of Wales, for example, rose from about 226,000 in the 1540s to about 342,000 in 1670; that of Scotland from about 500,000 in the fourteenth century to about one million by 1650. The biggest increase was in England – the population more than doubled from under 2.5 million in 1500 to about 5 million by 1651, thus increasing England's strength within the British Isles. However, the size of the Irish population, about a million in 1600, helped to underline its threat in English eyes, a theme that was to remain pertinent until the mid-nineteenth century. The population increase across the British Isles was due largely to a fall in mortality, though by modern standards mortality was still very high. The plague could still be savage in its effects: 30–33 per cent of the population of Norwich died as a result in 1587, 12 per cent of that of London in 1593, 40–50 per cent of that of Kendal in 1598, 12,000 in Edinburgh and its environs in 1644–9. Infected houses were marked with a sign and in effect quarantined, the only possible remedy for a society that lacked the scientific knowledge of transmission via rats and fleas. Alongside a fall in mortality, a rise in fertility due to a small fall in the average age of marriage was probably also important.

A rise in population led to a growth in economic demand and activity, a growth that helped the Tudor government at the same time that it created social problems. Economic expansion put pressure on living standards. While the area of cultivation was extended, former common land was enclosed, leading to riots. The labour shortage, high wages and low rents of the late medieval period were replaced by a price inflation, especially in 1540–53, that had an even greater effect from its following a period that had known scant inflation. Much of the peasantry lost status and became little different from poorly paid wage-labourers. Enclosure reflected not just capitalist opportunity but also a decline in paternal responsibility on the part of landlords: for example, in Norfolk gentry sheep farmers such as the Townshends benefited at the expense of tenants and lesser farmers. Although the impact of enclosure was very varied by region, in the sixteenth century it was generally designed to promote pastoral rather than arable farming.

Inflation in England was exacerbated by the debasement and increase in volume of the coinage. Rents and food prices rose faster than wages in England, and this contrast pressed hard on tenants and on those with little or no land. Very little data is available for Scotland, though the Scottish pound fell heavily in value against sterling. The high prices that helped English landowners also hit the poor, leading to a growth in the number of paupers and vagrants which greatly concerned the Tudors. The 1495 Act Against Vagabonds and Beggars was only the first of a number of statutes, including a series of poor laws (1531, 1536, 1572, 1598, 1601). Compulsory poor rates, a tax on property in each parish, were introduced in 1572, an Act of 1597 encouraged the provision of 'Abiding and working Houses' and in 1598 the relief of poverty was made the responsibility of the individual parish; but the situation was harsh, particularly for able-bodied men unable to find work, who were treated as rogues and vagabonds. The Poor Relief Act of 1662 established that the right to relief was dependent upon the pauper being settled in the parish, a practice that led to the expulsion of paupers deemed non-resident and their resettlement in their home parish. The system lasted until the Poor Law Amendment Act of 1834 which introduced the comprehensive workhouse system. In Scotland, there was a licensed begging system, a blue badge granting the right to beg in one's home parish. However, there was also suspicion of the able-bodied unemployed. In 1504, the Scottish Parliament banned begging by the able-bodied.

Economic pressure led to widespread malnutrition among the poor and to some starvation. Most folktales centred on peasant poverty and in many the need and wish to have an inexhaustible quantity of food is a central theme. Economic problems led to social pressure on the weaker members of the community and those judged most marginal, for example to measures against illegitimacy and bridal pregnancy, to the demand for a formal Church wedding as the source of marital legitimacy, and to attempts in some parishes to prevent the poor from marrying. Churchwardens and Church courts policed moral conduct, seeking to stop practices such as adultery, and the selling of alcohol at the time of Church services. This action was more intense in Scotland than England. It was in this context of social tension and coercion that concern about alleged witchcraft developed.

The poor were harshly treated by man and nature alike. They ate less, and less well, than the wealthier members of the community, and their housing was of low standard. Everywhere, the malnutrition of the poor reduced their resistance to disease and poor-health. Moreover, the wealthy might choose to seek compromise in their disputes with each other, but they generally showed no such willingness in disputes with their social inferiors. Social, political, economic and moral intimidation were frequently the lot of the poor. Unless through crime, charity or as servants, the poor were certainly cut off from the growing affluence and comfort of the wealthy, with their finer clothes and larger houses. Yet the highly public life of wealthy families made their affluence very visible to the poor: a powerful message of the nature of the social order.

The gentry were an important source of employment and patronage, and wealth was also spreading down the social scale to the yeomanry. There were more clothes and furniture, and more musical instruments and medicaments than a century earlier. Growing wealth had cultural and social consequences. There was much new building, particularly in brick in England. In Scotland, there was extensive building in stone in the sixteenth century; bricks were only used in ports that traded with the Low Countries, such as Aberdeen, where bricks were built into stone houses, particularly near the harbour. More material consumption was seen as a major cause of what was regarded with concern as a significant rise in crime. The breakdown of master–servant relations in a more volatile and less paternalistic society was also partly responsible for the rise in crime.

Aristocrats and gentry built prestigious houses, entertained liberally, showed great interest in sometimes spurious genealogical studies, and sought to adopt a code of aristocratic conduct. They were very interested in education, which secured their gentility, distinguished them from the rest of the community and provided valuable legal skills. Stately homes were built in new styles that reflected wealth and status and also, particularly in England, the more peaceful nature of the state: English, Welsh and Scottish aristocratic homes were no longer built like fortresses. Instead, houses such as Hardwick Hall, described by contemporaries as 'more glass than wall', and Longleat, had massive windows. The fortress quality of many sixteenth-century Scottish aristocratic houses was a matter of show and a statement of the valorous antiquity of the martial nation, rather than being designed for defence. These houses lacked moats, earthworks, and barbicans, and their gun-loops were not only so few as to suggest style not substance but also had poor angles of fire.

Landscaping in gardens and parks strengthened and reflected ideas of order and hierarchy. Hierarchy and the control of the countryside were also reflected in the limitations of rights to hunting by the English Game Acts of 1485 and 1604. Freeholders lost ancient rights to hunt on their own land, thanks to the greater property qualifications introduced by the second Act. Scottish social organisation remained more traditionally feudal.

Printing ensured that the records, both state and private, on which we base our historical accounts, became more common. Printing also brought books, offering the possibility of a more private and individual culture than that provided by the conspicuous consumption and display of Court splendour, public ceremonial and elaborate buildings. The first book printed in England was published by William Caxton in 1474, while Scotland gained its first printing press in 1508. A new reading public bought books, including religious literature, and helped to spur rising literacy. The publication of translations of the Bible transformed the religious culture of Britain and made it impossible to maintain the old order without change. Similarly, educational developments, not least the foundation of schools, ensured that public culture altered.

Aside from the cultural changes stemming from the Reformation, there was also more money available for cultural and leisure activities. The Theatre, the first purpose-built public playhouse in England, was opened in London in 1576, followed by the Curtain in 1577 and the Globe in 1599. The Lord Chamberlain's Men, a theatrical company in which William Shakespeare (1564–1616) had a stake, produced plays at the Theatre and the Globe. The degree to which theatrical companies were patronised by aristocrats such as the Lord Chamberlain and the Earl of Essex demonstrated the social leadership of the nobility, but the opportunities and exigencies of the commercial marketplace were crucial. In turn, Shakespeare's plays expressed the aspirations and tensions of the emerging nation-state, while their vocabulary and phrases came to occupy a major position in the language. Theatre developed in Scotland, not only in a court setting, with works by, for example, Sir David Lindsay; but also more popular performances.

Shakespeare himself responded to the possibilities offered by economic development, buying up local property, pursuing his debtors in court, and possibly speculating in grain. Although the drama of the age is principally remembered in terms of his plays, the London market was large enough to support other playwrights, including, in the late sixteenth century, Thomas Dekker, Robert Greene, Thomas Kidd and Christopher Marlowe and, early in the following century, Francis Beaumont, John Fletcher, Ben Jonson, Philip Massinger, Thomas Middleton, William Rowley and John Webster. The vitality of contemporary society was a major theme in their plays, as were the livelihood, pretensions and concerns of the population. For example, in *The Witch of Edmonton* (*c.* 1621) by William Rowley, Thomas Dekker and John Ford, Elizabeth Sawyer became a witch having made a pact with the Devil. In the same play, Susan Carter is murdered by Frank Thorney, who has bigamously married her to secure his inheritance, as she is his father's choice, and not his secret wife, the servant Winifred.

Urban growth was the most obvious aspect of the rise in sixteenth-century population, not least because it reflected both natural increase and migration from the countryside. By 1665 about 20–25 per cent of the English population was urban. This percentage owed much to the increase in London's population, from about 50,000–60,000 in 1500 to about 500,000–600,000 in 1700. It did so without serious unrest until the mid-seventeenth century, in part because of the cohesion of the city's elite and their willingness to respond to social ideals of reciprocal rights and obligations. Poor relief, though limited, thus contributed to social control in London. Growth, meanwhile, fostered urban culture, as in the spread of theatre or the increase in the number and importance of town halls.

Supplying the towns helped to fuel economic activity elsewhere in the country. The perishable nature of fresh food combined with transport problems to ensure that market gardening focused close to London. Pasture land was also located near cities, to provide milk and to secure pasturage for animals walked to towns to be slaughtered there for meat. At a very different scale, the coal industry in the north-east of England developed in the late sixteenth century in order to supply London. In the fifteenth century, 15,000 tons of coal were shipped annually from the River Tyne; by 1625, 400,000 tons. Both Gresham's Exchange and the Bourse were constructed in London, providing new foci for economic activity. Other cities also grew, but to nowhere near the same extent. Edinburgh's population rose to about 30,000–35,000 people in 1700, by when, if not well before, it was the third largest city after London and Dublin.

Throughout the British Isles, though most obviously in England and Wales, the role of the market economy became more insistent and consistent. However, the maintenance of the communication system was put under pressure by the disruption linked to the dissolution of the monasteries, while the obligation on the inhabitants of parishes to maintain the highway was often ignored. As an indication of the growing tendency to turn to Parliament, legislation was passed to fill the gap, an Act of 1555 seeking to enforce the obligation on parishes. The market economy increasingly affected areas that had formerly been characterised by subsistence agriculture and poverty. Welsh cattle and sheep were driven to English markets, especially London, the growth of which had a major effect on the economy. Food and coal were moved in greater quantities to London. The network of regular carriers' routes focused on London was instrumental in creating the national transport system.

In Scotland, the scale of cattle droving, which had been a major source of wealth interchange between the Highlands and Lowlands, rose greatly. An increasing number of animals were to find their way to England, although it is possible to argue that in the sixteenth century the Scottish economy was still autonomous. It was also dynamic, benefiting both from population growth and from other market opportunities. Notably, the expansion of coal production in central Scotland helped provide finance and fuel for other industries, such as salt panning. Entrepreneurs benefited from the introduction of important innovations.

Sir George Bruce (*c*. 1550–1625) was granted, in 1575, the lease of collieries in Culross, Fife, formerly owned by the Cistercian abbey. He overcame problems with drainage and ventilation, thanks partly to the 'Egyptian Wheel', which was turned by horses and operated thirty-six buckets on a chain to drain the mine; as a result, the depth at which coal could be worked increased from 30 to 240 feet. The new technology enabled Bruce to develop coal production in the area, and workings were extended under the Firth of Forth. Some of his wealth was spent in building a house later known as Culross Palace. He also built a jetty so that the coal could be more rapidly shipped.

Regional variations in prices in the British Isles became less pronounced than in the medieval period, but remained very significant in the eighteenth century. Economic developments meanwhile reflected both a rising population, although that faltered for much of the seventeenth century, and market opportunities. The latter were both regional and national. Thus, the enclosure of land in County Durham during the seventeenth century, so that it could be more easily cultivated and adapted to new agricultural methods, was a response to the rise in population associated with the development of lead and coal mining. Similarly, lead mining developed considerably in Derbyshire.

HENRY VIII (1509–47) AND THE REFORMATION

The extent to which a growing national economy was being created in England and Wales, feeding in particular the demand of the prosperous south-east of England, matched the greater political control being exercised by that region, both within England and in the British Isles. This control owed much to the political dimensions of the Reformation crisis. By force of personality, political skills, repression and the lack of a viable alternative, Henry VIII greatly strengthened the state; enough for it to survive the problems subsequently posed by the accession of a minor (Edward VI), two single women (Mary, Elizabeth I) and a new, foreign dynasty, the Stuarts from Scotland. He sought both to gain and to exercise authority.

There was little sign at the accession of the young Henry that his reign would be so dominated by religious issues. The Lollard heresy had had scant lasting impact, and, although criticism of the wealth and privileges of the Church had long been widespread, there were also many signs of popular piety, including much church building and the active veneration of local saints. Churches helped to ensure a detailed pattern of belonging. They served as the centres of identity for particular neighbourhoods and were fundamental to the organisation of social and cultural activity and in poor relief. The sense of local identity, ringing out with church bells and maintained by frequent processions, linked the generations, with churches the venues for baptisms, weddings and burials. The memory represented by a sense of family coherence focused upon churches, and the importance of this role helps explain the disruption caused by the Protestant Reformation.

Henry VII had gained his throne by battle in 1485, but had little personal interest in warfare. Henry VIII, in contrast, succeeded peaceably in 1509, but saw himself as a warrior king. In his early years, he devoted most of his energy to the highly competitive international relations of the period, a form of conspicuous display and dynastic pride rather than national interest. Henry campaigned in person against the French in 1513 and 1523, winning the battle of the Spurs in 1513. His leading minister, Thomas Wolsey, the clever and greedy son of an Ipswich butcher, rose simultaneously through Church and state thanks to Henry's favour, becoming Archbishop of York (1514), a Cardinal (1515) and Lord Chancellor (1515–29). Wolsey provided the funds for Henry's expensive foreign policy. Warfare, however, with its new costs of numerous cannon, new-style fortifications and warships, created serious financial problems. In 1525, the attempt to levy an 'amicable grant' to pay for Henry's foreign policy, led to riots and the abandonment of the tax.

Henry's position was challenged more by dynastic concerns than by popular hostility. His failure to have a legitimate son posed a serious problem for the continuity of the dynasty. Henry's first wife, Catherine of Aragon, had borne five children, but only a daughter, Mary, survived. In England, unlike France, rule by a woman was legal, but there was concern about how successful it might be. Henry was trying to end his marriage before he fell in love with Anne Boleyn who he determined to marry rather than have as a mistress. The Papacy, however, was unwilling to comply with Henry's demand for the annulment of his marriage because Catherine's nephew was Emperor Charles V, the most powerful ruler in Italy. Henry's mounting anger led first to the fall of Wolsey in 1529 and subsequently to the rejection of papal jurisdiction over the English Church.

The preamble to the Act in Restraint of Appeals [to Rome] of 1533 declared: 'this realm of England is an empire, and so hath been accepted in the world, governed by one supreme head and king having the dignity and royal estate of the imperial crown of the same'. This was the first claim of imperial status for the realm, rather than the Crown. By being declared an empire, England was proclaimed as jurisdictionally self-sufficient. Similarly, James V of Scotland (r. 1513–42) was interested in associating his power with the symbol of the closed imperial crown; although he did not advance Parliament to the extent seen in England in the 1530s.

The sovereignty of law made in Parliament was established by Henry VIII. In 1534, the term 'majesty' appeared for the first time in statutes and proclamations, and, by the Act of Supremacy of that year, Henry became the 'Supreme Head' of the English Church. His propagandists used the example of the Old Testament kings of Israel as their model. This supremacy reinforced Tudor government by its stress on obedience, and focused the impact of government on changing those aspects of Church organisation and practice deemed hostile or unacceptable, for example shrines and pilgrimages. Becket's shrine at Canterbury – a symbol of opposition to royal authority – was destroyed. Already, in 1533, an English court had granted Henry an annulment of his marriage and he had both married Anne and had a daughter, Elizabeth. The Act of Succession of 1534 placed the children of his current marriage first in the succession by bastardising Mary. However, Anne's failure to produce a son endangered her position, and she succumbed to factional hostility motivated by concern about her allies and policies. Anne was tried and executed on the possibly trumped-up charge of adultery in 1536, and her marriage declared void, thus bastardising Elizabeth. Henry then married the innocuous Jane Seymour. She produced a son, Edward, in 1537, but died soon after.

These shifts in direction interacted with a religious situation made volatile by the beginnings of the Protestant Reformation with Martin Luther's challenge to the Papacy in Germany in 1517. Initially there had been few signs that England would respond. William Tyndale's translation of the New Testament from Greek into English, which was influenced by that of Luther, was printed in Germany in 1525–6 and smuggled thence into England; but Henry was doctrinally conservative. In 1521 he wrote a book, *Assertio Septem Sacramentorum*, against Luther, earning the title 'Defender of the Faith' from Pope Leo X. Similarly, James IV of Scotland made annual pilgrimages to Whithorn, Tain and other Scottish shrines, while James V made frequent journeys to Our Lady of Loretto near Musselburgh.

There were few Protestants in England until Henry VIII's break with Rome encouraged them and weakened traditional authority. The question of what would have happened had Henry not broken with Rome is necessarily speculative. Protestant opinion was rising, but was still very much that of a minority with limited political influence, although the success of populist legislation against clerical pluralism in 1529–30 indicated the acceptability of attacks on the pretensions of the Church. In Scotland, there was significant Lutheran influence in the east-coast ports in the 1520s and subsequently. This may be the reason why the region was later to lean more to Episcopacy than to Calvinist Presbyterianism.

In the 1530s, Henry's breach with the Papacy and the growing influence of Protestantism in circles close to him led him to move in the direction of Lutheranism, though he himself was no Protestant and did not wish to see an abandonment of the Catholic faith. Furthermore, as a result of the royal supremacy, all religious questions became political; and dissent a direct challenge to the Crown. The Treason Act of 1534 extended treason to words (not just deeds) and to the denial of royal supremacy. The humanist intellectual Sir Thomas More, who had vigorously persecuted Protestants, resigned as Lord Chancellor (1532) in protest at Henry's divorce, was imprisoned for refusing to swear the oaths demanded under the Act of Succession, and was executed for treason in 1535 after a rigged trial. The duty of obedience to the king and of his accountability to God was pushed hard.

In the late 1530s, English policy moved in a more Protestant direction, in part under the influence of Henry's chief minister, Thomas Cromwell. The first complete translation of the Bible to be printed in English, that by Miles Coverdale, was dedicated to Henry in 1535. Henry argued that the 'word of God' supported the idea of royal supremacy and this view encouraged the translation of the Bible. An official English Bible was produced (1537) and every parish church was instructed to purchase a copy (1538). The availability of English Bibles contributed to standardisation of the language, changed reading habits and helped lead to a greater stress on personal piety, rather than on the lives and intercession of saints. Monasticism, one of the most visible symbols and important parts of the Catholic ecclesiastical order, an institution moreover that was attacked by Protestant reformers and was a longstanding source of popular anti-clericalism, was destroyed in 1536–40: the 1536 Act dissolving the smaller monasteries and transferring their property to the Crown was followed by the dissolution of the remainder of the houses.

The dissolution of the monasteries was very unpopular. Despite individual abuses, they still played a major role in the spiritual life of the population and were important in local economics. Furthermore, for a society that disliked change and found it difficult to view with confidence, such radical steps were very alarming, and also led to exaggerated rumours, for example in Lincolnshire that Henry intended to despoil the parish churches and to tax cattle and sheep. As a result of the unpopularity of royal policies, there were major risings in Lincolnshire and Yorkshire in 1536, as well as the Walsingham conspiracy in Norfolk in 1537. These risings, however, were weakened by the unwillingness of most who rose to overthrow the king. In Lincolnshire, the 'rebels' of 1536 clearly saw themselves as demonstrators: they administered an oath of loyalty, declared their loyalty to Henry, and argued that he was being misled by evil ministers, particularly Thomas Cromwell. Unpersuaded, Henry sent troops under the Duke of Suffolk to suppress the movement. In Yorkshire, a large rebel force of over 30,000 led by Robert Aske, who called the rising the Pilgrimage of Grace, pressed for the end of monastic dissolutions, the removal of Cromwell, and the restoration of papal authority and of Mary Tudor to the succession. Henry's promise of pardon and concessions led the rebels to disband the rising, but it was never implemented and the rebel leaders were executed in 1537. In 1541, the Wakefield Conspiracy revealed that opposition in the North was still strong, and led in response to a large armed progress to Yorkshire by Henry that was intended to reaffirm his control and the loyalty of the region.

The extensive monastic estates might have served as a permanent gain of wealth, and thus power, for the Crown, but, instead, they became centres of aristocratic and gentry influence, because they were sold to pay for Henry's military preparations against, and eventually unsuccessful wars with, France and Scotland. Much of the land went to already established families, but the Crown was able to reward key supporters and make 'new men'. For example, John Russell, who served Henry as diplomat, official, admiral and general, received many of the lands of the abbey of Tavistock in Devon from Henry, and Woburn Abbey in Bedfordshire from his successor, and was created Earl of Bedford in 1550. His successors, Dukes from 1694 to the present day, wielded political power in both Devon and Bedfordshire as a consequence of these grants. Thus, a new political geography, much of which was to last until the decline of aristocratic power in the late nineteenth century, was being established, and a vested interest, composed of many of the most powerful and talented members of the elite, was created to defend the changes. The dissolution of the monasteries both symbolised, and was an important aspect of, the process by which the Reformation led to a major shift within society towards lay control.

Aside from governmental moves, the popular appeal of Protestantism in England was growing, though support was patchy. The key areas of violent opposition to the Reformation were Yorkshire and Cornwall. It proved easier to destroy or change the institutions and public practices of medieval Catholicism – to expunge much of its artistic medium, such as stained glass and wall paintings in churches, or to prevent pilgrimages, than to create a new, and stable, national ecclesiastical order, or national enthusiasm for Protestantism. Nevertheless, the sense of a direct relationship with God seen with Protestantism inspired and channelled commitment and zeal, and the committed were to have an important role in England and Scotland. Illiteracy, which prevented reading of the translations of the Bible; a shortage of qualified Protestant preachers; and a reluctance to abandon the old religion, all limited the spread of Protestantism, although its impact at Henry's court and in London gave it a role beyond mere numbers. Thomas Cranmer, a secretly married reformer, whom Henry had used to further his divorce from Catherine, was made Archbishop of Canterbury in 1533 and actively backed Protestant measures.

In Henry's later years the king sought unsuccessfully to impose religious uniformity, and heretics, such as Anne Askew in 1546, were burnt, but there was considerable uncertainty over the direction of royal favour. Moves against Protestantism, especially the restatement of Catholic doctrines in the Act of Six Articles (1539) and the speedy rejection by Henry of his fourth wife, the unappealing Anne of Cleves (1540), were linked to the fall and execution of Cromwell in 1540. Anne was never a Protestant; her brother was a reforming Catholic, which was a major part of her attraction to Henry. Henry then married Catherine Howard, a member of the conservative Howard faction, but she was executed for adultery in 1542. His last wife was a widow, Katherine Parr, who was sympathetic to reform. At the end of his reign, Henry, although still faithful to many aspects of Catholicism, disgraced the Howards, leaving the succession to his only son, the young Edward VI. Power was left to Edward's uncle, Jane Seymour's brother, Edward, Earl of Hertford, who became

Protector and Duke of Somerset. Together, they were to take England in a Protestant direction.

Henry VIII's changes had consequences both within and outside England. Within England, they helped to lessen the autonomy of distant regions. Between 1536 and 1569, the Tudors crushed a series of rebellions. Some, particularly Kett's in Norfolk in 1549 and Wyatt's in Kent in 1554, were in the south-east, the area of strongest royal authority and greatest national wealth. Others were more distant: in the north and in Cornwall. These rebellions reflected the determination and ability of the Tudor state to enforce national policies. The Reformation led to greater concern about security and lawlessness and more acute sensitivity to the nature of government in regions remote from the centre of power in southern England. The nature of religion was such that changes, such as the dissolution of the monasteries or new prayer books, had to be introduced on a national scale, and this requirement placed a great strain on the authority of the Crown.

If the Reformation is seen, at least initially, as generally unpopular – and the thesis is a controversial one – then this has implications in terms of the strength of Tudor government. Changes in the parish churches were possible only because of the royal grip on the localities and on the elites who ran them. Though injunctions ordering liturgical change were disliked, they were normally obeyed, which suggests a fairly obedient population, and means that the local elite saw that changes were implemented. Thus, the Crown faced a challenge where the elite was recalcitrant.

ANGLO-SCOTTISH WARS

The English Crown also faced major challenges in the British Isles. In part, these reflected the continuation of earlier trends, specifically the determination of independent Scotland not to follow the English lead and the lack of English control over much of Ireland. The first of these trends led to war twice in Henry VIII's reign. Scotland looked to France as England's principal opponent and therefore the power with the greatest vested interest in Scottish independence. Scottish contingents had been very helpful to France in the war with England in the early fifteenth century. The Franco-Scottish alliance, renewed in 1512, brought Scotland and England to war in 1513 when Anglo-French hostilities broke out. James IV, irritated with his brother-in-law, Henry

VIII, for a number of reasons, including disputes over raids across the border, fulfilled his commitment to France by invading England with the largest army that had hitherto marched south, 26,000 men, including a French force intended to encourage the use of new military methods; 20,000 English troops under the Earl of Surrey blocked the Scottish advance at Flodden, where the Scottish pikemen were defeated by the more mobile English billmen. Flodden was a very significant battle for Scotland. James IV, and at least 5,000, possibly as many as 10,000, of his subjects, were killed.

His young successor, James V (r. 1513–42) was, initially, under the control of his stepfather, Archibald Douglas, 6th Earl of Angus, but, in 1515, John Stuart, 4th Duke of Albany, gained the regency and forced James's mother, Margaret, to hand the king over. Albany lost power in 1524, but in 1528, James used a hunt from Falkland Palace as a cover to escape Angus's control. Angus's castle at Tantallon was then besieged by royal forces under James, and Angus fled to England. Aristocratic opposition was crushed as James established his power with expeditions to the Borders in 1530 and to the Western Isles in 1540. The enforcement of royal power in areas where its sway had hitherto been weak was also a characteristic of Henry VIII's rule. Both were concerned to assert royal authority.

James resisted Protestantism, seeking, in the Parliament of 1541, to protect Catholicism, although he favoured a measure of reform and used papal anxieties to gain greater power over the Church. Allied to France, in 1542 James faced attack from Henry VIII, who sought to cover his rear before a projected invasion of France. A Scottish invasion of England was defeated at Solway Moss in November 1542, and James died the following month, leaving the succession to his newborn daughter, Mary, Queen of Scots. When Henry died in 1547, both England and Scotland faced a volatile situation, as each was headed by a weak and young monarch.

English pressure on Scotland increased from 1547 when the Duke of Somerset, who wanted to establish both Protestantism and English influence in Scotland, and to block the French there, invaded. At the battle of Pinkie, the Scottish army was badly battered by English cannon and archers. Somerset exploited the victory by taking a large number of positions where he established English garrisons, but this policy did not make English rule popular, proved ruinously expensive, and had to be abandoned in 1549 in the face of French intervention. Scotland was not to be conquered until 1650–2. Before then, the history of Scotland and England had become further intertwined as a consequence both of Scotland's acceptance of the Reformation, following the Reformation Parliament of 1560, and of the union of the two Crowns in 1603.

IRELAND

The acceptance of the Reformation by Scotland and Wales was crucial to their integration into a British consciousness and polity. Ireland, however, rejected the Reformation, an outcome that was central to the divergence of Ireland from the general model of British development. Henry VIII had sought to maintain his father's policy of increasing Tudor control in Ireland without major initiatives, but the Reformation altered the situation. In 1534, Thomas, Earl of Kildare, rebelled, offering the overlordship of Ireland to the Pope or the Emperor Charles V, in place of the schismatic Henry, whose forces defeated him the following year. The Reformation Parliament of 1536–7 acknowledged Henry as the 'supreme head' of the Irish Church, declared the succession to be in the heirs of Henry's marriage to Anne Boleyn, and, later, agreed to the dissolution of the monasteries. In 1541, the Irish Parliament accepted Henry as 'king of Ireland' rather than its lord. Gaelic nobles were offered English law and charters for their lands, an attempt to incorporate them peacefully into the structure of governmental control. Such a conciliatory policy was to be abandoned after Henry's death, but it already faced formidable difficulties given the precarious nature of the Crown's control over much of the island.

WALES

The Welsh accepted the Reformation with little opposition, which made changes in government easier. Henry VIII's legislation of 1536–43, the Acts of Union, assimilated all of Wales into the English governmental system. The 1536 statute gave parliamentary representation to the whole of Wales. Welsh subjects were made equal to the English under the law, although the language of the law was to be English. The Marcher lordships, which were regarded as badly administered, were converted into counties, and thus represented in Parliament. English inheritance practices, justice and county institutions were all introduced. Welsh land laws were abolished in 1543. The establishment of justices of the peace in Wales in 1536 gave the Welsh gentry an important measure of self-government.

Wales was not governed in precisely the same fashion as England as the Council in the Marches continued, while, from 1542, Wales had its own system of courts, the Great Sessions, which lasted until 1830. Yet Marcher independence had been destroyed, and a uniform system of government created for Wales. The Welsh had identified themselves by their customary law, and when it was abrogated the bards swiftly lamented the decline of 'Welshness'. Equality of status, however, was the basis for a more mutually beneficial relationship between the Welsh elite and the government. The preamble to the Act of Union of 1536 declared its aim to extirpate 'the sinister usages and customs' that caused differences between England and Wales, and it was declared that no Welshman could hold any post unless familiar with English, an objective that would have concentrated power where it already was: in the hands of gentry and clerics who could work with the English and were educated accordingly. Upwardly mobile Welshmen had for long been educated at Oxbridge or at the Inns of Court in London.

The Reformation had more of an immediate effect on the Welsh population than did the administrative changes. Although they were in serious eclipse by this time, the dissolution of monasteries and chantries had an impact on landholding, substantially to the benefit of the local gentry, and also disrupted the fabric of many communities. Education and poor relief were affected. Nevertheless, although enthusiasm for the Reformation was limited and areas of Catholicism remained, there was no equivalent to the opposition to religious change that existed in England, Ireland and Scotland. Indeed, the translation of the Bible into Welsh helped to sustain a sense of national identity. A translation of the Prayer Book and the New Testament was published in 1567 and William Morgan's readily comprehensible translation of the entire Bible appeared in 1588, although the metropolitan dominance of Britain was such that it had to be printed in London: by law only certain presses could publish Bibles anyway. Thanks to the translation, Welsh could be the official language of public worship and religious life in general, and the clergy had no need to catechise and preach in English. The Welsh language could develop from its medieval oral and manuscript characteristics into a culture of print.

MID-CENTURY CRISIS

The combined strains of the Reformation, weak monarchs, problems over the succession, aristocratic factionalism, regional particularism and foreign intervention plunged both England and Scotland into serious problems in the period *c*. 1542–68. Like the French Wars of Religion (1562–98), they indicate the precarious nature of the achievement of the 'new monarchies', although the Reformation posed new challenges, not least in imposing uniformity, resisting foreign intervention and coping with the extent to which religious dissidence sapped obedience and encouraged opposition.

ENGLAND UNDER EDWARD VI, 1547–53

During Edward's reign, England was open to the influence of continental Protestantism. Edward was strongly influenced by the Protestantism of his Seymour uncles. There was a surge of Protestant publishing and by 1553 there were about 10,000 foreigners in or near London, most of them Protestants. Moreover, a determined effort was made to educate future clerics as Protestants. Peter Martyr Vermigli and Martin Bucer were appointed regius professors of divinity at Oxford and Cambridge. Allied with Archbishop Cranmer, the Duke of Somerset introduced Protestant worship by the Book of Common Prayer (1549), which contained forms of prayer and church services for every religious event. Parliament passed a Uniformity Act decreeing that the Prayer Book alone was to be used for church services, which were to be in English.

Hostility to religious change, however, played a major role in the widespread uprisings in southern England in 1549, particularly in the south-west. There, the local gentry failed to suppress the rebellion, and professional troops from outside the region were used by the government. Slaughter in battle and in execution claimed a high proportion of the region's male population. A smaller-scale rising in Oxfordshire was also crushed.

In Norfolk, the rising centred not on religion but on opposition to landlords, particularly their enclosure of common lands and their high rents, and to oppressive local government. One of the rebels' articles, 'We pray that all bond men may be free', was an attack on the harsh nature of the social system. The rebels, under the leadership of Robert Kett, a landowner willing to act against enclosures, seized Norwich and chose governors for the hundreds into which Norfolk was divided. The refusal of an offer of pardon turned the movement into a rebellion and troops were sent to suppress it. At the battle of Dussindale (1549), John Dudley, Earl of Warwick, using professional troops including German mercenaries, cut the rebellion to pieces.

Protests and rebellions against Tudor government faced important political and military disadvantages. Peaceful protest was regarded as rebellion. Politically, ambiguity about the notion of rebellion ensured that there was an often-fatal confusion of purpose. Militarily, the untrained, amateur forces raised in the rebellions were no match for the troops the government could deploy. The rebels tended to lack cavalry, firearms and cannon; such forces could not challenge the government if it had firm leadership and the support of an important portion of the social elite. In Scotland the situation was different: the Protestant league formed by the Lords of the Congregation in the 1550s presaged a far higher degree of anti-monarchical militarisation than in England. In the 1560s Mary, Queen of Scots, a weak and discredited monarch, faced opposition from a group of powerful Protestant aristocrats and lacked the force to overcome them.

The English risings of 1549 were blamed in part on Somerset's opposition to enclosures, and led to his being overthrown as Protector by the council (1549). John Dudley, one of the leaders of the council, became its Lord President (1550–3) and Duke of Northumberland (1551), and had Somerset executed in 1552. Like Richard III, Northumberland was very able and determined, but self-serving and distrusted. This would not have mattered had he been successful and enjoyed a firm claim to government: Henry VIII had not lacked ambition, self-interest and cruelty. But, like Richard, Northumberland's faults helped to deprive him of success. He stretched the bounds of what was acceptable for a minister, trying to behave as a kingmaker in a political culture that did not want one; and, crucially, lacked both the weight given by the Crown and time to consolidate his position.

Overthrowing the hopes of those who thought that the fall of Somerset might lead to a more conservative religious settlement, Northumberland pressed on headlong towards Protestantism. Continental radical Protestant influence was especially strong in the Second Prayer Book (1552) and the statement of beliefs in the Forty-Two Articles (1553). The former expunged the remains of Catholic doctrine and practice: the bodily presence of Christ in the Eucharist was explicitly denied. The traditional trappings of Catholic religiosity – the special clothes of the clergy, the fittings of their churches, and the religious rituals of church calendar festivals – were removed.

Northumberland, however, was thwarted by Edward VI's deteriorating health, and the succession became the crucial issue. Edward excluded his half-sisters, Mary and Elizabeth, claiming that they were illegitimate, and Lady Jane Grey, grand-daughter of Henry VII through his second daughter, was declared next in line. She was married to one of Northumberland's sons, and, when Edward died, was proclaimed queen (1553). Mary, however, declared herself queen in Norfolk and began raising troops. Northumberland set out to defeat her, but, as support rallied to Mary, including London and the Privy Council, Northumberland surrendered. He and, eventually, Lady Jane were executed. If Northumberland had had the level of support Scots magnates opposed to Mary Queen of Scots were to command in the 1560s, a Protestant challenge might well have succeeded in England in 1553.

MARY, 1553–8

Mary, the daughter of Henry VIII and Catherine of Aragon, was a convinced Catholic. She swiftly restored papal authority and Catholic practice, although a papal dispensation allowed the retention of the former Church lands: their return would have alienated most of the propertied and the powerful. In 1554, moreover, in an attempt to secure the succession, Mary married her younger first cousin, Philip of Spain, a member of the leading Catholic dynasty, with the proviso that any child of the marriage would inherit England and the Netherlands, and, if Philip's son by an earlier marriage died, the entire Spanish monarchy: England would thus have been closely linked to the Continent. Mary granted Philip the title 'King Consort'.

The marriage was unpopular and led to a rising in Kent by Sir Thomas Wyatt. Designed to block the wedding, it may also have been intended to make Elizabeth queen. London, however, refused to rise and the rebellion was crushed. This outcome helped to give further impetus to the programme of re-Catholicisation. From February 1555, 284 Protestants, including Cranmer, Latimer and Ridley, as well as many poor individuals, were burnt at the stake. London, Kent and Sussex had a disproportionately high number of Protestant martyrs, being nearest to Continental Protestantism and most exposed to royal power. Protestant martyrology was to be important to the subsequent image of England as a Protestant nation, notably as its image was disseminated in *Acts and Monuments of the Church* (1563) by John Foxe, popularly known as the *Book of Martyrs*. Many other Protestants fled to the Continent from where they advanced the argument that there was a right to depose monarchs who defied God's will.

The Spanish marriage, however, brought an expensive and unsuccessful war with France from 1557 that led, in 1558, to the fall of Calais, England's last possession on the mainland of France. More seriously, Mary had no child, instead dying after long periods of dropsy, which appeared to some to be pregnancies. Philip had abandoned her for campaigning in the Low Countries, and she was more a tragic figure than a tyrant.

Mary was succeeded by her Protestant half-sister Elizabeth before re-Catholicisation had had much time to take root. Yet Protestantism had had only limited popular support when Mary came to the throne, and Mary met with little resistance to her religious legislation in Parliament. There was little opposition to the burnings. The Protestant reformers' earlier destruction of the old ways was a crucial limitation on the chances of successful re-Catholicisation, but, had Mary had a Catholic heir who had lived long enough to reach maturity, England might well have been a triumph for the Counter-Reformation. The altars and statues that had been destroyed under Edward VI were difficult to replace, but under Mary most stone altars were nevertheless reinstated, while Church literature such as Mass books was produced in large quantities. On the Continent, there were examples of persecution and repression working.

MID-CENTURY CRISIS IN SCOTLAND

The succession also created major problems in Scotland. By his second wife, Mary of Guise-Lorraine whom he married in 1538, James V left a daughter, Mary, who became Queen of Scots on his death in 1542. James's death gave the Protestants an opportunity for action, and in 1546 a group including John Knox murdered Cardinal Beaton and seized St Andrews Castle. However, the combination of war with England, French influence and troops (who recaptured St Andrews in 1547), and, from 1554, the regency of the Queen Dowager, Mary of Guise, led to opposition to Protestant activity, and the number of

Protestants was small. Mary, Queen of Scots, was sent to France in 1548, and in 1558 married Francis, the Dauphin (heir to the French throne), who became Francis II in 1559. Scotland therefore appeared firmly in the French camp.

This situation ended in 1560. The accession of Elizabeth in 1558 gave rise to hope of English support for Scottish Protestants, especially to the Lords of the Congregation – their noble supporters. Opposed to French influence, they deposed the Queen Regent and helped link Protestantism with patriotism. In 1560, English military intervention secured the expulsion of French garrisons. Francis II also died, leaving Mary a childless widow. A Parliament dominated by Protestants abolished papal authority and the Mass, and accepted a Protestant Confession of Faith.

Mary, who returned to Scotland in 1561, was less cautious than Elizabeth and did not ratify these changes, but she lacked the political ability to reverse them and to build up a strong body of support in the complex and bitter world of Scottish baronial factionalism. The Lords of the Congregation and their successors united against a Catholic monarch and the French alliance, while Mary's marital problems increased her unpopularity. Mary's second marriage, to her cousin, Lord Darnley (1565), was unsuccessful and in 1566 he played a role in the murder of her favourite, David Rizzio. Mary possibly then conspired with the brutal James, Earl of Bothwell, who murdered Darnley and married her (1567). This was an unpopular step and, in 1567, Mary was forced to surrender to the Protestant lords and to abdicate in favour of the infant James VI, her son by Darnley. The position of the Protestant Church was now consolidated.

A Catholic monarch had been overthrown by a Protestant realm. Mary escaped the following year, but was defeated at Langside and fled to England to the mercy of Elizabeth. The abdication of Mary encouraged the expression of ideas about the responsibility of Crown to people that qualified any authoritarian stress on the duties owed by subjects. This contractual theory of kingship was pushed by the leaders of the Church, not least George Buchanan who became tutor of James VI.

Nationhood was also developing in other ways. Thanks to mapping, the shape of countries was better understood, which underlined the importance of that level of identification. Although it was less extensive than in England, in the sixteenth and seventeenth centuries, the mapping of Scotland, nevertheless, greatly improved. In place of a contorted shape, there was a more accurate depiction of the coastline, although the Highlands remained poorly mapped. In the mid-sixteenth century, John Elder and Lawrence Nowell both produced maps of Scotland.

ELIZABETH I, 1558–1603

Queen for forty-four years, Elizabeth was the longest-reigning English monarch since Edward III, who had reigned from 1327 to 1377. Her longevity and personality played a major role in determining the political and religious character of Tudor England. Born in 1533, Elizabeth was the longest-living English monarch hitherto and was not to be surpassed until George II. Avoiding marriage and the perils of childbirth were clearly helpful, but her longevity was still remarkable; although in Scotland William the Lion lived from 1143 until 1214 and Robert II from 1316 until 1390. Had Elizabeth lived only as long as her half-brother, Edward VI, she would never have become queen; if she had matched her half-sister, Mary, or her grandfather, Henry VII, she would have died before James VI's mother, Mary, Queen of Scots, unless she had had Mary executed earlier than 1587.

Elizabeth's longevity, caution and political adeptness played a major role in restoring a measure of political stability after the confusion of mid-century, a restoration which was important both for the succession and for the religious settlement. There was also a return to fiscal stability, notably with a re-coinage. The fact that Elizabeth did not marry revived uncertainty over the succession. However, thanks to the execution of Mary, Queen of Scots, in 1587, there was a generally acceptable Protestant succession in the shape of her son, James VI of Scotland (born 1566), great-great-grandson of Henry VII through his elder daughter, Margaret, who had married James IV, although Elizabeth was reluctant to commit herself to James.

Elizabeth had benefited from a humanist education, an upbringing in which she had been obliged to accommodate two different regimes, and reversals of fortune; she was no fanatic. She lacked the religious zeal of her half-brother Edward and her half-sister Mary, and would have preferred a compromise religious settlement that was closer to her father's Catholicism: without pope, monks and some superstitions. But a lack of strong political support for such an option forced her to go further. Nevertheless, seeking to establish a single national Church broad enough to contain people of all views, Elizabeth introduced a Protestant settlement that was more conservative than that of Northumberland.

There were limits to her Protestantism, as she showed in her own religious practice, and in her concern for ceremonies and clerical clothes. She accepted those aspects of Protestant doctrine and practice which were consistent with order and rejected those aspects which were not. This settlement was an appropriate one for a people among whom many could recall the old religious traditions. Elizabeth compromised on 'externals' that affected popular attitudes, but was doctrinally Protestant. It was not until the 1580s that the Reformation gained general acceptance, that the old religion was dead for most people in most (not all) parts of England, and that Protestantism became identified with national survival and a rising English national consciousness in the war against Spain that began in 1585.

By then, most of the English population were conforming members of the Church. As such, they did not necessarily take much notice of the details of what the clergy taught, but most were probably God-fearing and sought to live as good Christians, not least because they hoped to enjoy eternal life as one of the saved. Moreover, the Church spanned nation, state and locality. Headed by the Crown, it provided a context of local and familial identity. Parishioners identified with their parish and their church building, with the churchyard where their ancestors were buried and they would follow, and with the community whose values and rites were celebrated by the Church.

Elizabeth was determined to keep royal control over the Church, its bishops, doctrine and liturgy, and once the Elizabethan church settlement had been introduced, she was unwilling to respond to pressure for further reformation. This was to lead to tension with the more radical Protestants. Puritanism was a tendency within the established Church calling for more radical church reform, leading to a more severe, Calvinistic theology and organisation. Similarly, James VI, who assumed power in Scotland in 1585, faced opposition from the Presbyterian General Assembly, notably in 1596. Like Elizabeth, he, instead, found the office of bishop an appropriate support in the Church, as well as an apt image of authority.

Elizabeth became the most experienced politician in her kingdom, keen on maintaining the royal prerogative, but knowing when to yield, dexterous in making concessions without appearing weak, and a skilled manipulator of courtiers who was able to get the best out of her ministers. She had favourites, but was prepared to sacrifice them for political advantage. Elizabeth did not condemn the contemporary stereotype of women as inferior to men, but instead claimed that she was an exceptional woman because chosen by God as his instrument. She was reasonably successful in coping with divisions among her advisors, but found it difficult to control her military commanders. She was intelligent and generally pragmatic, but found it hard to adjust to change.

Elizabeth's Protestant settlement aroused Catholic concern. About 500 clerics refused to accept it and a number went into exile on the Continent, where they established seminaries to train missionaries to proselytise for Catholicism in England. The most famous was Douai, founded in 1568 in the Netherlands, at that time ruled by Philip II of Spain. The same year, Mary, Queen of Scots, who was next in line in the succession, fled to England where she was imprisoned. Her presence acted as a focus for discontent.

In 1569, there was a conspiracy at Court to replace Elizabeth's leading minister, William Cecil, and to marry the Duke of Norfolk, a leading religious conservative, to Mary, Queen of Scots, and acknowledge her as heir to the throne. This conspiracy was thwarted at Court, but triggered a rising in the north by its supporters, particularly the earls of Northumberland and Westmorland, whose local positions were endangered by a lack of royal favour. The earls marked the start of the rising by occupying Durham Cathedral and celebrating Mass. Roman Catholic worship was restored in many churches. The earls, however, were unable to reach and release Mary when they marched south, and they subsequently fled when the more powerful royal army advanced. Northumberland was executed, while the titles and honours of the house of Neville, the family of the earls of Westmorland, were extinguished. Over 200 rank-and-file supporters were hanged in retribution in County Durham, a policy advocated by Elizabeth, while their homes were plundered. The wealthier rebels were better treated, and, as one commentator noted, 'the common people say the poor are both [de]spoiled and executed, and the gentlemen and rich escape'.

The Northern Rising was followed by the papal excommunication of Elizabeth and a proclamation of deposition of Elizabeth from the throne in 1570. There were then a number of conspiracies on behalf of Mary, particularly the Ridolfi (1572), Throckmorton (1582), and Babington (1586) plots. Elizabeth was reluctant to try Mary, a fellow sovereign and a relative, but in 1586 the interception of Mary's correspondence indicated that she had agreed to Elizabeth's assassination in the Babington plot. As a result, Mary was convicted of treason, a questionable charge since she owed Elizabeth no allegiance, and beheaded at Fotheringay

Castle (1587). Elizabeth was unwilling to confirm James's position in the succession, but she granted him an annual pension (payment).

By then England was involved in a major war. Elizabeth's support for the largely Protestant Dutch rebellion against her former half-brother-in-law, Philip II of Spain, particularly the dispatch of troops, under her favourite, Robert, Earl of Leicester, after the Treaty of Nonsuch with the rebels (1585), and her apparent connivance in raids on Spanish colonies and trade, led to war from 1585.

THE SPANISH ARMADA

The limited English commitment of troops made little difference to the conflict in the Netherlands, but it led Philip to decide on a major attack on England. Philip, however, failed to coordinate adequately two different plans: that of an amphibious invasion of England from Spain (the king of which was also King of Portugal from 1580 until 1640), and that for a crossing of the narrow Straits of Dover by the Spanish army in the Netherlands under Alessandro Farnese, Duke of Parma. The Spaniards were also delayed by the immensity of the necessary preparations and by Sir Francis Drake's successful spoiling raid on the main Spanish naval base of Cadiz in April 1587. The following year, the Armada, a massive force of 130 ships and 19,000 troops, left Lisbon, instructed to proceed up the Channel and then cover Farnese's crossing. Storm-damage led to refitting in Corunna and in July the slow-moving fleet appeared off the entrance to the Channel. As they headed for Calais, the Spanish warships, maintaining a rigid formation, were harried by long-distance English bombardment, but it did little damage and, during nine days of engagements, the Spaniards retained their formation. The English, however, had an advantage, not only in superior sailing qualities, but also because their guns were mounted on compact, four-wheeled truck carriages, and therefore could be readily reloaded, while the Spaniards lacked such equipment.

When the Spanish fleet anchored off Calais, it was discovered that Parma lacked the shipping necessary to embark his forces. The Spanish formation was disrupted by a night-time English attack with fireships and the English fleet then inflicted considerable damage in a battle off Gravelines. A strong wind blew the Armada into the North Sea and it returned to Spain via the north of Scotland and the west coast of Ireland, suffering heavy losses from storms and shipwrecks.

This storm was widely interpreted as God's providential support for England and Elizabeth.

The loss of so many trained and experienced men was a serious blow, but the fleet was rebuilt and the English themselves found it difficult to win a lasting victory. In 1589, Drake mounted a successful attack on Corunna, destroying Spanish warships, but thereafter the expedition was a failure. Drake was a poor naval strategist, Lisbon could not be taken and the attempt to intercept the Spanish treasure fleet from the New World off the Azores was unsuccessful. The English were driven back by storms, suffering much damage in the process. The Armada and the 'Counter-Armada' both illustrated the limitations of naval power in this period, not least vulnerability to storms, the difficulties of combined operations, and the major supply problems posed by large fleets.

THE PROBLEMS OF ELIZABETH'S LAST YEARS

The defeat of the Armada encouraged a sense of English national destiny that was reflected in the political language and the drama of the period. The winds that had helped were attributed to Providence. Subsequently, alongside the thwarting of the Gunpowder Plot in 1605 and the Glorious Revolution of 1688, this success created the patina of a divinely protected state.

The expense of the long war, however, created difficulties. Royal fiscal policies, particularly the sale of monopolies to manufacture or sell certain goods, and also additional taxes, led to bitter criticism in the Parliaments of 1597 and 1601; and also failed to provide sufficient resources to bring success in war. Monopolists sold permissions to produce and to trade, and therefore the monopolies acted as another form of taxation.

Puritanism led to disputes in Parliament, especially in 1587 when Puritan MPs tried to legislate for a Presbyterian church settlement, an unsuccessful move that caused an angry dispute between Elizabeth, who opposed changes in religious matters, and some MPs. Elizabeth found it difficult to create a stable government after the ministers who had served her for so long – William Cecil (Lord Burghley), Leicester and Walsingham – died.

There was a sense of crisis in society, with a shortage of food leading to rapid price rises, to widespread malnutrition, and to weakened resistance to disease. Death rates rose in the 1590s, and notably in 1597.

There was also a political dimension to social unrest, especially to opposition to the enclosure of common land by landlords. Rumours of rebellion spread and there were preparations for one in Oxfordshire in 1597. The traditional recourse, of action against vagrants and the allocation of stored grain, was matched by attempts to improve the situation, notably by building up stores, passing poor laws, and reviving legislation against enclosures. There was nothing uniquely harsh about the social politics of London, but the scale of the city was such that it represented a particularly bleak scenario, which in part was captured in Thomas Dekker's pamphlet *The Seven Deadly Sins of London* (1606), a recasting of the sins to take note of the energy of contemporary London.

The struggle with Philip II escalated in the 1590s, with Elizabeth sending troops to support the anti-Spanish side in the French Wars of Religion between 1589 and 1597. Expeditions to Brittany and Normandy were poorly executed, but were of some use in helping Henry IV consolidate his grip on the French throne as Elizabeth wished. Philip, in turn, conspired in the British Isles, with Catholic aristocrats in Scotland, and in Ireland.

THE SUBJUGATION OF IRELAND

The attempt under Henry VIII to assimilate Gaelic Ireland was replaced under his successors by a policy of the 'plantation' of districts bordering the area under English control with English ('New English') settlers. The plantations increased the security of the Crown's position, but the expropriation of Gaelic landowners was naturally unpopular. Begun under Edward VI, the policy expanded under Mary. From the late 1560s, English rule became increasingly military in character and intention, leading to fresh attempts to extend and enforce control. Regional councils were established for Connacht (1569) and Munster (1571) and, in the face of rebellions, the English resorted to the routine use of force. Authority was extended into outlying areas such as Sligo, Fermanagh and Monaghan.

This policy was not a conducive environment for the expansion of Protestantism, and, as Catholic energies were revived by the Counter-Reformation, religious differences became a more important feature of the Irish situation, symbolising, reflecting and strengthening a political rift and the hatred felt between what were increasingly seen as conquerors and a subject population. The 'New English' enjoyed office and the benefits of government support; while the Catholic 'Old English' felt alienated and excluded from office, and the Gaels (natives of non-English descent) harshly treated by a corrupt and brutal rule. Elizabeth failed to devote the necessary attention to Irish affairs and allowed a more unaccommodating policy to be pursued there than she would have accepted in England. Moreover, the Protestant Church did not minister successfully to the population as it proved difficult to find qualified Protestant clergy willing to serve the impoverished Church. One official reported in 1607 that the clergy of the archbishopric of Cashel were 'fitter to keep hogs than serve in the church'.

Gaelic resistance led to the Desmond rebellion of the 1580s and culminated in 1594 in a major rising ably led by Hugh O'Neill, Earl of Tyrone. O'Neill raised an army of 10,000 men, substantial by the standards of Ireland, extended the rebellion from the north into Munster and also sought Catholic 'Old English' support. From mid-century, firearms had been introduced into Ireland on a substantial scale and O'Neill's men were as well armed as the English. Many had served in the highly professional Spanish army, and O'Neill trained his entire force in the use of pikes and firearms. The wooded and boggy terrain of Ulster was well suited to guerrilla conflict and ambushes, and at Clontibret in 1595 O'Neill successfully ambushed an English army. Three years later, at Yellow Ford, another English force was badly battered when attacked on the march.

In 1599, Elizabeth's arrogant favourite, Robert, Earl of Essex, failed to defeat O'Neill. This led to his disgrace and loss of royal favour. Heavily in debt as a result of the loss of his monopolies, Essex tried to stage a coup in January 1601 in order to seize Elizabeth and destroy his rival, the chief minister, Burghley's son, Sir Robert Cecil. Essex sought more power for the nobility and remarked, 'to serve as a servant and a slave I know not'. Cecil outwitted the rash plan, the coup failed and Essex was beheaded. Not for the last time, Irish developments had had a crucial impact on mainland politics.

In 1600, the English sent a more effective leader to Ireland, the new Lord Deputy, Charles, Lord Mountjoy. He decided to campaign in the winter in order to disrupt O'Neill's logistical system; and also sought to immobilise the migrant herds of cattle which fed the Irish army on campaign. Enjoying numerical superiority, Mountjoy brought a new savagery to the conflict. English fears of foreign intervention were realised in September 1601 when Philip III of Spain sent 3,500 troops to Kinsale to support O'Neill. Mountjoy responded by blockading

Kinsale, but his force was rapidly weakened by sickness. O'Neill's relieving force, instead of blockading Mountjoy, decided to attack him. However, the night march on Mountjoy's camp was mishandled, and on the morning of 24 December O'Neill lost the tactical initiative, allowing Mountjoy to move first. The English cavalry drove their Irish counterparts from the field, and the Irish infantry retreated, those who stood being defeated. The Irish lost 1,200 men, but, more seriously, the pattern of victory was broken. No more Spanish troops were sent and O'Neill was to surrender in 1603.

For the first time, the English controlled the entire island. Thereafter, Ireland was to be contested as a unit, and it was to be assumed that the loss of part would lead, if unchallenged, to that of the whole. As with the Romans and England, foreign conquest had brought a new decree of unity. More immediately, the English victory was followed by the resumption and major extension of the policy of plantation. O'Neill and O'Donnell were restored to their lands when they submitted in 1603, but the imposition of English law and custom in Ulster led them to flee to Italy in 1607 with many of their supporters. James I (James VI of Scotland) then confiscated their lands: 3,800,000 acres of Ulster were seized. Some of the less fertile portion was granted to the native Irish, but the rest was allocated to English and Scottish settlers, Crown officials, the established (Protestant) Church, and, in return for financial support for the plantation, the City of London. At the same time large portions of Antrim and Down in Ulster were granted as private plantations, and also settled largely by Scots. By 1618 there were about 40,000 Scots in Ulster. Other plantations were established further south in, for example, Wexford, Leitrim, Westmeath and Longford; these, however, had fewer Protestant settlers. Across much of Ireland the native Irish landowners had been dispossessed in favour of Protestants, and in Ulster the native population as a whole saw their position deteriorate as large numbers of Protestants were settled. Discontent over land, religion and political status was to explode in the rising of 1641.

TRANS-OCEANIC EXPANSION

English power did not only increase in Ireland, though, having lost the vast bulk of their French possessions, the English did not immediately shift to trans-oceanic enterprise. They lacked both the 'stepping stones' provided to the Portuguese and Spaniards by the Azores, Madeira and the Canaries (as earlier the Vikings had had the Faeroes, Iceland and Greenland), and the tradition of expansion at the expense of the heathen that the Portuguese and Spaniards had acquired from their long wars against the Muslims. Nevertheless, the English soon took part in expansion, first across the Atlantic and then to southern Asia. Fishing expeditions from Bristol may have reached North America in the 1480s or 1490s, but the first precise information relates to the Italian John Cabot, who sailed west from Bristol in 1497 hoping to reach the wealth of the East Indies and, instead, probably reached Newfoundland. This route was soon followed by numerous English fishermen, while other explorers probed icy seas searching for a north-west passage to the East Indies. Martin Frobisher, John Davis and Henry Hudson entered major bodies of water – Baffin Bay and Hudson Bay – but in the 1610s William Baffin, Luke Foxe and Thomas James established that these led to further shores, not open ocean.

A north-east passage was also attractive. Sir Hugh Willoughby died on the coast of Lapland while searching for such a passage in 1553, but Richard Chancellor reached the White Sea and then travelled to Moscow, opening up a tenuous trade route that was explored further by Anthony Jenkinson in 1558–62 when he travelled thence to Central Asia and to Persia.

A sea route to South Asia seemed a better prospect and in 1600 an East India Company was founded to trade there. It was to be the basis of Britain's Asian empire. The company was a chartered monopoly trading body that spread the considerable risks of long-distance trade among a number of investors and thus drew on the wealthy mercantile resources of London. Trade with South Asia challenged the control of much of India's trade with Europe enjoyed by Portugal, then ruled by Spain. English schemes had clashed earlier, as with unsuccessful attempts to break into Portugal's trade with West Africa in the 1550s and the attempt to take a share in the profitable slave trade between Africa and the Spanish New World in the 1560s. As tension rose in the 1570s, privateering attacks on Spanish New World trade and settlements became more common. Francis Drake launched attacks in 1566–8 and 1570–3, and in 1577–80 became the first Englishman to circumnavigate the world, an expedition in which he sailed up the Californian coast and claimed it as 'Nova Albion' for Elizabeth.

The English also sought to establish a colony on the eastern coast of New America, called Virginia in honour of the unmarried Elizabeth. In 1585, 108 colonists were landed on Roanoke Island in what is now North Carolina, but they found it difficult to feed themselves and were taken off the following year. Another attempt was made in 1588, but when a relief ship arrived in 1590 it found the village deserted: disease, starvation or Native Americans may have wiped out the colonists. It was not until 1607 that a permanent colony was to be established in Virginia.

EARLY-MODERN WOMEN

The death of Elizabeth in 1603 is an appropriate place to review the position of women in the early-modern period. At the most elevated social level, this position was clearly in large part a matter of personality and politics, though the context was one of a male-centred, if not misogynist, culture. Thus, Elizabeth's Court preachers emphasised traditional stereotypes of feminine weakness, and presented the queen as a woman rescued by God, rather than as a warrior queen. God was given masculine attributes, unsurprisingly so, as all clergy were men. Elizabeth herself was no passive recipient of such nostrums, no more than her great-grandmother, Margaret Beaufort, who, having become pregnant by her second husband at the age of 12, intrigued strongly for the succession of her son, Henry VII, and then, in 1485, took the unusual step of having herself declared by Parliament a *femme sole* (independent woman), able to hold property and act like a widow, even though her fourth husband, the Earl of Derby, would live for another twenty years.

Yet cultural pressures were hostile to such independence and were represented in the legal system. Much was traditional, for example the different standards applied to male and female pre-marital and extra-marital sex. Elizabeth, indeed, had to cope with slanderous and politically compromising rumours about her preferences for men. The status and wealth of women continued to be derived from their husbands and fathers and thus defined by them. Margaret Tyler, the translator of *The Mirrour of Knighthood* (1578), criticised the traditional practice of arranged marriages to no effect. Dramatists frequently focused on the theme of love versus parental control in the choice of partners, as in Middleton and Dekker's *The Roaring Girl* (1610). In Francis Beaumont's play *The Knight of the Burning Pestle* (1607), Jasper, an apprentice, marries Luce, the daughter of his master, a merchant, against the latter's will, as he favours another suitor, only for Luce to be seized by her parents and locked up. Feigning death, Jasper is taken into the house in a coffin where he frightens the merchant by appearing as a ghost, and thus gains his consent. In Philip Massinger's play *A New Way to Pay Old Debts* (*c.* 1622), the greed of the villain Sir Giles Overreach is focused on the calculation of social advantage through family marriages, and failure thus leads to his becoming mad.

Wives were not normally allowed to make wills, because in law they could not own property separately from their husbands. Wealthy spinsters and widows, however, could be of considerable importance, as was indicated by educational and religious bequests, for example to several Oxbridge colleges. There is quite a lot of evidence that the position of women in Scotland was more independent, not least in leading to legal action against husbands for assault.

There were also changes in the position of women. Among the elite, alterations in inheritance practices led to daughters and widows receiving less, to the benefit of more distant male relatives. The Reformation offered new opportunities to female spirituality, and women were able both to claim and to exercise a right to conscience and self-determination in religious matters. These opportunities, however, did not fully transcend gender limitations. The attitudes of Protestant sects reflected traditional social ideals and practices, and few women rose to positions of authority within them. Convents, which had provided women with a world with some autonomy, were dissolved. Nuns were probably the group that lost most from the Reformation.

The Reformation did lead to a more sympathetic attitude towards marriage and sexual love within marriage, one that was reflected and strengthened by the fact that clergy now could be married. Yet concern about the disruptive nature of sexual desire focused on single and adulterous women. There was an important shift from regarding moral misdemeanours as matters for the Church courts, to bringing them under secular authority, so that prostitutes and women of ill-repute were increasingly dealt with by the justices of the peace, a process that preceded, but was furthered by, the Reformation and that matched the concern with social control expressed by moves against vagrancy. The sexual standards of the day, however, reflected female as well as male views, suggesting that women to some degree supported the maintenance of patriarchy.

After the Reformation, there were no major changes until the Civil War, which threatened to loosen Church controls over family behaviour. A new civil wedding ceremony was introduced in 1653, but traditional religious rites and social assumptions tended to prevail, and, after the Restoration in 1660, there was a re-imposition of earlier norms. Margaret Fell's defence of the right of women to preach in churches, made in 1666, was singularly inappropriate in its timing. Four years earlier, a Dutch visitor to London had witnessed the treatment of a woman convicted of murdering her husband, a crime treated with great severity and scant consideration of provocation:

> we saw a young woman, who had stabbed her husband to death . . . being burned alive . . . She was put with her feet into a sawn-through tar barrel . . . A clergyman spoke to her for a long time and reproved her, and said the prayer. Then faggots [sticks] were piled up against her body . . . and finally set alight with a torch . . . and soon it was ablaze all round.

Women punished as witches by a male-dominated legal system also suffered terribly. However, women were not simply the victims of witchcraft accusations; they were also actively involved in bringing prosecutions and acting as witnesses and searchers for marks supposedly revealing witches. Furthermore, there were also male witches. In general, women were more active in the legal process and thus had more control over their lives than patriarchal nostrums might suggest.

Similarly, women played a greater role in inheritance than was legally essential: 55 per cent of the wills from the Archdeaconry of Sudbury in 1636–8 named the wife as sole executrix (administrator of the will). Many husbands showed confidence in their wives in the phrasing of a will, and the interest in the well-being of widows indicates the degree of matrimonial love. Nevertheless, whatever their personal circumstances and legal position, hard work was the fate of most women, commonly alongside their husbands.

5
. . . .
1603–88

In 1603, for the first time, one individual came to power throughout the British Isles: James VI of Scotland and James I of England, Wales and Ireland. However, the male line of his family, the Stuarts, were expelled from Britain twice within the century, first in the British civil wars of the 1640s and early 1650s, generally known, inaccurately, as the English Civil War; and, secondly, in the civil war that began with the Glorious Revolution of 1688 and ended when the Stuart cause in Ireland capitulated in 1691. In retrospect, the period is usually so dominated by the (English) Civil War of 1642–6, its causes, course and consequences, that it is difficult to appreciate that both the war and its results were far from inevitable. The war was certainly a major struggle: more than half the total number of battles fought on English soil involving more than 5,000 combatants were fought in 1642–51. Furthermore, out of an English male population of about 1.5 million, over 80,000 died in combat and about another 100,000 of other causes linked to the war, principally disease. Possibly one in four English males served in the conflict.

Hostilities and casualties in the related struggles in Ireland and Scotland in 1638–51 were even heavier. In Scotland, where many prisoners were killed on the battlefield, about 6 per cent of the population died; and in Ireland an even higher percentage, greater than that in the potato famine of the 1840s. The civil war was more brutal in Scotland and Ireland than in England.

Bitter civil conflict was hardly without precedent, and more men may have fought at Towton (1461) during the Wars of the Roses than in any of the battles of the Civil War, but the sustained level of hostilities, the British scale of the conflict, and the degree of popular involvement and politicisation, were unprecedented. Attitudes were vicious.

During the Parliamentarian siege of Colchester in 1648, Royalist troops deliberately chewed and sanded their bullets to cause gangrenous wounds, while eight Royalist prisoners were mutilated. There was much looting, including a scarlet petticoat from Shakespeare's granddaughter. Trade was disrupted and charitable provision collapsed. In addition, the war came after a long period in which most of England, especially the more prosperous south, had been peaceful. Town walls had fallen into disrepair, castles into disuse.

The crisis of the mid-seventeenth century had a profound influence in shaping values, fears and ideologies in the century-and-a-half after the restoration of monarchy throughout the British Isles, in 1660. There was urgency and fear after the Restoration, fear that the world might again be turned upside down. What was crucial then was the need to recreate the habits of thought and patterns of the past, to destroy the work of the Civil War, and to exorcise its divisive legacy.

Though crucial in its consequences, the Civil War, like the French and Russian revolutions, was not inevitable either in its causes or its course. There had been serious political disputes during the reign of James I and the early years of Charles I, but they had been handled peacefully. Only marginal individuals resorted to violence. A small group of Catholics put gunpowder in the cellars under Parliament, planning to blow it up when James I opened the session on 5 November 1605. They hoped that the destruction of the royal family and the Protestant elite would ignite rebellion and lead to a Catholic England. The attempt to warn a Catholic peer, William, 4th Baron Monteagle, to be absent, led, however, to exposure of the plot and the brutal punishment of the conspirators. Guy Fawkes was tortured to force him to reveal the names of his co-conspirators in the Gunpowder Plot of 1605, and then executed. Twenty-three years later, George, Duke of Buckingham, Charles I's favourite and leading advisor, was assassinated; his assassin, John Felton, was executed. Such events, though, were far from typical.

JAMES VI AND I

James VI of Scotland (r. 1567–1625) and I of England (r. 1603–25) was faced in England by factionalism at court, tension over religious issues, the unpopularity of the pro-Spanish tendency of his policies, and bitter criticism of his heavy expenditure and consequent fiscal expedients. James's use and choice of favourites were questioned. A clever man, who lacked majesty and the ability to inspire or command support, but, nevertheless, had exalted views of his royal position and rights, James encountered problems similar to those of Elizabeth in her later years. However, the Treaty of London with Spain (1604), his subsequent care to avoid war until persuaded into one with Spain in 1624, and the absence of conflict in Scotland and Ireland, increased his political freedom of manoeuvre. James proved pragmatic and able to back away from poor decisions. He came to England determined to end some of Elizabeth's more elaborate monarchical values, but, within a year or two, he was restoring them. Royal 'touching', to cure scrofula, the King's Evil, a skin disease, was a quasi-magical sign of royal majesty. Having abolished it in 1603, James reinstituted the practice in 1605. The previous year, James established the panel that in 1611 produced the King James or Authorised Version, a translation of the Bible that was to prove very important to the development of the English language.

With the exception of the brief Addled Parliament of 1614, which neither voted money nor legislated, James ruled without Parliament between 1610 and 1621. The Addled Parliament could not have encouraged him to seek parliamentary approval. The two houses quarrelled, while the Commons were prickly about their privileges and independence, fearing that some politicians had been undertaking to manage them for the king, and reluctant to vote supply until grievances had been settled. In response to demands in 1621 that Parliament should be able to debate any subject, James tore the Protestation from the Commons Journal and dissolved Parliament. The 1624 Parliament, however, provided the basis for war with Spain, successfully linking the redress of grievances to the grant of supply and helping to channel popular and political enthusiasm for the conflict to effect. James saw himself as a European ruler, marrying his daughter Elizabeth to Frederick, Elector Palatine, the leading Calvinist ruler in Germany, and his son to a French princess.

The political system continued to display serious strains in Charles I's early years. His favour for Buckingham was unpopular, while the steps taken to finance unsuccessful wars with Spain (1624–30) and France (1627–9) led to public discontent and parliamentary protests, especially the 1626 parliamentary complaints about unauthorised levies on trade, and the Petition of Right (1628) which protested that imprisonment at royal will and taxes without parliamentary consent were illegal. The misuse of legal procedures in order to extend the Crown's lands was an example of an abuse that pressed hard on the elite. Of the two Houses of Parliament, the larger Commons was harder to influence through patronage and was particularly resistant to royal control.

The tensions of the period led to a major revival of ringing bells for the anniversary of the accession of Elizabeth I, recalling times past when the monarch had been clearly identified with the successful pursuit of what were generally seen as national interests. Yet there was nothing yet to match the crisis of 1638–42 in the British Isles, and no parallel to the serious problems that affected France and the Austrian Habsburgs in the 1610s and early 1620s. James I, and Charles I in his early years, did not have to campaign against their own subjects, as Louis XIII and Ferdinand II had to do. Not only did James succeed to the English throne peacefully in 1603, but the union of the Crowns was reasonably successful during his reign. However, despite James's hopes for a 'union of love', or at least a measure of administrative and economic union between England and Scotland, the union remained essentially personal. There was fear in England about the legal and constitutional implications, and the Westminster Parliament rejected a parliamentary or legal bond.

Meanwhile, the situation in Scotland changed. James went south to claim his new crown in 1603 and stayed there, except for one visit in 1618. He was less exposed than his predecessors to the impact of quarrels between Scottish barons and to their defiance of royal authority. Scotland was governed by the Scottish Privy Council and the absentee kingship proved relatively successful. The Presbyterians were persuaded to accept a modified episcopal system. James's succession to the English throne was followed by a firm campaign of repression against the border reivers or moss-troopers who dominated the border lands. Many were killed and one of the most persistently troublesome clans, the Grahams, was forcibly transplanted to Ireland in 1606. Moreover, the Highlands were brought under greater control from Edinburgh, although the situation remained troubled. There were particular problems on the borders of Highland estates, to which land-less men were driven. In the 1630s, Sir William Forbes of Craigievar in Aberdeenshire and his kinsmen at Corse suffered greatly from a band of Highland raiders led by Gilderoy. Finally, in 1636, twelve of the band, including the leader, were captured and hanged, and their heads displayed as a warning. England was less disturbed.

James's reign also saw the establishment of English colonies in North America. The Virginia Company, chartered in 1606, established a colony in the Chesapeake region in 1607; while, in 1620, the *Mayflower* made a landfall at Cape Cod, beginning what was to become Massachusetts. Whereas Virginia's settlers were largely conventional in religious terms, Massachusetts was a centre of Puritanism. Virginia and New England had a combined English population of 26,000 by 1640. Further north, Henry Hudson entered what became known as Hudson Bay in 1610. The English also colonised Bermuda (1613), and, in the West Indies, St Kitts (1624), Barbados (1627) and Nevis (1628). Trans-Atlantic trade and fishing grew, bringing new activity to ports on western coasts, for example Bristol and those in north Devon.

CHARLES I'S 'PERSONAL RULE', 1629–40

The situation in England eased in the early 1630s. Buckingham's death in 1628, Charles I's decision in 1629 to rule without Parliament, and the coming of peace with France (1629) and Spain (1630), all contributed to a reduction of tension. Neutrality, while most of Europe was involved in the Thirty Years War (1618–48), helped to bring a measure of prosperity. There was tension, however, over Charles's novel financial demands as the king sought to deal with his serious financial problems. The extension of ship money to support the navy to inland areas in 1635 was particularly unpopular, though most did not follow John Hampden in refusing to pay.

The toleration of Catholics at court, where the French Catholic queen, Henrietta Maria, was a prominent supporter, was more serious, as was the Arminian tendency within the Church of England associated with William Laud, whom Charles made Archbishop of Canterbury (1633). Laud sealed off the Church of England from Puritanism and Calvinism, but Arminianism, especially its stress on the sacraments and its favour for church services that emphasised the clerics not the congregation, was seen as crypto-Catholic by its critics. For example, the moving and railing in of communion tables was regarded as a reversal of Protestant practice. Laud's authoritarianism was also a major issue, as he sought to enforce uniformity on a Church that for decades had been diverse in many respects. Laud was unwilling to permit Puritan clerics to get round his regulations by complying with them only occasionally.

Charles lacked commonsense, was untrustworthy and could be harsh towards critics. He believed in order, sought to maintain the dignity of kingship, and was a keen supporter of Laud's religious policies. Charles supported needlessly provocative measures, such as the Laudian

Instructions of 1630 which forbade the appointment of clergy as chaplains by nobles unless strictly in accordance with a law of 1530. In practice, the instruction was unenforceable and provoked Puritan nobles. Charles was also authoritarian, intolerant and no compromiser. Prerogative courts under royal control, especially Star Chamber and High Commission, could give out savage penalties. Charles's attitude and policies contributed greatly to a polarisation of positions.

Nevertheless, despite differences over constitutional questions, such as the relationship between the monarch and the law, few in England wished to overthrow Charles. There was considerable public attachment to the role of Parliament and to the principle of parliamentary taxation, but the system of government was generally believed to be divinely instituted, and it was felt that, if Charles was a bad ruler, God would punish him in the next world, not man in this. Although religion was seen by some as providing justification for resistance, rebellion and civil war were regarded by most as akin to plagues in the body of the nation, and looked far from predictable in the mid-1630s.

THE CAUSES AND COURSE OF CIVIL WAR

The outbreak of civil war in England was the immediate result of political crisis in 1641–2 stemming from risings in Scotland (1638) and Ireland (1641). The crisis that engulfed Charles I was bound up with the fact that the Stuarts ruled over a multiple kingdom, whereas the Hanoverian kings, in 1715–16, 1745–6 and 1798, overcame crises that stemmed from the same cause. In Wales, there was criticism of the policies of Charles I in the 1620s and 1630s, and in particular of the activities of the Council of the Marches, but it was far less serious than that elsewhere. In Scotland, the absentee Charles's support for a stronger episcopacy and a new liturgy, and his tactless and autocratic handling of Scottish interests and patronage, not least on his visit to Scotland in 1633, led to a Presbyterian and national response which produced a National Covenant (1638) opposed to all ecclesiastical innovations unless they were agreed by the General Assembly. Instead of compromising, Charles stood firm. In the Bishops' Wars (1639–40) his folly of threatening violence in 1639 was followed by trying to make good that threat in 1640 without the means to sustain it. Charles made a poor choice of commanders, and inadequate finance wrecked logistics. The English army was poorly prepared and deployed, and therefore collapsed when attacked by the large and professionally officered Scottish army in 1640.

As with the last military commitment, the wars with Spain and France of the 1620s, the Bishops' Wars weakened Charles, first by undermining his finances, and then because he was unsuccessful. They also altered the relationship between Crown and Parliament in England. Charles's 'Personal Rule' had failed. Rulers of England lacked the resources to fight wars, unless they turned to Parliament. To raise funds, Charles summoned the 'Short Parliament' in April 1640, but, as it refused to vote them until grievances had been redressed, it was speedily dissolved. The Treaty of Ripon (October 1640) ending the Bishops' Wars, however, left the Scots in occupation of the north of England and in receipt of a daily payment by Charles until a final settlement could be negotiated. Charles was therefore forced to turn to Parliament again, and this 'Long Parliament', which met in November 1640, was to survive, albeit with many interruptions and changes of membership, until 1660: longer, in fact, than Charles.

Initially, Parliament was united in the redress of grievances and represented a sense of national identity and interest beside which the king's views appeared unacceptable. Parliament used the weapon of impeachment against Charles's much-feared ministers. Thomas, 1st Earl of Strafford, the autocratic Lord Deputy of Ireland, was attainted and executed (1641) for planning to bring Charles's Irish army to England, and Laud, abandoned by Charles, was imprisoned (he was executed in 1645). Restrictions on the Crown's power were even more important, and Charles's opponents thought them crucial. One, Lord Saye and Sele, subsequently wrote that it was necessary to resist Charles because he had determined 'to destroy the Parliament of England'. The opponents wanted to restore what they saw as the government of Elizabeth I: a system of clearcut Protestantism at home and abroad, and both Parliament and the aristocracy through the Privy Council playing a major role. A Triennial Act decreed that Parliament was to meet at least every three years. Other Acts forbade the dissolution of the Long Parliament without its own consent, abolished Star Chamber, High Commission and ship money, and limited the Crown's financial power.

Although these measures raised contentious points, while the obstinate Charles was hostile after the execution of Strafford, these changes were accomplished without causing the division that religious issues created at the end of 1641. Then the retention of episcopacy, traditional order and discipline in the Church proved very divisive and helped rally support for Charles. The possible abolition of episcopacy (bishops) was particularly divisive. Moreover, the need to raise forces to deal with a major Catholic rising in Ireland in 1641 led to a serious rift over how they were to be controlled. In an escalating crisis, Charles resorted to violence, invading Parliament on 4 January 1642 in order to seize his six most virulent opponents, including John Pym, but they had already fled by water to the City of London, a stronghold of hostility to the king. As both sides prepared for war, Charles left London on 10 January 1642 in order to raise forces. This departure was a crucial move as the history of civil conflict, up to and including the Jacobite rising in 1745, was to show that control of the resources and legitimating institutions of the capital was to be vital.

In 1642, many sought peace, and local neutrality pacts were negotiated, but determined minorities on both sides polarised the nation. Compromise and conciliation proved impossible, the product of the tensions and fears created by Charles I's policies and apparent intentions. Although it is dangerous to adopt a crude socio-economic or geographical determinism in explaining the divisions between the two sides, and it is clear that each had support in every region and social group, it is also true that parliamentary support was strongest in the most economically advanced regions: the south and east of England, many of the large towns, especially London and Bristol, and in industrial areas; while support for Charles in England and Wales was most pronounced in less advanced regions: the north, Wales and the west. Thus, religious and political differences were related to socio-economic situations, though not dependent on them. For example, the Derbyshire lead miners were split. Charles's supporters feared religious, social and political change, and were motivated by concepts of honour and loyalty. The sweeping parliamentary powers and reformation of the Church demanded by Parliament in the Nineteen Propositions of June 1642 seemed excessive to many moderates.

Fighting began at Manchester in July 1642, and, at Nottingham the following month, Charles, who lacked any military experience, raised his standard. He advanced on London, narrowly winning the battle of Edgehill (23 October), the first large-scale clash, but Charles failed to follow up after the battle and was checked at Turnham Green just to the west of London on 13 November 1642. An irresolute general, Charles did not press home an advantage in what were disadvantageous circumstances, and retreated to establish his capital at Oxford. His best chance to win the war had passed. In 1643 the royalists made gains in much of

England, particularly the West Country, where Bristol fell, but Charles's truce with the Irish rebels, which freed the royal forces in Ireland, was more than counteracted by the Solemn League and Covenant between the Scots and the parliamentarians. The royalist army had developed into an impressive force with good officers and sound infantry, and in 1644 an acceptable peace for Charles was not an impossible prospect. The Scots, however, entered England in January 1644, and, at Marston Moor near York on 2 July 1644, they and a parliamentary army under Sir Thomas Fairfax and Oliver Cromwell crushed the royalists under Prince Rupert and the Duke of Newcastle. The north had been lost for Charles. Now isolated royal garrisons rapidly fell.

The following year, in response to problems with the reliability of local forces, the parliamentary armies were reorganised with the creation of the New Model Army, a national army with a unified command under Fairfax, with Cromwell as commander of the cavalry. The army was more cohesive and professional and better cared for than other forces. Its initial effectiveness was in part due to it being paid with remarkable regularity for more than two years. In 1645, this force defeated the royalist field armies, with the victory at Naseby (14 June) being especially decisive. Charles had only 7,600 men to Fairfax's 14,000. Prince Rupert swept the parliamentary cavalry on the left from the field, but then attacked the baggage train, while Cromwell on the parliamentarian right defeated the royalist cavalry opposite and then turned on the royalist infantry in the centre, which succumbed to the overwhelming attack. The superior discipline of the parliamentary cavalry thus played a major role in the victory. By the end of the year, the royalists were reduced to isolated strongholds, and in May 1646 Charles gave himself up to the Scots.

Parliamentary victory in England was due to a number of factors, including the backing of the wealthiest parts of the country, the support of the Scots, London, the major ports and the navy, and the religious zeal of some of its followers. Cromwell saw himself as God's chosen instrument, destined to overthrow religious and political tyranny, a potent belief. On the other hand, the parliamentarians had also suffered from lacklustre and unsuccessful commanders, such as the Earls of Essex and Manchester and Sir William Waller, the leading generals in 1642–3. Moreover, the parliamentarians initially had far less effective cavalry than the royalists. Parliamentary taxation also aroused hostility. In turn, the royalists suffered from a lack of resources, from serious internal divisions, from uncertain command, and from only limited support in the areas they controlled.

As with the collapse of royal power in 1639–40, the defeat of Charles I owed much to the Scots, and it is not surprising that they played such a major role in the politics of the late 1640s, nor that England only became really stable when the rule of the Commonwealth government in England was forcibly extended to Scotland in the early 1650s. The union of the Crowns ensured that the political fate of the two countries could not be separated. The Cromwellian conquests of Scotland and Ireland were the consequence, and they prefigured the Restoration of Stuart monarchy throughout the British Isles (in very different circumstances), in 1660, in ensuring the end of any successful attempt by Scotland and Ireland to chart a different political trajectory from that of England.

THE WAR IN WALES AND SCOTLAND

The royalist cause was also defeated in Wales and Scotland. When the civil war broke out, the overwhelming majority of the Welsh were loyal to the king, while support for Parliament was strongest in Pembrokeshire, an English area. The Welsh gentry were overwhelmingly royalist and there was no large urban environment within which support for Parliament and Puritanism could develop. Wales produced large numbers of men and much money for Charles, and Welsh troops, especially infantry, played a major role, both in operations against nearby targets, particularly Gloucester, which was besieged unsuccessfully in 1643, and in more distant fields. However, the fall of nearby royalist bases in England, at Shrewsbury, Bristol and Chester, between February 1645 and February 1646, was crucial in undermining royalist confidence in Wales, and in the autumn of 1645 the royalist position in south Wales collapsed. The castles were left in royalist hands but they fell to the remorseless pressure of superior parliamentary forces, Harlech finally surrendering in March 1647.

After the Scots entered England in January 1644, Charles sent James Graham, Marquess of Montrose, to invade Scotland. He did so with a small army in April 1644, winning a series of victories from September 1644 to August 1645. In response, the Scottish army in England under General David Leslie marched north and at Philiphaugh (13 September 1645) Montrose's outnumbered army was surprised and defeated. Montrose fled back to the Highlands, his prestige shattered. The royalist troops in Scotland dispersed in 1646 when Charles I, having surrendered to the Scots in England, ordered them to lay down their arms.

CIVIL WAR IN IRELAND, 1641–9

In 1641, driven by anger at their treatment by Protestant overlords and settlers and under economic pressure, the Catholic Irish rose and slaughtered many of the Anglo-Scottish settlers. Their leader Rory O'More defeated government forces at Julianstown (29 November 1641) and then allied with many of the 'Old English' landowners of the Pale. Ulster was overrun by the rebels. Protestant churches were desecrated and bibles burned. The Scots sent an army to re-impose Protestant rule and it landed at Carrickfergus in April 1642. There was then a three-way struggle between Scots/Parliamentarians, royalists under James Butler, Earl of Ormonde, and the Catholic confederacy of Kilkenny: the Irish rebels. The last, under Owen Roe O'Neill, crushed the Scots army at Benburb in 1646. In 1647, with Charles I imprisoned, Ormonde surrendered Dublin to Michael Jones, a parliamentary colonel. His position there was challenged by the Catholic confederates under Thomas Preston, but, at Dungan Hill (8 August 1647), Jones heavily defeated Preston, capturing all his artillery. The parliamentary cause deteriorated in 1648 when the Second Civil War led Ormonde to return from Scotland. In 1649 he took Drogheda and Dundalk, and in June besieged Jones in Dublin. A sortie by Jones defeated Ormonde at Rathmines (2 August). Cromwell landed at Dublin 13 days later.

THE SECOND CIVIL WAR, 1648

As so often, victory led to disunity. After defeating Charles I, Parliament, the army and the Scots were divided. There were crucial divisions over Church government, especially the establishment of a Presbyterian system which the Scots demanded and many English parliamentarians as well as the army opposed; and divisions over negotiations with Charles I, who was handed over by the Scots when they left England in 1647. Radical social and political changes were advocated by the Levellers, who had some support in the army. The Levellers called for male suffrage as well as freedom of conscience in religion. The army, disaffected by the attitude of Parliament and the failure to pay its arrears of wages, increasingly took a political role. Charles was seized by the army in 1647, but he rejected Cromwell's proposed settlement of religious and political differences.

Cromwell, disenchanted with both the Presbyterians in Parliament and the Levellers, whose mutiny in the army he crushed, played the crucial role in ending the Second Civil War (1648). This conflict stemmed from royalist risings and a Scottish invasion on behalf of Charles, who had agreed, in the Engagement, in return for the invasion to introduce a Presbyterian system. Charles's stance illustrated his duplicity.

The risings were crushed. Cromwell advanced into south Wales and his opponents were defeated at St Fagan's. Fairfax moved into Kent and disrupted the royalists there in June. The royalists then concentrated at Colchester, resisted assaults by Fairfax and waited for news of the Scots. Having taken the surrender of Pembroke (11 July), Cromwell moved to intercept the Scots who, under the Duke of Hamilton, entered Cumberland on 8 July and pushed south. Cromwell advanced into Yorkshire and decided to attack the flank of his opponents' advance at Preston. Hamilton ignored warnings from the royalist Sir Marmaduke Langdale, and his uncoordinated forces were spread out when Cromwell pushed back Langdale's men and captured Preston on 17 August. The Scots surrendered.

The victorious army was determined to deal with Charles. Thanks to religious zeal, its leadership was not intimidated about confronting their anointed king. In order to stop Parliament from negotiating with Charles, the army purged Parliament in Pride's Purge on 6 December 1648. Those who were left, the 'Rump', appointed a court to try Charles for treason against the people. Parliament argued that Charles had given his word of honour not to fight again, and that he had broken it when he encouraged the Second Civil War. Charles refused to plead, arguing that subjects had no right to try the king and that he stood for the liberties of the people. He was found guilty and beheaded on 30 January 1649 at the centre of royal power, outside the Banqueting Hall in Whitehall.

REPUBLICAN ENGLAND

The formal trial and public execution of Charles I were markedly dissimilar to the killing of medieval kings, as they were intended as the centrepiece of the end of monarchy. England was declared a republic, The Commonwealth, and the House of Lords was abolished. Royal coats of arms and other devices were removed, and statues of Charles I were destroyed. Feudal dues had already been abolished in 1645. The

Church of England was effectively disestablished and a Presbyterian church settlement was established.

The republican regime in England was, however, faced with very different governments in Scotland and Ireland, and could not feel safe until these had been overthrown. In a tremendous display of military power, the republican forces conquered both Scotland, a success that had eluded many English monarchs, and Ireland, as well as the remaining English royalist bases in the Channel Islands, the Isles of Scilly, and the Isle of Man. Thereafter, there was not to be a lasting difference in military-political control between England, Scotland and Ireland until the British state lost most of Ireland in 1922. Short-term variations in allegiance – between England and Ireland in 1689 or England and Scotland in late 1745 – were unstable, and seen as such on both sides. Thus, irrespective of their precise constitutional relationship, England, Ireland and Scotland had become an inter-connected unit in the geography of military power.

THE CROMWELLIAN CONQUEST OF IRELAND, 1649–52

Cromwell crossed to Ireland and conquered most of the east and south in 1649, a task that was completed with the overrunning of the whole island by mid-1653. Cromwell's campaign, especially the capture of Drogheda and Wexford in 1649, has since become proverbial for cruelty, and as such plays a major role in the anglophobic Irish public myth. In fact, many Irish fought the royalists in what was an Irish civil war as much as an English invasion; massacres during conflicts in Ireland or in continental Europe were far from new, the Catholic uprising of 1641 in particular beginning with a widespread slaughter of Protestants; and at both Drogheda and Wexford there were no attacks on women or children. At Drogheda, however, where Cromwell's impressive train of siege artillery enabled him to fire 200 cannonballs in one day, the garrison of about 2,500 was slaughtered, the few who received quarter being sent to work the Barbados sugar plantations. Such harshness reflected not only anti-Cathlicism but also the memory of the 1641 atrocities.

After Wexford, Cromwell captured Ross, Carrick, Clonmel and Kilkenny, before leaving for England. His successor, his son-in-law Henry Ireton, defeated his opponents at Scarrifhollis (1650) and captured Limerick (1651). Galway fell the following year. Conquest led, as a result largely of famine, plague and emigration, to the loss of about 40 per cent of the Irish population, and was followed, especially in 1654–5, by widespread expropriation of Catholic land, as the Anglo-Irish Catholics lost power and status. Moreover, the Gaelic schools, in which bards were trained, were closed, a blow to the native cultural tradition, and the island was subjected to the Westminster Parliament.

THE CONQUEST OF SCOTLAND

Scottish quiescence was crucial to the early stages of the conquest of Ireland, but in 1650 Charles I's eldest son, Charles II, came to terms with the Scots. In response, Cromwell invaded Scotland on 22 July 1650. He could not, however, breach the Scottish fortified positions around Edinburgh and, outmanoeuvred by David Leslie, had to retreat to Dunbar. Cut off from retreat to England by a force twice as big, Cromwell launched a surprise attack that defeated the Scottish cavalry and then forced much of the infantry to surrender (3 September). Edinburgh was then captured.

The following summer, Cromwell used his command of the sea to outflank the Scots at Stirling and occupy Perth, but Charles then marched south into England, hoping to ignite a royalist rebellion. He reached Wigan on 15 August, but, short of recruits, decided to head for the Welsh borders and not march directly on London. Shrewsbury, however, resisted Charles and when he reached Worcester on 22 August he had few additional men. The parliamentarians under Cromwell, about 30,000 strong, drove on Worcester on 3 September from a number of directions. The royalists, about 12,000 strong, launched an initially successful frontal attack on Cromwell's position, but numbers told and the royalist army was overwhelmed. Hiding in an oak tree and supporters' houses *en route*, Charles II fled to France, but the royalist cause had been crushed.

By the summer of 1652 all Scotland had fallen. It could no longer serve as an alternative model to developments in England. The Scottish Parliament and executive council were abolished. In 1654, Scotland was asked to send members to the London Parliament, and measures were taken to adopt English law. Heavily garrisoned and governed by commissioners sent from England, Scotland faced many difficulties in the 1650s: the nobility were deprived of their hereditary jurisdictions, and the people were heavily taxed.

THE COMMONWEALTH

The strength, vitality and determination of the Commonwealth government was further displayed by its aggressive policy towards foreign powers. The Rump made commercial protection a key plank of its policy, and built up the navy to this end. The Navigation Acts of 1650 and 1651 excluded other powers from the trade of the English colonies and restricted most of the trade of England, Wales and Ireland to nationals. Commercial rivalry with the Dutch and suspicion of their political intentions led to the First Anglo-Dutch War (1652–4). The strength of the Commonwealth navy and the skill of its admirals, especially Robert Blake, led to success at sea, though the war was very expensive. Military strength and success helped to win the republic international recognition. Unlike Reformation England, it was clear that the republic would not have to fear foreign intervention; its principal challenges lay at home.

There were indeed serious divisions within the republican camp. Clashes over religious issues were related to disputes over the position of the army and the nature of the constitution. Having changed the latter thanks to the use of force, it was difficult to prevent further desire for change and recourse to force. Evidence of social and religious radicalism, however small-scale its support might be, was deeply disturbing to many supporters of the Commonwealth. A variety of sects, groupings and tendencies, including Muggletonians, Diggers, Quakers and Ranters, supported a variety of radical changes, including the communalisation of waste land, and abolition of the Church and of lawyers, proclaimed the superiority of personal revelation over scripture, and argued that the second coming of Christ was imminent. Seeing private property as the consequence of the Fall (the exclusion of Adam and Eve), the Diggers pressed the people's rights to common property. Their attempt to dig up commons in 1649 were dispersed by the army and angry locals.

OLIVER CROMWELL

Disputes led Cromwell, now head of the army, to close in April 1653 the purged 'Rump' Parliament which, like the army, only represented a minority of the political nation. A new, overwhelmingly military, council of state to administer the country, and a nominated 'Parliament', better known as the Barebone's Parliament after a radical member, Praise-God Barebone, were both appointed. In the sole systematic reform of the electoral system before the First Reform Act of 1832, rotten boroughs (constituencies with very few electors) were replaced by more county seats and separate representation for expanding industrial towns, such as Bradford, Leeds and Manchester. The franchise (right to vote) was extended. This Parliament was also the first to have representatives from Scotland and Ireland, although they were mostly Englishmen serving there. Most MPs were not from the traditional ruling elite, but were instead minor gentry. If anything, though, they were less representative than the usual parliamentarians, as they were not elected by any process, but chosen by the council of officers. Divorced from the bulk of the population, both elite and otherwise, by its background, attitudes and policies, the regime was, anyway, taking no steps to end this unpopularity.

Barebone's Parliament was divided between radicals, who wished, for example, to abolish tithes and the right of patrons to appoint clergy to livings, a property right and a source of gentry influence, and those who were less radical. This division led to the collapse of the Parliament in December 1653, creating a vacuum that Cromwell, as commander in chief, was obliged to fill. He did so by becoming Lord Protector. For a man born into the Huntingdonshire gentry, who had had no tenants and who had worked for a living, this was possibly the most dramatic example of upward social mobility in British history, though it was a side-effect of the most sweeping political revolution in that history. Cromwell told MPs in 1657 that he had taken on his position 'out of a desire to prevent mischief and evil, which I did see was imminent upon the nation'. That year, he initially backed the idea that he become king, although he eventually pulled back from accepting the offer of the throne. Cromwell's strong religious faith played an important role in his zealous ambition and policies and he worked hard to inculcate his sense of godliness, not least on the Welsh estates he acquired in 1648.

Until his death in 1658, Cromwell ruled, even if he did not reign, but he faced difficulties with the Parliaments that were called. Moreover, in the localities, the decision in 1655 to entrust authority to major-generals, instructed to preserve security and create a godly and efficient kingdom, was unpopular. It also made it harder to demilitarise the regime, although that military character helped to ensure stability. Cromwell's willingness to sacrifice constitutional and institutional continuity and his distrust of outward forms were not generally welcomed; nor were the religious 'reforms' of republican England, such as the introduction of civil marriage, attacks on the churching of women after childbirth, changes in baptism practices, the readmission in 1656 of the Jews (expelled by Edward I in 1290), and the toleration of a range of sects and practices that were anathema to many. Parliament had already banned the eating of mince pies and Christmas pudding on Christmas Day in 1646.

Political, social and religious conservatism were both strong and strengthened by the experience of the 1650s. The 'godly' were neither numerous nor united: some of their preachers compared England to Israel after Moses, ungrateful for the gifts of God. Repression of popular rituals deemed superstitious, popish or profane, such as Christmas and dancing round the maypole, as well as of theatre, led to antipathy. This conservatism was to ensure that the Restoration of Charles II in 1660 was generally popular. Daniel Defoe was later to claim that 6,325 maypoles were erected in the following five years. In the 1650s hostility to Puritanism fused with resentment towards the repressive, radical and illegal regime. War with Spain (1655–9) led to the capture of Jamaica, but hopes of gaining Cuba and Hispaniola proved wildly over-optimistic and the cost of the conflict caused a financial crisis.

Cromwell died in 1658 on the anniversary of his great victories of Dunbar and Worcester, but he was not an Alexander the Great cut short in his prime. When he died the unpopularity and divisions of the regime were readily apparent, and there was, in Charles II, a legitimate pretender still threatening the stability of the system. Cromwell had neither led the latter-day children of Israel to the promised land, as he had sought to do, nor created a stable government that would maintain and further his achievements. Cromwell's support for legal and educational reform was, however, forward-looking. His successor as Protector, his son Richard, was unable to command authority, but, in his last months, Oliver's leadership had also been faltering.

Parliamentary, army and financial problems crippled Richard's protectorate. Deposed in 1659 as a result of a military coup, he was followed by a restoration of the Rump Parliament and the Commonwealth, but the Parliament was dismissed by the army (October 1659), and, with anarchy apparently imminent and the army divided, the commander in Scotland, George Monck, marched south, and restored order and a moderate Parliament. Political instability, combined with the strains created by government policies, led to support for the return of monarchy which occurred in 1660. Charles II was invited to return from exile and did so in May, John Evelyn writing in his diary that 'it was the Lord's doing'. The Puritans' attempt to reform society and worship, to force their moral imperatives upon society, had failed. British society was to be more conservative as a result.

RESTORED MONARCHY

The Restoration Settlement brought Charles II (r. 1660–85) to the thrones of England, Ireland and Scotland. He was an appropriate figure to preside over the reconciliation and, still more, the stabilisation required after the 1640s and 1650s. Able and determined on his rights, Charles was nevertheless flexible and his ambition was essentially modest, the preservation of his position, rather than centring on any creation of a strong monarchy. He lacked the autocratic manner of his cousin, Louis XIV of France, who assumed personal power in 1661. If there was to be a royalist reaction, it would not be led by the king, although it was claimed that he told his trusted advisors in 1669 that he planned an autocracy. Charles's charm was also a definite asset and, if he was not trusted by all, and was seen as a tyrant and a rake by some, he was able to avoid the reputations and fates of his father, Charles I, and his brother, James II and VII.

Apart from those who had signed Charles I's death warrant, all parliamentarians and Cromwellians were pardoned. Royal powers were to be fewer than they had been in 1640, but greater than in late 1641, let alone later in the 1640s. Charles II was given a reasonable income and control over the army, but the prerogative taxation and jurisdictional institutions of the 1630s, for example ship money and Star Chamber, were not restored. There was to be no substantial landed estate under Crown control that might enable the monarch to maintain his financial independence. Proposals advanced in the 1650s for the reform of Parliament, the law and the universities, were certainly not welcome in the conservative atmosphere of the 1660s. Bradford, Leeds and Manchester lost their parliamentary seats.

The monarch might again reign by divine right, and a very different right from the providentialism claimed by Cromwell, but he was to rule thanks to Parliament: this was intended to be a parliamentary monarchy. The loss of prerogative powers and the need for parliamentary taxation ensured that Charles would also rule through Parliament, as was shown in 1661–2 when his hopes of a broadly-based established Church incorporating as many Protestants as possible, with toleration for the rest, were rejected by the 'Cavalier Parliament' (1661–79), following the failure in the Savoy Conference of 1661 to produce agreement between Anglicans and Presbyterians. The Corporation Act (1661) obliged town officials to accept an Anglicanism that clearly differentiated itself from Nonconformity, while the Test Acts (1673, 1678) excluded Catholics from office and Parliament, and Nonconformists from office. Ideological uniformity was pursued in a new repression. Thanks to the Act of Uniformity of 1662, Presbyterian clergy were ejected from their parishes, and worship with five or more people was forbidden unless according to Anglican rites; 130 ministers lost their livings in Wales, and in England the Baptist preacher John Bunyan was convicted of preaching without licence to unlawful assemblies and began writing *The Pilgrim's Progress* in prison.

Control over the world of print was also re-imposed. Under legislation of 1662, printing was strictly limited to the master printers of the Stationers' Company of London and the university printers. Only twenty of the former were permitted, and vacancies were filled by the authority of the Archbishop of Canterbury and the Bishop of London, who were troubled enough by the dissemination of heterodox opinions not to support a relaxation in the control of printing.

Fear as well as revenge conditioned the Restoration Settlement. A sense of precariousness, especially fears about republican conspiracies which indeed existed, led to treason and militia acts. Nevertheless, much of the legislation was undermined when Puritan gentry evaded it: gentry JPs often colluded in this evasion. Ejected Puritan clergy were frequently employed by Puritan gentry as private chaplains and tutors.

In Ireland, the Cromwellian land settlement was put into only mild reversal. In Scotland, Parliament, episcopacy, and aristocratic power and influence, were all restored. However, about a third of the Scottish parish ministers were unwilling to accept the new religious settlement. Presbyterian conventicles acted as centres of defiance, and government attempts to suppress them led to unsuccessful rebellions notably in 1679. John, Duke of Lauderdale, the Secretary for Scottish Affairs, maintained royal power based on military force.

Charles II was unhappy with the religious settlement and with attempts to restrict his freedom of manoeuvre. These attempts became more serious as a result of his apparent Catholic leanings. He was the ruler on whom the fictional King Bolloximian, of *Sodom: or, the Quintessence of Debauchery*, was modelled:

> Thus in the zenith of my lust I reign;
> I eat to survive and survive to eat again
> . . . And with my prick I'll govern all the land.

Vice and corruption at court were bad enough, to many, but an alleged Catholic as ruler was totally unacceptable. In a culture that knew little of religious toleration, such a king appeared to imperil national independence, the Church and society. Anti-popery and fear of arbitrary government were as important in the second half of the century as in the first. Yet, as later with George III, it would be unwise to exaggerate the king's unpopularity. Charles II touched a large number of people for the King's Evil (scrofula), evidence of faith in, and demand for, the curative powers of kingship.

Failure in the Second Anglo-Dutch War (1665–7), including an humiliating attack on the English fleet in the Medway (1667), was followed by the Secret Treaty of Dover with the most powerful Catholic monarch, Louis XIV (1670). Charles, in broad terms, promised to declare his conversion to Catholicism and to restore the religion to England. The two monarchs were to unite in attacking the Dutch, the leading Protestant power. This was the real Popish Plot, and suspicion about Charles's intentions helped not only to bedevil the rest of his reign, but also to ensure that his successor, his Catholic brother James II (1685–8), came to the throne in an atmosphere in which suspicion about Catholics had been both heightened and crucially linked to Louis XIV, whose moves against Protestants in France, culminating in the revocation of the Edict of Nantes (1685), were an apparent warning that Catholic rulers could not be trusted and would always be bitterly anti-Protestant.

THE POPISH PLOT

The Third Anglo-Dutch War (1672–4) was unsuccessful and it led to the fall of Charles's ministry, the Cabal. Such political storms could, however, be mastered by the adept Charles, always ready to sacrifice ministers to secure his own position, but the Popish Plot crisis of 1678 attacked Charles at his weakest points. Although he was the father of at least fourteen male bastards, the succession was a major problem for Charles. There were no legitimate children by his marriage to the Portuguese princess, Catherine of Braganza (who had brought Bombay and Tangier as her dowry in 1661), so his brother James, Duke of York, was his heir. The Popish Plot stemmed from false claims made by the adventurer Titus Oates, of the existence of a Catholic plot to assassinate Charles and replace him by James: an aspect of the process by which politics was understood and pursued through wild conspiracy stories. The murder of Sir Edmund Berry Godfrey, the magistrate who took the evidence, and the discovery of suspicious letters in the possession of James's former private secretary, Edward Coleman, inflamed suspicions and led to politics by orchestrated paranoia: a series of show-trials in which Catholics were convicted and then executed. The revelation by political rivals that Charles II's leading minister, Lord Treasurer Danby, had been negotiating with Louis XIV, fanned the flames. Danby fell from office, being sent to the Tower in 1679, and Court power collapsed.

THE EXCLUSION CRISIS

The Popish Plot became an attempt to use Parliament to exclude James from the succession and to weaken Charles's government: the Exclusion Crisis of 1679–81. Its leading advocate, Anthony, Earl of Shaftesbury, created what has been seen as the first English political party, the 'Whigs', an abusive term referring to Scottish Presbyterian rebels, originally used by their opponents, though the party should rather be seen as a faction held together by informal ties, ambition and ideology, not by party discipline and central control. The Whigs produced a mass of propaganda. The first unlicensed newspaper made clear its didactic nature in its title, 'The Weekly Pacquet of Advice from Rome . . . in the process of which, the Papists arguments are answered, their fallacies detected, their cruelties registered, their treasons and seditious principles observed'. Mistrust of the Court wrecked the possible success of an alternative to exclusion in the shape of the limitation of James's power.

Anti-Catholicism could help create a crisis that the Whigs could exploit, and royal powers were weakened, as with the Habeas Corpus Act of 1679 which made imprisonment without trial difficult. This legal principle was to be important to English political culture and to Britain's bequest to the world of liberal values.

The Whigs, however, suffered during the Exclusion Crisis from the determination of most people to avoid rebellion and a repetition of the chaos of the Civil War; the strength of Charles's position in the House of Lords and the king's right to summon and dissolve Parliament as he thought fit, both of which blocked exclusion in a legal fashion; the lack of a generally agreed alternative to James; and Charles's fixed determination. With Scotland and Ireland securely under control after the Covenanter rising of 1679 in Scotland was suppressed, Charles II did not face a crisis comparable to that of 1638–42, and he avoided foolish moves such as his father's attempt to arrest the Five Members.

In reaction to the Whigs, the 'Tories' developed as a conservative and loyalist grouping, supporters of the king and the Church of England. Whig failure to secure exclusion in 1681 led to a reaction that was eased by Charles's negotiation that year of a subsidy from Louis XIV that enabled him to do without Parliament for the rest of his reign. Whig office-holders were purged and Whig leaders fled or were compromised in the Rye House Plot (1683), an alleged conspiracy to assassinate Charles and James. This led to executions and stimulated an attack on Whig strongholds. Corporation charters, for example that of London, were remodelled in order to increase Crown influence, and Nonconformists (Protestants who were not members of the Church of England, many of whom were Whigs) were persecuted. In Scotland, the Test Act of 1681 obliged all ministers and office-holders to repudiate Covenants. James was based in Edinburgh in 1679–82 and Holyrood Palace in Edinburgh was rebuilt as a Court centre in the northern kingdom.

JAMES II AND VII, 1685–8

Thanks to the reaction against the Exclusion Crisis, James II (James VII in Scotland) was able to succeed his brother with little difficulty (1685). James was initially emollient, promising to protect the Church of England. His situation was strengthened that year by the defeat of rebellions in Scotland and England. Charles II's most charismatic bastard, James, Duke of Monmouth, had pressed a claim to be Charles's heir during the Exclusion Crisis, arguing that Charles had really married his mother, Lucy Walter. Monmouth landed at Lyme Regis in June 1685, and drew on opposition to James. That month, Katherine Hall, the wife of a London malt factor, was accused by her servant, Thomas Tothall, of saying that 'the late King [Charles II] was a black bastard and that the Duke of York, his present Majesty, was a duke of Devils'.

Monmouth won widespread support in Dorset and Somerset, and, at Sedgemoor on the night of 5/6 July, in a surprise attack on the royal army he nearly succeeded. His force, however, was routed with heavy casualties. Subsequently, Monmouth was executed and some of his supporters transported to the colonies or hanged after biased trials in the 'Bloody Assizes' of the West Country by Chief Justice George Jeffreys. A parallel rising in Scotland under the Duke of Argyle was also crushed and Argyle was executed.

Like Cromwell, victory gave James a conviction of divine approval, and the rebellion led him to increase his army, but Parliament was unhappy about this and especially with the appointment of Catholic officers. James prorogued Parliament in November 1685 and it never met again in his reign. With less constraint, he then moved towards the Catholicising of the government, which made him unpopular. The changes necessary to establish full religious and civil equality for Catholics entailed a destruction of the privileges of the Church of England, a policy of appointing Catholics, the insistent use of prerogative action, and preparations for a packed Parliament, all of which led to anger and suspicion. Furthermore, James took steps to develop the army into a professional institution answerable only to the king. And yet there was no revolution in the British Isles. Unlike in 1638–42, the Stuart monarchy was now strong enough to survive domestic challenges, and there was no breakdown of order in Scotland and Ireland.

The birth of a Prince of Wales on 10 June 1688 was a major shock to those unhappy with James's policies. 'It could not have been more public if he had been born in Charing Cross', noted the future Bishop Atterbury, but unhappy critics spread the rumour that a baby had been smuggled into the Queen's bed in a warming pan. Hitherto, James had had no surviving children from his fifteen-year-long second Catholic marriage, but had two daughters, Mary and Anne, living from his Protestant first marriage. Mary was married to James's nephew, William III of Orange, who was the leading Dutch political figure and a Protestant. It had been expected that they would succeed James and that therefore his changes would be temporary.

However, a male Catholic heir threatened to make James's changes permanent. Moreover, on 30 June, in an enormously popular verdict, Archbishop Sancroft of Canterbury and six bishops were acquitted on charges of sedition for refusing to read James's order that the

Declaration of Indulgence granting all Christians full equality of religious practice, a move that challenged the position of the Church of England, be read from all pulpits. Celebrations included a large number of bonfires. The importance of public opinion was emphasised by the extent to which James' supporters and opponents published tracts and books about such episodes. The acquittal was to be memorialised as part of the national tradition in the frescoes that were painted when the Houses of Parliament were rebuilt following the fire of 1834.

THE 'GLORIOUS REVOLUTION', 1688

The more volatile and threatening situation led seven politicians to invite William to intervene in order to protect Protestantism and traditional liberties. Motivated rather by a wish to keep the British Isles out of Louis XIV's camp, William of Orange had already decided to invade. In many respects his invasion was a gamble, dependent on whether Louis XIV decided to attack the Dutch, on the policies of other powers, the winds in the North Sea and Channel, and the response of the English fleet and army. After his initial invasion plan had been thwarted by storms, William landed at Torbay on 5 November 1688 with a substantial army as he expected a difficult campaign. William benefited from a collapse of will on the part of James, who had an army twice the size of William's. James had been a brave commander earlier in his life, but in 1688 he suffered from a collapse of resolve and a series of debilitating nose-bleeds, and failed to lead his army into battle. There was also a haemorrhage of support, culminating with the flight of Lieutenant-General John Churchill from James's camp at Salisbury to William's side, and that of Princess Anne from London. In turn, William refused to halt his march on London in order to allow negotiations to proceed, as the Tory leaders, who were less unfavourable to James than were the Whigs, would have preferred. James fled the capital, throwing the Great Seal of England into the Thames. Fear of the London mob and of anarchy led to the Archbishop of Canterbury and leading peers taking control of the city. Captured and returned to London, where his presence obstructed the creation of a new political and constitutional order, James was finally driven abroad by Dutch pressure.

A vacuum of power had been created within the context of a Dutch occupation that drew on significant English support. Most people did not want any breach in the hereditary succession, and William had initially claimed that he had no designs on the Crown. However, as the situation developed favourably for him, especially when James had been driven into exile, William made it clear that he sought the throne. This was achieved in 1689 by declaring it vacant and inviting William and Mary to occupy it as joint monarchs. All Catholics were debarred from the succession.

6

1689–1815

What was to become known as the Glorious Revolution was both the last successful invasion of England (and one that was largely bloodless) and a coup in which the monarch was replaced by his nephew and son-in-law, though William III's success also depended on an absence of extensive opposition in England, an absence reflecting apathy, reluctant compliance, and a measure of active enthusiasm in his favour. The change of monarch led to war with Louis XIV of France, who gave James II shelter and support; and the need for parliamentary backing for the expensive struggle with the leading power in western Europe helped to give substance to the notion of parliamentary monarchy. The financial settlement obliged William to meet Parliament every year, the Triennial Act (1694) ensured regular meetings of Parliament, and, by restricting its life-span to three years, required regular elections, thus limiting potential for the management of Parliament by corruption. William's was truly a limited monarchy.

The Glorious Revolution was to play a crucial role in the English public myth, to be seen as the triumph of the liberal and tolerant spirit, the creation of a political world fit for Englishmen, the taproot of the Whig interpretation of history. This interpretation never made much sense from the Scottish or Irish perspective nor from the perspective of the labouring class, and it has been seriously challenged. What was for long presented as an irresistible manifestation of a general aspiration by British society for progress and liberty, can now be seen, as it was by contemporaries, as a violent rupture, an ideological, political and diplomatic crisis. The cost of William's invasion was not only a civil war that brought much suffering to Scotland and Ireland, but also a foreign war. This war created considerable stresses within Britain, but was successful in restraining French ambition while it also left Britain with a new model of state finance based on a national debt guaranteed by Parliament.

From 1688, Britain diverged from a common European course, not only because of a more liberal constitutional regime in the Revolution Settlement, at least in England and Scotland, but as a result of the breach in the royal succession and the consequences of instability and civil war, certainly in Ireland and Scotland. Thus, there was a repetition, at a time when domestic political and religious order had been restored in most European states, of the divisions arising from the Protestant Reformation. From a different perspective, however, and albeit with the delays consequent upon the disruption of the Glorious Revolution, Britain thereafter took her place in the more general movement towards a reconciliation between Crown and social elite that was characteristic of Europe in the period.

James II and VII was resolved to regain his thrones, and the Glorious Revolution was thus responsible for Jacobitism, as the cause of the exiled Stuarts came to be known from the Latin for James, Jacobus. Initially, James had French backing, controlled most of Ireland and had considerable support in Scotland. This situation looked back to the last period of Stuart dispossession, the English civil wars and Interregnum, and there was no certainty that James would not be restored as his brother Charles II had been in 1660. This was a precedent that offered hope to the Jacobites. However, William III, like Cromwell before him, was to succeed in having the Stuarts and their supporters driven from Scotland and Ireland, thus forcing them to become reliant on foreign support that was offered in accordance with a diplomatic and military agenda, timetable and constraints that rarely suited the Jacobites.

James's standard was raised in Scotland in April 1689 by John Graham of Claverhouse, who was backed by the Episcopalians, the supporters of a Scottish Church controlled, like that of England, by bishops. This had been the established form of Church government under the Stuarts, but in Scotland the Glorious Revolution entailed the establishment of its Protestant rival, Presbyterianism, which also enjoyed the support of about half the population. At the battle of Killiecrankie on 27 July, Claverhouse's Highlanders routed their opponents with the cold steel and rush of a Highland charge, but their leader was killed and the cause collapsed under his mediocre successors. Most of the Highland chiefs swore allegiance to William in late 1691. The Massacre of Glencoe the following year, when Jacobite MacDonalds were killed, indicated the ultimate reliance of the new order on force.

WAR FOR IRELAND

The decisive battles were fought in Ireland, the Williamite conquest of which demonstrated the ability of a powerful and well-led military force to overcome a hostile population. Ireland was more accessible than Scotland to the major French naval base of Brest. James's supporters controlled most of Ireland in 1689, although Derry, fearing Catholic massacre, resisted a siege and was relieved by the English fleet that July. The following month, William's forces, mostly Danes and Dutch, landed and occupied Belfast and Carrickfergus. Naval power thus offered William military flexibility and prevented James from controlling all of Ireland.

Arriving in Ireland in June 1690, William marched on Dublin to find the outnumbered Jacobite and French army (21,000 men to 35,000–40,000) drawn up on the south bank of the River Boyne. Louis XIV's failure to attach the importance to Ireland that William III did was crucial in terms of the resources available to the combatants. Having beaten the Jacobites at the Boyne on 1 July, William easily took Dublin, though he failed to capture Limerick the following month. John Churchill, then Earl of Marlborough, captured Cork (September) and Kinsale (October). On 12 July 1691, Hugh Mackay turned the Jacobite flank at the last major battle, that of Aughrim, by leading his cavalry across a bog on which he had laid hurdles, and the Jacobite force broke, their infantry suffering heavy casualties in the rout. Galway fell and the Jacobite position collapsed with the capitulation of Limerick on 3 October. The war had done much damage. For example, the east town of Athlone was burnt in 1690, while the west town was badly damaged in 1691, receiving 12,000 cannon shot and 600 mortar bombs from William's artillery.

EIGHTEENTH-CENTURY IRELAND

By the Treaty of Limerick (1691), the Jacobites in Ireland surrendered, many, the 'Wild Geese', going to serve James in France. Ireland was then subjected to a Protestant ascendancy, which further entrenched the Protestant position in Ireland. The Catholics had held 59 per cent of the land in 1641 and 22 per cent in 1688. By 1703, this had fallen to 14 per cent and by 1778 to 5 per cent. Catholic officials and landowners were replaced, and parliamentary legislation against Catholics was passed. Catholics were prevented from freely acquiring or bequeathing land or property by legislation of 1704. They were also disenfranchised (lost the vote) and debarred from all political, military and legal offices, and from Parliament. Acts forbade mixed marriages, Catholic schools and the bearing of arms by Catholics. The Catholic percentage of the population did not diminish, however, because serious repression was only episodic, not consistent, while the Catholic clergy, wearing secular dress and secretly celebrating Mass, continued their work, sustained by a strong oral culture, the emotional link with a sense of national identity, by hedge-school teaching, by a certain amount of tacit government acceptance, and by support from parts of Catholic Europe.

As a result of the transfer of land ownership, absentee landlords became more common, with money thus drained from the rural economy. Jonathan Swift, no Catholic but the Church of Ireland (Protestant) Dean of St Patrick's, Dublin, the leading Irish writer of the period, bitterly denounced the situation. In his *A Proposal for the Universal Use of Irish Manufacture . . . Rejecting and Renouncing Every Thing Wearable that comes from England* (1720) Swift attacked landlords, who, he alleged, had 'reduced the miserable People to a worse Condition than the Peasants in France'. The government tried to suppress the pamphlet. Swift's *A Short View of the State of Ireland* (1728) was a bitter account of the impact of English dominance on the Irish economy. A lack of economic activity was linked to poverty, so that tenants 'live worse than English Beggars'. In *The Intelligencer* of December 1728 Swift argued that Irish impoverishment would lead to emigration to America. Swift also claimed that the condition of the poor was so bad that death was welcome.

Much of Ireland's economy remained basically pre-industrial. However, as it was drawn more fully into the market economy, its agricultural sector experienced growing diversification and commercialisation. Textile production developed markedly, while communications improved with the turnpiking of roads and development of canals. Recent scholarship has emphasised that Catholics of the period should be seen not as an amorphous mass of downtrodden victims, but as a more flexible group that interacted not only with civil disabilities but also with a growing economy. However, a combination of social stresses and agrarian discontents led to sporadic outbreaks of organised violence in certain parts of Ireland in the later eighteenth century: the Whiteboys of 1761–5 and 1769–76, the Oakboys of 1763, the Steelboys of 1769–72, and the Rightboys of 1785–8. The American War of Independence (1775–83) provided the spark for a reform movement on the part of Protestant nationalists and weakened government opposition, so that in 1782 the Dublin Parliament, then a Protestant body, secured legislative independence from the Westminster Parliament.

ENGLISH DOMINATION OF THE BRITISH ISLES

The Glorious Revolution had profound consequences for patterns of government in the British Isles, even if they were unintended. It institutionalised English domination of the British Isles, albeit domination that was helped by, and shared with, important sections of the Irish and Scottish population: Irish Anglicans and Scottish Presbyterians. The alternative had been glimpsed in 1689 when James II's Parliament in Dublin had rejected much of the authority of the Westminster Parliament. This path had, however, been blocked. Instead, Jacobitism, and the strategic threat posed by an independent Scotland and Ireland, pushed together those politicians in the three kingdoms who were opposed to it. Indeed, the Union of 1707 between England and Scotland arose essentially from English concern about the possible hazards posed by an autonomous, if not independent, Scotland, but this support was significant. It owed much to the view that Union would keep Catholicism at bay. Moreover, the consequences of the Glorious Revolution in England made Union more attractive to some: its support for religious and political freedoms offered advantages, including security for Presbyterianism and economic benefits. However, there was only limited support for the measure in Scotland. The passage of Union through the Scottish Parliament also depended in part on corruption. In addition, the Scottish Privy Council, the main instrument of absentee government for the past century, was abolished in 1708, ensuring that greater stress had to be placed on the non-institutional management of Scottish politics. The abolition encouraged the theme of the betrayal of Scotland, a theme that contributed to the extent to which a Scots-driven agenda increasingly took hold in the Jacobite movement.

In the early eighteenth century, there was some support for union with England among Irish Protestants, but it was unsuccessful. The preservation of a Parliament in Dublin enabled Ireland's Protestant politicians to retain a measure of importance and independence, but legislation in Westminster, the result of protectionist lobbying by English interests, hindered Irish exports, particularly to English and colonial markets, while the granting of Irish lands and pensions to favoured courtiers exacerbated the problem of absentee landowners and revenue-holders, with a consequent drain of money out of the country.

England clearly dominated the British Isles after 1691, but, for the politically involved groups at least, a sense of separate identity and national privileges continued to be important in Ireland and Scotland, though less so in Wales. Although the Parliament in Westminster claimed authority over Ireland, Ireland retained its Parliament until the Act of Union of 1800; while Scotland had a different national Church – 1689 bringing a Presbyterian establishment – and legal and educational systems. It continued to be governed by Scots and yet the sense of separate identity was weakened, especially at the level of the elite, by the decline of the Gaelic and Scots languages, and the growing appeal, at least among the elite, of English cultural norms and customs and the English educational system. Welsh, Irish and Scots sought to benefit from links with England. The Union brought access to a greatly expanded network of patronage. Scots came to play a major role in the expansion of empire, not least through service in the army and in the East India Company. Protestantism, war with France and the benefits of empire helped to create a British nationhood, which developed alongside the still strong senses of English, Scottish, Irish and Welsh identity.

EIGHTEENTH-CENTURY SOCIETY

The nature of British society in the period 1689–1815 has been a matter of some controversy. It is possible to stress modernity, to see a rising middle class and an age of reason, a polite and commercial people, aristocratic ease and elegance, urban bustle and balance, a land of stately homes and urban squares: Castle Howard, Blenheim, Bath, the West End of London, Dublin and the New Town of Edinburgh. The reign of Queen Anne (1702–14) saw the apogee of Tory Anglican triumphalism, with the building of many superb churches such as Nicholas Hawksmoor's masterpiece in east London. 'Georgian buildings', constructed in a new style, embellished the expanding towns of the period: buildings with large windows were built in a regular 'classical' style along and around new boulevards, squares and circles: in stone in Scotland and brick in England. Parks, theatres, assembly rooms, subscription libraries, race-courses, and other leisure facilities were opened in many towns. The first theatre in Lincolnshire, for example, was built, in Stamford, soon after 1718. Others followed in Lincoln

(c. 1731), Spalding (c. 1760), Gainsborough (1775), Boston (1777), Grantham (1777), Louth (by 1798), and Sleaford (1824). As elsewhere, most of the gates and walls of Newcastle were demolished, and the city gained assembly rooms (1776) and a theatre (1788). Such development served an increasingly urban population: it rose from about 5.25 per cent of the English population in 1500 to about 27.5 per cent in 1800, much of the growth being in London.

New construction was not restricted to England. In Carrickfergus in Ulster the wooden bridge was replaced in stone in 1740, a new market house was constructed in 1775, and a new county courthouse and gaol in 1779. Whereas earlier buildings in the town had been defensive in character, there was no sense of menace in the new urban landscape. Carrickfergus benefited from the development of the Ulster linen industry and many artisan houses were rebuilt in brick or stone with slate roofs.

Different images and views, however, can also be stressed, not least the view that society was in large part conservative, 'unenlightened', and dominated by superstitious lore, a landed elite and a providential monarchy. Serious disease played a major role in what was a hostile environment. The plague epidemic of 1665–6, which killed over 70,000 people in London and maybe close to 100,000 as a whole, was the last in England (bar a small outbreak of plague in Suffolk in 1906–19): mutations in the rat and flea population were probably more important in preventing a repetition than alterations in human habitat thanks to construction with brick, stone and tile, and a move away from earthern floors, let alone clumsy and erratic public-health measures. There were still, however, other major killers, including a whole host of illnesses and accidents that can generally be tackled successfully in modern Europe. Smallpox, typhus, typhoid, measles and influenza were serious problems: 38 per cent of the children born in Penrith in 1650–1700 died before reaching the age of six. Smallpox epidemics there were superimposed on the pre-existing cycle of mortality which was linked to movements in grain prices, leading to corresponding fluctuations in susceptibility to smallpox, thereby exacerbating the oscillations in child mortality. This, of course, is a modern analysis. Contemporaries lacked such knowledge and to them disease was a subject of anxiety and bewilderment.

The year, indeed, could be divided by the prevalence of different diseases: smallpox in spring and summer, dysentery in spring and autumn. Primitive sanitation and poor nutrition exacerbated the situation. Glasgow had no public sewers until 1790 and the situation thereafter remained totally inadequate for decades. The limited nature of the housing stock led to the sharing of beds, which was partly responsible for the high incidence of respiratory infections. In London, the stock of accommodation available to the bulk of the population declined in quality and shrank in quantity in the 1720s–50s as buildings deteriorated and there were few housing starts. Thus, the effective density of population increased, with all that that implied for potential exposure to infection. The substantial geographical variation in London's epidemiological regime was related to wealth.

Moreover, problems of food storage and cost ensured that the bulk of the British population lacked a balanced diet even when they had enough food. Poverty remained a serious problem. The Workhouse Test Act of 1723 encouraged parishes to found workhouses to provide the poor with work and accommodation, but too few were founded to deal with the problem, especially as the population rose from mid-century. Gilbert's Act of 1782 gave JPs the power to appoint guardians running Houses of Industry for the elderly and infirm. Workhouses, however, remained less important than out relief: providing assistance, and some-times work, to the poor in their own homes. Under the Speenhamland system of outdoor relief introduced in 1795, although never universally applied, both the unemployed and wage-labourers received payments reflecting the price of bread and the size of their family. Payments to families were made through the man.

The majority of children did not attend school, the distribution of schools was uneven, and the curriculum of most seriously limited. It was generally argued that education should reflect social status and reinforce the status quo, and thus that the poor should not be taught to aspire. The educational opportunities of women were particularly limited. Illiteracy was widespread, being more pronounced among women than men, and in rural than in urban areas. Belief in witchcraft, nevertheless, markedly diminished, although there were still episodes. *Lloyd's Evening Post and British Chronicle* of 2 January 1761 carried a report from Wilton in Wiltshire, not a remote 'marginal' environment:

A few days ago, one Sarah Jellicoat escaped undergoing the whole discipline usually inflicted by the unmerciful and unthinking vulgar on witches (under pretence that she had bewitched a farmer's servant maid, and a tallow-chandler's soap, which failed in the operation) only by the favourable interposition of some humane gentlemen, and the vigilance of a discreet magistrate, who stopped the proceedings before the violence thereof had gone to a great pitch, by binding over the aggressors by recognisance to appear at the next assizes, there to justify the parts they severally acted in the execution of their pretended witch law.

The Reverend Robert Kirk, Episcopalian minister in Aberfoyle, Perthshire, published in 1691 his *The Secret Commonwealth; or an Essay on the Nature and Actions of the Subterranean (and for the most part) Invisible People heretofoir going under the name of Faunes and Fairies, or the lyke, among the Low Country Scots, as they are described by those who have the second sight*. For revealing this knowledge, he was allegedly abducted by the 'little people' in 1692.

Although the occult was not absent, dread in cities took different forms. The painter William Hogarth (1697–1764) depicted the vigorous, if not seamy side of life in London, a thriving metropolis where alcohol, crime, prostitution and squalor were ever-present, and venereal disease and destitution much feared. Crime was linked to hardship: in Lincolnshire, the bad winter of 1741 led to a doubling of the theft figures. The criminal code decreed the death penalty, or transportation to virtual slave labour in British colonies, for minor crimes (although not in Scotland for nearly so many); the Game Laws laid down harsh penalties for poaching and permitted the use of spring guns by landlords. Under the Transportation Act of 1718, passed in order to deal with the rise of crime in perfunctorily-policed London, 50,000 convicts were sent to America from England and Wales by 1775 for seven or fourteen years or life; the loss of America was followed by consideration of transportation to Africa and finally, in 1788, the establishment of a convict settlement in Australia. The Scots began deporting criminals to America in 1766. Many who were transported died under the harsh conditions of their long journeys, a British counterpart to the cruel treatment of Africans sent to the New World as slaves.

A feeling of insecurity helps to explain that, in so far as there was an aristocratic and establishment cultural and political hegemony, it was in part bred from elite concern, rather than from any unchallenged sense of confidence or complacency. Aristocratic portraits and stately homes in part probably reflected a need to assert tradition and superiority and to project images of confidence against any potential challenge to the position of the elite.

There were certainly bitter political and religious disputes in the British Isles. The succession to the throne was a cause of division and instability until the crushing of James II's grandson, Charles Edward Stuart, 'Bonnie Prince Charlie', at the battle of Culloden in 1746. The disestablishment of Episcopalianism in Scotland after the Glorious Revolution, and the sense of 'the Church in danger' from Dissenters and Whigs in England and Wales, fed tension. The Toleration Act of 1689 gave Trinitarian Dissenters (but not Catholics or Unitarians) freedom of worship in licensed premises in England and Wales. Though William III (r. 1689–1702) and, to a greater extent, the first two rulers of the Hanoverian dynasty, George I (r. 1714–27) and George II (r. 1727–60), relied heavily on the Whigs, the continued existence of a popular and active Tory party was a challenge to the practice of Whig oligarchy, as was the existence of vigorous traditions of urban political activity.

Political division was echoed in culture: the politeness of much early eighteenth-century Augustan literature was co-extensive with the critical stance of writers like Alexander Pope and Jonathan Swift, much of whose work is spiked with bitterness and criticism. The impulse for order which has been seen as a dominant motif of the age should not be regarded as a simple reflection of some political and social reality. Rather, the commentators, writers and artists of the period stressed the need for order because they were profoundly aware of the threats to that order around them.

Likewise, far from being a secular age, as it is sometimes presented, the eighteenth century was one in which religious concerns still constrained and influenced the content of much cultural activity. This was a volatile and varied cultural world in which politics and religion were far from placid, and in which much that might seem today irrational was far from marginalised. By no means a cool age of reason, the century saw the religious enthusiasm that led to the foundation of Methodism, as well as almanacs, and millenarian and providential notions that were not restricted to a superstitious minority. There was a widespread interest in alchemy.

Methodism was initially a movement for revival that sought to remain within the Church of England, but, after its founder, John Wesley, died in 1791, it broke away completely, and his decision to ordain his own ministers in 1784 marked a point of division between Methodism and the Church of England. Intellectual advances were also affected by religion. Isaac Newton (1642–1727), from 1703 President of the Royal Society, a body established in 1660 to encourage scientific research, discovered calculus, universal gravitation and the laws of motion, but also searched for the date of the Second Coming and argued that comets, which he and Edmund Halley had analysed, should be seen as explaining the Deluge (Noah's Flood). Newton argued that God acted in order to keep heavenly bodies in their place. He was believed to act through the normal laws of physics; not to break them. Science was not therefore to be incompatible with the divine scheme.

More generally, there was a profound sense of disquiet about the very nature of society, coming not so much from radicals as from clergy, doctors and writers concerned about moral and ethical values. Morality, indeed, was a central cultural theme, and Hogarth's moral satires were a considerable success. The engravings of his series *A Harlot's Progress* sold over 1,000 sets and were much imitated. Similarly, the plays of Colley Cibber, George Colman, George Lillo and of Oliver Goldsmith, who had a good acquaintance with the street culture of his native Ireland, propounded a morality opposed to vice and indulgence. The etiquette of the period condemned dishevelment and slovenliness in clothing, and pressed for appropriate conversation and conduct as inherent to a polite, and thus stable, culture. Samuel Richardson's *Pamela* (1740), the first of the sentimental novels, was a very popular work on the prudence of virtue and the virtue of prudence.

Few contemporaries were as convinced as later historians that theirs was an age of stability. For them, stability in culture and politics was perhaps regarded as something which had existed in the past and was now increasingly lost, or as something which should be worked towards; it was hardly something which had been achieved in the present, or, if so, it could only be maintained through constant vigilance. Seen as a major help, education was presented in the later decades of the century in a progressive light within a Christian Enlightenment context. The prospectus of Christian communities that included the young as a means to regenerate society provided a powerful and pro-active vision of the potential of childhood.

EIGHTEENTH-CENTURY WOMEN

One measure of the position of any group in society is provided by crime and punishment. In late eighteenth-century Dublin, for example, women suffered greatly as victims of crime. Girls were raped and wives murdered and battered, without the judicial system taking much action. In comparison with the substantial number of hangings for theft, there were very few convictions for rape. Some women sought to respond by bringing prosecutions. Other women, however, were active participants in the world of crime, not in committing violence but in organising shoplifting and handling stolen goods.

Crime reflects both the basic dynamics of human interaction and more specific circumstances. The women involved in committing crimes responded to the opportunities created by the growth of wealth in society. This growth provided the general context for women's lives. There was still much poverty, not least in regions that were marginal to economic growth, and the rising population of the second half of the century placed much demand on available resources. Yet there were also more material goods and a slowly changing material fabric of life. This was most obvious in the cities, but it was not restricted to them.

The process was a long-term one that can certainly be traced back to the sixteenth century. The probate inventories of the village of Stoneleigh in Warwickshire in 1500–1800 present a picture of a community that steadily added to its material comfort and from time to time renewed its buildings. From 1600, there was a marked increase in housing. After 1600, the number of beds in large farms rose sharply: improved comfort and privacy may have led to more people having their own bed. Around 1700, goods appeared which were produced for mass distribution: Ticknall-ware for the dairy and tin dripping-pans for the hearth. There was a growth of separate rooms for different functions, such as dining rooms. Thus the domestic space in which many women lived was changing and they were increasingly gaining differentiated space for their own purposes.

Women also played an active role in the 'public spaces' of eighteenth-century society. Actresses such as Mrs Siddons were prominent on the London stage. Women played an important part in the debating societies that developed in London from the late 1770s, although less so in enlightened societies in Scotland. Less 'genteel' activities were also patronised. On 5 September 1759, *Lloyd's Evening Post and British Chronicle* reported:

> On Monday night was fought at Stoke-Newington [London], one of the most obstinate and bloody battles between four noted bruisers [boxers], two of each sex; the odds, before the battle began were two to one on the male side; but they fought with such courage and obstinacy, that at length the battle was decided in favour of the female.

The emotional position of many women was difficult. Love did not always feature in matrimony and the portrayal of marriage to a callous husband as imprisonment offered in Thomas Southerne's play *The Wives' Excuse* (1691) was not fanciful: Mrs Friendall, the perceptive and wronged protagonist, declared, 'But I am married. Only pity me.' Yet, an increasing feature of all Church courts was the predominance of actions for defamation of women, which suggests that their reputations were of growing importance. Prior to 1750 the majority of actions for divorce in the London Consistory Court were brought by women against their husbands for cruelty. In contrast, thereafter, the notion of romantic marriage and domestic harmony came to prevail among the prosperous, and the idea of divorce for incompatibility arose. It was still, however, a long and difficult process and the custody of any children was invested in the father so that separated and divorced women lost contact with them. Throughout, the treatment of the young reflected bias, as with the extent to which more boys at every level of society attended educational institutions.

THE BRITISH ISLES AS PART OF EUROPE

The Glorious Revolution is crucial to the Whig interpretation of British history, central to the notion of British uniqueness. This concept can, however, be queried by comparing Britain and the Continent in the post-1688 period in both a functional and an ideological light. Functionally, the crucial relationship in both was that of central government and ruling elite, a term that in the British Isles should be taken to include the peerage, the more substantial landed gentry, higher clerics and leading townsmen: the elite was more open to social mobility than was the case elsewhere in Europe. Members of the elite owned and controlled much of the land and were the local notables, enjoying social prestige and effective governmental control of the localities. In contrast, central government lacked the mechanisms to intervene effectively and consistently in the localities, unless with the cooperation of the local elite. Central government meant, in most countries, the monarch and a small group of advisors and officials, and the notion that they were capable of creating the basis of a modern state is misleading. In addition, in what was, in very large part, a pre-statistical age, the central government of any large area was unable to produce coherent plans for domestic policies based on the premise of change and development. Without reliable, or often any, information concerning population, revenues, economic activity or land ownership, and lacking land surveys and reliable and detailed maps, governments operated in what was, by modern standards, an information void.

Lacking the reach of modern governments, those of the early-modern period relied on other bodies and individuals to fulfil many functions that are now discharged by central government, and they reflected the interests, ideology and personnel of the social elite. Whatever the rhetoric and nature of authority, the reality of power was decentralised and consensual. Religion, education, poor relief and health were focused on the parish, which represented the interrelationship of Church and state at the local level. The parish was dominated by the laity and gentry.

Social welfare and education were largely the responsibility of ecclesiastical institutions or of lay bodies, often with religious connections, such as the Society for the Promotion of Christian Knowledge, established in 1698, which encouraged the foundation of charity schools in the early eighteenth century. Education in England had to be paid for either by the pupil's family, which was generally the case in the grammar schools, mostly sixteenth-century foundations, or by a benefactor, dead or alive; it was not supported by taxation, although in some parishes there was some free schooling. In Scotland, there was a stronger tradition of obligation: an Act of Parliament of 1496 made education compulsory for the eldest sons of 'men of substance'. An Act of the Privy Council of 1616 decreed that there should be a school in every parish. After the Reformation, schools and universities in Scotland came under the control of local authorities.

The regulation of urban commerce and manufacturing in Britain was largely left to town governments. The colonels of regiments were often responsible for recruiting their men, and for supplying them also, though the British navy was administratively, as well as militarily, impressive. Most crucially, the administration of the localities, especially the maintenance of law and order and the administration of justice, both in Britain and elsewhere in Europe, was commonly left to the local nobility and gentry, whatever the formal mechanisms and institutions of their authority. In this sense, Britain was an aristocratic society and this was not a system that could be readily circumvented. When James II had intervened and appointed Catholics as Lords Lieutenant of the counties, this had been of limited value to him as the new men lacked the stature and connections of traditional aristocratic holders of the office.

Despite the constitutional differences between the British Isles and most Continental states, the shared reality at the local level was self-government by the notables and their supporters, and, at the national level, a political system that was largely run by the elite; although this dominance was qualified, as far as politics and parliamentary rule were concerned, by strong traditions of popular independence, especially in the major towns. In the sixteenth canto of his ironic poetic epic *Don Juan* (1824), the Romantic poet Lord George Byron (1788–1824) stressed the dominance of electioneering by the elite, whatever their theoretical political differences: 'the "other interest" (meaning / The same self-interest, with a different leaning)'. As the radical Thomas Spence claimed in 1800, 'Are not our legislators all landlords?' He continued by stating, 'It is childish to expect ever to see small farms again, or ever to see anything else than the utmost screwing and grinding of the poor, till you quite overturn the present system of landed property.' Much urban and industrial property was also owned by aristocrats. For example, most of the town of Kildare belonged to the Earl of Kildare.

The key to stable government in the British Isles, as on the Continent, was to ensure that the local notables governed in accordance with the wishes of the centre, but this was largely achieved by giving them the instructions that they wanted. For the notables it was essential both that they received such instructions and that they got a fair share of governmental patronage. This system worked and its cohesion, if not harmony, was maintained, not so much by formal bureaucratic mechanism, as by the patronage and clientage networks that linked local notables to those wielding national influence and enjoying access to the monarch. The strength and vitality of the British aristocracy in the post-1688 world is readily apparent, not least because there was no sharp divide between them and the wealthy commoners, mostly landed, who, in large part, dominated and comprised the House of Commons.

At the local level, the gentry, as justices of the peace, were the dominant figures. They had been entrusted with much of the business of government in the localities from the fourteenth century, and their role continued whoever directed affairs in London. Law and order depended on the JPs and in Hanoverian Britain they were also the crucial figures in the local allocation of the land tax. Wales was particularly dominated by its gentry because, compared with England and Scotland, the peerage was sparse and relatively unimportant. The JPs played a smaller role in Scotland. The sheriff courts of Scotland, until 1747 hereditable jurisdictions, were increasingly staffed with professional lawyers. The distant Orkney and Shetland islands were ruled by the Earl of Morton, who held the lordship of Orkney and Shetland, and by the lairds (gentry) who sought to gain the property of the udallers (freeholders) and change them into tenants.

The system of aristocratic and gentry control cohered through patronage and personal connection, leaving copious documentation about such matters in the private correspondence of prominent politicians, such as Thomas Pelham, Duke of Newcastle, Secretary of State from 1724 to 1754, and First Lord of the Treasury from 1754 to 1756 and 1757 to 1762. Aside from this 'functional' similarity between Britain and the Continent, there was also an 'ideological' counterpart in the form of a shared belief in the rule of law, and of government being subject to it. The constitutional mechanisms by which this should pertain varied, but there was a common opposition to despotism.

Thus, the public myth of uniqueness that played such a major role in the Whig inheritance (by the 1770s most politicians could see themselves as Whigs), can be qualified and indeed was by domestic critics who charged, with reason, that the Whigs had abandoned their late seventeenth-century radical ideas, and who denied that the British system was different from, and better than, those across the Channel. Particular attention was focused on the way in which the 'executive' or central government had allegedly subverted the freedom of Parliament by corruption. What was in fact being witnessed was the re-creation of a measure of stable government in Britain by means of a new consensus, in which patronage and the avoidance of radical changes were dominant, smoothed by practices that lessened the chance of unpredictable developments. Therefore, despite the role of a permanent and quite effective Parliament, the ministerial Whigs could be seen as having created a stable state which, its critics claimed, bore comparison with both strong Continental monarchies and that attempted by the Stuarts. Such comparisons, voiced during the years of Whig hegemony in 1714–60, were also to be pressed home in the 1760s and early 1770s when George III (r. 1760–1820) broke with the tutelage of the 'Old Corps' Whigs, who had dominated politics under Georges I and II, and allegedly sought to create a stronger monarchy. Contemporaries searched for parallels in the crown-backed Maupeou 'revolution' in France (1771) and in Gustavus III's coup in Sweden (1772), both seen as measures designed to subordinate 'intermediate institutions' to Crown authority.

A counterpart to the role of the landed elite was provided by the stately homes of the period, which were, in part, a testimony to wealth, confidence, agricultural improvement and greater political and, to some degree, social stability after the restoration of Charles II. Such building activity revived after the Restoration, and flourished in the eighteenth century, with houses such as Sir Robert Walpole's mansion at Houghton. Sir John Vanbrugh (1664–1726), the exponent of the English Baroque, displayed at Blenheim, Castle Howard and Seaton Delaval a degree of spatial enterprise similar to that of the architects of princely palaces on the Continent. Robert Adam (1728–92), a Scot, rebuilt or redesigned many stately homes, including Culzean, Kenwood, Luton Hoo, Mellerstain House, and Syon House, his work redolent with Classical themes.

Landscape gardening, inescapably linked to wealthy landed patronage, flourished and was also influential abroad. The architect William Kent (1684–1748) developed and decorated parks (grounds of houses) in order to provide an appropriate setting for buildings. Lancelot 'Capability' Brown (1716–83) rejected the rigid formality associated with Continental models, contriving a setting that appeared natural, but nevertheless was carefully designed for effect. His landscapes of serpentine lakes, gentle hills and scattered groups of newly-planted trees represented a less insistent conquest of nature by man, and swiftly established a fashion in a world where the small number of patrons and their interest in new artistic developments permitted new fashions to spread swiftly, while their wealth enabled them to realise and develop the new fashions. Brown's ideas were developed further by Humphry Repton (1752–1818) in accordance with the concept of the 'picturesque', which stressed the individual character of each landscape and the need to retain it, while making improvements to remove what were judged blemishes and obstructions, and to open up vistas. A growth in privacy was inherent in the emergence of landscaped estates for they reflected a growing separation of the aristocracy from rural society.

There were obvious differences between society in Britain and on the Continent. These included the demographic and economic prominence of the capital, London, and the high percentage of the English labour force not engaged in agriculture. Common legal rights and penalties were more widespread in Britain than in most continental states, where the currency of privilege was more defined in the legal system. The rotation of crops and use of legumes that increasingly characterised East Anglian agriculture, and the growing use of coal, were not mirrored across most of Europe. Urban mercantile interests were more politically significant than in other large European states. And yet it would be inappropriate to focus on such differences and to suggest that therefore it is unhelpful to consider Britain in a European context. 'Progressive' features of British agriculture and industry were matched elsewhere. The agricultural techniques of East Anglia owed much to those of the province of Holland, while coal was already used for industrial processes in a number of continental regions, notably the Ruhr and the Pays de Liège. Industrial development was not restricted to Britain, but was also important in a number of continental regions, such as Bohemia and Silesia. The major variations between, and indeed within, regions in the British Isles were such that it is pertinent, as in more recent times, to note common indicators between individual British and continental regions rather than to stress the divide of the Channel. Moreover, in socio-economic terms, it is possible to stress similarity, rather than contrast, between Britain and the Continent, particularly in the first half of the century.

This approach is more problematic, however, as far as politico-constitutional aspects are concerned. The 'Glorious Revolution' led to a contemporary emphasis on uniqueness that has been of considerable importance since. The Whig tradition made much of the redefinition of parliamentary monarchy in which Parliament met every year, of triennial elections, the freedom of the press and the establishment of a funded national debt. The Revolution Settlement, the term applied to the constitutional and political changes of the period 1688–1701, was seen as clearly separating Britain from the general pattern of Continental development. Indeed, to use a modern term, it was as if history had ended, for if history was an account of the process by which the constitution was established and defended, then the Revolution Settlement could be presented as a definitive constitutional settlement, and it could be argued that the Glorious Revolution had saved Britain from the general European move towards absolutism and, to a certain extent, Catholicism. For fashionable intellectuals on the Continent, such as Voltaire, Britain offered a model of a progressive society, one that replaced the Dutch model that had been so attractive the previous century, though there was also criticism of aspects of British society. Many eighteenth- and nineteenth-century French and German historians and lawyers looked to Britain (by which they tended to mean England) as culturally and constitutionally superior, and thus as a model to be copied. With time, Britain also became more important as an economic model and a source of technological innovation.

Many foreign commentators underrated the divisions in eighteenth-century British society. Politics, religion, culture and morality, none of them really separable, were occasions and sources of strife and polemic, and the same was true not only of views of recent history, most obviously the Revolution Settlement, but also of the very question of the relationship between Britain and the Continent. Alongside the notion of uniqueness as derived from and encapsulated in that Settlement, there was also a habit, especially marked in opposition circles, of seeking parallels abroad. Thus, *Fog's Weekly Journal*, a leading Tory paper, could suggest in 1732 that the *Parlement* of Paris, an essentially judicial body, was readier to display independence than the Westminster Parliament. This habit was accentuated from 1714 by the Hanoverian connection, for, under both George I and George II, the contentiousness of that connection led to a sustained political discourse about the extent to which Britain was both being ruled in accordance with the foreign interests of her monarchs and being affected in other ways, especially cultural. Different British attitudes to the relationship with Continental Europe reflected internal political divisions, for example Tory hostility to the Dutch and to Protestant Palatine refugees.

POLITICAL IDEOLOGIES

The Glorious Revolution created major problems of adjustment, in terms of governmental activities, the situation within the British Isles, and relations with foreign powers. The frequent elections after the Triennial Act of 1694 created a new political world as did the clearer nature of ministerial accountability due to Parliament's newly-affirmed role in securing the financial system at a time of unprecedented national debt. Political parties provided a way to structure the resulting system, not least as a means to marshal parliamentary supporters, to organise election campaigns, and to energise electors.

However, party rule struck many as wrong, indeed as a form of factionalism that threatened division within the body politic; and such divisions were seen as potentially fatal, both to government as a whole and to the specific system of government established by the Glorious Revolution. The ideology and practice of policy witnessed a tension between an emphasis on party, and thus parties; and contrary principles and attempts focused both on the ideas of wider unity, patriotism and service to the Crown, and on the practice of mixed or broad-bottomed ministries. In part, this tension was one between politics and government – between organisation in political parties in order to maximise electoral opportunities and the seeking of a broad-based ministry in order to facilitate government. The king's government was a particularly important issue, as monarchy was central to assumptions about politics.

JACOBITISM

By the reign of George III (1760–1820) there was no question about who should be king; only about his powers. The situation had been very different earlier in the eighteenth century. The principal political threats to the Protestant succession and the Whig system were seen as coming from Jacobitism until mid-century, and from France. James II's exile meant that the direct line of the royal family had been subverted. With the deaths of his daughters (Mary and Anne) and the coronation of the distantly related (but Protestant) George I in 1714 a genuine crisis of conscience affected many in the British Isles, particularly in Scotland. Sympathy first for James II and VII, then his son ('James III and VIII') and grandson ('Bonnie Prince Charlie' or 'Charles III') led to serious security problems for eighteenth-century Britain. James II was succeeded in 1701 as the claimant to the throne by the 'warming-pan baby', 'James III', and, though the latter's attempt to invade Scotland with French support in 1708 was unsuccessful, his claim was a threat to the Hanoverian succession. The childless William III (r. 1689–1702) had been succeeded by his sister-in-law Anne (r. 1702–14), none of whose many children survived to adulthood. Under the Act of Succession (1701), she was to be succeeded by the German house of Hanover, descendants of James I's daughter Elizabeth. The Act of Security passed by the Scottish Parliament directly contradicted the settling of the crown on Hanover and this led to the Union and the forcing of the Act of Succession on Scotland by incorporation. The unexpectedly peaceful accession of George I in 1714 was a major disappointment for James, but the consequences were not completely unhelpful to his cause, for George's enthusiastic support of the Whigs alienated the Tories whom Anne had favoured in 1710–14 and helped to revive Jacobitism. Tories were excluded from most senior posts in government, the armed forces, the judiciary and the Church, and their role in county government was lessened.

THE '15

In 1715, the Jacobites planned three risings. 'James III' was to copy William III by landing in the south-west of England, where there was to be the major rebellion, followed by a march on London, while there were also to be risings in the Highlands and the Border counties, the latter including the north of England. The rising in the south-west was nipped in the bud in September 1715 as a result of prompt government action on the basis of intelligence, and Jacobite indecision. Nevertheless, on 6 September, John Erskine, Earl of Mar, raised the Stuart standard at Braemar, launching a serious challenge to the newly-established Hanoverian regime. Perth was seized and the royal forces under the Duke of Argyll were heavily outnumbered. Indecision on Mar's part, however, allowed the loss of valuable campaigning time. Mar should have attacked Argyll as soon as possible, so that Scotland could have been a base for assisting the risings in the borders and the north of England. Instead, he did not march on Edinburgh until November. On 13 November, Mar fought Argyll at Sheriffmuir, north of Stirling. Unaware of the dispositions of the other, each general drew up his forces so that their right wings overlapped the other's left. The left wings of both armies were defeated, but Mar failed to exploit his superior numbers. The indecisive battle was in practice a victory for Argyll, as Mar needed a triumph in order both to hold his army together and to help the Jacobites in the borders.

Rising there in October, the Jacobites had decided that Dumfries, Newcastle and Carlisle were too strong to attack, and had instead resolved to invade Lancashire, an area with many Catholics whom they hoped to raise. However, aside from being poorly led, the dependence on Catholic support weakened the appeal of the rising. There were only about 1,100 active English Jacobites in the '15. The Cumbrian militia offered no resistance, and on 9 November the Jacobites entered Preston, but it was to prove as unfortunate for them as it had been for the invading Scots in August 1648. Thomas Forster failed to defend the line of the Ribble against advancing government troops, and, instead of attacking the besiegers or trying to fight their way out, the Jacobites allowed their enemies to surround the town on the 13th and the weak Forster unconditionally surrendered on 14 November. Archbishop Wake and the bishops ordered declarations for George I to be read in all churches.

'James III' arrived at Peterhead on 22 December and at Scone, where his coronation was planned, on 8 January 1716. Yet, freed of concern about England, where the battle of Preston marked the end of the Jacobite rising, Argyll had now been provided with a far larger army, including 5,000 Dutch troops. Despite the bitterness of the winter and a Jacobite scorched-earth policy, Argyll marched on Perth on 21 January. The Jacobites were badly affected by low morale and desertion and James abandoned Perth. The army retreated to Montrose, but, rather than defending it, James and Mar sailed for France on 4 February, and their abandoned army dispersed.

George I and his Whig ministers sought to make frightening examples of the former rebels, the better to deter future uprisings. This vengeance was distinctly brutal in northern England. Most of the executions related to the fighting there, and all the prisoners transported to what George and probably many of his ministers envisaged as an early death in the colonies had surrendered at Preston. In Scotland, however, alongside exiles and a few executions after the suppression of the '15, there was a measure of *rapprochement* between the Scottish elite and the new regime. Indeed, when large-scale rebellion broke out again in 1745, the effective neutralisation of many Jacobites active in the '15 denied the movement the public support from influential members of the elite it so badly needed.

WALPOLEAN GOVERNMENT

In 1722 the Atterbury Plot, a Jacobite plan to seize London, was blocked by prompt governmental action, including the effective use of espionage and the creation of a large army camp in Hyde Park. The 1720s and 1730s were bleak years for the Stuart cause, because the leading minister, the venal but able Sir Robert Walpole, followed policies that were less aggressive and objectionable than those of his predecessors, and crucially kept Britain at peace for most of the period, thus denying the Jacobites foreign support. He was unwilling to support any further improvement in the legal position of Dissenters, a measure that threatened the position of the Church of England and its Tory supporters in the localities. Walpole was certainly corrupt and his ministry a Whig monopoly of power, but he caused offence principally to those who took a close interest in politics, rather than to the wider political nation, whose position was eased by his generally-successful determination to reduce taxation, especially on land. This policy was helped by Walpole's preservation of peace, although in 1733 the attempt to shift the burden of taxation from land to goods led to the Excise Crisis, a political storm that forced him to withdraw his financial plan. However, he survived pressure, both in Parliament and at court, and went on to win the 1734 general election.

The Walpolean system broke down in his last years. The collapse of Anglo-Spanish relations over vigorous Spanish maritime policing of what they claimed was illegal British trade with their Caribbean possessions, symbolised by the display to a committee of the House of Commons of the allegedly severed ear of a merchant captain, Robert Jenkins, led to war with Spain, the War of Jenkins' Ear (1739–48), a war that Walpole had sought to avoid. He did very badly in the general election of 1741, in part as a result of the support for the opposition, by Frederick, Prince of Wales, who had fallen out with his father, George II, and his father's ministers, rather as George himself had done in 1717–20 while Prince of Wales. Walpole sought to maintain his position, but declining majorities in the House of Commons created a crisis of confidence in the winter of 1741–2, and Walpole resigned in February 1742 after he lost his majority. He was made Earl of Orford by George II, who was very reluctant to lose his services, and opposition attempts to prosecute him for corruption were thwarted. The ministry which replaced Walpole's, in which the dynamic John, Lord Carteret, was a leading figure, sent British troops to the Continent in 1742 in order to resist French advances at the expense of Austria.

WAR WITH FRANCE

Britain had already fought France in 1689–97 (War of the League of Augsburg or Nine Years War) and 1702–13 (War of the Spanish Succession). These wars were designed both to prevent Louis XIV's domination of western Europe and to safeguard the Protestant Succession. William III had only limited success in the 1690s, as he struggled to resist the French conquest of the Spanish Netherlands (modern Belgium), but, in the second war, John, Duke of Marlborough, the husband of Queen Anne's cantankerous favourite, Sarah Churchill, won a series of crushing victories (Blenheim 1704, Ramillies 1706, Oudenaarde 1708) which drove French forces out of Germany and the Low Countries. Marlborough was dismissed by the Tory ministry of 1710–14 because they sought peace, but it was largely thanks to his victories that the government was able to negotiate good terms by the Treaty of Utrecht (1713). This accepted the British position in Newfoundland, Nova Scotia and Hudson Bay and the capture of Gibraltar (1704) and Minorca (1708). The French also recognised the Protestant Succession in Britain, while Louis XIV accepted a territorial settlement in western Europe that ended fears of French hegemony for a generation.

George I was able to negotiate an alliance (1716–31) with the regency government that followed Louis XIV, committing France to support the Hanoverian succession, and Walpole kept the peace with France. His successor's abandonment of this policy led to French support for Jacobitism. Carteret believed that Britain must resist French gains in Germany, and in 1743 the British defeated the French at Dettingen, George II being the last British king to command in battle. In 1744, the French responded with an attempted invasion of England on behalf of the Jacobites, only to be thwarted by Channel storms. Britain then formally entered the War of the Austrian Succession.

THE '45

The following year, 'James III's' eldest son, Charles Edward (Bonnie Prince Charlie), evaded British warships and landed in the Western Isles. He quickly overran most of Scotland, despite the reluctance of some Jacobite clans to rise for a prince who had brought no soldiers, and the antipathy of the many Scots who were not Jacobites. The British force in Scotland received very little local support, and fell victim to a Highland charge at Prestonpans outside Edinburgh (21 September 1745). Crossing into England on 8 November 1745, Charles Edward took Carlisle after a brief siege, and then, without any resistance, Lancaster, Preston, Manchester and Derby, which was entered on 4 December. The British armies had been outmanoeuvred and, if few English Jacobites had risen to help Charles, his opponents were affected by panic. But the lack of promised English and French support weighed most heavily with the Scots, and the Jacobite council decided on 5 December to retreat from Derby, despite Charles's wish to press on. There had been a crucial breakdown of confidence in the prince among his supporters, arising from the absence of the support he had promised. The Scots considered themselves to have been tricked into a risky situation.

Had the Jacobites pressed on, they might have won, capturing London and thus destroying the logistical and financial infrastructure of their opponents. By retreating, they made defeat almost certain, not least because, in combination with bad weather and the British navy, the retreat led the French to abandon a planned supporting invasion of southern England. Charles evaded pursuit, retreated to Scotland successfully, and, on 17 January 1746, beat a British army at

Falkirk. However, George II's inexorable second son, William, Duke of Cumberland, brought up a formidable army and, on Culloden Moor near Inverness, on 16 April 1746, his superior firepower smashed the Jacobite army. Cumberland's army included a substantial Scottish contingent. Cumberland recorded of his opponents that 'in their rage that they could not make any impression upon the battalions, they threw stones at them for at least a minute or two, before their total rout began'. He had secured the Protestant Succession established by William III.

SCOTLAND AFTER THE '45

The aftermath was harsh. The Hanoverian regime had been overthrown in Scotland and the army humiliated, and the government was determined to ensure that there was no recurrence of the '45. The Highlanders were regarded as barbarians, and Cumberland's successor, William, 2nd Earl of Albemarle, offered his solution for 'the bad inclination of the people in most of the northern counties and their stubborn, inveterate disposition of mind . . . nothing could effect it but laying the whole country waste and in ashes, and removing all the inhabitants (excepting a few) out of the kingdom'. Such a harsh policy was not in fact followed, but the 'pacification' of the Highlands was to be characterised by killings, rapes and systematic devastation, and by a determined attempt to alter the political, social and strategic structure of the Highlands. The clans were disarmed, and the clan system broken up, while roads to open up, and forts to awe, the Highlands were constructed. Hereditable jurisdictions were abolished, and the wearing of Highland clothes prohibited. Those Scottish MPs in the Westminster Parliament who did not agree with this policy had little choice but to acquiesce in its implementation since they had no national and autonomous powerbase from which to oppose it. The rebellion and its suppression, therefore, gave cause and opportunity for the sort of radical state-directed action against inherited privilege, especially regional and aristocratic privilege, that was so rare in Britain.

More long-term political changes were also important. In effect, Scotland, like many dependent parts of multiple kingdoms or federal states, was losing its capacity for important independent political initiatives. This loss affected both the Highlands and the country as a whole. Yet, it was not a case of English pressure on an unwilling people, for political changes profited, and were in part shaped by, local politicians.

Many Scots, particularly the numerous Presbyterians, were firm opponents of the Stuarts and supporters of the Protestant Succession. London relied not on Englishmen but on Scottish politicians to govern Scotland, such as Archibald, 3rd Duke of Argyll, and, at the close of the century, Henry Dundas. Moreover, clerics, burgesses and city provosts conducted a great deal of local administration. The Scottish professional classes and minor lairds who stayed at home contributed a great deal to the administration and character of their country.

The '45 revealed the vulnerability of the Hanoverian regime, and yet also led to its firm establishment. It thus closed a long period of instability, and provided the basis for a fundamental recasting of British politics in which Toryism lost its Jacobite aspect, thus facilitating the dissolution of the Whig–Tory divide over the following 17 years. Attempts to conciliate opponents and comprehend them within ministerial ranks, and expectations concerning the future behaviour of the heir to the throne, first Frederick, Prince of Wales, who died in 1751, and then the future George III, along with the behaviour of the latter after he came to the throne in 1760, compromised the cohesion and identity of the Tories, and brought some of them into government. In addition, the relationship between England and Scotland became essentially one of the willing co-option of the powerful Scots through patronage, with no alternative Jacobite or nationalist focus of loyalty and with a diminishing emphasis on coercion.

This process was helped by the great economic expansion of central Scotland, particularly the area round Glasgow, that began in the third quarter of the eighteenth century. Urbanisation in Scotland was more concentrated than in England. The urban population there grew by 132 per cent in 1750–1800 and Aberdeen, Edinburgh and Glasgow were the setting for a major explosion of intellectual life known as the Scottish Enlightenment. Many new ideas about government, society and science were advanced. The most famous individual work was Adam Smith's masterpiece of free-market economic analysis, *The Wealth of Nations* (1776). Similarly, James Hutton's *Theory of the Earth* (1785) was the foundation of modern geology. The New Town proposals of Sir Gilbert Elliott and Lord Provost Drummond sought to make Edinburgh a fitting metropolis for the chief city of North Britain.

Scotland after the Union of 1707 and the suppression of Jacobitism retained a distinctive structure of local government, a contrasting legal system and a different established Church, but the Scots came to play a major role in the expansion of empire, a policy actively pressed by

Dundas, who rose to be Home Secretary, Secretary of State for War, President of the Board of Control for India, First Lord of the Admiralty and Viscount Melville. The political elites of England and Scotland turned together against the domestic radicalism inspired by the French Revolution, leading from 1793 to a repression that suppressed demands for a more democratic political system. The avoidance of revolution in Scotland was not, however, only due to repression. Radical sentiment was limited, while paternalism, in the form of a more responsive poor law and subsidised grain prices, helped to lessen discontent. The Scottish Enlightenment had been politically conservative and aristocratic dominance of society was still strong, helped by the extent to which Scotland remained an overwhelmingly agrarian society.

THE GROWTH OF THE EMPIRE

Britain was not the only European maritime and trans-oceanic imperial power, although her naval strength and colonial possessions had grown considerably since the mid-seventeenth century. Her control of the eastern seaboard of North America north of Florida had been expanded and consolidated with the gain of New York from the Dutch (1664), the French recognition of Nova Scotia, Newfoundland and Hudson Bay as British (1713), and the foundation of colonies including Maryland (1634), Pennsylvania (1681), Carolina (1663) and Georgia (1732). Possibly 200,000 people emigrated from the British Isles to North America during the seventeenth century, far outnumbering the French settlers in Canada and Louisiana, and the settlements founded included Charleston (1672), Philadelphia (1682), Baltimore (1729) and Savannah (1733). The English also made a major impact in their West Indian islands where they developed a sugar economy based on slave labour brought from West Africa; British coastal bases there included Accra (1672). The East India Company, chartered in 1600, was the basis of British commercial activity, and later political power, in the Indian Ocean. Bombay was gained in 1661, Calcutta in 1698. Scottish hopes of colonisation, which led to the unsuccessful Darien scheme, an attempt in 1698–1703 to establish a colony in Central America, played a role in the background to Union between England and Scotland. There were to be more opportunities once the latter had been negotiated.

Trade outside Europe became increasingly important to the British economy, and played a major role in the growth of such ports as

Bristol, Glasgow, Liverpool and Whitehaven. Trade with the North American colonies rose greatly from the mid-seventeenth century. The mercantile marine grew from 280,000 tonnes in 1695 to 609,000 in 1760, the greater number of experienced sailors providing a pool from which the Royal Navy could be manned, in part through the agency of the dreaded press gangs. This navy was to be crucial in the struggle with France that was a central theme from 1689 to 1815.

THE SEVEN YEARS WAR, 1756–63

The unification of Britain was important in her longstanding conflict with France. The decisive struggle was the Seven Years War (1756–63). It ended with the Thirteen Colonies on the eastern seaboard of North America, and the British possessions in India, secure, with French Canada, Spanish Florida, and many Caribbean islands acquired, and with Britain as the leading maritime power in the world, thus fulfilling what Thomas Arne and James Thomson had seen as the national destiny in the ode 'Rule Britannia' (1740): 'Rule Britannia, rule the waves: / Britons never will be slaves'. This was the achievement of the ministry of William Pitt the Elder and Thomas, Duke of Newcastle (1757–61), and of a number of able military leaders, including Wolfe, Clive, Hawke and Boscawen. Robert Clive's victory at Plassey, over the vastly more numerous forces of the Indian Nawab of Bengal, Surajah Dowla, in 1757, laid the basis for the virtual control of Bengal, Bihar and Orissa by the East India Company from 1765. The French were subjugated in India in 1760–1, and Britain emerged as the most powerful European state in the Indian subcontinent.

The French attempt to invade Britain on behalf of the Jacobites was crushed by the British naval victories of Lagos and Quiberon Bay in 1759. That year, British troops also beat the French at Minden in Germany, while, after a hazardous ascent of the cliffs near Quebec, that city was captured, General James Wolfe dying at the moment of glorious victory on the Plains of Abraham. The bells of victory rang out across Britain: the ringers at York Minster were paid four times between 21 August and 22 October for celebrating triumphs, beginning with Minden and ending with Quebec. The victories were also a tribute to the national unity that had followed the defeat of Jacobitism: Scots played a major role in the conflict. In 1762, British forces campaigned round the globe. They helped the Portuguese to resist successfully a Spanish invasion, fought the French in Germany, and captured Martinique from the French, and Havana and Manila, the major towns in Cuba and the Philippines, from the Spaniards. This was an extraordinary testimony to the global reach of British power, particularly the Royal Navy, and to the strength of the British state.

ECONOMIC DEVELOPMENT

Britain was to have to defend the maritime and colonial position it gained in the mid-eighteenth century from serious challenges in the period 1775–1815: rebellion in America and Ireland, and war with Revolutionary and Napoleonic France. The society that did so was changing both socially and economically. Many of the social features that were to be associated with economic transformation were already common. Far from the British Isles being a rural Elysium, the rural world had already in the fifteenth and sixteenth centuries witnessed massive disruptions of land and labour. Neither enclosure, sweeping changes in land use, rural proletarianisation nor the social and economic changes wrought by industrialisation, technological change and the rise and decline of specific areas and economic activities, were new. They were, however, both to increase in scale and pace from the late eighteenth century, and never to cease to do so thereafter. This process of continual change, more than anything else, marked the birth of modern times.

After a century of limited growth, if not stagnation, population growth rates shot up, leading to a rise in the population of England and Wales from, in millions, 5.18 (1695), 5.51 (1711), 5.59 (1731), 6.20 (1751), and 6.97 (1771) to 8.21 (1791), with the growth rate being highest in 1781–91 at 0.83 per cent per annum. The Scottish population rose from 1.26 million in 1757 to 1.6 million in 1801. As the labour force expanded, Britain had to import grain to feed the growing numbers and real wages were put under pressure, although they remained roughly stationary until the 1790s. The rising population was sustained and high growth rates continued. This achievement owed more to an increase in fertility from the 1780s to the 1820s than to a decline in the death rate. Moreover, rural fertility triumphed over urban mortality, for the towns were particularly dangerous as incubators and spreaders of disease, and their population increased only as a result of migration from rural areas. In London, however, infant mortality fell with different methods of infant care and feeding.

Agricultural improvement, the construction of canals and better roads, and the development of industry and trade led to a growth in national wealth and a different economy. Thus, the percentage of the male labour force employed in industry in England and Wales rose from 19 in 1700 to 30 in 1800, while that in agriculture fell from 60 to 40, though agricultural productivity increased, thanks in part to the use of lime as a fertiliser. As a reminder of the multiple linkages of economic growth and efficiency, the limekilns were fired by coal.

Canals played a major role in improving the transport of bulky goods, notably coal. The Bridgewater Canal, begun in 1761 to bring coal from the Duke of Bridgewater's mines at Worsley to Manchester, was particularly influential. Having viewed it in 1767, Joseph Banks reflected 'The benefits accruing to the country are almost invaluable. Trade is opened between two very large towns [Manchester and Liverpool] before labouring under great inconveniences . . . and a plan is struck out before deemed impracticable which has already been followed in several parts of the kingdom.' In 1790, indeed, the Oxford Canal linked Oxford and the Midlands, creating the final link in a network joining the rivers Trent, Mersey and Thames. In turn, the requirement for more capacity led to the decision to improve the London–Birmingham route by digging a new canal, the Grand Junction Canal, from the Thames near London to join the Oxford Canal. The legislation passed in 1793, the same year in which the opening of the Monkland Canal stimulated the development of the Lanarkshire coalfield to serve the rapidly-growing Glasgow market.

Knowledge was important both to economic growth and to a sense of greater potential. Scientific advances were made in a number of fields. William Brownrigg (1711–1800) formulated the concept of a multiplicity of chemically distinctive gases. Joseph Black (1728–99), professor of chemistry at Glasgow and later Edinburgh, discovered latent heat and first fixed the compound carbon dioxide. Henry Cavendish (1731–1810), a master of quantitative analysis, was in 1766 the first to define hydrogen as a distinct substance and in 1781 the first to determine the composition of water by exploding a mixture of hydrogen and oxygen in a sealed vessel. Joseph Priestley (1733–1804) discovered a number of gases and oxides, as well as electricity.

The spread of fodder crops, such as clover, coleseed and turnips, helped to eliminate fallow land and to increase the capacity of the rural economy to rear more animals, sources of the 'roast beef of old England', as well as of woollen cloth and crucial manure. The percentage of enclosed land increased greatly: during the century, about 21 per cent of England was affected by enclosure acts. They were especially common during the 1760s and 1770s when the heavy clay soils of the Midlands were enclosed and there was widespread conversion from arable to pasture, and again during the long war with Revolutionary and Napoleonic France in 1793–1815 when high prices brought an extension of arable cultivation particularly to unused or lightly used land. Hedges became even more characteristic of lowland Britain.

Enclosure did not necessarily raise efficiency, and also caused work. Agriculture, moreover, remained very labour-intensive, while, far from enclosure being vital, there are examples of unenclosed areas that witnessed agricultural improvement. Enclosure, however, made it easier to control the land through leases, was often linked to innovation, and was frequently accompanied by a redistribution of agricultural income from the tenant farmer to his landlord. Progressive landowners disrupted traditional rights and expectations and the enclosure of common lands led to particular bitterness.

Enclosure was helped by the extent to which, unlike in Continental Europe, peasant ownership of the land was limited. The system of tenure in Britain helped to perpetuate landlord control. To underline the theme of regional variety, it is, however, worth noting that the social context of enclosure varied: in some areas, such as Northamptonshire, landlords secured parliamentary acts to further their interests, but in others, for example Hampshire and Sussex, enclosure was by private agreement and caused less tension. The rise in population combined with war with France resulted in a boom in agriculture from the 1790s to the 1810s. This led to more rental income, which was reflected in extensive building by landlords: the Georgian houses for which much of particularly rural England is still noted. Substantial stately homes were also constructed in Scotland and Ireland, for example Culzean and Inveraray in the former.

There were, however, also many losers from agrarian change. From the early 1790s, the Highland clearances in Scotland reflected the move to an agricultural system, imposed by landlords, that required fewer people. The Countess of Sutherland cleared 794,000 acres of clan land in 1814–20. In Ireland, in contrast, intensive cultivation of the potato supported a major expansion of the population.

INDUSTRIALISATION

Even if the rate of industrialisation was less impressive than used to be believed and was restricted to only a few regions and sectors, the qualitative impact of economic change was obvious to contemporaries. A sense of economic change and the possibilities of progress was powerfully present amongst many people in the later eighteenth century. There were important changes in the intensity of work, the organisation of labour and in material conditions. The impression was of Prometheus Unbound, of extraordinary opportunities offered by technological innovation. John Kay's flying shuttle of 1733, which was in general use in Yorkshire by the 1780s, increased the productivity of handloom weavers. James Hargreaves's spinning jenny (1764–5), Richard Arkwright's water-frame (1769) and Samuel Crompton's mule (1779) revolutionised textile spinning.

In 1769 James Watt patented a more energy-efficient use of steam engines. Steam pumping got water out of deep coalmines while steam-powered winding engines were introduced in coalmines in the early 1790s. Visiting Coalbrookdale in 1754, Reinhold Angerstein noted 'It is amazing how far the art of casting iron has been developed in this place.' In 1776, Jabez Fisher toured the copper-smelting site at White Rock near Swansea founded in 1737:

Here are 43 Furnaces constantly in Blast, all employed in their proper departments, and 150 Men who appear like what we might conceive of the Inhabitants of Pandaemonium. The greatest decorum is however preserved; they all move like a Machine.

Less significantly, steam power was also used in agriculture, being employed from 1798 to drive threshing machines.

Economic growth was linked to Britain's wars and the burgeoning demands of her empire, as well as to home demand and to changing foreign markets. Thanks in part to war, metallurgical industries, especially gun founding, developed, and ironmasters were keen to adopt new technological developments. Canals and waggonways were built to move coal. The fourth Duke of Portland built a new harbour at Troon on the west coast of Scotland in 1808 and linked it to his coalpits at Kilmarnock by a waggonway which in 1839 carried over 130,000 tons of coal. In 1812–13, the first locomotives at work in the Greater Manchester Region used a geared driving wheel engaging with racks cast on the iron rails to haul coal from the colliery to the Leeds and Liverpool Canal. In 1816, Napoleon, then a British prisoner on St Helena, told his British captor, 'Your coal gives you an advantage we cannot possess in France.'

In turn, success in war was important. The French Revolution, which began in 1789, was followed by warfare involving France from 1792 until 1815 that led, thanks to eventual defeat, to the loss of France's relative position as a powerful threat to British economic superiority. Moreover, the perception of British military superiority enhanced the ability to repay war debts and thus helped ensure the self-financing character of British growth. Finance was important, not only as a resource but also as an institutional practice and political product. The British financial system was more resistant to shock than its Dutch and French counterparts, in large part because of its rich mixture of varied financial institutions and its pattern of interrelated financial markets. This situation matched the way in which Britain made better use than other states of its raw materials and external trade.

TRANSPORT AND THE PACE OF CHANGE

Better communications were important to a changing Britain, and not just for economic reasons. Spreading news and fashions, greater ease of communication helped to unify the elite, facilitating education, socialising, and travel for business or political reasons. Many Turnpike Acts were passed in the late eighteenth century, enabling local trusts to take over sections of roads and to finance improvements through tolls, a process that had begun in the 1660s. The Edinburgh–Glasgow road was turnpiked in the 1780s. The introduction from the 1780s of the macadamised and cambered road gave a harder and drier surface and thus permitted greater speeds for horse-drawn carriages. Bridges were also built, replacing fords and ferries. Stage-coaches stopped at inns at each stage of the journey obtaining fresh horses, and thereby travelling faster. London newspapers were sent to the provinces in increasing numbers, and postal services improved considerably, Royal Mail coach services starting in 1784, to the benefit of the expanding banking system as well as to the letter writer, that central character in two recent and rapidly developing literary forms, the novel and the magazine. By 1835, there were 28 mail coaches leaving London each night and another 75 travelling between provincial towns, while others travelled in the reverse direction.

GEORGE III, 1760–1820

For those few who wielded power, however, political challenges were foremost. The Whig–Tory two-party alignment that had played a major role since the beginning of the century gradually gave way in the 1760s to a number of essentially personal political groups, the rivalries of political leaders and the changing preferences of George III fostering instability. As much as any Continental ruler who did not have to face a powerful representative institution, George, the first of the Hanoverian monarchs born in Britain, was determined to reject what he saw as the politics of faction and to thwart the efforts of unacceptable politicians to force their way into office.

As did other rulers, George found it most difficult to create acceptable relationships with senior politicians at his accession, when he had to persuade those who had had a good working relationship with his predecessor, and those who had looked for a dramatic change, to adjust to his wishes. George broke with William Pitt the Elder in 1761 and with Thomas, Duke of Newcastle, in 1762, and made his favourite, John, 3rd Earl of Bute, First Lord of the Treasury in 1762, only to see the weak-willed Bute resign in 1763 in the face of bitter domestic opposition. George complained to the French ambassador in 1763 about 'the spirit of fermentation and the excessive licence which prevails in England. It is essential to neglect nothing that can check that spirit.' He was determined to uphold the Revolution Settlement as he understood it, but the ambiguity of a number of constitutional points, such as the collective responsibility of the Cabinet and the degree to which the monarch had to choose his ministers from those who had the confidence of Parliament, exacerbated the situation, as did the volatile political atmosphere in London. Dissatisfaction there, part of which stemmed from economic difficulties after the end of the Seven Years War, was exploited by a squinting anti-hero, John Wilkes, an entrepreneur of faction and libertine MP, who fell foul of George as a result of bitter attacks on the king in his newspaper the *North Briton*. Not until 1770, did George find a satisfactory minister who could control Parliament: he was Frederick, Lord North.

THE LOSS OF AMERICA

The discontent and divisions of the 1760s over the determination of George III to pick ministers of his own choice paled into insignificance, however, beside the collapse of the imperial relationship with America. The determination to make colonies, which were not represented in Parliament, pay a portion of their defence burden was crucial, though so also was increasing democratisation in American society, a stubborn rejection of British authority, concern about British policy in Canada, and the borrowing of British conspiracy theories about the supposed autocratic intentions of George III.

The Seven Years War had left the British government with an unprecedentedly high level of national debt and it looked to America to meet a portion of the burden. The Americans, however, no longer felt threatened by French bases in Canada and were therefore unwilling to see British troops as saviours. The Stamp Act of 1765 led to a crisis as Americans rejected Parliament's financial demands, and, thereafter, relations were riven by a fundamental division over constitutional issues. The fact that Britain's most important colonies in the western hemisphere, those in the West Indies, did not rebel, despite the sensitivity of their elites on questions of constitutional principle, suggests, however, that there was no inevitable crisis in the British imperial system, but rather that factors particular to the American colonies were crucial. Similarly, there was no rebellion in Ireland.

Fighting broke out near Boston in 1775 as a result of the determination of the government of Lord North to employ force, and the willingness of sufficient Americans to do likewise. An ill-advised attempt to seize illegal arms dumps led to clashes at Lexington and Concord, and the British were soon blockaded by land in Boston. Their attempt to drive off the Americans led to very heavy losses at the battle of Bunker Hill.

The British were driven from the thirteen colonies from New Hampshire to Georgia in 1775, and the Americans declared independence the following year. However, the British held Canada against invading Americans, before counter-attacking to regain New York (1776). The following year, the British seizure of Philadelphia was matched by defeat at Saratoga. After the French entered the war on the revolutionary side (1778), the British lacked the resources necessary for America and were pushed onto the defensive in a world war. Spain joined France in 1779, and, at the end of 1780, the Dutch were added to the list of Britain's enemies in what became a global conflict.

Though the Franco-Spanish attempt to invade England failed (1779), and the British held on to Gibraltar, India and Jamaica, defeat at Yorktown (1781) was followed by a collapse of the will to fight on and by the acceptance of American independence. This split the unity of the English-speaking world. America, inhabited by an independent people of extraordinary vitality, was to be the most dynamic of the independent states in the western hemisphere, the first and foremost of the decolonised countries, the people that were best placed to take advantage of the potent combination of a European legacy, independence, and opportunities for expansion and growth. At the same time, America was to play a crucial role during the First and Second World Wars, helping to ensure the success of the alliances that included Britain; and also ensured that aspects of British culture, society and ideology, albeit in altered forms, were to enjoy great influence, outside and after the span of British empire.

THE MINISTRIES OF WILLIAM PITT THE YOUNGER, 1783–1801, 1804–6

As so often in British history, defeat led to the fall of the government. Lord North's resignation in 1782 was followed by a period of marked ministerial and constitutional instability. Forced to accept ministries that he disliked, first that of Charles, Marquess of Rockingham, George threatened abdication. In 1783–4, he breached several fundamental political conventions in engineering the fall of the Fox–North ministry and supporting that of the 24-year-old William Pitt the Younger, the severe but sometimes drunk second son of Pitt the Elder, although the new ministry lacked a Commons majority. Pitt's victory in the 1784 general election was also, therefore, a triumph for George and it began a period of largely stable government that lasted until Pitt's resignation in 1801. Like Walpole and North, Pitt understood the importance of sound finances, and, although he was interested in electoral reform, he did not push this divisive issue after it had been defeated in Parliament in 1785. The War of American Independence more than doubled the national debt, but Pitt's prudent financial management and reforms, and a dramatic growth in trade, not least with America, stabilised the situation.

As so often in a monarchical state, continuity was, however, threatened by the succession, for George, Prince of Wales, later George IV, was not only opposed to the frugality, virtue and duty of his father, but also to Pitt. The Prince of Wales preferred instead the latter's chief opponent, Charles James Fox, who, unlike the prince, had talent, but, like him, lacked self-control. When, in late 1788, an attack of porphyria led to the conviction that George III was mad and near death, the resulting Regency Crisis nearly produced the fall of the government, but, fortunately for Pitt, the king recovered in early 1789.

Defeat at the hands of America had led to reform, especially in the Royal Navy, and this was to help Britain in the more serious challenge that lay ahead. She bounced back from the loss of the Thirteen Colonies, Florida and various Caribbean islands (Treaty of Versailles, 1783), to establish the first British foothold in Malaysia (Penang, 1786), and the first European colony in Australia (1788), and to thwart Spanish attempts to prevent her from trading and establishing settlements on the western coast of modern Canada (Nootka Sound crisis, 1790).

WAR WITH FRANCE

Though buffeted seriously during war with Revolutionary and then Napoleonic France, and most worryingly with the Irish rising of 1798 and the threat of invasion by Napoleon from 1803, Britain survived, thanks in particular to a series of naval victories, culminating in Horatio Nelson's triumph at Trafalgar (1805). The war against Revolutionary France revealed, however, that the British were unable to defend the Low Countries, and subsequent expeditions there – the 1799 landing in Holland under George III's son Frederick, Duke of York (now best remembered in a nursery rhyme for marching troops up and down hills), and the 1809 attack on Walcheren – ended in failure.

War with France involved Britain from 1793 to 1802, 1803 to 1814 and again in 1815, and this struggle placed a major strain on British resources. Moreover, defeats led to, or exacerbated, political problems. Pitt the Younger discovered that wartime leadership was considerably more difficult than the period of reform and regeneration he had earlier helped to orchestrate, and he died in 1806, worn out in office. The cost and economic disruption of the war pressed hard throughout society, leading to inflation, the collapse of the gold standard under which paper currency was met by the Bank of England (1797), the successful introduction of income tax (1799), the stagnation of average real wages, and widespread hardship, especially in the famine years of 1795–6 and 1799–1801. The real wages of Lancashire cotton weavers fell by more than a half in 1792–9. Radicals found their activities prohibited or limited, while trade unions were hindered, though not ended, by the Combination Acts of 1799 and 1800 which made combinations of unions of employees for improved pay or conditions illegal. There was a nationalist dimension to radicalism in both Ireland and, to a lesser extent, Scotland.

Napoleon's domination of much of the Continent from 1806 to 1813 was a major challenge to British interests. He sought in the Continental System, which was inaugurated in November 1806, to bring Britain to her knees by economic means. The Berlin Decrees declared Britain blockaded and banned trade with her. Further economic difficulties arose from the war with the United States of America (1812–15) over the British regulation of neutral trade. The British burnt Washington DC in 1814 and defended Canada successfully, but were defeated outside New Orleans in 1815.

That conflict, the only war Britain fought with the United States after 1783, was only a diversion, however, from the struggle with Napoleon, and the British were fortunate that they fought the Americans after the French navy had been defeated and when Napoleon's system was beginning to collapse as a result of his unsuccessful invasion of Russia in 1812. Eventual triumph over Napoleon came as part of an alliance to which Britain contributed money (£66 million in subsidies and armaments to her allies) and Arthur, Duke of Wellington's victories in the Peninsular War (1808–13) in Portugal and Spain, such as Vimeiro (1808), Talavera (1809), Salamanca (1812), and Vitoria (1813). The disciplined firepower of the British infantry played a major part in these triumphs. Wellington never had more than 60,000 British troops under his personal command and was always outnumbered in both cavalry and artillery, but he was a fine judge of terrain and, as at Vimeiro, the well-positioned British lines succeeded in blunting the attacking French columns.

British commitment culminated in the major roles taken by Britain at the peace congress of Vienna (1814–15) and, under Wellington, on the battlefield of Waterloo on 18 June 1815. Though British troops composed less than half of the Anglo-German-Dutch force that Wellington commanded, they played a decisive role in stopping the successive advances of French cavalry and infantry, until finally Napoleon's veteran guard units were driven back. Their major role at Waterloo sealed the rehabilitation of the Highlanders and made possible the 1822 pageant in Edinburgh to welcome George IV.

UNION WITH IRELAND

The Act of Union with Ireland in 1800 was a response to the rising of 1798. Increasing Catholic wealth in the second half of the century and divisions among the Protestants were important to the long-term process by which the Catholics came to play a more central role in politics and a more active role in society. The harnessing of Irish manpower for war with France also strengthened pressure for improvement in the position of Catholics. Moreover, concern about the possible impact of the French Revolution led the government in London to improve the legal condition of Catholics. The French Revolution had radicalised Irish discontent and provided the possibility of foreign support for a rebellion. When in 1791 Wolfe Tone founded the United Irishmen, until 1796–7 largely a Presbyterian Ulster movement, he put forward a programme advocating manhood suffrage, equal electoral districts and annual parliaments which, if implemented, would have destroyed the oligarchical regime at Dublin. Pitt the Younger overruled the Lord Lieutenant, John, 10th Earl of Westmorland, and the wishes of the Protestant Ascendancy in Ireland, and placated the Catholic agitation by granting better-off Catholic freeholders the vote in 1793. The Place and Pensions Act and the Catholic Relief Act allowed Catholics to bear arms, sit on juries and hold minor civil and military office. Pitt was already thinking about the possibility of a parliamentary union between Britain and Ireland. The Irish Catholic Church, concerned about the hostility to the Catholic Church, and indeed to the atheism of the French revolutionaries, preached the religious duty of obedience to the government of George III.

Important initiatives were, however, blocked. William, 2nd Earl Fitzwilliam, Lord Lieutenant 1794–5, sought to remove the remaining legal disabilities barring Catholics from Parliament and government office, but was disavowed and recalled. Fitzwilliam had believed that concessions were necessary in order to prevent the spread of revolutionary sentiment, and his failure helped in the alienation of Catholic opinion, and confirmed radicals in the view that the only means to achieve their aims was revolution. The United Irishmen, who had been banned in 1794, had re-formed as a secret society that was openly republican and increasingly Catholic, and had already begun to plot revolution. Tone sought support in America and France. He managed to persuade the French to mount a major invasion attempt in 1796, but it was thwarted by adverse winds. When the French fleet reached Bantry Bay in December 1796 it failed to land any of the 12,000-strong force it carried. The United Irishmen developed a military organisation, but the British army disarmed its Ulster cells in 1797. As the United Irishmen increasingly sought to win Catholic backing, they alienated Protestant support.

Rising sectarian violence culminated in rebellion in 1798. The arrest of the Leinster provincial committee of the United Irishmen and of the organisers of the projected uprising in Dublin gravely handicapped the rebels, who were only able to mount a serious military challenge in Wexford where the local garrison was weak. The rebels were smashed at Vinegar Hill. The rebellion, which was supported by an unsuccessful French invasion of Connacht, was firmly suppressed by Cornwallis, who had been defeated by the Americans and their French allies at Yorktown in 1781.

This rebellion demonstrated that the Protestant Ascendancy could not keep Ireland stable, and encouraged the British government to support union. The Act of Union of 1800 abolished the separate Irish Parliament in return for Irish representation at Westminster. The House of Commons had to accommodate 100 new MPs, although a number of Irish 'rotten' boroughs lost their seats. Four spiritual lords and twenty-eight temporal lords were added to the House of Lords. The established churches were combined into one Protestant Episcopal Church, called the United Church of England and Ireland, although this union never amounted to much.

However, Pitt's attempt to follow Union by admitting Catholics to Parliament and to most public offices was thwarted by George III, who argued that this would breach his promise in his coronation oath to protect the position of the Church of England. In the medium term (or even by the 1820s at any rate) the insistence on Protestantism and civil rights going together may have undermined the Union, but a fair share of informed high political opinion thought it could go forward on that narrow basis. Catholics could not become MPs in the new Parliament until 1829. The marginalisation of Catholics was demonstrated by the ecclesiastical geography of Ireland. In the town of Kildare, for example, where the overwhelming majority of the population were Catholic, the sole place of Catholic worship was a chapel in a remote part of the town. Nevertheless, Catholics had more rights than ever before.

EXPANSION OF THE EMPIRE

Naval power permitted Britain to dominate the European trans-oceanic world during the Revolutionary and Napoleonic Wars. Danish, Dutch,

French and Spanish naval power were crippled, notably with Horatio Nelson's victory over a Franco-Spanish fleet at Trafalgar on 21 October in 1805. Britain was left free to execute amphibious attacks on the now isolated centres of other European powers, and to make gains at the expense of non-European peoples. The route to India was secured: Cape Town was captured in 1795 and then again, after it had been restored in 1802, in 1806; the Seychelles in 1794; Reunion and Mauritius in 1810. The British position in India and Australasia was consolidated, while her gains at the Congress of Vienna in 1814–15 included Ceylon (Sri Lanka), the Seychelles, Mauritius, Trinidad, Tobago, St Lucia, Malta, Cape Colony and Guyana. The Pacific became a British rather than a Spanish lake, while India served as the basis of British power and influence around the Indian Ocean. The establishment of the British imperial position owed much to success in war, and it was not surprising that the pantheon of imperial heroes defined and depicted in the nineteenth century was largely composed of military figures, such as Horatio Nelson. In 1828–30, Wellington was the only former general in British history to be a prime minister.

The nature of the British empire and of the European world had both altered dramatically between 1775 and 1815. In 1775, the majority of British subjects outside Britain were white (though the population of the West Indian colonies was predominantly black slaves), Christian, of British or at least European origin, and ruled with an element of local self-government. By 1815 none of this was true. By then, most of the trans-oceanic European world outside the western hemisphere was British; while, by 1830, this was true of the vast majority of all European possessions abroad. The situation was not to last; indeed, 1830 was the date of the French occupation of Algiers, the basis of their subsequent North African empire. Nevertheless, the unique imperial oceanic position that Britain occupied in the Revolutionary, Napoleonic and post-Napoleonic period was to be of crucial importance to its nineteenth-century economic and cultural development. France was to revive as a great imperial power; Portugal and the Dutch were to make gains, and Germany, Italy, Belgium, and the United States were to become imperial powers, but for none of these was empire as important, or as central a feature of public culture, as it was for Britain, by the late Victorian and Edwardian period.

The rise in British imperial power had a great influence on the British economy, on the British elite, who were provided with a new sense of role and mission and, in many cases, with careers, and on British public culture. Service in the colonies, particularly in India, came to be prestigious, more so than anything similar for France or Germany. Sir Walter Scott referred to India, where many Scots pursued a career in the army, administration and commerce, as the 'corn chest for Scotland'. The sense of Britain playing a major role in resisting challenges to the European system, which had characterised opposition to Louis XIV, the Revolution and Napoleon, ebbed, as empire, especially from the mid- and late 1870s, instead set the themes of Britain's role and identity, a process that was furthered by the development of widespread emigration to certain colonies. Britain's destiny as the world's leading empire appeared clear.

7

Age of Reform and Empire, 1815–1914

In this century, the British Isles, from 1801 the United Kingdom of Britain and Ireland, were affected by the economic transformation summarised as the Industrial Revolution, by a process of political transformation, and by Britain's position as the world's leading empire. In turn, these changes threw up fresh problems, while the 'Irish Question' increasingly became a vexed issue in British politics.

THE INDUSTRIAL REVOLUTION

The rise of Britain to become the greatest imperial power in history was not alone responsible for the major divergence between her and the other European powers, a divergence that very much struck contemporaries. Economic development and the rise of nationalism further constituted and accentuated the process of divergence. Historians have been deeply divided on the speed of industrial change. For long, it was seen as very fast, then there was an emphasis on evolution rather than revolution, but now there has been a swing back to a stress on revolutionary development. The harnessing of technological change led to an economic transformation of the country, not least as a consequence of the benefits of readily-available capital and labour, and the burgeoning markets of growing home, colonial and foreign populations.

The Industrial Revolution fundamentally altered the nature of the British Isles. Previously 'underdeveloped' and inaccessible areas, such as the Cumbrian coast, became, through the presence of coal, astonishingly vigorous and dynamic. Coal was central to the production of energy (steam power), to transport (railways) and to new industrial processes (for example, iron smelting), and Britain produced the most coal in the world.

The energy available made a dramatic difference to contemporaries. The Wheal Virgin steam engine of 1790, produced by the Birmingham partnership of Matthew Boulton and James Watt, could do the work of 953 horses. Widespread use of the abundant and easily-worked British supplies of coal to fuel mechanical power freed the economy from its earlier energy constraints, reducing costs and increasing the availability of heat energy. This potential was exploited in a host of industries such as soap production, glass-works and linen bleaching. As a mobile source of energy, the steam engine permitted the concentration of industrial production in towns and was also responsible for a growth in the range of products for the growing middle class.

Alongside major changes, however, it is also appropriate to stress the two-tier, gradual and evolutionary nature of part of the Industrial Revolution. In particular, technological change was generally slow in the early decades of the century and there was great variety within industries. Handloom weaving, for example, persisted on an appreciable scale in Lancashire into the 1840s; London and Birmingham were primarily cities of workshops, not factories; 86 per cent of London's employers in 1851 had fewer than ten employees. Moreover, water, rather than coal, continued to provide much of the power for Scottish industry before 1830. Despite the railway, much of Britain remained a horse-drawn society. Furthermore, the chronologies of the growth in the use of steam power and in urban population do not tally.

Nevertheless, the notion of an Industrial Revolution is still justified. The potential and character of much of British industry changed dramatically. Many of the fastest-growing cities of the early nineteenth century were centres of industrial activity, for example Bradford, Dundee and Merthyr Tydfil. Moreover, the Industrial Revolution gave Britain a distinctive economy. The annual averages of coal and lignite production for 1820–4, in million metric tons, were 18 for Britain, and 2 for France, Germany, Belgium and Russia combined. The comparable figures for 1855–9 were 68 and 32, and for 1880–4, 159 and 108. Raw cotton consumption in thousand metric tons in 1850 was 267 for Britain and 162 for the rest of Europe, and in 1880, 617 and 503. The annual production of pig-iron in million metric tons was in 1820, 0.4 for Britain, and the same for the rest of Europe, in 1850, 2.3 and 0.9, in 1880, 7.9 and 5.4; of steel in 1880, 1.3 for Britain, 1.5 for the rest of Europe.

The British population (excluding Ireland) rose from an estimated 7.4 million in 1750 to 29.7 in 1881, with that of England and Wales rising from 8.9 million in 1801 to 32.5 million in 1901. Much of this growing population lived in the shadow of mill, mine and factory, and most was urban. In 1801, only a third of the population of England and Wales lived in towns with over 2,500 people, but, by 1901, the percentage was nearly 80; and, within that growth, that of large cities was particularly important. For example, the population of Manchester and Salford grew by more than five times between 1801 and 1891. The 1851 census showed that, for the first time, the English urban population exceeded its rural counterpart. A growing population at home and abroad helped fuel demand.

THE TRANSPORT REVOLUTION

The Great Exhibition of the year 1851 was a tribute to manufacturing skill and prowess, as was the evolution from the stationary to the locomotive steam engine and the consequent railway revolution. The Stockton and Darlington Railway was opened in 1825; the Liverpool to Manchester in 1830. The locomotive that began services on the Stockton and Darlington Railway had a speed of twelve to sixteen miles an hour, but when Goldsworthy Gurney's steam-jet (or blast) was applied to George Stephenson's *Rocket* locomotive in 1829, the engine reached a speed of twenty-nine miles an hour. In the following two decades, a national system developed, one constructed and run by competing companies. Services from London reached Birmingham in 1838, Southampton in 1840, Bristol in 1841, Exeter in 1844 (cutting the journey time from twenty-one to less than six hours), Norwich in 1845, Lincoln in 1846, Plymouth in 1847, Holyhead, the postal port for Ireland, in 1850 (cutting the journey time from forty to nine-and-a-half hours), and Truro in 1859. Scotland had a separate network from the 1830s and initially travellers had to go by sea to Liverpool and then by rail to London. In 1849, the Caledonian Main Line via Carstairs to London opened, a Scottish initiative intended to open routes to England. By 1850, the now joined rail network covered most of the country apart from north Scotland, Cornwall and most of Wales.

The network subsequently spread throughout the British Isles and was far more extensive than the canals. The expansion of the network involved not only spur lines, for example to Buntingford in

Hertfordshire, completed in 1863, but also new main lines, for example the Midland Mainline from London to Bedford in 1868, and the Great Central from London to Nottingham in 1899. In 1911, there were 130 staffed stations in Devon and Cornwall alone. Canals were not immediately eclipsed by the railways. Their cheaper tariffs still made them an attractive prospect where heavy goods did not need to be moved rapidly and as feeders for railways. Yet, in the end, the railways largely consigned them to decay.

The railways transported goods and people round the country and brought new sounds and smells, as well as the dramatic engineering of bridges, such as Isambard Kingdom Brunel's across the Tamar (1859), and the Forth Bridge (1890), viaducts, and tunnels, such as the Severn Tunnel (1886). The extent of passenger journeys rose from 60 million miles in 1850 to near 300 million in 1870. Moreover, the manufacture and maintenance of trains became an important aspect of Britain's industry, with major workshops at towns that were newly founded or greatly expanded, such as Crewe, Doncaster, Swindon and Wolverton. Even towns that are no longer noted for their railway works could be heavily dependent on them. In Brighton and Gateshead, for example, the railway was the largest employer.

Thanks in part to developments in transport, economic patterns changed, not least the nature of marketing. Small market centres collapsed and the position of towns in the urban hierarchy altered. Railways competed with coastal shipping, supplanting it in the crucial movement of coal from the North-East to London and East Anglia. Their speed ensured that trains were used to move perishable goods, such as fruit, flowers and milk, to the major cities: over 15,000 tons of Cornish broccoli annually by 1900; a special daily refrigerated van carrying Devon rabbit carcasses to London before the Second World War. Use of the railway from the 1840s enabled the brewers of Burton-upon-Trent to develop a major beer empire. Dairy farmers switched to produce 'railway milk' rather than farmhouse cheese. Train travel also encouraged the growth and popularisation of domestic tourism, not least the development of the seaside resorts that changed much of coastal Britain, such as Newquay, Ramsgate, Bournemouth, Hove, Eastbourne, Margate, Southend, Yarmouth, Skegness, Cleethorpes, Bridlington, Scarborough, Morecambe, Blackpool and Largs.

The very building of the railways, with large gangs of migrant workers moving across rural Britain, disrupted local social patterns and assumptions. The cultural impact of change in transportation was also dramatic. It brought the standardisation of time, and a new speed to news and changing fashions. Local trends and towns were eclipsed by metropolitan fashions. The railways needed standard time for their timetables, in order to make connections possible; and, in place of the variations from east to west in Britain, they adopted the standard set by the Greenwich Observatory as 'railway time'. From its offices on the Strand, the Electric Telegraph Company communicated Greenwich time from 1852: clocks were kept accurate by the electric telegraph that was erected along railway lines. The train, moreover, transformed postal services, which were organised from London, where, in 1840, the Penny Black, the world's first postage stamp, was released.

SOCIO-ECONOMIC CHANGE

In Britain, the nineteenth century was an age of dramatic economic change, possibly most so in Bradford, whose population climbed from 16,012 in 1810 to 103,778 in 1850, as the Yorkshire city became the global centre of worsted production and exchange. Factory horsepower in Bradford rose 718 per cent between 1810 and 1830. Mechanisation there brought profit, larger factories and a wave of immigrants. Innovation was continual: the mechanisation of yarn spinning was followed, in 1826, by that of worsted weaving, despite riots by hostile workers. By 1850 the work formerly done in Bradford by thousands of handloom weavers, working in the countryside, was now performed by 17,642 automatic looms contained in factories and mass-producing women's dress fabrics.

Mechanisation was crucial to uniformity, the production of low-cost standardised products. As a result, brands of mass-produced goods, such as chocolate and soap, could be consumed and advertised nationally. Though factory production did not predominate until the second half of the century, industry and trade changed the face of the nation and the life of the people. In *Isabella* (1820), the poet John Keats wrote: 'many a weary hand did swelt / In torched mines and noisy factories'.

The consequences of economic growth were varied. Overcrowding was serious. The Bradford Sanitary Committee visited over 300 houses in 1845 and found an average of three people sleeping per bed. At the great seaport of Liverpool, about 30,000 sailors were ashore at any one time, leading to a major rise in prostitution: there were about 300 brothels in 1836, and 538 in 1846, and in 1857 there were at least

200 regular prostitutes aged under twelve. Industries such as steel were 'sweated' and created a workforce whose leisure centred on the company pub where men could rehydrate, sometimes with four quarts a day paid for by the employer.

As the British Isles had a number of regional economies and not a national one, industrial growth was far from uniform across the country. It was concentrated in areas with coal: the North-East, the Midlands, southern Lancashire, the West Riding of Yorkshire, South Wales, Fife and Strathclyde. 1910 was the peak year for the number of collieries in South Wales: 688 in all. Heavy industries, such as iron and steel, engineering and shipbuilding, were attracted to coal and iron-ore fields. Thus, Workington on the Cumbrian coast developed as a major centre of iron and steel production from 1857 onwards: railways built in the 1840s and 1850s created ready access to nearby iron-ore fields and to the coke supplies of County Durham. Many of the migrant workers for the town came from Ireland.

Middle-class professions developed to 'service' these new industries: new professions such as accountants emerged, as did new 'industries' such as leisure and tourism. Conversely, previously important areas, such as East Anglia and the South-West of England, suffered de-industrialisation, and therefore, depopulation, in part because they lacked coal. Norfolk, once a county with an important textile industry, saw this collapse from the 1790s in the face of competition from factory-produced cottons. Many small market towns, such as Diss and Swaffham in Norfolk, had little growth and were not to change greatly until they expanded again from the 1960s.

AN AGE OF ENTREPRENEURS

The structure and nature of wealth in the country were only partly changed by the growth of industrial capitalism. The values of the metropolitan (London) elite were different from those of the factory owners of the north and more akin to the gentlemanly lifestyle of the traditional landed elite. At the same time, the wealthy businessmen of the industrial areas purchased landed estates, patronised the arts and increasingly sought political and social influence. One of the greatest was William Armstrong (1810–1900), and his career epitomised the opportunities the intertwined forces of technology and industry presented in the Victorian age. Grandson of a Northumberland yeoman farmer and son of a Newcastle corn merchant, he became a solicitor, but was also an amateur scientist, with a particular interest in hydroelectrics. His development of the hydraulic crane led him to establish an engineering works at Elswick (1846). Armstrong subsequently expanded into both armaments and shipbuilding, his Elswick Ordnance Company becoming one of the largest engineering and armaments concerns in the world. The 110-ton, nearly 44-foot-long Armstrong breech-loaders manufactured for *HMS Victoria*, which was launched in 1887, were the largest and most powerful guns in the world. Warships were also built for a host of foreign powers, including Japan, Italy, Argentina and Chile. When he died, Armstrong was employing 25,000 people.

Armstrong was at the forefront of technological application, responsible for the installation of the world's first hydroelectric power station, and the mock-baronial stately home he built at Cragside was in 1880 the first house to be properly lit by lightbulbs. Armstrong supplied the hydraulic equipment to raise Tower Bridge in London, opened in 1894 and a potent symbol of empire. He was also responsible for the hydraulic lifts that were necessary if the London underground railway system was to expand with deep stations. A great local benefactor, who helped provide Newcastle with a better water supply and supported local education and health, Armstrong gained great wealth and became a peer in 1887. He was President of the Arts Association and a purchaser of the works of contemporary British painters, such as Dante Gabriel Rossetti. It was appropriate that in 1894 this greatest of the Victorian, or indeed modern British, warlords should have purchased Bamburgh Castle, the centre of Northumbrian power for much of the Anglo-Saxon period, and a great medieval royal fortress.

Isambard Kingdom Brunel (1806–59) was less successful than Armstrong, but shared his desire to apply technological innovations. Brunel's formidable engineering triumphs, the Clifton suspension bridge, his achievements as chief engineer on the Great Western Railway 1833–46, and his large iron-clad steamships, the *Great Western* (1838), *Great Britain* (1845) and *Great Eastern* (1858), reflected his work at the forefront of technical innovations, on, for example, screw propellers. The *Great Western* was, when launched, the largest steamship afloat and it was the first to sail regularly to America; the *Great Britain* the first large ship using a screw propeller; the *Great Eastern* the largest steamship yet built, and one constructed by new methods. Scots also played a major role in inventions and entrepreneurships, including the tyre (Dunlop), the first electric locomotive (Davidson), the motion picture camera (William Dickson), the bicycle (Macmillan), the waterproof (Macintosh), the steam hammer (Nasmyth), chloroform (Simpson) and the vacuum flask (Dewar).

Not all entrepreneurs came from outside the landed order. In 1859 Rowland Winn began developing the iron industry on his family's Lincolnshire estates. This supplied an iron and steel industry in Scunthorpe. In 1885 Winn, by then Lord St Oswald, replaced manual labour in his mines with grab cranes. By 1917 the St Oswald mines were supplying one-twelfth of Britain's output of iron ore.

Inventors and entrepreneurs combined to expand the nature of capabilities and possibilities across a wide range of human activity. For example, the chemical industry helped to develop a plethora of new products that greatly affected material life by transforming such areas as fabric colours and foodstuffs.

ECONOMIC LINKS

Economic growth did not, however, mean that there were no fears of Continental economic competition. France was much feared as an industrial rival down to the 1840s, while concern about German competition was a major reason for the repeal of the Corn Laws which kept the price of grain high for the benefit of British agriculture, but also raised the food costs of workers. In the parliamentary debates of February–March 1839 on the Corn Laws, in response to the depression, almost every speaker was aware of the threat from foreign manufacturing, especially because of the German *Zollverein* (customs union) of 1834. Economic confidence was most developed in the 1850s and 1860s, which were abnormally prosperous decades, and even then it was not unqualified.

Nevertheless, it was not simply the scale of British economic development that was of importance, but also the links that were being created, as well as, literally, forged. Britain became, from the 1870s and 1880s, part of a global agrarian system. Moreover, by establishing a more stable currency, the Bank Charter Act of 1844 allowed Britain to expand her financial control. British investment was central to economic developments across much of the world.

The end of protection for British agriculture with the repeal of the Corn Laws (1846) was important to global economic links, as were technological changes, including steamships, barbed wire, long-distance railways and, in the 1880s, refrigerated shipholds, which led to the development of agricultural production for the European market in other temperate climes and to the ability to move products rapidly without spoilage. Britain looked for food to empire, both formal and informal, rather than to Europe; grain from Germany, Poland and Russia was only bought in significant quantities in some years. Some Continental agricultural products were important, most obviously fruit and vegetables, such as German sugar-beet. By the end of the century, Danish bacon and eggs were the staple of the British breakfast. Nevertheless, it was North American grain, Argentine beef and Australasian lamb and mutton that were crucial sources of food, all opened up by British technology, particularly railways, and helped by British finance.

In combination, these imports led to the end of the golden age of 'high farming' in Britain and, instead, to a severe and sustained agricultural depression from the 1870s which badly affected farm-workers and rural craftsmen, and led to high rates of rural depopulation until the end of the century. There was a general stop in the construction of mansions by landlords in the same period. The spread of new technology, for example combined reaping and mowing machines, also affected the rural labour force. The total area devoted to agriculture in Britain fell by half a million acres between the 1870s and 1914.

The cheap imported food that fed the growing workforces of the industrial north of England helped to lead to a sustained depression throughout much of the more agrarian south, a regional disparity that was to be reversed the following century. Sunderland, today a city with many urban problems, was in 1850 the greatest shipbuilding town in the world, with high wages and a high rate of owner-occupation of housing. Thanks to cheaper food, industrial workers were able to spend a lower proportion of their wages on food than hitherto, thus becoming important consumers, as well as producers, of manufactured goods.

EMPIRE

Britain was the leading imperial power in the nineteenth century. At the end of the century, she ruled a quarter of the world's population (largely thanks to India) and a fifth of the land surface (with much help from Canada). The bases of imperial union were supposed to be twofold. There was a stress, sometimes misleading, on common British origins, customs, race, language and constitutions, but secondly, also, an emphasis on the degree to which each part of the empire complemented the others, especially economically. Thus, the Dominions and Crown colonies could exchange primary products for manufactured goods with industrial Britain, their common interests resting on the differences between the parts. This was also the relationship with trans-oceanic trading partners that were not part of the empire, most obviously South America. The theme of common British origins was matched by an emphasis on England, Scotland and Ireland as local component parts of empire with an international reach, as in the huge number of Caledonian Societies.

Between 1860 and 1914, Britain owned approximately one-third of the world's shipping tonnage and by 1898 about 60 per cent of the telegraph cables, a crucial aspect of imperial government and defence planning. In 1890–1914, she launched about two-thirds of the world's ships and carried about half of its marine trade. In his poem *Cargoes* (1903), John Masefield was able to present the three ages of marine trade through a 'Quinquireme of Nineveh', a 'Stately Spanish galleon', and lastly, a 'Dirty British coaster' carrying a cargo of British exports: 'cheap tin trays', a mass-produced product. Financial links played a major role in British imperial expansion, which was expressed by investment and shipping as much as by the export of manufactured goods. Investment abroad ensured that overseas income as a percentage of United Kingdom gross domestic product rose from 2 in 1872 to 7 in 1913: an ability to export finance was crucial to Britain's economic position in regions such as South America, especially Argentina. London, the centre of world finance and shipping, grew greatly in economic importance.

British strength spread throughout the oceans of the world. Between 1850 and 1914, in a process unique in world history, her list of island possessions was enlarged by the Andaman, Nicobar, Gilbert and Ellice, Kuria Muria, South Orkney, South Shetland and Cook islands, Malden, Starbuck, Caroline, Pitcairn, Christmas, Phoenix, Washington, Fanning and Jarvis islands, Fiji, Rotuna, the Solomon islands, Tonga, Socotra, and South Georgia. British naval power was supported by the most numerous and wide-ranging bases in the world, a testimony to the global reach of the British state. In 1898 these included Wellington, Fiji, Sydney, Melbourne, Adelaide, Albany, Cape York (Australia),

Labuan (North Borneo), Singapore, Hong Kong, Weihaiwei (China), Calcutta, Bombay, Trincomalee, Colombo, the Seychelles, Mauritius, Zanzibar, Mombasa, Aden, Cape Town, St Helena, Ascension, Lagos, Malta, Gibraltar, Halifax (Nova Scotia), Bermuda, Jamaica, Antigua, St Lucia, Trinidad, the Falklands and Esquimalt (British Columbia).

As today, the peacetime army was always overstretched to meet its numerous commitments. It grew in size to 195,000 men in 1898, and this force was supported by a substantial body of native troops in the Indian army, the basis for powerful expansion of British power in southern Asia in the Victorian period. Sind, a reluctantly-acquired territory, was conquered in 1843, Baluchistan and Kashmir became British vassals in 1843 and 1846 respectively, the Punjab was annexed in 1849, and by 1886 all Burma had followed. The Indian Mutiny of 1857–8 was a severe shock, and the Afghan tribes successfully resisted invasions during the wars of 1838–42 and 1878–9, but, in cooperation with the landlords and native princes, the British governed India with considerable success. British explorers, particularly James Bruce, David Livingstone, Mungo Park and John Speke, explored much of Africa. Others explored Australia and Canada, while the Royal Navy charted the oceans of the world.

The last decades of the century were years of still-spreading territorial control, although there was considerable disagreement among politicians about the wisdom of particular steps, and some were highly reluctant imperialists. Several prominent Liberal politicians, including William Gladstone, Liberal Prime Minister in 1868–74, 1880–5 (when Egypt was invaded), 1886, and 1892–4, were critical of jingoism, of imperial expansion for its own sake, and of many advances of British power, for example into Uganda.

Nevertheless, Britain gained the most important share of the two leading colonial carve-ups of the period, the scramble for Africa and the seizure of hitherto unclaimed island groups. She became the leading power in east and southern Africa: reluctantly, but successfully invaded Egypt in 1882, defeated the Mahdists of Sudan at Omdurman (1898), a battle in which the young Winston Churchill served, gained the territory that was to become British Somaliland, Kenya, Uganda, Northern Rhodesia (Zambia), Malawi and Southern Rhodesia (Zimbabwe), and eventually defeated the Afrikaner republics of southern Africa, the Orange Free State and Transvaal, in the Boer War of 1899–1902. The war proved far more difficult than had been anticipated, but the ability of Britain to spend £250 million and deploy 400,000 troops was a testimony to the strength of its economic and imperial systems, while her unchallenged control and retention of the South African ports allowed her to bring her strength to bear. On the other hand, many contemporaries were deeply worried by the army's performance and the war was followed by a budgetary crisis.

Historians have been divided in their stress on economic, political or strategic factors in the growth of the New Imperialism of the late nineteenth century. Economic exploitation, the Marxist account, is no longer the prime explanation of imperialism. Empire, however, was not simply a matter of power politics, military interests, elite careers and an ideology of mission and purpose that appealed to the propertied and the proselytising. It also had relevance and meaning throughout a society affected by the growth of popular imperialist sentiment. This influence was reflected in the jingoistic strains of popular culture: the ballads of music hall and the images depicted on advertisements for mass-produced goods. On the other hand, many of the workers appear to have been pretty apathetic about imperialism.

Empire reflected and sustained widespread racist assertions and assumptions, both of which were amply demonstrated in the literature and press of the period. Empire also provided the occasion and stimulus for a new concept of exemplary masculinity focusing on soldier heroes, such as Wolseley, Gordon, Roberts and Kitchener, who, in a fusion of martial prowess, Protestant zeal and moral manhood, were seen as national icons. Their victories were gained at the expense of numerous non-Europeans, often slaughtered by the technology of modern weaponry, as in Kitchener's victory at Omdurman (Sudan) in 1898. The zealous Charles Gordon, who died defending Khartoum in 1885, was presented as a quasi-saint resisting a vast force of Muslims. The impact of such controversial imperial events was enough to threaten prominent politicians such as Gladstone.

The sieges of the Indian Mutiny (1857–8) and the Second Boer War (1899–1902) offered drama for the entire country. Imperial clashes were re-enacted in open-air spectacles in Britain: the tableau and pageant became art forms. Newspapers spent substantial sums on the telegraphy that brought news of imperial conflict. Moreover, army service was a glorious route out of the slums for many working-class men. The Protestant and Catholic churches of Britain devoted their resources to missionary activity outside Europe, particularly, though not only, within the empire, which they endorsed as a means of facilitating Christian missions.

BRITAIN AND EUROPE

With the succession of Queen Victoria in 1837, the dynastic link with Hanover was broken: only men could succeed there, so her uncle Ernest, Duke of Cumberland, became King of Hanover. Britain's global responsibilities meant that she took a view of the world in which Europe was simply one element, though it was a very important element. Prominent Foreign Secretaries, such as George Canning, 1807 and 1822–7, Prime Minister 1827, and Henry, Viscount Palmerston, Foreign Secretary 1830–41 and 1846–51, Prime Minister 1855–8 and 1859–65, were extremely concerned with Continental international relations, for example in Iberia, Greece and the Near East. In addition, imperial issues could have a European dimension, most obviously with 'the Eastern Question', the problem created by Russia's growing influence and ambitions in the Balkans as the Ottoman (Turkish) empire declined. Furthermore, the absence of challenges on the Continent could free Britain for imperial ambitions.

British governments worried about the plans and actions of their Continental counterparts. Invasion by France, including through a planned (but not built) Channel tunnel, was feared in 1847–8, 1851–2 and 1859–60, while Russian moves in the Balkans led Britain to go to war with her: the Crimean War (1854–6). This was the last war that Britain fought with a European power until the First World War broke out in 1914, an unprecedented length of time. The Crimean War was characterised by administrative incompetence, which provided evidence of the need for army reform. There were heavy losses in manpower, and a series of military misjudgements, most famously the Charge of the Light Brigade into the face of Russian artillery at Balaclava in 1854. Nevertheless, the war also indicated Britain's continued ability to project her power around the world, naval attacks being mounted on Russian coasts as far as Kamchatka on the Pacific, and in this she was assisted by technological advances. The warships sent to the Baltic in 1854 were all fitted with steam engines, and also benefited from Brunel's work on gun-carriages.

More generally, educated Victorians were acutely aware of what they shared with other European peoples as a result of a common culture based upon Christianity and the legacy of Greece and Rome. Gladstone published three books on the Classical Greek writer Homer and edited Bishop Butler's sermons. The growing number of public schools made the Classics the centre of their teaching. Those who could afford to do so performed and listened to German music, read French novels and visited the art galleries of Italy. The British were involved, intellectually and at times materially, for most of the century, in what was happening on the Continent. This was obviously true of the Napoleonic and Crimean wars in which Britain participated, but, in addition, the Greek War of Independence and the *Risorgimento* (Italian unification) aroused enormous interest, and more so than many of the British minor colonial wars and acquisitions of colonial territory. The manner in which the Italian hero Garibaldi was mobbed by working-class crowds when he visited England in 1864 testified to the way in which Victorians of all social classes were able to relate many of the events taking place on the Continent to their own struggles and aspirations: the logbooks of Southampton's schools show massive truancy when he landed in the city. In 1876, moreover, Gladstone was able to embarrass Disraeli's ministry seriously over the massacre of Bulgarians by the Turks. Continental news remained very important in the British press, though more attention was devoted to imperial questions from the 1870s. Furthermore, most Britons by 1901 probably saw their 'family of nations' in the Dominions and Empire.

A major difference between Britain and Continental countries, especially in the mid-nineteenth century, was that Britain traded abroad far more than they did, and far more widely. Continental economies were more self-sufficient; what foreign trade they did was mainly with other European countries. So Britain was dependent on foreign trade, and on the wider world outside Europe, in a way they were not. From this followed many aspects of Britain's difference from the Continent: Britain's outward-looking perspective and internationalism; her interest in peace, which was believed to create the best conditions for trade, and which determined her diplomatic isolation from the Continent (except during the Crimean War) – to avoid being dragged into European wars; and her opposition to a large and expensive army.

BRITAIN AND AMERICA

The British attitude towards America was ambivalent and vice versa. Many Victorians wrote about it, for example Charles Dickens, Anthony Trollope and James Bryce, all of whom were popular in the USA and taken by its energy and drive, yet often shocked by its 'vulgar' (populist) politics. A standard means of criticising a politician was to accuse him of the 'Americanisation' of British politics, and Gladstone and Joseph Chamberlain both suffered accordingly. There was also much down-right hostility between the two states: over the Crimean War, when the British, being very short of troops by 1855, tried to recruit American mercenaries; the American Civil War, when the British were considered too favourable to the South; and in disputes over clashing imperial inter-ests in the New World and the Pacific, for example involving Venezuela in the 1890s, although Britain had accepted America's Monroe Doctrine with its demand for non-intervention in the Americas. The Civil War (1861–5) divided British public opinion fairly widely. The South sought to win diplomatic recognition, a step that would have legitimated seces-sion. The Foreign Secretary, Lord John Russell, and, even more, the Chancellor of the Exchequer, Gladstone, were sympathetic, but fears that recognition would lead to war with the Union prevented the step. It was not only power politics that led to hostility. There were also cultural and economic rivalries, for example over copyright law in the 1850s.

On the other hand, despite disagreements over the Maine frontier and, more seriously, tension over the fate of modern British Columbia, the British and the Americans managed to agree the course of the long Canadian border without war. Similarly, cross-border raids on Canada by the Fenians, American-based Irish terrorists, did not trouble relations for long. There was massive British investment in America, particularly in railways, the transfer of British technology, again in railways, and important cultural and social links. A number of American women married peers or their heirs in 1870–1914, some bringing great wealth, as when Consuelo Vanderbilt married the Duke of Marlborough in 1895.

MORAL POLITICS

Empire was a crucial component of British nationalism, especially towards the end of the century. The imagery of government fuelled this: Victoria, the Christian ruler of a largely Hindu country, was made Empress of India in 1876; the journal *Punch*, an influential creator of images, popularised empire in its cartoons; and public buildings were decorated with symbols of empire. The expansion of empire was seen as furthering moral, as well as national, goals by spreading what was seen as liberal government and the rule of law, and providing opportu-nities for Christian proselytism. A sense of the strengths of the British constitution was another major aspect of nationalism. Though political expedients, compromises and the search for short-term advantage played a major role in the details of political reform, a sense of idealism was also important. Moral campaigns, for example against slavery, cruelty to animals and alcohol, aroused widespread support, fuelling a major expansion in the voluntary societies that were such a characteristic feature of Victorian Britain. The numerous hymns of the period meanwhile made clear the commitment to a Christian society: faith was far from being a matter of personal salvation alone.

RADICALISM

Domestic radicalism was initially encouraged by the French Revolution (1789), as part of the process by which the American and French Revolutions resulted in a flourishing of political ideology that helped politicise much of society. In turn, the growing violence and radicalism of the Revolution led, especially from 1792, to reaction, a rallying to Church, Crown and nation, with which the name of the politician-polemicist Edmund Burke will always be linked; although he was more liberal on slavery and on British policy in America, India and Ireland. This conservative surge helped to see Britain through years of defeat at the hands of France, before finding victory. However, serious economic strains and social discontent did not end with the war, and were indeed exacerbated from 1815 by post-war depression and demobilisation. Population growth led to under-employment and unemployment, and thus low wages and poverty, both for those in and for those without work. Unemployment, which also owed something to new technology (and thus inspired Luddites to destroy new industrial machines in Yorkshire in 1811–12), the unbalanced nature of industrial change and the economic problems it caused, poor harvests, and agitation for political reform, combined to produce a volatile post-war atmosphere.

Parliament, dominated by the landed interest, in 1815 passed the Corn Laws, which prohibited the import of grain unless the price of British grain reached 80 shillings a quarter. Thus, the price of the essential component of the expenditure of the bulk of the population was deliberately kept high. The result was food riots amongst hungry agricultural labourers, with attacks on farmers and on corn mills, and demands for wage increases. Threshing machines, which replaced the hand-flailing of cereal crops, also led to anger and there were outbreaks of machine-breaking, for example in south Norfolk in 1822. Income tax, seen as an emergency wartime measure, was repealed in 1816. William Cobbett (1762–1835), a leading political writer, denounced 'The Thing' – the Anglican, aristocratic establishment that dominated society, politics, religion and learning by means of patronage.

Luddism was not only about destroying machinery. It was, also, in areas such as Nottinghamshire, about strengthening the wage-bargaining position of trade unions, but governmental attitudes in the 1810s were hostile to these aims and not conducive to the development of popular activism outside the context of self-consciously 'loyalist' activity. Discontent and violence led to repressive legislation, most prominently the Six Acts of 1819; although, by the standards of modern totalitarian regimes, there was no police state. Nevertheless, the Peterloo Massacre in Manchester (1819), a panic charge by the Yeomanry (militia), ordered on by the over-excitable Manchester magistrates, on an enormous crowd gathered to support demands for parliamentary reform by speakers such as Henry 'Orator' Hunt, led to eleven deaths and many injuries. It elicited widespread revulsion. The radical poet Percy Bysshe Shelley (1792–1822) referred in *The Mask of Anarchy* to 'Trampling to a mire of blood / The adoring multitude', and called for a popular rising: 'Ye are many – they are few.'

However, the radicals were divided and most, including Hunt, rejected the use of force after Peterloo, which received so much attention because it was untypical. A small group of London revolutionaries, under Arthur Thistlewood, plotted to murder the entire Cabinet and establish a government, but they were arrested in Cato Street in 1820. Thistlewood, who was hanged for treason, declared at the end of his trial, 'Albion [England] is still in the chains of slavery.' A rising in Huddersfield, also in 1820, was unsuccessful, while Hunt was imprisoned for his role at Peterloo.

There was also tension in Scotland, culminating in the so-called 'Radical War' of 1820. The Glasgow Police Commission appointed 700 new constables in 1817 and in 1819 took the threat of rebellion seriously. The radicals there used the slogan 'Scotland Free or a Desert'. About 60,000 people went on strike in Glasgow and Strathclyde. Across Britain, arson and animal-maiming were common in many rural areas. The invention of friction matches in 1826 by the Stockton chemist John Walker, and their subsequent manufacture as 'strike anywhere Lucifers', made arson easier.

George IV, Prince Regent 1811–20 while his father, George III, was incapacitated by porphyria, and King 1820–30, was very unpopular, especially for his extravagance and, to a lesser extent, his conservatism: he thanked the Manchester authorities for their conduct at Peterloo. George's unpopularity climaxed in 1820 when he tried to divorce his separated wife, Caroline, and to remove her royal status. Her cause was taken up by public opinion and the government felt obliged to abandon its campaign for a divorce, though she was successfully denied a coronation. Though George's visits to Ireland and Scotland, neither of which had been visited by the monarch since the seventeenth century, were very successful, *The Times* remarked in 1830, 'Never was there a human being less respected than this late king . . . what eye weeps for him?'

THE FIRST REFORM ACT, 1832

Tensions eased during the prosperous years of the early 1820s and in response to a more moderate government policy, but in the late 1820s an industrial slump and high bread prices helped cause a revival in popular unrest. In 1830 'Swing' riots affected large parts of southern and eastern England. Machine-breaking, arson and other attacks often followed letters signed by 'Swing' threatening trouble if labour-saving, and thus job-destroying, machines were not removed. Over ninety threshing machines were broken in Wiltshire; and there were at least twenty-nine cases of arson in Lincolnshire. The identity of 'Captain Swing', a pseudonym appropriated by the protestors, is unclear, and the riots probably spread spontaneously, rather than reflecting central control. Some industrial machines were also attacked. Wage and tithe riots contributed to the atmosphere of crisis in 1830: in much of rural England it was the last episode of riot until the period of trade-union activity in the 1870s.

In 1830, alongside continued Tory criticism of the Whigs as radical, there was also much pressure for reform of Parliament to make it more representative of the wealth and weight of the community. The Whig government of Charles, 2nd Earl Grey, that took power after the elections of 1830 believed such reform necessary as part of a confidence in a future they could determine. However, the Tory-dominated House of Lords opposed reform. Grey thought the situation 'too like what took place in France before the Revolution'. Commons' majorities for reform, and popular agitation, including riots in Bristol, Merthyr Tydfil and Nottingham, resulted in a political crisis, and George IV's brother, William IV (r. 1830–7), a former naval officer, eventually felt it necessary to agree that he would make new peers in order to create a majority for reform in the Lords. This willingness led the Lords to give way.

The First Reform Act (1832), described by its authors as final, fixed a more uniform right to vote that brought the franchise to the 'middle class', and reorganised the distribution of seats in order to reward growing towns, such as Birmingham, Bradford and Manchester, and counties, at the expense of 'rotten boroughs', seats with a small population that were open to corruption. The size of the English electorate was increased by 50 per cent, albeit from a low base so that it remained small. The growth of the Scottish electorate under the Reform Act (Scotland) of 1832 was even more spectacular: the vote was granted to one in eight adult males, as compared with one in 125 before, and representation was extended to industrial centres such as Paisley. Political rights were extended at the same time, however, as inequality was preserved. Most men still could not vote, voting qualifications still differed between the boroughs and the counties, the size of electorate continued to vary greatly by seat, and women were still excluded from the vote.

The 1832 Reform Acts were not alone. Instead, they began a process of continuous reform. The Municipal Corporations Act of 1835 reformed and standardised the municipal corporations of England and Wales. Elected borough councils, based on a franchise of rated occupiers, were given control over the local police, markets and street lighting. This legislation made town governments responsible to the middle class and was a crucial precondition for a wave of reforming urban activism, although much of this was slow in coming, and there had also been considerable improvement before 1835.

Reform aroused mixed feelings. Grey was to complain in 1837 that the Reform Act had made 'the democracy of the towns paramount to all the other interests of the state', which was not what he had intended, for the Whigs had little time for radicalism. The following year, William Wordsworth (1770–1850), one of the greatest of the Romantic poets and initially a radical and a supporter of the French Revolution, revealed in his *Protest Against the Ballot* the extent of the conversion to reaction that was to help him gain a civil list (government) pension (1842), and the poet laureateship (1843). It began:

> Forth rushed from Envy sprung and Self-conceit,
> A Power misnamed the SPIRIT of REFORM,
> And through the astonished Island swept in storm,
> Threatening to lay all Orders at her feet
> That crossed her way.

Wordsworth continued by urging St George, patron saint of England, to stop the introduction of the secret ballot as it threatened to spawn a 'pest' worse than the dragon he had slain. Not one of Wordsworth's masterpieces, the poem underlines the hostility and fear that reform aroused in many circles, and the sense that concessions to change had to be balanced by containment.

CHARTISM

Others, however, were dissatisfied with the limited extent of reform. The radicals had long seen the Whigs as exponents of oligarchy. 'Orator' Hunt, whose address had triggered the violence at Peterloo and who supported universal manhood suffrage (right to vote), opposed the First Reform Act because he feared it would link the middle and upper classes against the rest. Dissatisfaction led in the late 1830s to a working-class protest movement, known as Chartism, that called for universal adult male suffrage, a secret ballot and annual elections. The Six Points of the People's Charter (1838) also included equal constituencies, the abolition of property qualifications for MPs, and their payment, the last two designed to ensure that the social elite lost their control of the representative system. Although Chartists disagreed over tactics, there was general support for the argument that peaceful agitation should be used. Many Chartists argued that force could be employed to resist what they saw as illegal action by the authorities, but, in practice, there was great reluctance to endorse violent policies.

The general Chartist Convention held in Birmingham in 1839 presumed that Parliament would reject the Chartist National Petition, and called on the people to refrain from the consumption of excisable goods and thus hit tax revenues, a means of putting pressure on the government and the middle classes, and pressed for the people to exercise a right to arm. This was seen as a preparation for a general strike or 'sacred month' for the Charter, which was in fact not implemented, due to disagreements over appropriate action and lack of preparedness. In the event, Parliament resisted Chartist mass-petitions (1839, 1842, 1848), and Britain did not share in the disorders of 1848, the year of revolutions on the Continent, although there was support for action in Scotland.

The reason for the failure of Chartism is controversial. It is unclear whether it failed because of the iron fist of the state, because the government met some of its demands and left it looking passé, because of its failure to achieve its objectives, or because of growing prosperity: mass support for Chartism was apparent only in times of recession. Similarly, rural protest movements against heavy rent and tithe burdens did not change the situation in the countryside.

THE CONDITION OF THE PEOPLE

The pressure that economic circumstances placed on the bulk of the population is indicated by the decline in the average height of army recruits in the second quarter of the century, although, as Britain had a voluntary army, this decline is only a limited guide to the physical stature of the population as a whole. The strains of industrialisation in the early nineteenth century certainly caused much social and political tension. Unlike cotton textiles, many other industries were slow to experience technological transformation, with the result that general living standards only rose noticeably from mid-century. Working conditions were often unpleasant and hazardous with, for example, numerous fatalities in mining accidents. Poor ventilation helped the build-up of gas, leading to explosions such as that at Haydock in Lancashire in 1878 which killed 189 men and boys. Other processes were also dangerous. The manufacture of matches from yellow phosphorus contributed to jaundice, psoriasis, chronic diarrhoea and phosphorus-rotted jaw. The Factory Acts regulating conditions of employment in the textile industry still left work there both long and arduous. The 1833 Act established a factory inspectorate and prevented the employment of under-9s, but 9–10-year-olds could still work eight-hour days (which by 1836 would also apply to those under 13), and 11–17-year-olds twelve hours. The 1844 Act cut the hours of under-13s to six-and-a-half hours, and of 18-year-olds and all women, to twelve; those of 1847 and 1850 reduced the hours of women and under-18s to ten hours. There were still about 5,000 half-timers aged under 13 in the Bradford cloth industry in 1907.

If the bulk of the working population faced difficult circumstances, the situation was even worse for those who were more 'marginal' to the economy. Henry Stuart, who reported on East Anglian poor relief in 1834, found three main groups of inmates in the often miserable parish workhouses: the old and infirm, orphaned and illegitimate children, and unmarried pregnant women, the last a group that was generally treated harshly, and far more so than the men responsible for their pregnancies.

The Poor Law Amendment Act (1834) introduced national guidelines in place of the former more varied parish-based system, but the uniform workhouse system that it sought to create was not generous to its inmates. Outdoor relief was abolished for the able-bodied and they were obliged to enter the workhouse, where they were to be treated no better than the conditions that could be expected outside in order to deter all bar the very destitute from being a charge on the community. Bastardy and indigent marriage and parenthood were to be discouraged. The national system was to be overseen by the Poor Law Commissioners in London. In Wimborne, Dorset, workhouse beds had to be shared, meat was only provided once a week, there were no vegetables other than potatoes until 1849, men and women were segregated, and unmarried mothers had to wear distinctive clothes. In general, expenditure was severely controlled, discipline was harsh and the stigma attached to dependent poverty grew.

There was some popular opposition to the workhouses. The one at Gainsborough in Lincolnshire was destroyed while it was being built in 1837 and there were also disturbances elsewhere, for example at Todmorden in Yorkshire which was for many years the sole English Poor Law Union area without a union workhouse. Opposition there owed much to John Fielden, a wealthy cotton manufacturer and radical MP. Moreover, a degree of outdoor relief continued in many places.

Social differentiation also characterised the care of the insane. Ticehurst Asylum, founded in the 1790s to cater for the wealthy, followed a 'no-restraint' policy, offered pleasant surroundings and plentiful food, and permitted visits, as did the York retreat. Elsewhere the situation was far more bleak, although the Asylum Act of 1845 brought a measure of reform.

Social assumptions and conventions pressed harder on women than on men. Women, not men, were blamed for the spread of venereal disease. Under the Contagious Diseases Acts (1864, 1866, 1869), passed because of concern about the health of the armed forces, women suspected of being prostitutes, not men who also might have spread disease, were subjected to physical examination and detention, if infected, in garrison towns and ports. After an extended campaign, in which women acquired experience of acting as political leaders in the Ladies National Association for the Repeal of the Contagious Diseases Acts, the Acts were repealed in 1886.

Charity could temper hardship, but it often entailed deference if not subordination for its recipients. Andrew Reed's charity, established in

1813 for the education of orphans, led to the foundation of schools, first at Clapton and then at Watford (girls and boys were, as was usual, educated separately). Subscribers to the charity were awarded votes and widows had to lobby them to gain entry for their offspring. Parliament made the first grants towards education in 1833, but the Newcastle Commission of 1858 showed that only one in eight children was receiving elementary education.

> Hell is a city much like London –
> A populous and a smoky city.

The poet Shelley's statement in *Peter Bell the Third* (1819) seemed increasingly appropriate. Fast-expanding towns became crowded and polluted, and a breeding ground for disease: 8032 of the 9453 houses in Newcastle in 1852 lacked toilets. Mortality rates remained high, though, thanks in part to vaccination, smallpox declined. In both town and countryside infant mortality was especially high. In largely rural Norfolk, one-quarter of all deaths in 1813–30 were of children less than one year old. Sewer systems were particularly deficient, as large amounts of waste were discharged into rivers without treatment, and up-river of where water supplies were obtained. Cholera, a bacterial infection largely transmitted by water affected by the excreta of victims, hit first in Britain in 1831, in slums such as the overcrowded east end of Sunderland. In *The Times* in 1855, Michael Faraday described the Thames between London and Hungerford bridges as a 'fermenting sewer'. By 1866 about 140,000 people had died of cholera. Disease struck most at the poor living in crowded and insanitary urban squalor, but also threatened the rich and helped lead to public alarm, for example about the health implications of the use of public transport.

The highest in the land were vulnerable. Edward, Prince of Wales, nearly died of typhoid, another water-borne infection, in 1871; his father, Queen Victoria's husband Prince Albert, had been killed by it in 1861. Dysentery, diarrhoea, diphtheria, whooping cough, scarlet fever, measles, and enteric fever were significant problems and frequently fatal. The death or illness of breadwinners wrecked family economies, producing or exacerbating poverty and related social problems.

Neither these, nor political discontents, however, led to revolution in 1848. There was no equivalent in Britain to the unsuccessful attempted insurrection by the Young Ireland nationalist movement. Instead, change came gradually. The year 1848 saw the Health of Towns Act, which created a General Board of Health and an administrative structure to improve sanitation, especially water supply. The new Act enabled the creation of local boards of health. The one that was constituted in Leicester in 1849 was instrumental in the creation of a sewer system and in tackling other aspects of the urban environment, such as slaughter-houses and smoke pollution. Despite its limitations and the opposition that it encountered, the Act was a definite advance in awareness of, and organisation for, public health.

THE VICTORIAN ETHOS

The contrast with the violent nature of political development on the Continent led to a measure of complacency. Having suffered from defeat and colonial rebellion in 1791–1825, Britain's colonial and maritime rivals were to be absorbed in domestic strife and Continental power politics over the following half-century. Meanwhile, as reform legislation was passed within Britain, so British imperial power spread throughout the world, and the two processes were fused as, first, self-government and, later, Dominion status were granted to the 'white colonies'. New Zealand achieved self-government in 1852, Newfoundland, New South Wales, Victoria, Tasmania and South Australia in 1855, and Queensland in 1859; while the Dominion of Canada was created in 1867.

It is scarcely surprising that an optimistic conception of British history was the dominant account. A progressive move towards liberty was discerned, a seamless web that stretched back to Magna Carta in 1215 and the constitutional struggles of the barons in medieval England, and forward to the nineteenth-century extensions of the franchise. These were seen as arising naturally from the country's development. This public myth, the Whig interpretation of history, offered a comforting and glorious account that seemed appropriate for a state that ruled much of the globe, was exporting its constitutional arrangements to other parts of the world, and could watch the convulsions on the Continent as evidence of the political backwardness of its societies and the superiority of Britain. The leading British role in the abolition of the slave trade and the emancipation of the slaves also resulted in self-righteousness and a degree of moral complacency, not least about the position of the poor in Britain, although even when there was moral concern, it was often hardly helpful to the poor.

The extension of civil rights to those outside the established Church, most obviously with the repeal of the Test and Corporation Acts in 1828 and the passing of an Act for Catholic Emancipation in 1829, could be seen as another aspect of British reason and superiority. In addition, the nineteenth century was very much a period of evangelicalism, which was by no means confined to the middle class, and this evangelicalism further encouraged a sense of national distinctiveness and mission. This sense remained pertinent into the mid-twentieth century, contributing to collectivist solutions to social welfare, but then falling victim of the rising role of the state, as well as the social liberalism of the 1960s.

The Victorians sought to provide and secure a stable civic order, based on the rule of law, through which liberties could be safeguarded, prosperity enjoyed and progress maintained. This prospect required what was seen as responsible and rational conduct and the control of emotionalism. There was confidence in the present, and faith in the future. In 1857, the painter William Bell Scott stated that 'the latest is best . . . not to believe in the 19th century, one might as well disbelieve that a child grows into a man . . . without that Faith in Time what anchor have we in any secular speculation'. His painting *The Nineteenth Century, Iron and Coal* (1861) was set in the major industrial city of Newcastle and sought to capture, as he stated, 'everything of the common labour, life and applied science of the day'. It depicted workers at Robert Stephenson's engineering works, one of the largest manufacturers of railway engines in the world, an Armstrong gun, the steam of modern communications, and telegraph wires.

ECONOMIC AND IMPERIAL CHALLENGES

However, the process of late Victorian expansion took place in a context of European competition that was far more serious, and gave rise to more concern than the position in 1815–70, worrying as that had been at times. The British economy remained very strong, and new industries, such as engineering and automobiles, developed. The pace of scientific advance and technological change was unremitting, and British scientists led in a number of fields. Michael Faraday (1791–1867), the son of a Surrey blacksmith, had discovered electromagnetic induction in 1831, making the continuous generation of electricity a possibility. His work was expanded by two Scots, James Clerk Maxwell, the first professor of experimental physics at Cambridge, and Lord Kelvin. Maxwell played a key role, being crucial to electromagnetic and light field theory. The development of commercial generators led to the growing use of electricity. New distribution and retail methods, particularly the foundation of department and chain stores, helped to create national products.

The international context was less comforting. This was due to the greater economic strength of the major Continental powers, their ability to take advantage of new technology and their determination to make colonial gains in pursuit of their own place in the sun. These combined and interacted to lead to a relative decline in British power and to produce a strong sense of disquiet in British governmental circles. The growth of German economic power posed the starkest contrast with the situation earlier in the century. The annual average output of coal and lignite in million metric tons in 1870–4 was 123 for Britain, and 41 for Germany; by 1910–14 the figures were 274 to 247. For pig-iron the annual figures changed from 7.9 and 2.7 in 1880 to 10.2 and 14.8 in 1910; for steel from 3.6 and 2.2 (1890) to 6.5 and 13.7 (1910). The number of kilometres of railway rose in Britain from 2411 (1840) to 28,846 (1880) and 38,114 (1914); in Germany the comparable figures were 469; 33,838; and 63,378. In 1900, the German population was 56.4 million, that of Britain excluding Ireland, 37 million, and including her, 41.5 million. In the Edwardian period, Britain's second most important export market, after India, was Germany.

The tremendous growth in German power posed a challenge to Britain, in whose governing circles there had been widespread support for German unification and a failure to appreciate its possible consequences. France and Russia were also developing as major economic powers, while American strength was ever more apparent in the New World and, increasingly, the Pacific. Given the importance of imperial considerations in governmental, political, and popular thinking, it is not surprising that British relations with and concern about the Continental powers registered not in disputes arising from European issues, but from differences and clashes centring on distant, but no longer obscure, points on the globe, ranging from Fashoda in the forests of the Upper Nile, to the islands of the western Pacific. French and German expansion in Africa led Britain to take counter measures: in West Africa, the occupation of the interior of the Gambia in 1887–8, the declaration of the Protectorate of Sierra Leone in 1896, the establishment of the Protectorates of Northern and Southern Nigeria in 1900, and the annexation of the Gold Coast in 1901. German moves in East Africa helped result in the establishment of British power in Uganda in the 1890s. Suspicion of

Russian designs on the Ottoman empire and French schemes in North Africa led the British to move into Egypt in order to protect the route to India. Concern about French ambitions contributed to the conquest of Mandalay (1885) and the annexation of Upper Burma; while Russia's advance across Asia resulted in attempts to strengthen and move forward the 'north-west frontier' of British India and the development of British influence in southern Persia. The Russian advance was the biggest single on-going concern of British generals from the late 1870s and posed a military challenge which they never satisfactorily resolved, until Russia's defeat by Japan solved it for them in 1905.

Specific clashes of colonial influence interacted with a more general sense of imperial insecurity. The idea of Social Darwinism, with its stress on inherent struggle as the context for progress, the survival of the fittest, had unsettling consequences in attitudes towards international relations. Pressing the case for imperial preference, Joseph Chamberlain argued in 1903 that free trade threatened Britain's economic position: 'Sugar has gone; silk has gone; iron is threatened; wool is threatened; cotton will go.' In the 1880s, there was concern about British naval weakness: in 1889 public pressure obliged the government to pass the Naval Defence Act, which sought a two-power standard, superiority over the next two largest naval powers combined. Expenditure of £21,500,000 over five years, a vast sum, was authorised. The importance of naval dominance was taken for granted. In the preface to his *History of the Foreign Policy of Great Britain* (1895), Captain Montagu Burrows RN, Professor of Modern History at Oxford, wrote of 'this fortress-isle of Britain, safely intrenched (*sic*) by stormy seas, confronting the broadest face of the Continent, and, later on, almost surrounding it with her fleets, was and was not, a part of Europe according as she willed'. The myth of national self-sufficiency peaked in these years. Naval strength was a prerequisite of such an ideal. These were the years in which the British built battleships of the class of the *Magnificent*: the first ships carrying cordite-using big guns.

By the mid-1900s, it was Germany, with its great economic strength and its search for a place in the sun, that was the principal threat. British resources and political will were tested in a major naval race between the two powers, in which the British launched HMS *Dreadnought*, the first of a new class of battleships, in 1906. It was also the first capital ship in the world to be powered by the marine turbine engine, which had been invented by Sir Charles Parsons in 1884. A projected German invasion was central to *The Riddle of the Sands* (1903), a novel by

Erskine Childers that was first planned by him in 1897, a year in which the Germans were indeed discussing such a project. Military discussions with France following the Anglo-French *entente* of 1904 were to play a major role in leading Britain towards the First World War. From 1905 Britain began to plan seriously for war with Germany and to see her as a major threat to Britain's overall future, as opposed to simply a commercial challenge and an irritant in the spread of empire.

THE VICTORIAN PRESS

The state that was taking part in this growing confrontation with imperial Germany was different from that of the early years of Victoria's reign. Britain had become more urban and more industrial. Her population was more literate and educated and was linked by modern communications and a national press. Changes in the press were symptomatic of the modernisation of the country. One of the many ways in which Victorian London was at the centre of British life and that of the British empire was in the provision of the news. Through its press, which laid claim to the title of the 'fourth estate' of the realm, London created the image and idiom of empire and shaped its opinions. Aside from this political function, the press also played a central economic, social and cultural role, setting and spreading fashions, whether of company statements or through theatre criticism. In what was increasingly a commercial society, the press played a pivotal role, inspiring emulation, setting the tone, fulfilling crucial needs for an anonymous mass-readership, and pandering to the lowest tone in the 'yellow press' of the 1880s.

The press was itself affected by change, notably by the energising and disturbing forces of commercialisation and new technology. It was to be legal reform and technological development that freed the Victorian press for major development. Newspapers had become expensive in the eighteenth century, in large part due to successive rises in stamp duty. In the mid-nineteenth century these so-called 'taxes on knowledge' were abolished: the advertisement duties in 1853, the newspaper stamp duty in 1855, and the paper duties in 1861. These steps opened up the possibility of a cheap press and that opportunity was exploited by means of a technology centred on new printing presses and the continuous rolls or 'webs' of paper that fed them. A steam press was first used, by *The Times*, in 1814, while web rotary presses were introduced in Britain from the late 1860s. Mechanical typesetting followed towards the end of the century.

New technology was expensive, but the mass readership opened up by the lower prices that could be charged after the repeal of the newspaper taxes justified the cost. The consequence was more titles and lower prices. The number of daily morning papers published in London rose from eight in 1856 to twenty-one in 1900, and of evenings from seven to eleven, while there was a tremendous expansion in the suburban press. The repeal of taxes also permitted the appearance of penny dailies. The *Daily Telegraph*, launched in 1855, led the way, and by 1888 had a circulation of 300,000. The penny press was, in turn, squeezed by the halfpenny press, the first halfpenny evening paper, the *Echo*, appearing in 1868, while halfpenny morning papers became important in the 1890s with the *Morning Leader* (1892) and the *Daily Mail* (1896), which was to become extremely successful with its bold and simple style. The *Echo* peaked at a circulation of 200,000 in 1870. The papers that best served popular tastes were the Sunday papers, *Lloyd's Weekly News*, the *News of the World* and *Reynold's Newspaper. Lloyd's*, the first British paper with a circulation of over 100,000, was selling over 600,000 weekly copies by 1879, and in 1896 rose to over a million. The Sunday papers relied on shock and titillation, drawing extensively on police-court reporting.

In comparison, an eighteenth-century London newspaper was considered a great success if it sold 10,000 copies a week (most influential papers then were weekly), and 2,000 weekly was a reasonable sale. Thus, an enormous expansion had taken place, one that matched the vitality of an imperial capital, swollen by immigration and increasingly influential as an opinion-setter within the country, not least because of the communications revolution produced by the railway and better roads. The development of the railways allowed London newspapers to increase their dominance of the English newspaper scene. Thanks to them, these papers could arrive on provincial doorsteps within hours of publication, although the provincial press remained very strong. Railways also led to the massive development of commuting into London, which provided new opportunities for newspaper sales. There was a separate Scottish national press.

REFORM

The press gave Charles Dickens (1812–70) early employment. His subsequent novels reflected many of the concerns of mid-Victorian society. Knowledge about prison conditions and other such social issues was spread by the Condition of England movement, which was linked to the cult of novels that was so strong from the 1840s. Dickens himself was a supporter of reform in fields such as capital punishment, prisons, housing and prostitution. His novel *Bleak House* (1852–3) was an indictment of the coldness of law and Church, the delays of the former and the smugness of the righteous Reverend Chadband; *Little Dorrit* (1855–7) an attack on aristocratic exclusiveness, imprisonment for debt, business fraud and the deadening bureaucracy exemplified in the Circumlocution Office.

Dickens's friend and fellow-novelist Wilkie Collins (1824–89) was criticised by the poet Algernon Swinburne for sacrificing his talent for the sake of a mission. Collins's novels indeed dealt with issues such as divorce, vivisection and the impact of heredity and environment, the last a major concern to a society influenced by the evolutionary teachings of Charles Darwin and thus, increasingly, concerned with living standards. Darwin's *The Origin of Species* (1859), which advanced the theory of evolution, aroused much attention. Concern over the state of the population led to a widespread determination to 'reform', i.e. change, popular pastimes. Leisure was to be made useful: drink was to be replaced by sport. The teetotal movement was well developed by 1833, and temperance excursions were developed by the Secretary to the South Midland Temperance Association, Thomas Cook, as the basis for an industry of leisure trips.

In the mid-nineteenth century, reform was the leading divisive issue, reform of the protectionist system and reform of the franchise. The repeal of the Corn Laws (1846) by Sir Robert Peel, Tory Prime Minister in 1834–5 and 1841–6, badly divided the Tories. It was followed by the repeal of the Navigation Acts (1849) and by Cobden's Treaty with France (1860), which cut duties on trade, as did Gladstone's free-trade budget of the same year. Free trade became a central theme of British policy.

Reform was linked to the growth of middle-class culture and consciousness in the great northern cities such as Newcastle and Leeds. The civic gospel was expressed architecturally in their grandiose town halls: Manchester's was opened in 1877. The basis of authority in such towns had moved greatly from traditional to innovative. Their newspapers played a major role in orchestrating opinion in favour of reform. Although Peelite conservatism appealed to an important segment of the middle class, the Anti-Corn-Law League was a symbol of middle-class aggression, while the scandalous mismanagement of the Crimean War (1854–6) helped to boost middle-class values of efficiency in politics at the expense of the aristocracy. This tendency was linked to the movement of Whiggism to Liberalism in the 1850s and 1860s, as, in acquiring middle-class support, the Whigs became a party fitted for the reformist middle class. Reform was central to their appeal.

More active local government was an important source and instrument of reform with, for example, the public health movement from the 1840s, the laying out of public parks, especially following the Recreation Grounds Act (1859) and the Public Health Act (1875), and the building of libraries and art galleries for workers, though much was funded by charity or public subscription. Parks and other open spaces were seen as crucial to public health in offering fresh air. Thus, Halifax opened the People's Park, paid for by Sir Francis Crossley, the MP and owner of the local carpet mills, in 1857; Leeds opened Roundhay Park in 1871; and Liverpool Corporation purchased farmland from the Earl of Sefton and in 1872 the 265-acre Sefton Park was opened, typically by a member of the royal family, the Duke of Connaught. The 1862 Highways Act enabled the combination of parishes into highway districts in order to improve the roads.

A professional police force replaced the yeomanry and the, sometimes incompetent, constables and provided a much more effective check on working-class immorality, offering a powerful weapon of middle-class cultural dominance. Scotland's first constables were appointed in 1617, but city and burgh police forces were not established until the nineteenth century, largely replacing town guards of citizens or old soldiers, although a small, but short-lived, professional police force had been established in Glasgow in 1778. The Glasgow Police Act of 1800 was the first United Kingdom Police Act, and another eleven Scottish cities and burghs established police forces under individual police Acts of Parliament before Peel's Metropolitan Police was founded. As Home Secretary in 1822–7 and 1828–30, Sir Robert Peel believed that society could survive in turbulent times only if secular authority was resolutely defended. He was a determined supporter of the death penalty, while his Metropolitan Police Act (1829) created a uniformed and paid force for London. This process was extended by Acts of 1835 and 1839, and the County and Borough Police Act (1856) made the formation of paid forces obligatory. The new police largely replaced individuals as prosecutors in cases of criminal justice in England and Wales.

The Hanoverian legal code was transformed. From the 1830s, hanging was confined to murderers and traitors, while the transportation of convicts to Australian dumping grounds ceased by the 1860s. Instead, prisons were built and reformatory regimes developed. From 1868, hanging was no longer carried out in public.

The police and judiciary served in the regimentation of society. Practices judged unacceptable, such as public drunkenness, were subject to regulation and action. The courts dealt with unacceptable beliefs that led to action that could be monitored, for example witchcraft: related crimes led to court cases, including eight in Birmingham and the Black Country in the 1860s.

The emphasis in society was on knowledge as uplifting. There was a great expansion of reading, and the expanding middle class also patronised a great upsurge in art, poetry and the performance or production of music, leading to popular art movements, notably that of the Pre-Raphaelites: William Holman Hunt, John Millais and Dante Gabriel Rossetti, who enjoyed considerable popularity from the mid-1850s. Cities such as Glasgow, Liverpool, Manchester, Leeds, Newcastle and Birmingham founded major art collections, musical institutions, such as the Halle Orchestra in Manchester (1857), and educational bodies. Civic universities were created. Mason Science College, which eventually became part of the University of Birmingham established in 1900, was founded in 1880 by Sir Josiah Martin, a self-educated manufacturer of split-rings and steel pen-nibs. He spent part of his fortune on local orphans as well as on his new foundation, which was designed to be especially useful for local industries. Men such as Martin set the tone of much of urban Victorian Britain. Their views and wealth were a tremendous stimulus to the process of improvement, civic and moral, in origins an eighteenth-century idea that was so central to the movement for reform.

Reform, however, did not only originate with the middle class. After Chartism failed and hopes of gaining political citizenship for the working class receded, there was a resurgence of interest in building up its own institutions, such as co-operatives and friendly societies (self-help sick and burial clubs), and in schemes for the improvement of the moral and physical condition of the working people through education and temperance. The Victorian age also witnessed the reform of most institutions, including the Church of England and public schools. Rational organisation, meritocratic conduct and moral purpose were the goals.

NINETEENTH-CENTURY IRELAND

The Union of 1801 ensured that the politics of Ireland were far more closely linked with those of Britain than heretofore. It is possible to write a brief survey of Ireland in this period centred on hardship and discord: the potato famine of 1845–8 and the struggle for Irish political autonomy. Both were of great importance. Yet, it is also important to recall that other themes can be advanced. Ireland remained within the empire, largely speaking English, there was no collapse into anarchy or civil war, and the Irish economy grew as part of the expanding imperial economy, although the canal network was less extensive than in Britain and the railway system was established more slowly. Belfast developed as a great port and with manufacturing industry based on linen, ship-yards and tobacco. Its expansion, however, saw the development of patterns of urban segregation based on religion.

Throughout Ireland, the closing decades of the century brought economic and social change, commercialisation, anglicisation and the dismantling of landlord power, and by 1914, Ireland had gained a large share of its economic independence. Thanks to legislation in 1860, 1870, 1881, 1885, 1891 and 1903, landlords were obliged to settle the land question largely on their tenants' terms, and farmers increasingly owned their holdings. The position of the Catholic Church markedly improved. For example, in Kildare a convent was established, soon followed by a church and schools, and, in 1889, a magnificent Catholic Gothic church whose spire dominated the town was opened. Ireland was more closely linked to Britain by economic interdependence and the rapid communi-cations offered by railways and steamships, but its Catholic areas were at the same time becoming more socially and culturally distinct.

The reform process that characterised Britain was matched in Ireland. Thus, for example, through the Municipal Corporation (Ireland) Act of 1843, elected municipal commissioners replaced the traditional town governments, which had often been characterised by oligarchy and corruption. The Irish Local Government Act of 1898 brought to Ireland the system of elected local councils introduced in England by Acts of 1888 and 1894. Thus, alongside the far greater peasant proprietorship stemming from land legislation, local government was also transferred to the control of the largely Catholic bulk of the population. Landlords were a declining power economically and politically.

In Ulster, the position of landlords also declined, but, because of the power of local Unionists (unlike in the South, where Unionists were few), they managed to retain a foothold in politics. This, however, was shaky. The Belfast and East Ulster business classes took over the leadership of the Ulster Unionists from 1906, a year after the formation of the Ulster Unionist Council, and, although the landlords were a presence and had some influence, they were not a major force.

Nineteenth-century Ireland also had an important and growing nationalist movement. Part was violent, mounting terrorist attacks in Britain, Ireland and elsewhere. The Fenians, a secret organisation founded in 1858, tried to launch a rebellion in Ireland in 1867 and were responsible for terrorist acts in Britain and for an attempted invasion of Canada from the United States. Reconstituted as the Irish Republican Brotherhood in 1873, they continued to mount terrorist attacks, and in 1882 another secret society, the Invincibles, murdered Lord Frederick Cavendish, the Chief Secretary for Ireland, in Phoenix Park, Dublin, leading to new measures designed to maintain order. Some Irishmen served with the Boers in South Africa against the British army.

Most Irish nationalism, however, was non-violent. Daniel O'Connell organised a party that in the 1830s and 1840s campaigned for the repeal of the Act of Union. The government responded by attempts to improve the lot of the population through reform and by firm action aimed at limiting extra-parliamentary agitation. The extension of the franchise in 1867 and 1884 greatly increased the number of Catholic voters, and most of them supported Home Rule, which would have left an Irish Parliament and government in control of all bar defence and foreign policy. The Home Government Association of 1870 was followed by the Home Rule League (1873). Charles Parnell (1846–91) became leader of the MPs pressing for Home Rule in 1879, and this group became an organised and powerful parliamentary party with sixty-one MPs in 1880, and eighty-six in 1885. Their role in Parliament helped ensure that Home Rule came to play a major role in the political agenda.

IRISH MIGRATION

Earlier migration across the Irish Sea and to North America swelled in the mid-1840s as the potato blight drove hundreds of thousands to flee. The potato played a major role in feeding the expanding population of the early nineteenth century, in part because animal husbandry was uneconomic on Irish smallholdings; but reliance on one crop and over-population created a vulnerable situation. Crop blight began in 1845, and the 1846 and 1848 crops were disastrous. About 800,000 people died as a result of starvation or diseases made more virulent by malnutrition. The government's attempts to bring relief were of little effect. Thanks also to emigration, mostly to the USA, the Irish population fell by 2–2¼ million. Migration was helped subsequently by the introduction of steamships which cut the time needed to cross the Atlantic from six weeks in the 1850s to one in 1914. Migration was one of the defining factors in the Irish experience in the nineteenth century.

As a result of immigration, the Irish-born population of England and Wales rose to 602,000 in 1861, about 3 per cent of the total population. The equivalent statistics for Scotland in 1851 were 207,000 or 7 per cent. The impact was increased by concentration in a few cities, such as Glasgow, where 23.3 per cent of the adult population in 1851 were Irish-born; London, where the Irish were 5 per cent of the population in 1861; and Liverpool, where the percentage was near 25. Other port cities, such as Portsmouth and Plymouth, also had many migrants. Irish migration into Britain peaked in around 1860, declined until about 1870, rose again until 1877, and then fell until the end of the century.

Overwhelmingly poor, and attractive as labour precisely because they were paid badly, the Irish migrants lived in the areas of cheapest rent, which were invariably the most crowded and least sanitary. Thus, in Newcastle, where the percentage of Irish-born migrants rose from 5.73 of the population in 1841 to 8.02 in 1851, the majority were housed in poor living conditions in areas such as Sandgate. The men were generally employed as labourers or in other casual employment, the women as washerwomen, flower sellers or other poorly paid jobs. In Glasgow, the majority of Irish immigrants did not gain jobs offering reasonable pay, conditions and status, and their position contrasted with that of migrants from the Scottish Highlands. However, an appreciable number of Irish immigrants emerged into the middle class.

Irish migrants focused and exacerbated anti-Catholic feelings, and sometimes undercut native workers, as in the Lanarkshire coalfield in Scotland where they were used for strike breaking and wage reductions. In 1850, thanks to their acceptance of lower wages, they took over hoeing from women near Dunfermline, leading to an anti-Irish riot there in which migrants were brutally driven out. However, outside Lancashire, such a violent response was unusual. Moreover, many Irish immigrants did not live in ghettos but were dispersed across working-class areas, and a certain number 'married out'.

GLADSTONE AND DISRAELI

Middle-class interests and views increasingly set the legislative agenda in late nineteenth-century Britain, although aristocratic influences on policymaking remained strong. The Second Reform Act, passed by a minority Tory government (1867), nearly doubled the existing electorate and, by offering household suffrage, gave the right to vote to about 60 per cent of adult males in boroughs.

The Liberal victory in the following general election (1868) led to the first government of William Gladstone, who pushed through a whole series of reforms, including the disestablishment of the Irish Church, the loss of the special position of the (Protestant) Church of Ireland, in 1869, and the introduction of open competition in the civil service (1870), and of the secret ballot (1872), both the latter attacks on patronage. Bank holidays were created in 1871, providing holidays with pay, and thus more leisure time for the workforce. In 1872, the powers of turnpike trusts were ended and road maintenance was placed totally under public control. Again replacing private patrons by a paternalist state, the 1870 Education Act divided the country into school districts and required a certain level of educational provision, introducing the school district in cases where existing parish provision was inadequate. The provisions of the Act were resisted, as in Ealing where tenacious efforts by the Church of England to protect voluntary education and block the introduction of public board schools, ignoring the implications of rapid population growth, left 500 children unschooled twenty-five years after the Act. The end of long-established distinctions, variations and privileges played a major role in the reform process. The Endowed Schools Commission established in 1870 redistributed endowments and reformed governing bodies. The Church of England underwent a similar change.

Driven by a sense of providential agency, Gladstone was a formidable and multifaceted individual of great determination and integrity, a Classical scholar and theological controversialist, a hewer of trees and a rescuer of prostitutes. He had a library of 20,000 books. A Tory Treasury minister in the 1830s, he became the leading Liberal politician of the age, committed to reform at home and a moral stance abroad, both aims joined in a conviction that religion was a key element and purpose of government and politics. Gladstone's writings included his books *The State in its Relations with the Church* and *Church Principles Considered in their Results*. His political skills bridged the worlds of

Parliament and of public meetings, for, under his leadership, Liberalism became a movement enjoying mass support. Gladstone appealed from Parliament to the public and sought to gain mass support for his politics of action and reform.

The Tories or, as they were now called, Conservatives, came to power again in 1874 under Benjamin Disraeli, an opportunist and skilful political tactician who was also an acute thinker, able to create an alternative political culture and focus of popular support around the themes of national identity and pride, and social cohesion, that challenged Liberal moral certainty. Legislation on factories (1874), public health, artisans' dwellings, and pure food and drugs (1875) systematised and extended the regulation of important aspects of social welfare. The Factory Acts of 1874 and 1878 limited work hours for women and children in industry. The Prison Act (1877) established central government control. These were, however, less important for Disraeli than his active foreign policy which involved the purchase of shares in the Suez Canal (1875), designed to secure British control over the new short route to India; the creation of the title of Empress of India for Victoria (1876); the acquisition of Cyprus (1878); and wars with the Afghans (1878–9) and Zulus (1879).

Economic difficulties, stemming from agrarian depression and a fall in trade, and political problems, skilfully exploited by Gladstone in his electioneering Midlothian campaigns (1879–80), led to Conservative defeat in the 1880 election. Imperial and Irish problems, however, affected Gladstone's second government (1880–5), with the unsuccessful First Boer War (1880–1) in South Africa, the occupation of Egypt (1882–3), the massacre of General Gordon and his force at Khartoum (1885), and the Coercion Act designed to restore order in Ireland (1881). In 1884 the Third Reform Act extended to the counties the household franchise granted to the boroughs in 1867, so that over two-thirds of the adult males in the counties, and about 63 per cent of the entire adult male population, received the vote. As in 1868, the Conservatives were defeated, in 1885, in the first election held with the new franchise: many rural electors voted against their landlords.

The process of reform, both political and social, continued with the Redistribution of Seats Act (1885), which revised the electoral map; the Local Government Act (1888), creating directly elected county councils and county boroughs, and the London County Council; and the Workmen's Compensation Act (1897), obliging employers to provide compensation for industrial accidents. A collectivist state was developing, and in some respects it looked towards the later welfare state. State intervention in education helped in the decline of illiteracy. Greater social intervention by the new, more formal and responsive, mechanisms of local government encouraged a general expectation of state intervention in the life of the people, especially in health, education and housing.

The political situation was, however, complicated by the consequences of the economic downturn of the 1870s, by uncertainties stemming from the expansion of the electorate, and by the longstanding malaise over the Irish question. Fenian terrorism in Ireland, England and Canada led to casualties, and there was both pressure for land reform and agitation for Home Rule for Ireland. Proposals for Home Rule, introduced by Gladstone, were defeated in 1886 and 1893 at Westminster, where they helped to divide politicians. Conservatives led the resistance, and the Conservative Party changed its name to the Unionist Party in 1886, but the defeat of the First Home Rule Bill in 1886 was due to the defection of ninety-three 'Liberal Unionists' from Gladstone's third government. Home Rule split the Liberals, not the first nor the last occasion when Ireland was of great significance for British politics. In Easter 1887 Gladstone wrote in his diary, 'now one prayer absorbs all others: Ireland, Ireland, Ireland'.

The political hegemony of the Liberals, who had returned to office in January 1886 after a brief Conservative ministry, was destroyed that July, as the Conservatives, under Robert Cecil, 3rd Marquess of Salisbury, won the general election. Though the Liberals, still under Gladstone, now elderly, half-blind and half-deaf, won the 1892 election, the Conservatives dominated the period 1886–1905 with the support of the Liberal Unionists. Salisbury (Prime Minister 1885–6, 1886–92, 1895–1902) and his successor and nephew, Arthur Balfour (1902–5), opposed Home Rule and followed a cautious policy on domestic reform. The cultural basis of Liberalism was under challenge and the mix of Conservative policies, attitudes and resonances were more attractive to the electorate. In 1900, Liberalism lost its overall majority of Scottish seats for the first time since 1832. Salisbury, a Marquess and owner of Hatfield House, one of the palaces the British domesticate as 'stately homes', derived most of his disposable income from urban property, including London slums. Two-thirds of his Cabinet were peers, although it did nothing to advance the landed interest other than not passing budgets like the Liberal one of 1894 which had greatly increased death duties. Salisbury's government was nicknamed 'Hotel

Cecil' as it contained so many Cecil family members. When his nephew Arthur Balfour became Chief Secretary for Ireland in 1887, this gave rise to the expression 'Bob's [Robert's] your uncle'. In 1894, Gladstone was succeeded as Liberal leader and Prime Minister by Archibald, 5th Earl of Rosebery, whose landed wealth had been enhanced by marriage to the Rothschild heiress.

There was also, however, growing pressure for more radical political and social policies. Political opinion began increasingly to coalesce and polarise along social and class lines. The landed interest largely broke from the Liberals after 1886. Joseph Chamberlain's 'unauthorised' Liberal programme of 1885 called for land reform and was followed in 1891 by Gladstone's Newcastle programme which also called for Home Rule, Welsh and Scottish disestablishment, free education, a reduction in factory work-hours, electoral reform and the reform or abolition of the House of Lords. That year, the Scottish Liberals pressed for land reform in the Highlands, an eight-hour day for miners and an extension of the franchise. The social order could be harsh as well as inegalitarian. In 1891, Tom Masters, a 13-year-old Northamptonshire farm labourer, was whipped by his employer for insolence. However, calls for a more radical Liberalism led to accusations that Liberalism was increasingly a threat to stability and a product of sectional interests. This pressure encouraged an opposing coalescence of opinion in defence of property and order in the shape of the Conservatives.

NINETEENTH-CENTURY WALES

Developments in Wales serve as a valuable prism through which wider processes can be understood. Growth there became more sustained from the 1790s and was also increasingly concentrated in coal- and iron-rich south Wales. The production of pig-iron there rose from 5,000 tons in 1720 to 525,000 by 1840; 36 per cent of the British total. The tremendous industrial expansion in Monmouthshire and east Glamorgan, at for example Ebbw Vale and Merthyr Tydfil, created numerous jobs and helped lead to a permanent demographic shift; the growth in the south Wales coalfield was also important. Welsh coal was suited for coking for iron furnaces and for steamships, and Welsh anthracite coal was ideal for the hot-blast process for the iron and steel industry. Production (in million tons) rose from 1.2 in 1801 to 13.6 by 1870, and 57 by

1913. The majority was exported and the coal industry employed about a third of the Welsh male labour force. The development of the port of Cardiff by the 3rd Marquess of Bute, and the spread of the railways, especially the Taff Vale line between Cardiff and Merthyr Tydfil (1841), permitted the movement of large quantities of coal. Cardiff's population rose from 10,000 in 1841 to 200,000 in 1921; that of the coalmining Rhondda from under 1,000 in 1851 to 153,000 in 1911. Glamorgan and Monmouthshire had about 20 per cent of the Welsh population in 1801, but 57.5 per cent in 1901 and 60.5 per cent from 1921.

Economic and demographic growth in the industrial regions led to a decline in the relative importance of agriculture and rural Wales, and played a major role in the reorientation in the standard images of Welshness. Anglicans became outnumbered and the growth of Dissent played a major role in reshaping Wales culturally and politically. In place of the dominance of conservative Anglican gentry, the Liberal Party, based on Nonconformity, was dominant from 1868 to 1918.

Industrialisation was not achieved without traumatic change, and the work that was required of people was back-breaking, dangerous and alienating. Even so, and in spite of the fact that it was a process of transformation from without, largely by wealthy English people, indus-trialisation met with relatively little violent resistance. Nevertheless, Merthyr Tydfil, the centre of early industrialisation, had a full range of industrial disputes in the early decades of the century, with particular bitterness in 1831. The Merthyr Rising collapsed in the face of military action and its own divisions, but at least twenty rioters were killed. In 1839, a Chartist rising of over 5,000 men in Newport was stopped when a small group of soldiers opened fire and the rioters dispersed.

Also in 1839, the Rebecca Riots began in south-west Wales. The tollgates that handicapped the rural economy were attacked. The riots persisted until 1844 and extended their targets to include attacks on unfair rents and workhouses. 'Mother Rebecca', the symbolic leader of the protests, with a white gown and red or black face, was named from the Rebecca of Genesis, 'possessing the gates of those which hate them'. The 293 crowd attacks on tollgates in 1838–44 reflected considerable social alienation, the product of the industrial depression of 1839–42, the inflation of land rents during the Napoleonic Wars, and hostility to landlords, church tithes and the loss of common land through the widespread enclosures of 1750–1815, as well as to the high charges of the turnpike trusts. Hostility was also expressed by poaching and arson.

The Rebecca disturbances faded after an Act of 1844 replaced turnpike trusts with highway boards in south Wales, but the following decades saw a series of serious coal strikes in Glamorgan. Nevertheless, it is necessary to put this militancy in context. Strikes were a natural response to a poorly regulated industry. What is more obvious is that the revolutionary sentiment that did exist did not lead to a full-blown revolution. There was nothing to compare with the Year of Revolutions (1848) on the Continent. Troops from the garrison at Brecon did play an important role in a number of disputes, but the number of regular troops in south Wales in 1839 was only raised to 1,000. This scarcely compared with Habsburg (Austrian) forces in Hungary and Italy. Far from south Wales being 'held down', revolutionary sentiment was limited, while most industrial disputes were restricted to specific grievances. There was only a limited sense of worker solidarity and it was unusual for agitation to be far-reaching. Trade unionism emerged only slowly.

Political pressures, however, are not only expressed through violence. The new socio-economic order created through industrialisation was one that sat ill with traditional hierarchies, allegiance and practices. Industrialisation, moreover, brought great demands for labour, particularly in the coalfields and iron works of south and north-east Wales. Initially, most of the necessary labour came from rural Wales, easing rural poverty, although an appreciable Irish contingent also settled in Merthyr Tydfil, Swansea and Cardiff. The consequence is that the Catholic Church is important in modern South Wales. From the 1850s large numbers of English immigrants settled in south Wales; 11 per cent of Swansea's population in 1861 had been born in south-west England. Wales, indeed, was unusual in Europe in having a net immigration rate in the nineteenth century. The immigrants had no commitment to Welsh culture, which was anyway in a state of flux in the rapidly industrialising regions. As a result, the Welsh language came to be of far less consequence in the areas of Wales that were increasingly the centres of economic power and political representation; although over half the population of Wales still spoke Welsh in 1901, while industrial towns like Merthyr and Swansea were the most important centres for Welsh culture throughout the nineteenth century.

It was not only thanks to immigration, however, that the Welsh language became less widely used. The use of English was encouraged by members of the emerging middle class. Gentry landowners were commonly English-speaking, but they had less of a linguistic impact than groups that were becoming more important, as the economy of all of

Wales was affected by economic growth and integration: cattle dealers and drovers, merchants, shopkeepers, master mariners. English was the language of commerce, the language in which financial records were kept. It was also the language in which the elite was educated.

As the use of English became more common, it also became more politically charged, a consequence in part of debates over the role and nature of public education. Furthermore, in the second half of the century, language came to play a role in a powerful political critique directed against Conservative landowners and the Anglican Church and in favour of Liberalism and Nonconformity, both of which were presented as truly Welsh. There was a parallel with the Irish Home Rule movement and the late nineteenth-century Gaelic cultural revival.

There was a greater interest in Welsh cultural history and identity, a growth in Welsh poetry, the development of choral singing and, in 1858, two years after the Welsh national anthem was composed, the 'revival' of the *eisteddfod*. A range of new institutions, from St David's College, Lampeter (1822) and University College Aberystwyth (1872) on, testified to a stronger sense of national identity, the institutionalisation of which created bodies that had an interest in its furtherance and that provided a vital platform and focus for those seeking to assert Welsh identities. Both the National Library and the National Museum were authorised by royal charter in 1907.

In political terms the assertion of Welsh identities was largely represented by Liberalism. With David Lloyd George, Chancellor of the Exchequer 1908–15 and Prime Minister 1916–22, Welsh liberalism reached the apex of political power, but, as later with the Scot Ramsay MacDonald and Labour, this was as part of a British political consciousness. The key Welsh issues of the late nineteenth century – land reform, disestablishment and public education – could be presented in radical Liberal terms and thus incorporated in British politics. Agitation over rents and tithes led to riots, particularly in 1887, but landlords were not shot: the Welsh wished to differentiate themselves from the more bitter contemporary agitation in Ireland.

NINETEENTH-CENTURY SCOTLAND

Much of Europe was inspired by nationalism, or, depending on one's perspective, suffered from it in the nineteenth century. Multinational empires, particularly Austro-Hungary and Russia, were challenged by the rise of nationalist politics and the same was true for Britain in Ireland and India. Yet in Scotland this was less the case, largely because of Scottish identification with the idea of Britain and the benefits of the British empire. At the same time, Scottish distinctiveness is lost in a unitary British approach. Scotland functioned in many respects separately in developing education, police and technology.

Yet, Scotland was affected by the same trends as England and Wales, not least the industrialisation, migration and urbanisation that reflected the development of coal-based industries and the new technology of steam. Thus steamships and the railway ended such centuries-old practices as droving (the driving of animals), while regions lacking coal, such as most of south-west Scotland, saw only limited growth. By 1861 the majority of the population were living in towns. Scotland was a powerhouse of innovation and entrepreneurs.

Industrial growth was particularly rapid from the 1830s and was especially concentrated in Strathclyde, where it led to a major growth of population, largely due to migration from the countryside. Glasgow's population grew from 77,385 in 1801 to 274,533 in 1841, despite annual average death rates of 33 per 1,000 in 1835–9, the highest in Scotland. Thanks to industrialisation, the percentage of the Scottish population in the central belt rose from nearly 40 in 1755 and nearly 50 in 1821 to 80 today. Edinburgh and Glasgow were linked by railway in 1841, and the railway provided Scotland with a network of rapid land communication to match coastal shipping. Service industries also developed, especially banking and life assurance in Edinburgh, which emerged as a major financial centre. By the mid-nineteenth century, fewer than 10 per cent of those employed in the central-belt counties of Lanarkshire, Midlothian and Renfrewshire worked in agriculture, forestry and fishing. Despite a very high rate of emigration, Scotland's population as a whole rose from 1,265,380 in 1755 and 1,608,000 in 1801 to 4,472,103 in 1901. Economic growth encouraged immigration, mostly from Ireland.

As in England, urbanisation and poverty led to serious social problems. Dundee, for example, which, on the basis of imports of raw material from India, became the leading jute-working city in the world, suffered from slums, disease and high infant mortality. Glasgow was hit by a serious outbreak of cholera in 1832, and of typhus in 1817–18 and 1837.

Change also pressed in more remote areas. Most of the population of the Highlands and Islands became bilingual in English and Gaelic.

Gaelic alone was spoken only by a minority in the north-west and the northern Hebrides. The sentimentalised Highland landscape helped to bring the area to the attention of the outside world. Tourism flourished. In 1864 the original fort at Fort William was demolished to make room for the railway station through which English tourists reached the Highlands. Socially there had been a major shift in the region. The clan system had declined during the eighteenth century, to be replaced by a more aggressively commercial attitude towards land tenure, social relations and economic activity, helping to lead to extensive emigration. After the Napoleonic Wars, the labour-intensive economy, in which fishing, military employment and illicit whisky-making had played a major role, was replaced by a more capital-intensive economy based on sheep-ranching, which required less labour. Most of the Highland population possessed no secure and long-term legal rights to land, and were therefore easily displaced in the 'clearances'. As in Ireland, there was a serious potato famine in the Highlands in the late 1840s. Hunger led to migration from the Highlands and Islands, a policy encouraged by landowners who did not wish to bear the burden of supporting the poor. Large numbers moved within Britain, but also to North America. Nearly two million Scots emigrated there and to Australasia.

Those who remained reacted with increasing bitterness to the effects of change. In part the clearances were for leisure purposes: by 1884, 1.98 million acres, over 10 per cent of Scottish land, were reserved for deer, and thus the hunting interests of a small minority. In the 1880s, crofting MPs, opposed to clearances, won five seats in northern Scotland, while the 'Battle of the Braes' in Skye grew more intense. There was an Irish-type resistance to clearing: the Land League, modelled on the Irish Land League, had 15,000 members by 1884. The crisis led to the Napier commission and the Crofters' Holding Act of 1886 which established crofting rights and ended the major phase of the clearances. This resistance is now memorialised with commemorative monuments.

The nineteenth century saw the development of a sense of Scottishness centring on a re-emergent cultural identity that did not involve any widespread demand for independence: kilts and literary consciousness but no Home Rule party. The religious dimension, so obvious in Ireland, was lacking. Furthermore, the Highland peasantry were being evicted by their clan chiefs, rather than by English absentees. The National Association for the Vindication of Scottish Rights was launched in 1853: 2,000 people came to its first meeting at Edinburgh; 5,000 in Glasgow. The Association strongly urged Scottish rights, including administrative devolution and Cabinet-level representation, but was not explicitly nationalist. Later, some Scottish nationalists, such as Theodore Napier, identified with the Boers. The Scottish Patriotic Association, the Scottish Home Rule Association (SHRA), and other bodies all played a role in the development of a stronger sense of political separateness. The SHRA regarded the exerting of pressure on the most sympathetic political party as the best political strategy. In place of the notion of North Britain, which was rejected by the late nineteenth century, that of Scotland returned, although it was an increasingly anglicised Scotland. The Secretaryship for Scotland was restored in 1885.

WOMEN IN THE NINETEENTH CENTURY

Industrial urban society served women little better than rural society had done. Women were affected by social and ecological challenges similar to those of men, but they also faced additional problems. Like most men, most women had to cope with gruelling labour and debilitating diseases, but their legal position was worse, a reflection of a culture that awarded control and respect to men, and left little role for female merit or achievement. The restrictive nature of the work available to women and the confining implications of family and social life together defined the existence of the vast majority of women.

A large proportion of the working classes lived together out of wedlock. Social and economic pressures helped to drive women towards co-habiting or marriage and also, whether they were unmarried or married, towards employment. Co-habitation or marriage offered most women a form of precarious stability. The marital prospects of unmarried mothers were low, with the significant exception of widows with children of a first marriage, particularly if they possessed some property. As a result, single women often resorted to abortion, which was both treated as a crime and hazardous to health, while unmarried mothers often became prostitutes or were treated as such. The absence of an effective social welfare system and the low wages paid to most women ensured that prostitution, either full- or part-time, was the fate of many. Part-time prostitution was related to economic conditions.

Women, single, co-habiting and married, suffered from the generally limited and primitive nature of contraceptive practices. Frequent childbirth was exhausting, and many women died giving birth, ensuring that many children were brought up by stepmothers. Near the apex of society, Joseph Chamberlain's first two wives died in childbirth, leaving him with responsibility for six children. Female pelvises were often distorted by rickets during malnourished childhoods, while there was no adequate training in midwifery. As a result, obstetric haemorrhages were poorly managed and often fatal. It was not until the introduction of sulphonamides after 1936 that mortality figures fell substantially. Birth control was, however, developing: in Scotland marital fertility declined appreciably between 1881 and 1901.

Women often did very arduous jobs, such as coal-carrying in the mines, or work in the fields. In 1851, 229,000 women were employed in agriculture, but this number fell to 67,000 in 1901 in large part due to the agricultural depression. A common form of work, the largest category of female employment in Wales in 1911, was domestic service. Household tasks, such as cleaning and drying clothes, involved much effort. It was possible in the hierarchy of service to gain promotion, but, in general, domestic service was unskilled and not a career. Wages were poor and pay was largely in kind, which made life very hard for those who wished to marry and leave service. The working conditions, however, were generally better and less hazardous than in the factories of the age, where repetitive work for many hours was expected.

Women from the social elite came to have more opportunities. In 1796, Anderson's Institution in Glasgow admitted women to its classes, and a group round John Anderson were strong advocates of women's education. Subsequently, higher education for women began in both Cambridge and Oxford, though they were not permitted to take degrees for many years. At Aberdeen University it was formally agreed in 1892 that women be admitted to all faculties, but none studied law or divinity, they were not offered equivalent teaching in medicine, and there was unequal access to the Bursary Competition. Women students took no positions of influence and the student newspaper, *Alma Mater*, was hostile, presenting them as unfeminine or flighty and foolish: the men clearly found it difficult to adjust to female students, although their numbers and influence increased in the 1900s and especially during the First World War. Indeed, by 1939, nearly a quarter of British university students were women.

The general notion of equality was one of respect for separate functions and development, and the definition of the distinctive nature of the ideal female condition was one that, by modern standards, certainly did not entail equality. Women's special role was defined as that of home and family, and was used to justify their exclusion from other spheres.

To a certain extent, such issues were meaningless for most women because their economic conditions and the nature of medical knowledge and attention ensured that their circumstances were bleak.

At the same time it is important to notice nuances and shifts: it is only from the misleading perspective of hindsight that Victorian society and culture appears as a monolith. Recent work, for example, has re-evaluated notions of Victorian sexuality in order to suggest that the image of universal repression was misleading, not least in Queen Victoria's own enjoyment of sex. However, while sexual pleasure was given generally discreet approval within marriage, it was harshly treated, in the case of women, outside it. Thus some workhouses made 'disorderly and profligate women' wear distinctive yellow clothes, though the practice was stopped in the 1840s. The Foundling Hospital in London, founded in 1741 to deal with abandoned babies, only accepted in the nineteenth century infants from mothers who could prove that they had had sex against their will or on promise of marriage and were otherwise of irreproachable conduct, a policy designed to exclude prostitutes, who were a large group.

Industrialisation ensured that more, predominantly single, women worked in factories, although it reduced rural opportunities, such as spinning. Women generally moved into the low-skill, low-pay 'sweated' sector as they were denied access to the new technologies. Female factory workers were generally worse treated than men, a practice in which the trade unions (which were male organisations) cooperated with the management. Both condemned the women woollen workers of Batley and Dewsbury for organising themselves in a dispute in 1875. Definitions of skills, which affected pay, were controlled by men and favoured them; skilled women, such as the weavers of Preston or Bolton, were poorly recognised. In contrast, women in the pottery industry were able to maintain status and pay despite male opposition.

A potentially important change was the institution of divorce proceedings in 1857. Before the 1857 Act, divorce required a private Act of Parliament, a very difficult process only open to the wealthy, or a separation achieved through the ecclesiastical courts, which did not allow remarriage. Even after the Act, divorce still remained costly and therefore not a possibility for the poor. As a result, former practices of 'self-divorce' continued, while co-habitation was another option, though offering most women no economic security. Women suffered because marital desertions were generally a matter of men leaving, with the women bearing the burden of supporting the children: poverty made some men heedless of the Victorian cult of the family and patriarchy. This cult was strengthened by the belief that the Home was the key way to maintain morality. Meanwhile, successive extensions of the franchise did not bring the vote to women, though they were socially less dependent than is generally assumed and than their legal situation might suggest.

THE RISE OF TRADE UNIONISM

Pressures for social reform from within the Liberal Party were supplemented in the late nineteenth century by the development of more explicitly working-class movements, both political and industrial. Early trade unions tended to have an origin in the skilled crafts and to focus on sectional interests. In protecting the right of their members against others, there was, in fact, only slow growth towards trade-union unity.

Nevertheless, the rise of trade unions reflected the growing industrialisation and unification of the economy, the growth of larger concerns employing more people, and, by the end of the century, a new, more adversarial and combative working-class consciousness. Trade unionism, in turn, contributed to the politicisation of much of the workforce, although many trade unionists were not political activisits. The Trades Union Congress (TUC), a federation of trade unions, began in 1868. Unionism spread from the skilled craft section to semi-skilled and unskilled workers, and there were major strikes in the London gasworks and docks in 1888–9.

The 1890s were a crucial decade in the definition of 'mass' unionism. Keir Hardie, Secretary of the Scottish Miners' Federation, founded the Scottish Labour Party (1888) and the Independent Labour Party (1893). The latter pressed for an eight-hour day and 'collective ownership of means of production, distribution and exchange'. Six years later, the Trades Union Congress advocated an independent working-class political organisation, which led in 1900 to the formation of the Labour Representation Committee, the basis of the Labour Party. Some working-class militants looked to a Marxist tradition: the Social-Democratic Federation pioneered the development of socialism in the 1880s and was Britain's first avowedly Marxist party. However, the TUC was relatively slow to develop and never really operated as a unified body until the 1920s when the General Council was formed (1921) with the power to call on member unions to bring out their members in a strike.

LATE VICTORIAN SOCIETY

The rise of trade unions was one of the developments that helped cause and reflected a situation of sustained doubt, if not a crisis of confidence, in late Victorian society. This society did not seem beneficent to the growing numbers who were gaining the vote and becoming more politically aware; while many commentators were concerned about the relative weakness of Britain, economically and politically, compared with the leading Continental states. British industries no longer benefited from cheaper raw materials, energy and labour. Foreign competition was responsible for closures, as in 1901 of the Tudhoe ironworks in County Durham which employed 1,500 men. There was less confidence that British institutions and practices were best. In the 1890s and early 1900s, there was much interest in the German educational system, and much envy of its 'practical' orientation. The Marquess of Salisbury was not alone in being pessimistic about the future of the empire. These varied strands of disquiet were to lead to fresh pressure for reform and new political divisions in the period up to the First World War.

The British could take pride in the spread of empire and the triumphalism of Queen Victoria's Gold and Diamond Jubilees in 1887 and 1897, but the domestic divisions of the first half of the century, which had diminished or disappeared in its prosperous third quarter, were re-emerging, taking on new forms, and being accentuated by fresh sources of tension. Economic change brought significant levels of social disruption.

There was also persistent and justified concern about the 'state of the nation'. Infant mortality rates were high: in the mining communities of north-east England, half the total deaths occurred in the range 0–5 years, and a high proportion in the range 5–15. Many families lived in only one room: about 7,840 out of the 20,000 in Newcastle in 1854. In 1866, 43 per cent of the city's population was still living in dwellings of only one or two rooms; in 1885, 30.6 per cent. Furthermore, industrial pollution was a serious problem there and elsewhere. Gastro-intestinal disorders linked to inadequate water and sewerage systems were responsible for Bradford's very high infant mortality rate. More generally, the supply of fresh cow's milk became badly infected in the 1880s and 1890s, leading to a serious increase in diarrhoea in inner cities in hot weather and a rise in infant mortality in the 1890s, especially as the practice of breast feeding decreased. In the Irish town of Kildare, although the water supply was improved in 1886, no adequate sewerage system was installed until 1900. Much of the town's population continued to live in thatched-roofed one-room cabins with overcrowding, lack of privacy and poor refuse disposal.

Poor urban sanitation, housing and nutrition were blamed for the physical weakness of much of the population. The army found this a serious problem at the time of the Boer War and the First World War, the Metropolitan Police thought their London recruits physically weak, and defeats at the hands of the visiting New Zealand All Blacks rugby team in 1905 led to discussion about a supposed physical and moral decline arising from the country's urban and industrial nature. The social surveys of Charles Booth in east London in the late 1880s and of Seebohm Rowntree in York in 1899 revealed that over a quarter of their population were living below what they saw as the level of poverty. There was also concern at the apparent extent of atheism among the urban working classes, while some politicians, such as Winston Churchill, emphasised the threat to imperial stability allegedly posed by social distress within Britain, and advocated reform as the best means of defence. William Booth had already founded the East London Revival Society in 1865, and in 1878 it was reorganised as the Salvation Army. The Boy Scout movement was launched by Robert Baden-Powell in 1908 in order to occupy and to revive the martial vigour of the nation's youth. The movement rapidly became a national institution.

Government action was another response. 'We are all Socialists nowadays', declared Sir William Harcourt, Liberal Chancellor of the Exchequer, in a speech at the Mansion House in 1895. He was referring to the creation of public utilities, 'gas and water socialism', and to the concern for social welfare that was such an obvious feature of late Victorian values and that played a role in the amelioration of living conditions, especially the decline of epidemic disease. Urban and rural sanitary authorities and their districts responsible for the maintenance of sewers and highways were inaugurated in England and Wales by the 1872 Public Health Act following the recommendations of the report of the Sanitary Commission (1871). These districts were based on town councils and existing local boards of health in urban areas and on boards of guardians in rural areas. The Rating and Local Government Act of 1871 set up the central machinery, viz, the local government board. In respect of the local machinery of rural and urban sanitary authorities, the Public Health Act of 1875 was a consolidating measure. The Public Health (Scotland) Act of 1867 established the appointment of sanitary inspectors.

Meanwhile, the supply of clean water was improved or begun and London at last acquired a sewerage system appropriate for the capital of a modern empire. From 1859, under the direction of the determined but effective Joseph Bazalgette, Chief Engineer to the Metropolitan Commissioner of Sewers (a body established in 1847), an effective drainage system was finally constructed. Fully completed in 1875, this pioneering system contained 82 miles of intercepting sewers. These took sewage from earlier pipes that had drained into the Thames, and transported it instead to new downstream works and storage tanks from which the effluent could be pumped into the river when the tide was flowing into the North Sea. A large number of steam pumping stations provided the power. Storm-relief sewers followed from the 1880s. In part, the storm-relief system used London's rivers other than the Thames, completing the process by which these had been directed underground. This concealment of the rivers made their use for this sewerage system acceptable.

Meanwhile, the 1852 Metropolitan Water Act obliged the London water companies to move their water supply sources to above the tidal reach of the Thames. The improvement in the water supply produced a large fall in mortality figures.

In Glasgow, the civic government was associated with the provision of pure water and with the individual purity of teetotalism. The provision of plentiful supplies of clean water was not only an engineering and organisational triumph, but also part of the process by which rural Britain was increasingly subordinated to the cities. Manchester, for example, looked to the distant Lake District to supplement supplies from the nearby Pennines. The Corporation purchased the Wythburn estate, stopped the local lead industry in order to prevent water pollution, and, despite overwhelming local opposition, gained parliamentary approval in 1877 for the drowning of the Thirlmere valley.

Across the country, typhus virtually disappeared by the 1890s, typhoid was brought under partial control, and death rates from tuberculosis and scarlet fever declined. The sole infection seriously to affect adults in 1900 was tuberculosis, but the childhood killers were still rampant. The burial records of the Bonner Hill cemetery in Kingston indicate that from 1855 to 1911 one-third of all burials were of children aged four or under. Diphtheria and measles were particularly serious killers, but neither was tackled adequately by medical provision, and the situation was exacerbated by the number of damp houses.

Improved diet, thanks, in part, to a significant fall in food prices, played an important role in the decline in mortality rates, which in Newcastle fell from 30.1 to 19.1 per thousand between 1872 and 1900. Medical advances, not least the replacement of the 'miasma' theory of disease by that of 'germs', helped, though mortality contrasts between registration districts persisted: from 17.1 to 41.5 per thousand in Newcastle in 1881. There was a noticeable, though not invariable, relationship between life expectancy and population density and thus poverty: crowded cities, such as Liverpool, having very much higher mortality rates.

Public health problems, however, also existed in small towns and rural areas. Edward Cresy reported to the General Board of Health on the small Sussex town of Battle in 1850, 'Typhoid and other maladies have arisen here in consequence of putrescent matters having been retained too close to the dwellings of the poor from the want of a proper supply of wholesome water, and thorough ventilation . . . the town is at present entirely devoid of proper sewers.' Reports on the situation in the small Somerset town of Bruton in the 1870s and 1880s graphically described insufficient and defective toilet arrangements, inadequate sewerage disposal and a lack of clean water. A reluctance to spend money ensured, however, that, as in mid-century London, plans to improve the situation were delayed, and, though the sewerage system was finally improved, Bruton did not construct a water supply system in the Victorian period.

Social welfare was linked to the growing institutionalisation of society that led to the construction of schools, workhouses and asylums. The Wiltshire asylum was opened in Devizes in 1851, replacing private institutions for the insane run for profit. By 1914 a basic national network of infant and child welfare centres had been created. Health-visiting was expanding. Educational authorities had been made responsible for the medical inspection of schoolchildren. Isolation, tuberculosis, smallpox and maternity hospitals and sanatoria were established by local authorities. Far from unconstrained capitalism, this was increasingly a regulated society. In 1888, the county councils assumed responsibility for most of the turnpike roads and the turnpike trusts were wound up.

At the same time, there were serious policy and political differences, reflecting fundamental disagreements over Ireland, trade union relations and the nature of the British political system. Ireland was the most threatening issue from 1910, for the determination of the Ulster

Protestants to resist Home Rule took the country to the brink of civil war in 1914. The formation of the Ulster Unionist Council (1905) and the Ulster Volunteer Force (1913) revealed the unwillingness of the Ulster Protestants to subordinate their sense of identity to Irish nationalism. They were assisted by the Conservatives, from 1912 the 'Conservative and Unionist Party', who did their best to resist the Home Rule Bill introduced by the Liberal government in 1912. The Bill, twice rejected by the House of Lords, was finally passed in an amended form in 1914, with the proviso that it was not to be implemented until after the First World War. The crisis defined the political forces in Ireland and gave a powerful impetus to the consciousness of the Ulster Protestants. The authority and power of the British state was challenged in a fashion that was far more potent and threatening than the imperial challenges of the Indian Mutiny and the Boer War.

LIBERAL GOVERNMENT, 1905–15

After nearly twenty years in power, for most of the period 1885–1905, the Conservatives were replaced by the Liberals, who from 1903 were allied with the new Labour Party. Victors in the landslide 1906 election over the Conservatives, then divided over free trade, the Liberals governed until a coalition wartime government was formed in 1915, although they lost their overall majority in both the 1910 elections and thereafter continued as a minority government dependent on Labour and Irish nationalist support. Some Liberals, particularly the dynamic David Lloyd George, Chancellor of the Exchequer 1908–15, were determined to undermine the power and possessions of the old landed elite, and keen to woo Labour and the trade unions. In 1906, the Liberals passed a Trade Disputes Act that gave unions immunity from actions for damages as a result of strike action, and thus rejected the attempts of the courts, through the Taff Vale case (1901), to bring the unions within the law. The Mines Regulations Act (1908) limited the number of hours that miners could spend underground.

Lloyd George wished to move the Liberals to the left, and in 1909 announced a people's budget, introducing new taxes for the wealthy: land taxes, supertax and increased death duties. He declared in a speech at Newcastle, not a city where the aristocracy were popular, that 'a fully equipped duke costs as much to keep up as two Dreadnoughts [battleships]', and that the House of Lords comprised 'five hundred men, ordinary men, chosen accidentally from among the unemployed'. His Liberal predecessors had never been so critical. The opposition of the Conservative-dominated House of Lords to this policy, only overcome in 1910, led to the Parliament Act (1911), which removed their right to veto Commons' legislation and weakened the self-confidence of the aristocracy. That year, Lloyd George had also defused the first general railway strike. As the President of the Board of Trade (1908–10), Winston Churchill, a keen advocate of Lloyd George's budget, tried to improve wages in the 'sweated' trades where they were harsh and to develop unemployment insurance. As Home Secretary (1910–13), he attempted to reduce sentences for petty offences, although he dealt forcibly with both the militant suffragettes and labour unrest.

Welfare measures were a key legacy from the pre-war Liberal governments. These measures owed much to the failure of the Royal Commission on the Poor to find a solution to the increasing burden of the Poor Laws. The Majority Report wanted more of the same and more money, while the Minority Report wanted government departments to deal with children and the old. In the end, it was expedient to reduce the burden upon the Poor Law by removing some categories of workers from it by a combination of health, insurance and old-age pension measures. In 1911, Lloyd George's National Insurance Act provided for all males eligible for insurance to be registered with a doctor, who was to receive a fee per patient irrespective of the amount of medical attention provided. There were also provisions for unemployment assistance. Another Liberal, Herbert Samuel, was responsible for legislation extending governmental responsibility to all children, rather than only paupers or victims of cruelty. The birching of young boys was restricted, child imprisonment was ended, and a national system of juvenile courts was created.

There were a number of major strikes in 1910–12, particularly in mining, transportation and shipbuilding; as well as the continued growth of trade union membership, and a vociferous, though largely middle-class, suffragette movement demanding the vote for women. The militant tactics of the Women's Social and Political Union were designed to force public attention. Labour, which was associated with most of the leaders of the movement, officially endorsed women's suffrage in 1912. The situation seemed increasingly volatile. Labour won twenty-nine seats in the general election of 1906 and forty in that of 1910, though it was not until 1922 that it emerged as the second largest party in Parliament. Although Labour benefited from a growing sense of class-consciousness, the radical programme of 'New Liberalism', with its emphasis on state-directed social reform and the redistribution of wealth by taxation, was more attractive to most electors outside Labour strongholds.

Aside from the apparent imminence of conflict in Ulster, strikes also brought widespread violence in Britain. These took place against a recent history of often bitter labour relations. Workers were no longer prepared to accept the idea that their pay should fall during recessions. Instead, they were prepared to fight for what they perceived as a 'just' living wage. The growing socialism of the unions was a victory for the more militant elements among the working population, such as dockers and gasworkers.

In Britain in 1914, however, the Liberal Party still displayed few signs of decline at the hands of Labour, while over 75 per cent of the working population were not members of trade unions, and divisions existed within the workforce, between skilled and unskilled, between Protestants and Irish immigrants, and between and within different regional economies. Much of the working class was, as in the Black Country and Scotland, prepared to vote Liberal or Conservative. Ethnic, religious, regional and occupational division were as important as class issues. Thus, in the cotton finishing industry, elite foremen engravers had little in common with poorly-paid bleachers.

THE PERSISTENCE OF HIERARCHY

Britain, on the eve of world war, was still in many respects an hierarchical society. George V (r. 1910–36) summoned 'My loyal subjects' to war in 1914. Hereditary monarchy remained important, though it had lost much of its power. Queen Victoria could influence but not control politics. In his important *The English Constitution* (1867), Walter Bagehot claimed that 'a republic has insinuated itself beneath the folds of a monarchy' and argued that the monarchy was useful as an image rather than a source of authority: 'It acts as a disguise. It enables our real rulers to change without heedless people knowing it.' He stated that the monarch had three rights, none of them commanding: 'the right to be consulted, the right to encourage, the right to warn'.

Society was obviously scarcely egalitarian. Third-class passengers were not allowed on Great Western Railway expresses until 1882. In 1880, over half of the fertile county of Norfolk was owned by landowners with more than 1,000 acres, and all those with estates there of more than 15,000 acres were members of the aristocracy, with the Earl of Leicester owning 43,000. In 1874, the Duke of Buccleuch owned 37 per cent of the land in the counties of Selkirk and Dumfries and 25 per cent in Roxburghshire. Elected county councils following the Local Government Act of 1888 ended the oligarchy of JPs and squirearchy in favour of elected control of roads, housing and other functions, but the first elections for the new county councils led in 1889 to the Duke of Richmond and Lord Monk Bretton becoming chairmen of the West and East Sussex county councils respectively.

The aristocracy survived as major players in political and social life until the very end of the nineteenth century, but, thereafter, they suffered major blows. Their debts rose as a consequence of the economic problems of agriculture, while death duties were greatly increased in 1894. Greatly expanded institutions with a meritocratic ethos – the civil service, the professions, the universities, the public schools and the army – were all very significant in the creation of a new social and cultural establishment to replace the aristocracy in the late nineteenth century. This development had, significantly, taken place rather earlier in Scotland. The armed forces played a much less dominant role in Victorian Britain than in the leading Continental states, where they served as a base for continued aristocratic, or at least, landed, influence: the army in particular was not popular with politicians. In Britain, the old landowning political elite had had its dominance of the electoral process challenged in 1832, and, thereafter, a steadily decreasing percentage of MPs came from it. Mr Merdle, the great 'popular financier on an extensive scale' in Charles Dickens's novel *Little Dorrit* (1855–7), was 'a new power in the country . . . able to buy up the whole House of Commons'.

This was an exaggeration, but reflected a sense of new economic forces and political interests. Joseph Chamberlain (1836–1914), a major Birmingham manufacturer of screws, who employed 2,500 workers by the 1870s and became Mayor of Birmingham, sold his holdings in the family firm and became a professional politician, despising the amateurism and inherited privilege of aristocratic politicians such as the Marquess of Harrington, later Duke of Devonshire, who was Liberal leader in 1875–80; although he had to work with them. Moves against the Game Laws, by which rural sporting rights were controlled by the elite, reflected challenges to their position. The Game Act of 1880 reflected urban agitation and a different moral and socio-political world from that which had extended the privileges of the sporting interest by the Night Poaching Act of 1828 and the Game Act of 1832.

The aristocracy opposed the Liberal Party in the 1900s because they sought to preserve their political position, as well as to resist what appeared to be an entire ethos of change centring on the policies of the extension of the power of the state, collectivism and the destruction of the Union with Ireland. They grasped the danger that democracy might entail the poor plundering the rich, or, in the eyes of its supporters, the social justice of redistribution. Social and political change operated in tandem. Whereas Disraeli, an outsider, had acquired a country estate in 1848, the Liberal Herbert Asquith, a barrister, was in 1908 the first Prime Minister not to have his own country house, though he was to end up with an earldom. Asquith was more hesitant than his predecessors about accepting the claims of hereditary aristocrats to high office, although most of his Cabinet came from the old upper classes.

RELIGION

The political, religious, intellectual and educational authority of the Church of England had also been challenged. The role of the parish in education and social welfare declined in favour of new governmental agencies. Municipal and county government was better able than the Church to implement the aspirations of society for reform and control, and in many towns the prestige and authority held by the vicar passed to the mayor. The universities of Oxford and Cambridge, hitherto Anglican monopolies, where all the teaching was conducted by clerics, were opened to non-Anglicans by legislation of 1854 and 1856. The Church of Ireland was disestablished by Gladstone in 1869. Nevertheless, the Church of England continued to play a major role in a society which was still very much Christian in its precepts. There were numerous clergymen. The Church also reformed itself, rationalising its structure and revenues, and improving its pastoral care. In Lincoln Cathedral, for example, after a long period of nepotism and corruption under the Pretyman family from the 1780s to 1860s, there were attempts to improve the frequency of services, the care of the poor and education.

The principal challenge to the Church of England came not from atheism, but from the rise of Nonconformity. The vitality of Nonconformity led to many new congregations. Without the authority of an established church it was, however, difficult to prevent splits. Thus, for example, the Primitive Methodists formed in 1811 and the Wesleyan Reform Methodists in 1849. Six years earlier, in the Disruption of 1843, the Church of Scotland divided on the issue of lay patronage, a dispute that had a nationalist dimension because of the issue at stake.

The re-emergence of 'public' Catholicism, with the legal re-establishment of the Catholic hierarchy in England in 1850–1 and massive Irish immigration, caused tension. Between 1850 and 1910, 1,173 new Catholic churches were opened in England and Wales, the largest number in London and Lancashire. The number of Catholics in Scotland, where the hierarchy was re-established in 1878, rose from about 146,000 in 1851 to about 332,000 in 1878, largely as a result of Irish immigration. Catholicism came to be accepted as part of the religious scene, albeit as clearly secondary to the established Church. This acceptance was strengthened by a strong Anglo-Catholic strand in the Church of England, 'the Oxford Movement'.

Although Jewish immigration increased greatly, the British Isles remained overwhelmingly Christian. Religion was an important prism through which the outside world was viewed. In addition, racial pride was of considerable importance. The right of the British to rule over other peoples was still taken for granted, and Darwinism, with its stress on natural selection, seemed to give new force to it. Social Darwinism led to a view of the nation-state as an organic entity that needed to grow if it was to avoid decline, an inherently aggressive attitude.

SOCIAL CHANGE AND LEISURE

There had also been major social change stemming from the new mass electorate, universal compulsory primary education, and widespread urbanisation and industrialisation. These developments had brought widespread social dislocation, instability and fears. Deference and traditional social patterns, never as fixed as some thought, had ebbed, and the new and newly-expanded cities and towns created different living environments in which the role and rule of the old world was far less. Only 10.4 per cent of the United Kingdom's workforce was employed in agriculture in the 1890s, compared with 40.3 per cent in France.

As part of a process of change, organised sport expanded. This expansion was a response to the clearer definition of leisure time in an industrial and urban society, to the reduction in working hours, to the increase in average real earnings in the last quarter of the century, and to the role of the middle classes in developing 'rational recreations'. In part, this was a result of changing religious attitudes. John Wesley, the Methodist leader in the eighteenth century, had believed that leisure would lead the poor to sin. In contrast, Victorian attitudes were more favourable so long as the Sabbath (Sunday) was respected. Professional football developed, becoming very popular, and driving out cricket in Scotland. The Football Association, formed in 1863, sought to codify the rules and football was organised on a large scale from the 1880s. In 1901, 111,000 spectators stood on the banks of Crystal Palace – the football stadium that hosted FA Cup finals from 1895 until 1914 – to watch Tottenham beat Sheffield United in the final. In 1913, 121,919 fans made often long journeys to watch Aston Villa beat Sunderland in the final.

Across Britain, there was also a boom in middle-class sports, such as golf and lawn tennis, whose rules were systematised in 1874. Northumberland Cricket Club had a ground in Newcastle by the 1850s, while Newcastle Golf Club expanded its activities in the 1890s. By 1895 the *Daily News* covered racing, yachting, rowing, lacrosse, football, hockey, angling, billiards, athletics, cycling and chess. Less respectable traditional sports and pastimes, such as cockfighting, ratting and morris dancing, lost popularity or were suppressed. The holiday trade also developed, although the type, character and destination of holidays reflected social divisions as did sport: few among the working class played golf, while the wealthy rarely watched football.

As a key medium of change, railways offered an affordable system of rapid, mass transport and created new economic and social relationships, as well as new leisure and commuting options. Their construction destroyed or damaged many of the most prominent sites of the past, including Berwick and Newcastle castles and Launceston Priory, and wrecked the canal system. The geography and townscape of London was changed by the train, including underground railways, by the tram, and by new roads, such as Kingsway and Northumberland Avenue, which respectively destroyed a red-light district and the splendour of Northumberland House. In 1862, Gladstone joined the directors of the Metropolitan Railway on the first run over the full length of their underground railway in London. Glasgow also developed an underground system.

TECHNOLOGY

Technology itself was like a freed genie, bringing ever more novelties and developments. The railway and telegraphy were succeeded by the motor car and the telephone, electricity and wireless. The growth of the genre of 'scientific romance' testified to the seemingly inexorable advance of human potential through technology. In *The Coming Race* (1871), by Sir Edward Bulwer Lytton, one of the leading men of letters of his age and a former Conservative Secretary for the Colonies, a mining engineer encountered at the centre of the earth a people who controlled 'Vril', a kinetic energy offering limitless powers, which has left its legacy in the British diet with Bo(vine)vril. Science fiction played a greater role in the work of H(erbert) G(eorge) Wells (1866–1946), who had studied under Charles Darwin's supporter, the comparative anatomist T. H. Huxley. Man's destiny in time and space was a central question for Wells, reflecting in part the intellectual expansion and excitement offered by the evolutionary theory outlined by Darwin in his *Origin of Species*, and by interest in manned flight. His first major novel, *The Time Machine* (1895), was followed by *The War of the Worlds* (1898), an account of a Martian invasion of England.

Developments were in fact less lurid than those outlined by Wells, but they still changed many aspects of human experience. The first demonstration of electric lighting in Birmingham was in 1882; the Birmingham Electric Supply Ltd following seven years later. The electric lighting industry developed and spread rapidly: the installed capacity in the local-authority sector in Scotland rose from 6,332 kilowatts in 1896 to 84,936 in 1910. Electricity was also regarded as a means to improve the social environment. The first original, full-size British petrol motor was produced in 1895; the first commercial motor company was established at Coventry in 1896; motor buses were introduced in about 1898. 'Cinematograph Halls' showed films: by 1913 there were fourteen cinemas in Lincolnshire alone. The following year, Manchester had 111 premises licensed to show films. In 1909, the first successful flight across the Channel led the press-baron Lord Northcliffe to remark that 'England is no longer an island'.

Meanwhile, the Motor Car Act of 1903 extended the rights of the motorist, the motor bus was introduced in London in 1905, and, four years later, the national Road Board was founded to lend energy and cohesion to road construction. Motor transport led to the widespread tarring of roads from the early 1900s, a major visual and environmental change. Indeed, there was concern in some circles about what the poet Gerard Manley Hopkins termed 'the strokes of havoc' created by technological change and economic development. Similar views were expressed by such leading literary figures as Matthew Arnold, William Morris and John Ruskin. Efforts were made to save open spaces from development.

By 1914, there were 132,000 private car registrations. There were also 124,000 motor cycle registrations, and 51,167 buses and taxis on the road. Cars ensured that bicycling, which had boomed following the development of the safety bicycle in 1885, descended the social and age scales. A new world of speed and personal mobility, with its own particular infrastructure, was being created. If cars were still a luxury, every such innovation contributed to a powerful sense of change that was possibly the most important solvent of the old order.

8

The Twentieth Century

TECHNOLOGY, CHANGE AND THE STATE OF THE NATION

War and the loss of empire framed the political experience of Britain from the outbreak of the First World War (1914) to the 1960s, but the environmental, medical, social and economic contexts, as well as the nature of personal experience, were all to be transformed totally as a result of technological innovation and application. The nineteenth century had brought major changes, but the twentieth century truly witnessed revolutionary transformations in theoretical and applied science and in technology in most fields, whether transport, the generation and distribution of power, medicine, contraception, agricultural yields, or the accumulation, storing and manipulation of information. The wealth was created, and means provided, to make feasible the suggestion that man's lot on earth could be substantially improved. Change would be so all-encompassing that fears of permanent damage to the environment and to mankind itself would become a major issue from the 1960s, though worried voices had been raised earlier. In his *To Iron-Founders and Others*, the Yorkshire poet and dramatist Gordon Bottomley (1874–1948) warned:

> When you destroy a blade of grass
> You poison England at her roots . . .
> Your worship is your furnaces,
> . . . your vision is
> Machines for making more machines.

In this brave and troubled new world, it was possible for people to travel and transmit ideas as never before, to create and destroy in new ways and on a scale hitherto only graspable in imaginative fiction, to synthesise and manufacture new substances, textures, tastes and sounds, and to create, from the fertile human mind, a world in which mankind itself, its desires, needs and imagination, seemed the sole frame of reference, the only scale.

For an elderly person at the close of the twentieth century, it was not only the individual major technological innovations of their lifetime, whether atomic energy or contraceptive pill, television or microchip, jet engine or computer, bio-technology or artificial hip, that were of importance in affecting their life, directly or indirectly, insistently or episodically; it was also the cumulative impact of change. The past ceased to be a recoverable world, a source of reference, value and values for lives that changed very little, and became, instead, a world that was truly lost, a distorted theme-park for nostalgia, regret or curiosity. A potent element in twentieth-century English life was an obsession with a particular kind of romantic landscape, reflected, for example, in the popularity of the poetry and novels of Thomas Hardy, the music of Ralph Vaughan Williams and in the success of ramblers' clubs.

Change was first a matter of displacement. Migration had always been important in British history, especially in the nineteenth century with mass movement to the new industrial areas and emigration to the colonies, but in the twentieth century the pattern of the people changed even more radically. Much of rural Britain became like a skeleton, without its people, a skeleton clothed increasingly by commuters who lived there, but worked elsewhere. In 1921–39, the number of agricultural labourers fell by a quarter, and the pace quickened after the Second World War (1939–45). Horses were replaced by tractors, and local mills, both windmills and watermills, fell into disuse as they were replaced by electricity. Hand-milking was replaced by machines. Agriculture became increasingly a solitary, rather than a communal, activity, although these changes did have some benefits. The bothies (one-roomed huts) in which many male Scottish farm workers lived in claustrophobic and insanitary conditions, disappeared in the 1960s.

Other non-urban activities, such as forestry, mining and quarrying, also either declined or dramatically cut their workforces. These changes led to the depopulation of many rural regions, especially upland areas and those beyond commuting distance from towns, for example north Norfolk, the Lincolnshire Wolds and much of Cornwall and Wales.

Many small rural schools closed. This was not a case of the destruction of age-old lifestyles, for the rural world of 1900 was in many respects merely the result of the major changes of the period 1500–1900, while the depopulation of some rural areas had been a major problem in Tudor England and earlier. Change was constant, and yet, in terms of the sense of place and identity of the British population of this century, the scale of change seemed revolutionary. The countryside became, for many of its inhabitants, a place of residence and leisure, rather than of work, and urban attitudes were introduced, as in complaints about the noise produced by farm animals and especially about the hunting of wild animals, principally foxes and stags, for sport. At the same time, the newly-formed 'Countryside Alliance' staged a demonstration in London in 1998 in opposition to a Bill to end foxhunting, and a quarter of a million people took part. In much of rural Britain, housing became scarce and expensive as a result of purchase by commuters and buyers of second homes, while the problems of the agrarian economy led to a large number of rural households living below the poverty line.

At the other end of the social scale, though the wartime boosts to production and state subsidies for agriculture under the 1947 Agriculture Act helped farmers and landowners, Lloyd George's tax changes of 1909–10 and the disappearance of the vast labour force of cheap servants had already hit country-house life, and many country houses were demolished or institutionalised. Over 1,200 were destroyed or abandoned between 1918 and 1975; many others were transferred to the National Trust, became reliant on paying visitors, or became schools or other institutions. The dominance of much of the rural life of the British Isles by the aristocratic estate became a thing of the past, especially in England and Ireland. Massive land sales after the First World War, in which many heirs to estates died, broke the traditional landlord–tenant relationship. For example, the Lincolnshire estate of the Earls of Yarborough, 60,000 acres in 1885, fell to about half after land sales in 1919, 1925, 1933, 1944 and 1948, although their links with tenants in north Lincolnshire remained close and extensive. The growth of owner-occupation of farmland after 1918 ensured that the tenurial relationship upon which landowner control had rested became less important: the influence of landowners in the politics of agriculture was replaced by that of farmers. The poor economic conditions in farming during the inter-war years were partly responsible for this. In so far as new country houses were built, they were not for landed families, but for rich businessmen or foreigners, who intended to play no role in local government and politics and who did not wish to build up extensive landholdings.

Some families maintained control of their estates, but often they shrank: more than half of the great estates in the East Riding of Yorkshire sold much or all of their land. The aristocracy also sold their town houses. Again, these were demolished or converted to institutional use. In Scotland, some traditional landholding patterns survived. The Dukes of Buccleuch and Sutherland, and Cameron of Lochiel each owned major estates at the close of the century, but, although large-scale traditional landholding continued, the number, extent and role of such estates were less than in the past. Meanwhile, the position of Anglo-Irish landowners collapsed due to land reform and civil violence in the first quarter of the century.

Visually and environmentally, the rural British Isles also changed greatly. New crops had an impact, most obviously the striking yellow colour of oil-seed rape and, in the 1990s, the pale blue of European Union-subsidised flax. Redundant farmsteads fell into ruin or were destroyed. Traditional occupations and activities that used and maintained habitats such as meadows declined. The amalgamation of fields and bulldozing of hedges led, from the 1950s, to the replacement, as in East Anglia, of the earlier patchwork of small fields surrounded by dense hedges, by large expanses of arable land, bounded often by barbed-wire fences. These changes had serious environmental consequences, as had those in the use of more marginal lands. Marshlands were drained and became intensively farmed. Upland valleys, such as the North Tyne, the Durham Derwent and several in Wales, were drowned for reservoirs. Large plantations of coniferous trees were established on upland moors and on the Norfolk and Suffolk Breckland. Throughout the British Isles, pesticides were used extensively in agriculture, and entered the groundwater system. The conquest of nature became ever more comprehensive and insistent.

People not only moved off the land, but also away from declining industrial regions. Areas that were collectively the nineteenth-century 'workshop of the world' became industrial museums and regions of social dereliction, designated as problems requiring regional assistance, as under the Special Areas Act (1934), which in fact provided only limited assistance. During the slump of the 1930s, unemployment in Sunderland rose to 75 per cent of shipbuilders and half of the working population, and was associated with hardship and higher rates of ill-health. Jarrow, another shipbuilding town in north-east England, also had unemployment levels of over 70 per cent. People moved from such towns to areas of greater economic opportunity, mostly in the Midlands and south-east England.

In addition, particularly since the Second World War, crowded inner-city areas lost people as slums were torn down. Instead, people moved to new developments on 'greenfield' sites in the countryside, or on the edge of older settlements. The former were new towns, the first garden city being Letchworth (1903), the latter suburban sprawl, the suburbia where a far greater percentage of the population now came to live. This was especially the case around major cities, particularly London, which expanded greatly in a contiguous fashion in the 1920s and 1930s. The Restriction of Ribbon Development Act of 1935, which attempted to prevent unsightly and uncontrolled development along new or improved roads, such as those leading from London, was an admission of a serious problem.

Once Green Belt legislation was passed from the late 1930s, sprawl was limited. New Towns were designed to complement Green Belts. London was to be contained, with a Green Belt, and New Towns were to be built outside the Belt. The first, Stevenage, was chosen in 1946, the year of the New Towns Act, which was followed by a new Town and Country Planning Act in 1947. The London Green Belt, which was given legislative aspiration in 1938, was finally secured with an Act of 1959. Many new and greatly expanded towns, however, for example Cumbernauld, Crawley, Peterlee and Basingstoke, translated old social problems to new, often poorly-planned, sites, but also exacerbated them by destroying the 'old communities'.

Designed to allow the growing middle class to realise their earning potential, to escape from the crowded and polluted conditions of the city, and to join in the expanding hobby of amateur gardening, new housing was both cause and consequence of a massive expansion of personal transport. Commuting led to an increase in, first, train and, later, car use. In the 1920s and 1930s, the development of the London 'tube' underground railway system allowed a major spread of the city to the north, while national private ownership of cars increased more than tenfold and, by 1937, over 300,000 new cars were being registered annually. 'The sound of horns and motors', referred to in T. S. Eliot's poem *The Waste Land* (1922), was becoming more insistent and creating a national mass culture. The railways had often pioneered feeder bus services, but, from the 1920s, competition from road transport became serious for them. There were half a million road goods vehicles, nearly two million cars, and 53,000 buses and coaches by September 1938.

This expansion in road traffic contributed to a crisis in the rail network. Among the 'Big Four' railway companies, the Southern Railway was alone in paying a regular dividend to shareholders before nationalisation in 1948. About 240 miles of track and 350 stations were closed completely in the inter-war period and another 1,000 miles and 380 stations to passenger traffic. After a fall in car ownership during the Second World War, its rise accelerated rapidly, especially after petrol rationing stopped in 1953. In terms of thousand million passenger-miles, private road transport shot up from 47 in 1954 to 217 in 1974, an increase from 39 to 79 per cent of the total. This gain was made at the expense of bus, coach and rail transport. The percentage of goods traffic moved by road rose from 37 in 1952 to 58.3 in 1964.

The railways lost money from the late 1950s, and the Beeching Report of 1963 led to dramatic cuts in the network. Freight and passenger services were greatly curtailed, the workforce cut, lines were taken up, and many stations became unmanned halts, or were converted to other uses. One of the major 'public spaces' of Britain, the railway, was thus greatly diminished in favour of the more 'individual' car. In 1991, Britain spent less per head on rail improvements than any other country in the European Union (EU) apart from Greece and Ireland, neither of which has a substantial network. Nevertheless, there was a degree of electrification, notably with the line from London to Edinburgh electrified by 1991. In 1997, the railways were privatised, the last of the privatisations by the Conservative governments of 1979–97.

Compared with America, however, rail transport still played an important role in the British Isles, particularly in travel between the major cities and in commuting into them, and traffic grew greatly in the late 2000s. Paradoxically, the relative decline of rail travel did not end its grip on the popular imagination, although that focused on the now-discarded system of steam trains. Preservation groups and other enthusiasts re-opened a few lines and stations, while the nostalgic story-book character 'Thomas the Tank Engine' remained a figure of great popularity for children of about four, and some adults. With the rise of leisure activities, several former railway trackbeds were turned into long-distance footpaths.

There were 12.2 million cars in Britain in 1970, 21.9 million in 1990. Car ownership rose from 224 per 1,000 people in 1971 to 380 per 1,000 in 1994. Only 42 per cent of those who worked in Newcastle in 1971 lived in the city and most of the rest commuted by car. A survey of British Social Attitudes in 1999 by the National Centre for Social

Research showed that those who lived in big cities were the group keenest to move.

Increased use of the car and the construction of more roads interacted. As road usage grew, it became necessary progressively to supplement existing roads. Every town required its bypass: Newbury's, built in the 1960s, quickly became congested and it needed another. Trunk roads with dual carriageways were constructed, and a motorway system was created, beginning with the M6 Preston bypass, opened, in December 1958, by Harold Macmillan (Conservative Prime Minister, 1957–63). The M25 around London, completed in 1986, became the busiest route in the country.

Greater personal mobility for the bulk, but by no means all, of the population enabled, and was a necessary consequence of, lower-density housing and declining subsidies for public transport. Employment patterns changed. In place of factories or mines that had large labour forces, most modern industrial concerns were capital-intensive and employed less labour. They were often located away from the central areas of cities, and on flat and relatively open sites with good road links. A growing number of the rising percentage of the population who were retired left the cities to live in suburban, rural or coastal areas, such as Colwyn Bay and Worthing. New shopping patterns developed, with the rise of the supermarket in the 1950s and the hypermarket, mainly out of town, in the 1980s. By 1992, 16 per cent of the total shopping space in Britain was made up of shopping centres, such as Brent Cross in north London, Lakeside Thurrock in Essex, the Glades in Bromley, Kent, Meadowhall in Sheffield, and the Metro Centre in Gateshead, the last applauded by Margaret Thatcher, Conservative Prime Minister from 1979 to 1990. Shopping centres were moulders of taste and spheres of spending activity at the heart of the consumer society. Almost all of their customers came by car, abandoning traditional high-street shopping with its gentler pace and more individual service.

Related changes in location were also of great importance in such areas as education and health. Whereas, in 1971, 14 per cent of junior school children were driven to school, by 1990 the percentage had risen to 64. The percentage walking or going by bus fell markedly, again an aspect of the declining use of 'public space', and one related to the marked increase in obesity and unfitness among children. Parking space for cars came to take a greater percentage of city space. Multi-storey carparks disfigured many townscapes, while the problems of parking became a major topic of conversation.

Greater mobility for most, but not all, of the population also exacerbated spatial segregation. The division of the population into communities defined by differing levels of wealth, expectations and opportunity was scarcely novel; indeed in most towns had developed greatly from the eighteenth century. It became, however, more pronounced during the twentieth century, and an obvious aspect of what was termed the 'underclass', in both town and countryside, was their relative lack of mobility.

Consumerism and technology, the two closely related, were crucial features of the century. Their impact was very varied. Thus, the spread in the 1930s of large numbers of affordable cars with reliable self-starter motors, so that it was not necessary to crank up the motor by hand, led to a wave of 'smash and grab' raids as the criminal fraternity took advantage of the new technology. Greater mobility totally changed the pattern of crime. In response, London's Metropolitan Police experimented with mounting ship's radios in cars and was able to develop a fleet of Wolseley cars thus equipped with which to mount an effective response. More generally, the car changed the nature of policing. In 1900, only about 3 per cent of committals were to do with transport and cars, but, by the 1930s, this rose to well over 50 per cent. In the early 1930s, deaths on the road from just over a million motorised vehicles rose to more than 7,000 per year, often up to 70 per cent of them children. With barely any extra members of the force in the inter-war years, the police devoted much effort to keeping the motorist and the pedestrian apart. High car death rates also led to road safety campaigns and to attempts to look at road design and layout.

The post-Second World War era was to see computer fraud, but also the use of computerised information and of sophisticated forensic techniques by the police. Traffic offences brought middle-class individuals into contact with the police and the courts. 'Flying pickets' (mobile groups of trade unionists) used cars to spread strike action, as in the 'Winter of Discontent' strikes of 1978–9 and the miners' strike of 1984–5. By the early 1990s, 45,000 children were being injured on the roads every year and, among those aged 5–15, two-thirds of deaths were the result of road accidents. In 1992, 4,681 people were killed in car accidents, compared with 499 by murder. Alarmist and often lurid reports about the latter fed popular concern about crime. In contrast, deaths and injuries due to cars aroused less public interest and concern and were treated as a fact of life.

Labour-saving devices, such as washing machines, vacuum cleaners, and dishwashers, also had a major impact on society. They reduced the burden of housework and replaced domestic servants, easing the struggle with dirt and disease, though they also ensured that household use of water increased considerably. The sights and smells of life changed. In his 1938 novel *Invisible Weapons*, John Rhode captured the linkage with altering social patterns:

'Everything here's absolutely up to date. The cottage wasn't anything like this in Squire Gunthorpe's time, of course. The gardener and his wife lived here, and they didn't trouble much about appearances. But when the estate was sold Mr Whiteway bought the place. And the first thing he did was to pull it about to suit himself. Spent quite a lot of money on it, too, one way and the other. Put in all the latest gadgets – tiled bathroom, latest type of gas cooker, electric refrigerator, coke boiler for constant hot water, pretty well everything else you can think of. It's what Mrs Whiteway calls a labour-saving house, and she's about right. But it wouldn't suit me, for there isn't a coal fire in the house . . . of a winter's evening I like to draw my chair up in front of a good blaze. Coal, with a nice ash log on top of it. That's what I call comfort.' (John Rhode, *Invisible Weapons* (London, 1938), p. 145)

The communication of messages was revolutionised by the spread of technology. Telephone ownership rose to a high level, while fax machines and mobile phones became important from the 1980s. The growing numbers of personal and company computers facilitated the explosion of electronic mail. By 2001, it was estimated that 40 million text messages were sent daily in the United Kingdom.

The number of radio and television channels multiplied. Radio broadcasts began in 1922; the British Broadcasting Corporation, a monopoly acting in the 'national interest', and financed by licence fees paid by radio and later television owners, was established in 1926; and it began television services from Alexandra Palace in 1936. However, commercial television companies, financed by advertising, were not established in Britain until 1955, and the first national commercial radio station, Classic FM, was not founded until 1992. Television ownership shot up in the 1950s, the numbers of those with regular access to a set rising from 38 per cent of the population in 1955 to 75 per cent in 1959. As a result, the cinema declined in popularity: by 1966, over half of those in the north-west of England had closed, although, in the 1990s, there was to be a significant resurgence of cinemas with the building of multiplexes. After an all-time peak in 1946, Hertfordshire had an all-time low in cinema attendances in 1984, while multiplexes appeared in the county from 1991.

By 1994, 99 per cent of British households had televisions and 96 per cent had colour televisions. In the 1990s, the larger number of regular television channels were supplemented for many by satellite channels, the receiving dishes altering the appearance of many houses as television aerials had earlier done. Moreover, more than 70 per cent of British households had video-recorders, giving them even greater control over what they watched.

Television succeeded radio as a central determinant of the leisure time of many, a moulder of opinions and fashions, a source of conversation and controversy, an occasion of family cohesion or dispute, and a major feature of the household. A force for change, a great contributor to the making of the 'consumer society', and a 'window on the world', which demanded the right to enter everywhere and report anything, television also became increasingly a reflector of popular taste. Just as radio helped to provide common experiences – royal Christmas messages from 1932, King Edward VIII's abdication speech in 1936, the war speeches of Winston Churchill, heard by millions (as those in the First World War of Lloyd George could not be) – so television fulfilled the same function, providing much of the nation with common visual images and messages. Over twenty million viewers watched Morecambe and Wise Christmas programmes in the 1980s.

This process really began with the coronation service for Elizabeth II in 1953, a cause of many households purchasing sets or first watching, and, thanks to television, the royals almost became members of viewers' extended families, treated with the fascination commonly devoted to the stars of soap operas. The *Royal Family* documentary of 1969 exposed monarchy to the close, domestic scrutiny of television. Indeed, both the 'New Elizabethan Age of optimism', heralded in 1952, and discontents in the 1990s about the position and behaviour of some members of the royal family, owed much to the media; the same had been true with Queen Victoria in the 1860s and 1870s.

Television was central to much else: the trend-setting and advertising that are so crucial to the consumer society, and the course and conduct of election campaigns. Parliament was televised and much of public politics became a matter of sound bites aimed to catch the evening news bulletins. Television increasingly also set the idioms and vocabulary of public and private life. Thus, on 14 July 1989, the Prime Minister, Margaret Thatcher, was attacked by Denis Healey of the Labour Party for adding 'the diplomacy of Alf Garnett to the economics of Arthur Daley', knowing that listeners would understand his references to popular television characters.

Technological change contributed to an economic situation in which the annual output of goods rose appreciably for most of the century, while personal output, consumption and leisure similarly rose alongside a major growth in British population: including Northern Ireland, up from 44.9 million in 1931 to 58.6 million in 1997.

Despite the Depression, for most of those in work, the 1930s was a decade of improved housing, wider consumer choice and a better quality of life. It was a period of new and developing electrical goods, of cars, radio, television and the 'talkies'. Large numbers of cinemas were constructed: despite their relatively low population, Suffolk had forty in 1937 and Lincolnshire fifty-eight.

A similar contrast was true of the recessions at the beginning of the 1980s and the 1990s. Alongside high unemployment, and social strains, manifested in rising crime rates and urban riots, many of those in work had high living standards. Average British disposable income rose by 37 per cent between 1982 and 1992. The real income of the bottom 10 per cent in Britain increased by 10 per cent in 1973–91, although the top 10 per cent gained 55 per cent, and average income differentials thus rose. Ownership of telephones, washing machines, dishwashers, cars and video-recorders all rose: by 1996 nearly 90 per cent of households had a deep freezer and 20 per cent had a dishwasher.

Economic growth and changing political and social assumptions in Britain had led earlier to the development of national social security and educational provision and, from 1948, of a national health service, ensuring that the indigent and ill were offered a comprehensive safety net, while a range of services were provided free at the point of delivery to the whole of the population. Measures such as free school meals (1906), non-contributory old-age pensions (1908), labour exchanges (1909), the National Insurance Act (1911), the Education Act of 1918, which designated 14 as the minimum school leaving age, and the creation of the Unemployment Assistance Board (1934), were limited, but still an improvement on the earlier situation, and the establishment of antenatal screening in the 1920s was important. The Local Government Acts of 1929 abolished poor law unions, replacing boards of guardians by public assistance committees, which were committees of the counties and county boroughs, and encouraged local authorities to take over workhouses (since 1913 called poor law institutions) as hospitals. Philanthropy, mutual aid and voluntary activity, however, all remained important in the practice and policy of social welfare.

Further developments were widely supported in the three decades after the Second World War, a period when 'one-nation Toryism' and 'Butskellism' (a merging of the Tory 'Rab' Butler and the Labour Hugh Gaitskell) reflected a measure of continuity and consensus between Conservative and Labour policies. The Conservatives did not dismantle the National Health Service (NHS) after they were returned to power in 1951. Both parties responded to Keynesian economic theory with its emphasis on economic stimulus, an expanding money supply and full employment.

The creation of the welfare state reflected a conviction that social progress and economic growth were compatible; that indeed a major purpose of the latter was to achieve the former. The Beveridge Report of 1942 envisaged a welfare state able to end the 'five giants' of want, disease, ignorance, squalor and idleness. The Education Act of 1944 obliged every local education authority to prepare a development plan for educational provision, and the Ministry of Education imposed new minimum standards in matters such as school accommodation and size. The minimum school leaving age was raised to 15 and fees in state-supported secondary schools were abolished; legislation in 1947 extended the provisions to Scotland and Northern Ireland. Stable employment and social security were seen as important goals.

There were also major changes in housing. Following the 1915 Rent and Mortgage Interest Restrictions (War) Act, which owed something to the Clydeside rent strikes of that year, private landlordship became less profitable, tenants' rights more secure and renting from local authorities, 'council housing', more important. Partly due to the 'fair rent' system, which allowed rent officers to fix rents below the market level, supposedly to protect tenants from rapacious landlords, the private rental sector fell from an 80 per cent share of British housing in the 1940s to 8 per cent in 1988, which greatly lessened the flexibility of the property market and helped to stoke up demand for owner-occupation.

Meanwhile, the 'Greenwood' Housing Act of 1930 gave local authorities powers to clear or improve slum (crowded and substandard housing) areas, and, after 1945, slums were swept aside and their inhabitants moved into new publicly-owned housing estates, reflections of the priority given to rehousing the masses and creating an acceptable living environment. Prefabricated methods of construction ensured that multi-storey blocks of flats could be built rapidly, and local councils, such as Glasgow, Gateshead and Newcastle in the 1960s, took pride in their number, size and visibility. Moreover, municipal housing policies helped in the consolidation of Labour's working-class base, for example in Clydeside and London. Extolled at the time, and illustrated alongside castles and cathedrals in guidebooks of the 1960s, municipal multi-storey flats were subsequently attacked as ugly, out of keeping with the existing urban fabric, of poor quality, as lacking in community feeling, and as breeders of alienation and crime. Alongside much unattractive and poor-quality municipal housing in the 1960s, there was also a brutal rebuilding of many city centres, for example Birmingham, Manchester and Newcastle.

In contrast, the Conservative governments of the 1950s fostered owner-occupation, while the Conservative government that came to power in 1979 felt little sympathy for public housing and, under the 'right to buy' Housing Act of 1980, introduced a policy of the sale of council housing to tenants. This expanded opportunities for home ownership, but also depleted the stock of public housing. Whereas 29,290 new homes were built by local authorities in England and Wales in 1984, the figure for 1994 was only 528. Rent control was restricted in the 1950s, and, after 1979, the 'fair rent' system was abolished. The number of private-renting households rose by 22 per cent in 1989–93.

There has been much disagreement about the social and educational consequences of the comprehensivisation of British education, the abandonment, in the 1950s and especially from 1965, of streaming of children by ability into different schools after examination at the age of 11 (12 in Scotland). Grammar and secondary-modern schools were replaced by comprehensive schools, a policy actively supported by the 1964–70 Labour government and further implemented under the 1970–4 Conservative government. Labour politicians regarded grammar schools as elitist, unfair, and simply serving the middle classes, and favoured a more egalitarian approach. In practice, comprehensive schools varied greatly, often reflecting the social nature of their catchment area. Another major shift was away from single-sex and towards co-educational schooling, by the 1990s overwhelmingly the norm in the state sector. Educational standards in the state sector were the cause of much controversy, while private education was perceived by some as both the basis and the consequence of class distinction.

Major expansions in higher education in the 1960s, 1990s and 2000s dramatically increased the percentage of school-leavers continuing in full-time education and thus eventually the graduate population. The number of students from lower-income families rose considerably. Nine new universities were founded in 1958–66, and the number and importance of polytechnics also increased from the late 1960s. The Robbins Report of 1963 recommended places in higher education for all suitably qualified candidates, and the government responded. Students were also given free tuition, and a grant for their maintenance in proportion to their parental income. The percentage of 18-year-olds entering university in the United Kingdom rose from 4.6 in 1961 to over 30 by the mid-1990s, by which time the polytechnics and several other colleges had also become universities. It is not clear that the hopes inspiring this process, especially those of fulfilling the economy's requirements for skills and widening opportunity, were met. Similar uncertainty surrounded the attempt from 1989 to establish a national curriculum at primary- and secondary-school level in England and Wales.

The National Health Service (NHS), established by the Labour government in 1948, brought about a fundamental change in the medical provision of the nation, and was for long regarded as one of the triumphs of social welfare policy. It caught up with the ill-health and inequality that had allowed many people, especially women and children, to receive little or no medical provision before 1948. However, the NHS was harmed from the outset by the problems of nationalised entities, including (frequently inconsistent) political intervention, inflexible national policies, funding problems, and poor management and labour relations, and was also harmed by the measures taken in order to win the consent of interest groups, especially doctors and dentists. The NHS also suffered, from the outset, from rising expectations of care, the greater cost that stemmed from an ageing population, and the rising costs of medical treatment. From 1950 to 2010, the NHS budget grew twice as fast as Britain's economy.

Although there were serious inefficiencies, the NHS, nevertheless, was able to maintain the policy of medical (but not dental) treatment free at the point of delivery, so that many of the anxieties about the availability and cost of medical treatment that the poor faced earlier in the century ended. The NHS invariably wins top rating in popular esteem in public opinion polls. The NHS also established a much fairer geographical and social allocation of resources and skills than existed hitherto, and there was a positive effort to develop medical education and specialised services spread across the regions, rather than concentrated, as earlier, in a few centres, principally London.

Uniform health provision through the NHS played a major role in the dramatic change in the medical condition of the population that characterised this century, though other factors, such as improved diet, were also of great importance. Britain was in the forefront of medical research and development throughout the century, and, as general medical knowledge rose greatly, so the ability to identify and treat disease increased exponentially. These improvements touched the lives of millions and totally altered the condition of the people. In Norfolk, for example, death rates fell from about 22 to 12 per 1,000 people between 1851 and 1951. The discovery of insulin in 1922 and its use (developed from pigs' pancreases) from the mid-1920s enabled young diabetics to live. Moreover, Britain played a major role in the understanding and treatment of mental illness. The twentieth century brought recognition of the importance of psychological and mental processes, and the diagnosis and treatment of mental illness were revolutionised. The development, from the 1940s, of safe and effective drugs helped in the treatment of major psychoses and depression, dramatically improving the cure rate.

British scientists, such as Sir Alexander Fleming, the discoverer of what he called penicillin, played a major role in the development of antibiotics. They were of enormous benefit for dealing with infections, which, of one kind or another, were a very common cause of death in the first half of the century. Tuberculosis was conquered, thanks to the use, from the 1940s, of an American antibiotic, streptomycin, as well as to better diet, earlier diagnosis and the programme of mass BCG vaccination. It had killed one adult in eight at the beginning of the century, including, in 1930, the novelist D. H. Lawrence at the age of 44, and in 1950 his counterpart George Orwell at 47, and was still serious in the 1930s, particularly among the urban poor.

Antibiotics also helped with other bacterial infections such as venereal disease. Diarrhoeal diseases diminished; while urinary infections could be more readily treated. The common childhood diseases which caused high mortality and high morbidity in children in the early part of the century, such as measles, whooping cough, polio, diphtheria, mumps and rubella (German measles), were dramatically reduced by the post-war introduction of immunisation programmes for the entire child population. However, an erroneous theory that the MMR vaccine against measles, mumps and rubella could cause autism led to a significant fall in the percentage of children vaccinated: from 92 in 1996 to under 80 in 2003, resulting in a marked rise in the diseases. By 2011, vaccination rates had returned above 90 per cent and cases of the diseases had fallen.

From the 1970s, there was also the introduction of population screening for the early detection and treatment of other diseases, such as breast and cervical cancer. The 1980s saw the increasing development and use of anti-viral agents for the treatment of viral infections. Health education improved and become more important.

The range of surgical treatment dramatically increased. The two world wars, especially the second, saw a major improvement in surgical techniques, with, for example, the development of plastic surgery. A major increase in anaesthetic skills, due to greater knowledge and the introduction of increasingly sophisticated drugs, meant that complex surgical operations could be performed. Once serious operations, such as appendectomies, became routine and minor. There were major advances in the treatment of the heart, and bypass and transplant surgery were completely developed after the Second World War. Key-hole surgery became common.

Medical advances led to dramatic changes in the pattern of causes of death, although related developments in public health were also of great importance. The poor, insanitary and overcrowded housing, low incomes and overcrowded maternity hospitals that were such serious problems as late as the 1930s, pushing up infant mortality rates and malnutrition among the poor and unemployed, lessened with post-Second World War social welfare policies. The Clean Air Act and other environmental measures, safety at work awareness, and the Health and Safety at Work Act, as well as a growing understanding of the dangers of working in smoke-filled buildings and with carcinogenic asbestos, all contributed to changes in health, not least to the decline of chest illnesses. Most milk sold after 1949 was pasteurised. The hazards of drinking to excess and, particularly, of smoking became generally appreciated and were addressed by government action, but with only mixed success.

Large numbers of children died in the first half of the century: although it had fallen greatly from the start of the century, the United Kingdom infant mortality rate was still 58 per 1,000 in 1937, and infections were then a major cause of death for the entire population. By the end of the century, in contrast, later-onset diseases, such as heart disease and cancers, were far more important, and infections generally only killed people who were suffering from associated disorders and were at the extremes of life. Birth in hospital became the norm: in 1993, only one in every sixty-three births in England and Wales occurred at home. Infant mortality fell by nearly two-thirds between 1971 and 1994.

Average life expectancy for all age-groups persistently rose during the century, the major exception being those aged between 15 and 44 during the 1980s. Average lifespan increased by an average of two years every decade in the 1960s–90s. The rise in life expectancy led to a new age structure, as a result of the increasing number of pensioners, and to problems of dependency posed by the greater number of people over 85: 12.6 per cent of Norfolk's population were over 65 in 1951; only 9.2 per cent a century earlier. But by 1990 the percentage was 19.6. Britain's dependency ratio (of working-age to retirement-age citizens) is predicted to be 2.4 by 2050.

Not all illnesses retreated. Possibly as a result of increasing car exhaust emissions, respiratory diseases, such as asthma, definitely rose. Tuberculosis made a comeback after 1987, partly due to refugees and immigrants from countries where it was more common, but also due to HIV infection, homelessness, and the appearance of drug-resistant strains. The massive increase in the importation, treatment and burying of hazardous waste from the 1980s led to concern about possible health implications. High rates of obesity helped to explain high rates of type 2 diabetes and of heart disease: the latter was particularly acute in Scotland. In England, blood-pressure rates were especially high in the north and the west Midlands. Lung cancer rates fell as people gave up smoking. However, due in part to increased testing, prostate cancer rates rose from 7.7 to 51 cases per 100,000 people from 1979 to 2008, while greater exposure to the sun led to an increase in skin cancer. During that period, cancer rates as a whole rose from 329 to 388 per 100,000 people, with rates rising particularly strongly among women, with better detection for breast cancer, increased drinking, later childbirth and obesity all being significant. At the same time, cancer survival rates doubled in the period 1979 to 2008.

If the age-structure of the population changed totally as a result of medical advances, so too did many aspects of people's lives. Contraceptive developments dramatically increased the ability of women to control their own fertility and played a major role in the emancipation of women, as well as in the 'sexual revolution', a change in general sexual norms, from the 1960s on. After 1921, when Marie Stopes founded the Society for Constructive Birth Control, it became increasingly acceptable socially for women to control their own fertility. Contraceptives became widely available. The number of legal abortions in the United Kingdom was 184,000 in 1990. The fertility of the approximately 20 per cent of couples who were infertile was enhanced by new techniques such as in-vitro fertilisation. Though AIDS (Acquired Immune Deficiency Syndrome) developed in the 1980s as a new killer, leading to an emphasis on 'safe sex', antibiotics dealt with most other sexually transmitted diseases. More generally, pain was increasingly held at bay by more effective and selective painkillers, bringing relief to millions suffering from illnesses such as arthritis and muscular pain. Thus the condition of the people really changed. They became healthier and longer-living. Nutrition improved considerably, average height increased for both men and women, and the country became affluent and health-conscious enough to emphasise (correctly) the newly-perceived problem of the overweight.

ECONOMIC PROBLEMS

Yet the modern age was also a period when Britain's relative economic performance declined appreciably by comparison with traditional and new competitors. There had been long-term decline from the 1870s, but, between 1960 and 1981, Britain's annual growth in gross domestic product was lower than that of all the other eighteen OECD countries. The average standard of living fell beneath that of Germany, Japan, France and Italy in the post-1960 period. There were serious problems with under-investment, low industrial productivity, limited innovation, poor management, especially production management, and obstructive trade unions. A sense of decline, pervasive at times, was especially characteristic in the 1970s. The cover of the satirical magazine *Private Eye* on 10 January 1975 showed the oil-rich king of Saudi Arabia, then visiting London, with the caption 'Britain Sold Shock. New Man at Palace'. Ironically, the discovery of oil in the North Sea in 1970, and its production from 1975, was to help ease Britain's balance-of-payments problem, though it did not prevent continued economic decline relative to competitors who lacked that resource. Thus, the oil masked the consequences of this decline from most of the population, creating, at the same time, a dangerous dependence.

   In addition, longer-term structural changes in the British and world economies created major problems, particularly with widespread unemployment in the early 1980s and early 1990s, a decline in manufacturing, especially heavy manufacturing industry with associated regional problems, and difficulties in maintaining a stable currency. In both recessions, the rising ownership of goods was in part met by increased imports, while British industry was harmed by the high exchange-rate of sterling as the interests of producers were subordinated to those of finance, not least due to a determination to reduce inflation. The post-war commitment to full employment was not met, and was increasingly regarded as unrealistic. The decline of manufacturing continued so that by 2010 it represented only about 12 per cent of the economy, half the percentage in the early 1990s.

These problems interacted with aspects of the 'political economy', not least the rising power of trade unions with their generally perceived determination to put sectional interests first, the conviction of politicians that they could improve the economy, and a variety of interventionist policies that generally did not have this result. Trade union membership rose from 1½ million in 1895 to over 13 million in 1979. Union leaders, such as Ernest Bevin, General Secretary of the Transport and General Workers Union 1921–40, Walter Citrine, Jack Jones, General Secretary of the Transport and General Workers Union 1968–78, and Hugh Scanlon, the engineers' leader, wielded great influence from the late 1930s until the Conservatives came to power in 1979. The trade unions played key roles in what was a corporatist state. During the Second World War, despite strikes, labour relations were far better than in the earlier world war, and the institutional freedom of the unions was preserved alongside central planning and wage restraint. The post-war Labour government realised many of the unions' political aims, including nationalisation of much of industry (coal, steel, railways, electricity supply, gas), universal statutory social services, and the goal of full employment; and a wages policy was maintained until 1950. The unions' refusal to continue the wages policy helped lose Labour the general election in 1951, although it won more votes than the Conservatives (who won more seats in Parliament). In 1974, Jack Jones forged a social compact (generally known as the social contract) with the Labour government of Harold Wilson (Prime Minister 1964–70, 1974–6) under which the unions were to moderate wage demands in return for acceptance of their views on legislation.

Relations between the unions and Conservative governments were more acrimonious, not least because political differences were matched by an absence of common assumptions, experiences and history.

Nevertheless, the Conservative Party and governments attempted to keep on good relations with the trade unions from 1946 until 1964, which was one aspect of 'Butskellism'. In contrast, strikes by the National Union of Miners, some of whose leaders were motivated by political hostility, defeated the Conservative government of Edward Heath in 1972 and, crucially, 1974. In the 1970s, thanks to television and power cuts, people became accustomed respectively to the immediacy of picket-line violence and to taking baths in the dark.

Trade union power and economic problems helped to discredit the post-war social democratic consensus, particularly the notion of the planned, corporatist state, and led to a reaction in the form of 'Thatcherism'. Unions engaged in wasteful demarcation disputes and many shop stewards adopted the language and attitudes of class warfare and economic conflict. A 'winter of discontent' in 1978–9, with strikes by hospital ancillary staff, ambulancemen and others in which 'secondary picketing' (disrupting work at concerns not otherwise involved in the dispute) had played a major and disruptive role, helped Thatcher to victory in 1979. She had little time for discussions with trade union leaders, believing that they played too large and disruptive a role in the economy, and she secured legislation to limit their powers, a task that Wilson had failed to achieve in 1969 when the bill based on the 'In Place of Strife' white paper (proposed legislation) was withdrawn due to trade union and Labour Party opposition. Meanwhile, the miners' strike in 1984–5 was only beaten after a long struggle, and then in part because the miners were divided and the weather good.

Under Thatcher, there was a thorough and widespread assault on trade unionism in order to further her goals of economic growth and individual freedom: picketing and secondary strike action were greatly limited, pre-entry closed shops largely abolished, and unions forced to ballot members by post before strikes were called. Fixed-term contracts for employees became more common. In the late 1980s, trade union militancy, which had been a very serious problem, became less common, and the level of industrial action (strikes) continued to fall in the early 1990s. By 1990, only 48 per cent of employees were union members and the number covered by closed-shop agreements had fallen to 0.5 million, compared with 4.5 million a decade earlier. Trade Union Congress membership fell to 7.3 million by January 1994, although this was not the total trade union membership, which remained well over 8 million. Far more wage negotiations were at a local level, there were fewer demarcation disputes, and the spread of 'single-union agreements' eased industrial tension. Thanks to privatisation in the 1980s and early 1990s, fewer trade unionists were the employees of state-owned companies. Thatcher found it harder, however, to foster and manage economic growth.

Aside from difficulties with the unions, there was also a lack of continuity in economic policy, for example over regional aid. The steel industry was nationalised in 1949 and 1967, and privatised in 1953 and then again after 1979, this time alongside gas, electricity, telephones, water, rail and much else, as the Conservatives under Thatcher, and then (from 1990) John Major, strove to diminish the role of the state and to revive economic liberalism. Their success was limited: in 1995, one in five of the British workforce was still employed in the public sector.

Despite the pursuit of a variety of economic policies since the Second World War, economic growth did not match political expectations, leading to disagreement over expenditure priorities. A major increase in government expenditure and employment since 1914 increased the importance of these disputes. The national budget was unable to sustain the assumptions and demands of politicians on behalf of, for example, social welfare and defence. Thus, the devaluation of the pound by 30.5 per cent in 1949 was followed by public-expenditure cuts, leading to resignations by left-wing Labour ministers, especially Aneurin Bevan and Wilson. Alongside the often unsuccessful management of the economy by politicians, notably the delay until 1967 by the Wilson government in devaluing sterling, there was also at times a serious neglect of aspects of the economy, symbolised by the remark of Sir Alec Douglas-Home, who renounced his earldom to become Conservative Prime Minister (1963–4), that his grasp of economics was of the 'matchstick variety'.

Poor economic management and trade union power, which thwarted the connection between high unemployment and low inflation, were in part to blame for high rates of inflation, which rose to an annual average of 15.8 per cent in 1972–5, and for the subsequent need to turn for assistance to foreign sources of finance, in the shape of the International Monetary Fund (1976). All post-war premiers, with the possible exception of James Callaghan (Labour, 1976–9), probably spent too much time on foreign policy and certainly found it difficult to abandon the expensive habit of seeing Britain as a major international player, a habit unhelpfully continued by Tony Blair (Labour, 1997–2007).

POLITICAL CULTURES

Higher living standards and an overall low rate of economic growth were scant consolation to those with diminished experiences and disappointed expectations. And yet a striking feature of the domestic and international problems that Britain encountered is that they did not lead to a consistent or massive radicalisation of British politics. There were exceptions: Strathclyde's militancy resulted in it being termed 'Red Clydeside' from the First World War, and unrest there in 1919 led to tanks on Glasgow's streets. The British Communist Party was formed in 1920. However, the TUC-organised General Strike in 1926 in support of the coal miners who had been locked out (allowed to return only if they accepted wage cuts), was swiftly brought to an end by the firmness of the Baldwin government and the resulting lack of nerve of the trade union leadership. The TUC did not want a protracted crisis and the miners were abandoned.

The 1930s saw the formation, by Sir Oswald Mosley, of the New Party, which subsequently evolved into the British Union of Fascists. Mosley, who had been successively a Conservative, Independent and then Labour MP, was a would-be dictator whose changing views revolved around a fixed point of belief in himself. He deliberately staged marches by his paramilitary Blackshirts in areas of Jewish settlement, particularly the East End of London and Manchester, in order to provoke violence. Mosley was discredited by his demagoguery, violence and links with Nazi Germany, and was imprisoned during the Second World War.

Some writers of the period expressed the fear that sinister conspiracies lay behind political and industrial problems, although this was only true to a very limited extent. This was the theme of the popular adventure novel *Bulldog Drummond* (1921) by 'Sapper' (Lieutenant-Colonel H. C. McNeile). John Buchan (1875–1940), a Scottish writer who served in intelligence during the First World War, before becoming an MP and Governor-General of Canada, discerned in his popular adventure novel *The Three Hostages* (1924), 'wreckers on the grand scale, merchants of pessimism, giving society another kick downhill whenever it had a chance of finding its balance, and then pocketing their profits . . . they used the fanatics . . . whose key was a wild hatred of something or other, or a reasoned belief in anarchy'. In *The Big Four* (1927) by the detective writer Agatha Christie (1890–1976), the best-selling author of all time, 'The world-wide unrest, the labour troubles that beset every nation, and the revolutions that break out in some . . . there is a force behind the scenes which aims at nothing less than the disintegration of civilisation.' Technology was at the service of this force: 'a concentration of wireless energy far beyond anything so far attempted, and capable of focusing a beam of great intensity upon some given spot . . . atomic energy', so that the Big Four could become 'the dictators of the world'. Such sinister threats facing Britain were to become a staple of spy thrillers, as in the novels of Ian Fleming (1908–64), beginning with *Casino Royale* (1953). Adventure stories, many of which testified to the imaginative potency of the new technology, Fleming's series of James Bond thrillers also revealed a sense of the nation under threat, an imaginative extension of the challenges facing the country.

Yet, radicalism directed to the overthrow of the political system was to make little impact in Britain and the continuity of parliamentary government was not broken. Arguably the most successful of those who called for change were the suffragettes, who won votes for women in 1918. The combined total membership of the Communists and the Fascists never exceeded 70,000, and the economic upturn of 1934 stemmed rising support for Mosley. Despite their subsequent reputation, far more Cambridge undergraduates of the 1930s were interested in sport than in Communist activism. The widening of the franchise in 1918 and the growth and nature of the Labour Party helped to limit radicalism.

The limited extent of radicalism was even more true after the Second World War. Nazi activities had discredited the extreme right, while the policies and eventual failure of the Soviet Union struck successive blows at the credibility of the far left. Harry Pollitt, General Secretary of the British Communist Party 1929–39 and 1941–56, became disillusioned with the Stalinism he had served so faithfully after Krushchev's revelations about its nature, while, in 1968, the Communist Party of Great Britain condemned the Soviet invasion of Czechoslovakia. The Labour Party drifted to the left in the 1970s and was affected by 'entryism' by far-left groups, so that there was little to choose in the 1980s between the views of some Labour MPs and western European Communists. Yet this situation helped to lead to four successive Labour defeats in the general elections of 1979, 1983, 1987 and 1992, the most unimpressive record of any major political party since the decline of the Liberals after the First World War, and one that was achieved despite serious economic difficulties for Conservative governments at the beginning of the 1980s and before the 1992 election.

The attempt to create a collectivist society by means of state action, a new-model society planned in accordance with socialist principles, was rejected not only by the electorate, but also, in the late 1980s and early 1990s, by the Labour Party itself under the leadership of Neil Kinnock (1983–92), John Smith (1992–94) and Tony Blair (1994–2007). The rising popularity of the party under Blair was directly linked to the espousal of policies deemed moderate, and he easily defeated John Major in the general election of 1997, going on to win strong majorities in 2001 and 2005. Similarly, successive public opinion polls in the 1980s and early 1990s revealed limited support for much of the agenda of the 'new right', with its emphasis on self-reliance and a limited role for the state and, instead, there was clear popular backing for the welfare state, especially the National Health Service. Similarly, the recessions of the early 1980s and early 1990s did not lead to a revival of left-wing radicalism. The hardcore of the Communist Party who refused to accept reconfiguration into Democratic Left put up four candidates in 1992, only for them to win an average of 150 votes.

The relationship between the lack of defeat in war and the absence of a successful challenge to the political system, or at least a major transformation of it, is unclear but suggestive. Germany, Japan, France, Italy and Austria all suffered serious defeat in the First and/or Second World Wars, leading to a political and institutional transformation which has been as important for the subsequent success of most of those societies as the rebuilding of economic systems on which attention is usually focused. No such process took place in Britain. Whereas for most European countries, the history of the twentieth century was one of shame, defeat and/or repression, for Britain it was not.

Indeed, in several respects, the essential features of the political system in early 1997 were still those of before 1914: a hereditary monarchy with limited, essentially consultative powers, albeit one that adopted the British name of Windsor in 1917 in place of that of Saxe-Coburg and Gotha, a bicameral Parliament, with the House of Commons being the most powerful and only elected chamber, national political parties with recognisably different regional and social bases of support, a largely two-party system, an absence of proportional representation, and a centralised British state without regional assemblies, or, still more, devolved or independent parliaments for Scotland and Wales. Britain remained in some respects an elective dictatorship, with the Prime Minister enjoying great power as head of both the executive and the leading party in the legislature, and national leader of that party. The social system was still markedly inegalitarian, and the political system, the civil service, the armed forces, the professions, the banking system, large companies and the universities were disproportionately dominated by those whose background cannot be described as working class. The Conservatives stressed the modest origins and difficult upbringing of Major, Prime Minister from 1990 to 1997, but neither circumstance was true of the bulk of his Cabinet and parliamentary colleagues.

IRISH INDEPENDENCE

And yet, there had also been major changes during the century, which can be summarised under the headings of Ireland, empire, Europe, mass immigration, democratisation and the decline of British cohesion. War hit the British empire hard, weakening it in resources and morale. The first major loss was Ireland. Although not strictly comparable, it is instructive to note that half a million men of Irish descent, both Protestant and Catholic, volunteered to fight for King George V in 1914; while, in contrast, Sir Roger Casement's attempt to raise an Irish Brigade for the Germans from prisoners of war failed. Moreover, fewer than 2,000 rose in the Easter Rising of 1916 in Dublin, an unsuccessful attempt to create an independent Irish Republic, although in part the numbers reflected the many who heeded Eoin O'Neill's countermand to the Rising. The numerous soldiers' wives of Dublin, when informed by the rebels that the establishment of a republic meant that the payment of separation allowances had now ended, responded not with national- ist enthusiasm but with anger. Outside Dublin, the planned nationalist uprising failed to materialise.

The firm British response, however, served to radicalise Irish public opinion. Martial law was declared and a series of trials, executions and internments provided martyrs for the nationalist cause. In the 1918 general election, 73 out of the 105 Irish parliamentary seats were won by the Sinn Fein party, nationalists under Eamonn de Valera, who refused to attend Westminster and demanded independence. They rejected the policy of 'home rule within the empire' which John Redmond (1856–1918), the leading pre-war Irish politician, had supported and which had been the basis of the Home Rule Act in 1914. Redmond's brother, a home rule MP, had died fighting for George V in the First World War. Sinn Fein replaced the home rule Irish Party as the focus of Irish nationalism.

Instead, in January 1919, a unilateral declaration of independence was issued by a new national assembly (Dáil Eireann), and the nationalist Irish Volunteers, soon to rename themselves the Irish Republican Army (IRA), staged their first fatal ambush. British refusal to accept independence led to a brutal war in 1919–21, followed by the Anglo-Irish Treaty of December 1921, which brought partition and effective independence for the new Irish Free State, which governed most of the island. The Irish Free State became a self-governing Dominion within the British empire with a Governor-General appointed by the Crown, although on the recommendation of the Taoiseach by the 1930s. The Protestant Unionists of the north refused to accept this, and six out of the nine counties of Ulster opted out and became Northern Ireland, which remained part of the United Kingdom and was represented at Westminster by twelve MPs (increased after 1979 to seventeen). It was self-governed and became very much a Protestant state, its Catholic minority suffering discrimination; although the extent of this is controversial and arguments that Catholics were worse treated in the allocation of public housing have been challenged. The partition was opposed by much of the IRA, which mounted a terrorist campaign in Ulster in 1921 and fought the newly-independent government in the south in 1922–3, the latter a more bloody conflict than the War of Independence. The IRA was beaten in both Ulster and the Irish Free State: IRA terrorism led to a vigorous response from the Irish government, which executed 77 rebels and imprisoned 12,000. Thereafter IRA terrorism remained a minor irritant, in both north and south, until the late 1960s.

De Valera, who had been leader of Sinn Fein in 1917–26 and had rejected the Anglo-Irish Treaty in 1921, won the 1932 election with the Fianna Fail party he had founded in 1926, and was, thereafter, President of the Executive Council (1932–7), Prime Minister (1937–48, 1951–4, 1957–9), and President (1959–73). Much of the IRA was willing to accept his leadership and, indeed, he took some of its members into the government and the police. Others, however, wished to fight on for a united Ireland and this led them into conflict with de Valera, not least when they raided army bases, in order to gain arms, and took money and arms from Hitler. De Valera responded with imprisonment and executions, and, like the British government in Northern Ireland in the early 1980s, faced IRA hunger-strikers. He was unwilling to fight to push Ireland's territorial claim to Northern Ireland, although it was expressed in the 1937 constitution. Under that constitution, the oath of allegiance to the Crown that MPs had been obliged to take under the

Anglo-Irish Treaty of 1921 was abolished. Vestigial British authority was extinguished by the Republic of Ireland Act (1948).

The IRA terrorist campaign of 1958–62 in Northern Ireland had no success, but, later in the decade, a civil rights movement, essentially complaining about the position of Catholics, led to a harsh and insensitive response and to violence, resulting in the intervention of British troops (1969), the suspension of the Unionist provincial government and its replacement by direct rule from London (1972). By September 1992, 3,000 people had died in the 'troubles', many as a result of terrorism by the Provisional IRA, though with an increasing number killed by Protestant paramilitary groups determined that Ulster should remain part of the United Kingdom. IRA terrorism on the British mainland began in 1972, included attacks on the Conservative Party conference at Brighton (1984), and the Cabinet (1991), and led to the deaths of three Conservative MPs. Talks between the British and Irish governments produced, on 15 December 1993, the Downing Street Declaration, agreeing to a shared sovereignty that would guarantee the rights of nationalists, while Unionists were assured that they would not be forced into a united Ireland. A paramilitary ceasefire followed in 1994 and negotiations in 1995. The ceasefire broke down in 1996, in large part over the decommissioning (handing over for destruction) of IRA weapons, but it was resumed in 1997 and in 1998 the Good Friday (10 April) Agreement laid the basis for the resumption of provincial self-government. The settlement was endorsed by 71 per cent of the voters in Northern Ireland who voted in a referendum in May 1998. An Assembly and an Executive were both created, and the Assembly met for the first time in July 1998.

THE FIRST WORLD WAR, 1914–18

The loss of Ireland in 1922 (although, initially, it remained part of the Empire with Dominion status) revealed the weakness of the British empire when confronted by a powerful nationalist movement. The First World War, in which Britain had played a major role on the victorious side, mobilising her resources of people and wealth as never before, was, however, followed by the expansion of the British empire to its greatest extent. The war began with pistol shots in Sarajevo, the assassination by Serbian terrorists of Archduke Franz Ferdinand, the heir to the Austro-Hungarian empire. The conflict pitted a large coalition, in which Britain, France, Russia, Italy and, from 1917, the USA were the major powers, against Germany, Austria-Hungary, Bulgaria and Turkey.

The German invasion of Belgium, as a means to out-flank French forces, led Britain, which had guaranteed Belgian neutrality, to declare war on 4 August 1914. The German drive, first on Paris and then on the Channel ports, was thwarted, and, late in 1914, both sides dug in across north-eastern France on Germany's 'western front'. The concentration of large forces in a relatively small area, the defensive strength of trench positions (particularly thanks to the machine gun), and the difficulty of making substantial gains even if opposing lines were breached, ensured that, until the collapse of the German position in the last weeks of 1918, the situation was essentially deadlocked. British attacks, as at Neuve-Chapelle and Loos (1915), the Somme (1916), and Arras and Passchendaele (1917), led to unprecedentedly enormous losses of men with little gain of territory. Scottish losses were disproportionately high: 10 per cent of male Scots aged between 16 and 50, one in six of the imperial war dead. Nevertheless, public support for the war effort remained strong.

The Western Front dominated British strategy, not least because of concern about French stability, and was responsible for most of their 750,000 dead. The blocking of German offensives there in 1914, 1916 and 1918 were essential preconditions of victory, and British battlefield success in 1918 was crucial. There were also attempts to search out a weaker front and to strike at Germany's allies. These attempts led to the disastrous expedition to the Dardanelles (1915), whose forceful advocate, the energetic First Lord of the Admiralty, Winston Churchill, resigned, and to failures in Iraq (1916) and at Salonika (1916), but also to Allenby's successful campaign in Palestine (1917–18). The German colonies were overrun. The threat from the German surface fleet was blocked at the indecisive battle of Jutland (1916), but their submarines took a heavy toll of British merchant shipping, until their impact was lessened by the use of convoys and the entry of America.

The scale and duration of the struggle resulted in an unprecedented mobilisation of national resources, including, after over two million men had already volunteered to fight for king and country, the introduction of conscription (1916), and state direction of much of the economy. The war gave a tremendous boost to the role of the state and the machinery of government. The Cabinet Office was created in 1916. The allocation of resources by the new Ministry of Food led to a rise in civilian living standards and an improvement in the life expectancy of those of the worst-off sections of the pre-war working class who were exempt from war service. State regulation increased in all spheres so that the nature of rural socio-economic relationships was changed in 1917 with the introduction of statutory agricultural wage boards and the control of agricultural rents.

Victory owed much to the German defeat on the Western Front, although the war was in part won as a result of the collapse of Austria-Hungary and the exacerbation of the military, economic and domestic problems facing the Germans which destroyed their will to fight. The German overseas empire was distributed among the victors, Britain gaining League of Nations mandates for Tanganyika, part of Togo and a sliver of the Cameroons, all in Africa, and Nauru Island in the Pacific. War with Germany's ally Turkey led to the annexation of Egypt (1914), and the gaining of mandates over Palestine, TransJordan and Iraq when Turkey's empire was partitioned at the end of the war. Ardent imperialists, such as Lord Milner and Leo Amery, pressed for the strengthening of the empire, partly in the hope that this would mean that Britain need never again be dragged into the Continental mire. British influence increased in both Persia and Turkey, and British forces, operating against the Communists in the Russian Civil War that followed their coup in 1917, moved into the Caucasus, Central Asia, and the White Sea region, and were deployed in the Baltic and the Black Sea. George, Viscount Curzon, Foreign Secretary in 1919, suggested the annexation of parts of the Russian empire.

THE POLITICS OF THE 1920s

This high tide of empire was to ebb very fast. The strain of the First World War, the vast number of men lost, the money spent, and the exhaustion produced by constant effort, left Britain unable to sustain her international ambitions, and this problem was exacerbated by political division. Lloyd George had split the Liberal Party when, in order to bring more decisive war leadership and further his own ambition, he had replaced Asquith as Prime Minister at the end of 1916, and he was dependent on Conservative support, a measure that strained post-war Conservative unity. Thus, despite the major role that Britain played in the making of the Versailles Peace Treaty (1919) and Lloyd George's strutting on the global stage, there was an absence of stable leadership.

In 1922, there was a Conservative revolt from below, by back-benchers, junior ministers and constituency activists: a meeting of the parliamentary Conservative Party at the Carlton Club, led to the decision to abandon the coalition. Lloyd George now fell, but so too did the Conservative leader Austen Chamberlain, who had sought continued support for the coalition. Chamberlain's predecessor, Andrew Bonar Law, returned as party leader, formed a totally Conservative government, and easily won the 1922 general election. Far from having broken the mould of British politics, Lloyd George was consigned to the political wilderness. When he had held power, he had been unwilling to support electoral reform, the proportional representation that would have helped the Liberals in the 1920s (and today), and, once out of power, he certainly could not obtain such a change.

Liberal disunity, and the decline or obsolescence of distinctive Liberal issues, helped in the rise of Labour, which became the official opposition after the 1922 election. The number of Labour MPs rose from 29 in 1906 to 288 in 1929. Its trade union alliance allowed Labour to identify itself as the natural party of the working class, and thus to benefit from the extension of the franchise, and from the doubling of trade union membership from 4 million in 1914 to 8 million in 1920. The party constitution of 1918 consolidated male trade union domination of Labour. Liberalism survived best in areas such as Cornwall where trade unions were weak, and is still strong there. The 1918 Reform Act gave the vote to men over 21 fulfilling a six-months residence qualification and to women over 30 (with some important social restrictions), increasing the electorate from 8 to 21 million. A Redistribution Act was based on the principle of equal size of constituency electorates, but the opportunity to introduce proportional representation was lost.

The new electorate, which was not interested in such pre-war Liberal Nonconformist causes as the disestablishment of the Church of England, the temperance movement and church schools, was potentially volatile. Winning its support posed a considerable challenge to politicians, similar to that which had confronted Disraeli and Gladstone when the Victorian electorate expanded. Politics became more professional as the management of constituencies and political parties was now more a matter of full-time activity. Under Stanley Baldwin, Conservative leader 1923–37 and Prime Minister 1923–4, 1924–9 and 1935–7, the media were harnessed to create a political image for a mass electorate. Baldwin 're-packaged' himself energetically for the voters, and during the General Strike of 1926 he used the *British Gazette* to spread government views.

The 1920s were a period in which British governments drew in their horns. At home, spending was cut, the 'Geddes Axe' – the report of the Geddes committee (1922) – leading to cuts in education, housing and the armed forces. The homes that had been promised to those 'heroes' who had survived the mud and machine guns of the Somme and Passchendaele, and the other mass graves of humanity on the Western Front, were not all built, as the financial austerity of the Treasury thwarted some of the aspirations of the 1919 Housing Act. As Chancellor of the Exchequer (1924–9), Churchill, who had left the Liberals for the Conservatives in 1924, cut taxes and, in 1925, put Britain back on the Gold Standard at the pre-war rate with the dollar. Designed as a sign of financial strength, this rate over-valued the pound, hit exports and harmed manufacturing. Britain had to abandon the Gold Standard in September 1931 and the pound then dropped rapidly against the dollar.

The complex manoeuvres of three-party politics resulted in minority Labour governments under Ramsay MacDonald in 1924 and 1929–31. The second was badly affected by the world economic crisis that began in 1929. The government divided over the cuts that were believed necessary, in the midst of a European banking crisis, to balance the budget in order to restore confidence in sterling, especially a cut in unemployment benefit. Unwilling to accept the last, the divided Labour Cabinet resigned on 23 August 1931, leading, next day, to a cross-party National Government headed by MacDonald. Largely composed of Conservatives and supported by only a few Labour and Liberal MPs, the National Government continued in power until the wartime coalition was formed in 1940. MacDonald was succeeded as Prime Minister by Baldwin (1935) and by Baldwin's successor as Conservative leader, Neville Chamberlain (1937); and the government won the general elections of 1931 and 1935. The Conservatives benefited from the economic upturn of 1934 and from the consolidation of propertied and business interests into one anti-socialist party.

Although the cinema provided escapism, the new electrical goods, however, were of scant value to the unemployed: nearly 3 million in late 1932, and, despite a strong recovery in 1934–7, still above one million until 1941. Heavy industry was especially badly hit by the Depression, although it had already encountered serious problems after the First World War; 238,000 tons of shipping were launched from shipyards on the Tyne in 1913, but fewer than 7,000 in 1933. More than a quarter of the Scottish labour force was out of work in 1931–3, as was about one-third of Derbyshire's miners; and the 1933 Derbyshire march of the National Unemployed Workers' Movement used the slogans of the movement: 'We refuse to starve in silence . . . We want work schemes.' The decline of the Cornish tin industry was such that unemployment in Redruth in 1939 was 25 per cent; in Cornwall as a whole, the percentage was 18–20. Many of those who had work faced low wages, a life of shifts and expedients, inadequate food and poor housing; but, for many others, the 1930s was a period of prosperity and this prosperity helped to account for the sweeping victory of the Conservative-dominated National Government in the 1935 British election. About half the working class voted Conservative in the 1931 and 1935 elections, with working-class women particularly prone to do so.

EMPIRE IN THE 1920s AND 1930s

Abroad, intervention in Russia against the Communists had been a failure and was abandoned. In the Middle East, revolts in Egypt (1919) and Iraq (1920) led to Britain granting them independence, while British influence collapsed in Persia (1921), and the British backed down in their confrontation with Turkey (1922–3), the last being a crucial factor in Lloyd George's fall. These failures were a consequence of what had already been obvious in the decades prior to the First World War: the problems created by the rise of other states and Britain's global commitments, as well as of the particular strains that arose from that conflict and from subsequent developments. There was a lack of resources and will to sustain schemes for imperial expansion.

And yet the empire was still very much a living reality in the inter-war period. The loss of most of Ireland under the Anglo-Irish Treaty of December 1921, which took effect from 1922, was not followed by any further reduction of cohesion within the British Isles. The Labour government failed to deliver on hopes of Scottish home rule in 1924, and elements in the Scottish Home Rule Association began to think that a national party would be more effective. The National Party of Scotland, founded in 1928, and the Scottish Self-Government Party, founded in 1932, united in 1934 to form the Scottish National Party, but it did not win a parliamentary seat until 1945.

In many respects imperial links developed further, a process given concrete form in the majestic buildings designed by Sir Edwin Lutyens and Sir Herbert Baker for the official quarter in New Delhi, from where

India was governed, and finished in the 1930s. Economic relations between Britain and the empire became closer, while communications improved. Imperial Airways, a company founded with government support (1924), produced new routes for the empire. Weekly services began to Cape Town (1932), Brisbane (1934) and Hong Kong (1936); in contrast, thanks to the problem of flying the Atlantic, they only began to New York in 1946. It took nine days to fly to Cape Town in 1936, and fourteen to Adelaide, but these were far less than sailing times. Commitment to the empire was demonstrated in a different form by the building of a major new naval base for the defence of the Far East at Singapore. Empire Day was important in the 1920s and 1930s.

The empire faced serious problems in the 1930s, not least pressure from the Indian National Congress and serious disturbances in Palestine, where there was violent Arab opposition to Jewish immigration. As with Ireland in 1914, it is not clear what would have happened in India had there not been war from 1939. The Government of India Act (1935) was bitterly opposed by Conservatives such as Churchill, who saw its moves towards self-government as a step towards the abandonment of empire, but was designed to ensure the British retention of the substance of power; however, the provincial elections of 1937 were a success for Congress. Nevertheless, it was the Second World War that undermined the empire, even as it brought the British occupation of a little more territory, Somaliland and Libya, both formerly Italian, and led Churchill to consider the annexation of the latter, a move the American government successfully opposed.

THE SECOND WORLD WAR, 1939–45

The Second World War cost fewer British lives than the First, and the British army was spared from being put through the mangle of the trenches, but Britain came closer to defeat. As in 1914, she went to war to resist German aggression and to fulfil the logic of her alliance politics, but in 1939–40 Hitler's Germany destroyed the system of British alliances. The eastern front was ended within weeks as Poland was defeated (1939), Stalin's Soviet Union (Russia plus) taking its share after it also had attacked Poland; while the western front was rolled up in 1940 in a German *blitzkrieg* (lightning war) that overran the Netherlands, Belgium and France and brutally exposed the military failure of the Anglo-French alliance. Expelled from the

Continent – though able by bravery, skill and luck to save much of the army in the evacuation from Dunkirk – Britain had the valuable support of its empire and control of the sea; but the first was threatened by Italy and Japan and the second under attack from German airpower and still more from German U-boats (submarines).

Britain appeared to have lost the war, and it is not surprising that several major politicians were willing to consider a negotiated peace with Hitler, although it was clear from Hitler's conduct that he could not be trusted to respect any agreement. Hesitation in Britain was ended in May 1940 by the replacement of Neville Chamberlain, a Prime Minister identified with the appeasement of Germany in the late 1930s and with failure in war, by the egotistical, but effective, Churchill. Convinced in 1940 of the total rightness of the British cause and the utter untrustworthiness of Hitler, he was determined to fight on, however bleak the situation might be. Churchill pinned his hopes on bringing the United States into the war. The blunting of German airpower in the Battle of Britain led Hitler to call off Operation Sealion, his planned invasion of Britain (1940). However, British successes against the Italians in North Africa that winter were followed, in 1941, by a German offensive there and by their conquest of Yugoslavia and Greece, the latter entailing the defeat of British forces in Greece and Crete.

The loss of the Greek island of Crete in May 1941 was the last major defeat for an isolated Britain. Hitherto, her European allies had offered little as London had become a collecting house for defeated governments in exile. The German assault on the Soviet Union (June 1941) and the Japanese attack on Britain and the United States, followed by the declaration of war on the Americans by Japan's ally Germany (December 1941), totally altered the situation as Britain was now a member of a powerful coalition. There were still to be serious blows, especially in early 1942, and the Battle of the Atlantic against U-boats was not won until early 1943, but Britain was now part of an alliance system, linked to the strongest economy and financial power in the world, and, as Britain and her new allies successfully blunted German and Japanese offensives in late 1942, the long and stony path to victory appeared clearer: the Soviet victory at Stalingrad in the winter of 1942–3 was crucial. In May 1943 the Germans surrendered in North Africa to the British and Americans, who subsequently landed in Italy, which surrendered unconditionally in September 1943. The following June, Anglo-American forces landed in Normandy, and in May 1945 the Germans surrendered.

As with the last campaigns against Napoleon, Russian/Soviet strength had played a crucial role. However, the Anglo-American achievement had also been considerable, not least because they were responsible for the important sea and air wars against Germany, defeated the German forces in western Europe, provided the Soviet Union with valuable supplies, and were also bearing the brunt of the war with Japan. This conflict ended with Japanese surrender in August 1945 just a few days after the dropping of American atom bombs. Nuclear weapons were the most spectacular application of technology to warfare, but, in both world wars, British technology, especially in metallurgy and electronics, had made major contributions to advances in weaponry, not least tanks in the First World War and radar in the Second.

THE LOSS OF EMPIRE

The war had fatally weakened the empire. Britain had lost prestige and resources, her Dominion allies, especially Australia when menaced by Japan in 1942, had had to look to America for support, and there was a loss of confidence within Britain in the legacy of the past. The surrender of 'impregnable' Singapore to the Japanese on 15 February 1942, after a poorly-conducted campaign in Malaya and the loss of the *Prince of Wales* and the *Repulse* to Japanese bombers, was either the most humiliating defeat in modern British history, or one to rank with Cornwallis's surrender at Yorktown in 1781. The surrender of Singapore to Japan in February 1942 gravely weakened British prestige in Asia. Combined with the need for Indian support in the war against advancing Japanese forces, this defeat spelled the end of empire in the Indian subcontinent, the heart of the British imperial experience. In 1942, the Congress Party was offered independence after the war, in return for support during it, an offer that it spurned with its 'Quit India' movement.

In line with Gallup poll results since 1942, the Labour Party became a majority government for the first time in 1945. In large part, this result was a reaction against the Conservatives, as the party of privilege and pre-war division, and, instead, a vote in favour of the collectivism and social welfare offered by Labour. Labour was committed to Indian independence and this was achieved in 1947, although at the cost of partition into the new states of India and Pakistan and of large numbers of deaths in Hindu–Muslim clashes.

Despite Indian independence, that of Burma and Ceylon (1948), and the ending of the Palestine mandate in 1948, Britain was still a major imperial power and the Labour government, especially its Foreign Secretary, Ernest Bevin (1945–51), had high hopes of using imperial resources, particularly those of Africa, to strengthen the British economy and make her a less unequal partner in the Anglo-American partnership. Wartime conscription was continued. Bevin acted in a lordly fashion in the Middle East, but empire ran out in the sands of rising Arab nationalism and a lack of British resources, leading to a succession of crises starting with that in 1947 over sterling convertibility. The British faced a number of imperial problems in the early 1950s, including the Malayan Emergency (a Communist uprising, which was eventually tackled successfully), but it was the Suez Crisis of 1956, an attempt to destabilise the aggressive Arab nationalist regime of Gamal Abdul Nasser in Egypt, that clearly exposed their weakness.

Just as echoes of the appeasement of dictators in the 1930s were initially to be voiced when the Argentinians invaded the Falklands in 1982, and it was misleadingly thought that the British government would not respond, so in 1956 the Prime Minister, Anthony Eden (1955–7), who had resigned as Foreign Secretary in 1938 ostensibly in protest at appeasement, was determined not to repeat its mistakes and accept Nasser's nationalisation of the Suez Canal. Secretly acting in concert with France and Israel, Eden sent British forces to occupy the Canal Zone. The invasion was poorly planned, but it was American opposition and its impact on sterling that was crucial to weakening British resolve and thus leading to a humiliating withdrawal.

A lack of American support has been seen by some historians as a major problem for the empire ever since the Second World War; in 1956, American anger made Britain's dependent status obvious. However, once the 'Cold War' with the Soviet Union began, the Americans sought to sustain Britain's role as a world power. They were interested in preserving many of Britain's overseas bases, either to maintain Britain's utility as an ally, or to have them ready for American use. Nor did they want premature decolonisation to result in chaos and perhaps Communism. The Americans supported the continued British military presence east of Suez in the 1960s, notably in Aden, the Persian Gulf and Malaysia, and in the Suez Crisis itself saw themselves as rescuing a friend from a fit of madness. They sought to persuade Arab, Asian and African opinion that the USA was anti-imperialist in order to reduce the dangers posed by Soviet exploitation of the Suez Crisis, and by further Afro-Asian alienation from the West.

The fourteen years after the Suez Crisis witnessed the rapid loss of most of the rest of the British empire. The British people might not have been European-minded after 1950; but neither were they imperial-minded. After 'Suez' many leading Conservatives, especially Harold Macmillan, Prime Minister 1957–63, and lain Macleod, whom he appointed Colonial Secretary, became deeply disillusioned with the empire and ready to dismantle it. However, decolonisation was criticised by some right-wing Conservatives. Moreover, anti-colonialism was also a minority view.

Empire, however, was proving too expensive, too troublesome, and too provocative of other powers. Decolonisation was hastened by a strong upsurge in colonial nationalist movements, particularly in Ghana, which policy-makers did not know how to confront, as they sought to rest imperial rule on consent, not force. The American government encouraged decolonisation, while the logic of Britain's self-proclaimed imperial mission – bringing civilisation to backward areas of the globe – ensured that the granting of self-government could be presented as the inevitable terminus of empire. Independence was granted to Ghana and Malaya in 1957, Nigeria and Cyprus in 1960, Sierra Leone and Tanganyika in 1961, Jamaica and Uganda in 1962, and Kenya in 1963. Although in 1964 Wilson foolishly declared, 'We are a world power and a world influence or we are nothing', by 1969 none of Africa remained under British rule, and the 'east of Suez' defence policy, supported by both Labour and the Conservatives, had fallen victim to the consequences of the devaluation of sterling in 1967. British forces withdrew from Aden in 1967, the Persian Gulf in 1971, and Singapore in 1974 (most had left in 1971). Decolonisation was largely peaceful, although there were difficult struggles in some areas, notably Malaya, Cyprus, Kenya and Aden. Their legacy has helped compromise the reputation of empire, but, in practice, decolonisation proved less traumatic than was the case for Dutch, French, Belgian and Portuguese empires.

BRITAIN AND THE WORLD SINCE 1945

Britain's status as a major power was no longer territorial, no longer a consequence of empire, let alone economic strength. Instead, this status was a consequence of her being, from 1952, one of the few atomic powers, and of her active membership, both in American-led international organisations, especially NATO (the North Atlantic Treaty Organisation of which she was a founder member in 1949) and, from the 1970s, in the EEC (European Economic Community), which she eventually joined in 1973, and which later became the European Union (EU).

NATO was designed to defend western Europe against the Soviet Union, for the defeat of Germany in the Second World War was followed by fears of Soviet plans and by a Cold War that lasted until the collapse of the Soviet Union in 1991. Already, in mid-1944, planners for the Chiefs of Staff were suggesting a post-war reform of Germany and Japan so that they could play a role against a Soviet Union whose ambitions in eastern Europe were arousing growing concern. On 14 March 1946, the British embassy in Moscow asked if the world was now 'faced with the danger of the modern equivalent of the religious wars of the sixteenth century' with Soviet Communism battling against Western European social democracy and American capitalism for 'domination of the world'.

American assistance became a key point. Denied American expertise, by January 1947, Clement Attlee, Labour Prime Minister from 1945 to 1951, had decided to develop a British nuclear bomb; the first one was exploded in 1952. In contrast, in 1947, Britain and the USA signed a secret treaty for cooperation in signals intelligence. The Berlin Crisis (1948), in which the Soviet Union unsuccessfully blockaded Berlin, made clear the vulnerability of western Europe and furthered dependence on the United States. It led to the stationing of American B-29 strategic bombers in Britain.

In the Far East, British forces played a major role in resisting Communist aggression as part of United Nations forces in the Korean War (1950–3), while, in 1951, the Chiefs of Staff warned that the Soviet Union might be provoked by western rearmament into attacking in 1952. Under American pressure, Britain embarked on a costly rearmament programme in 1951 that undid many of the economic gains that had been made since 1948, and helped to strengthen the military commitment that has been such a heavy economic burden on post-war Britain. Defence spending took a higher percentage of gross national product than for other western European powers. The anti-Soviet political and strategic alignment was continued by subsequent governments, both Conservative (1951–64, 1970–4, 1979–97) and Labour (1964–70, 1974–9), until the Cold War closed with the dissolution of the Soviet Union in 1991. From 1960, American nuclear submarines equipped with Polaris missiles began to operate from the Holy Loch in Scotland and, by the Nassau Agreement of 1962, Macmillan persuaded President Kennedy to provide Britain with Polaris, which offered Britain a small but survivable, and therefore a not insignificant, submarine-based strategic nuclear force. That year, *Dr No*, the first of the James Bond adventure films, had the hero of the British secret service saving American missile tests. In the 1980s, despite the protests of the Campaign for Nuclear Disarmament, American Cruise missiles were deployed in Britain, and American bombers attacked Libya from British bases.

Empire was replaced by NATO, the Commonwealth and Europe. The Dominion status given to the 'white' colonies was a preliminary to the establishment of the British Commonwealth as an association of equal and autonomous partners (1931). In 1949, the prefix 'British' was discarded and it was decided that republics might remain members, a measure that enabled India to stay in. The Commonwealth was seen for a time as a source of British influence, or as the basis for an international community spanning the divides between first and third worlds, white and black, and its unity was fostered by a secretariat, established in 1965, and by heads-of-government meetings. However, disputes over relations with South Africa, then ruled by a white-minority government, over immigration policies, and over the consequences of British concentration on Europe, all led to serious differences between Britain and Commonwealth partners; although the absence of common interests and views was of greater long-term significance.

Economic, military and political links with former imperial possessions became less important. New Zealand and, even more, Australia looked to Japan, and later China, as economic partners, while Canada became part of a free-trade zone with the United States and Mexico. The United States replaced Britain as Canada's biggest export market after the Second World War, and as the biggest source of foreign investment there from the 1920s. The British share of this investment fell from 85 per cent in 1900 to 15 per cent in 1960, while the American share rose from 14 to 75 per cent. The percentage of the Australian and Canadian populations that could claim British descent fell appreciably after 1945. Britain had little role to play as the Pacific became an American lake and, in 1951, Australia and New Zealand entered into a defence pact with the United States. In the mid-1970s, members of the former sterling area largely switched their foreign reserves from pounds to dollars, putting further pressure on sterling.

BRITAIN AND AMERICA

The United States, in some respects, served Britain as a surrogate for empire, providing crucial military, political, economic and cultural links, and offering an important model. Part of the attraction was ideological. The American stress on the free market appealed to more groups in British society, not least to commercial interests, than the more statist and bureaucratic Continental societies. Anglo-American links slackened from the 1970s, not least because anglophilia became less important in America, and Britain had less to offer in terms of any special relationship. On the other hand, particularly through the role of American programmes on British television, American or American-derived products in British consumer society, the American presence in the British economy and its more diffuse, but still very important, mystique as a land of wealth and excitement, America remained very important to Britain, especially to British culture, in the widest sense of the word.

For linguistic and, to a certain extent, commercial reasons, post-war American cultural 'hegemony' was stronger in Britain than elsewhere in Europe, and thus accentuated differences. The Atlanticism of the 1960s led to the creation of Schools of English and American Studies in new universities such as East Anglia and Sussex, separate from those of European Studies. Few Victorians would have thought it sensible to study their literature and history within this sort of a context. British film audiences were under the sway of Hollywood, and American influence on television was considerable. When 'J.R.', the leading character in the television series *Dallas*, was shot, it was reported on the BBC news, the fictional world displacing its less exciting real counterpart. In the last quarter of the twentieth century, transatlantic air travel became much less expensive in real terms and the range of routes increased as large numbers visited America on holiday, notably to Florida. In addition, America was the largest market for popular music, a field in which Britain led. America also played a major role in the British economy, especially in car manufacture, oil drilling and refining, and electronics. In 1986, for example, 58 per cent of the foreign-owned manufacturing firms in Wales had American parent companies.

BRITAIN AND EUROPE SINCE 1945

The post-war movement towards western European unity reflected the particular interests of the participant states. Britain did not share the concern of Italy and Germany to anchor their new democracies, nor the willingness of France to surrender a portion of her sovereignty in order to restrict German independence, and so she was not one of the founding members of the European Economic Community (EEC), the basis of the modern European Union. The different nature of British commerce and investment was also important. Joining the EEC would have been far more disruptive for Britain than it was for the other states, because their trade was overwhelmingly Euro-centric, while less than half of Britain's trade was. Thus, joining entailed a major economic dislocation; which, for a country whose foreign trade was so vital, was bound to make her adjustment to membership more difficult.

It soon became apparent, however, that the EEC was going to be a success, at least in terms of economic growth, and the costs of staying out seemed greater than those of joining. As a result, successive governments, both Conservative and Labour, applied to join in 1961 and 1967, only to be rejected by the veto of the President of France, Charles de Gaulle, who argued that Britain's claim to a European identity was compromised by her American links. Ireland, which had planned to join with Britain, did not pursue membership. De Gaulle's resignation in 1969, and a fresh application in 1970, by the Conservative government under Edward Heath (1970–4), led to the successful negotiation of British entry. Britain joined in January 1973 (as did Ireland).

Division over the issue led the next Labour government, in 1975, to hold the first national referendum: 67.2 per cent of those who voted did so to remain in the EEC, though voters' interest in, and knowledge of, the issues were limited, they were misled about the political goals of the EEC, and they were more influenced by the support for membership displayed by most politicians. The only areas showing a majority against staying in were the Shetlands and the Western Isles, but only 59 per cent of the Scots who voted supported membership. Moreover, Protestant suspicion of continental Catholicism was probably responsible for the relatively low pro-vote in Ulster. In contrast, smaller percentages voted for devolution for Scotland and Wales in 1979, although they included the majority of those who voted in Scotland in 1979. Under the terms of the devolution referendum, which required a majority of the electorate (as opposed to votes cast), Scotland would have failed to vote yes to EEC membership in 1975; while, under the terms of the EEC referendum, Scotland voted yes to Labour's devolution proposals in 1979 by a not very different margin. Thus, the English and Welsh, but not the Scottish, electorate of the 1970s appeared to favour both membership of a European body with supra-national institutions, rationale and pretensions, and the retention of the configuration of the traditional British nation-state.

Concern about the European dimension grew as the limited objectives of most of the politicians who constructed the EEC developed in more ambitious directions, with the call to create stronger institutions, and to transfer a considerable measure of authority, and thus sovereignty, from the nation-states. Changing nomenclature registered new objectives: the EEC became the European Union, which developed wide-ranging political pretensions. In response, the nature and defence of national sovereignty became important issues and there was much debate about the meaning of sovereignty, particularly in the 1990s.

Politics was not the only sphere in which Britain interacted with the Continent. With increased numbers travelling for pleasure, as a consequence of greater disposable wealth among the bulk of the population, the development of the package holiday, the use of jet aircraft and the spread of car ownership, far more inhabitants of Britain than ever before visited the Continent, and far more than ever before also made a regular habit of doing so. Many of the metropolitan middle-class households that would have had servants in the 1930s, by the 1990s had a second home in France, and *The Times* could carry regular articles on where and how best to purchase such properties.

In addition, the opportunity of learning at least one foreign language was offered to all schoolchildren. Social differences, however, played a major role, both in language-learning and in leisure. By the mid-1990s, more than a quarter of Britons had still never holidayed abroad, regarding it as a luxury; and of the 56 million holidays taken in 1993, 32.5 million were in Britain. Holiday patterns were a clear sign of social difference but also, increasingly, of technology. Individual booking on-line greatly hit the travel industry in the 2000s and 2010s and was also associated with the rise of new low-cost airlines.

The British were also reluctant to learn foreign languages. In 1991–2, their schools taught an average of only 0.9 languages per pupil, which was the lowest in the EU, bar Portugal. French was the commonest foreign language in Britain's secondary schools, but it was studied by only 59 per cent of pupils in 1991–2; German was next at 20 per cent. The comparable percentages in Ireland were 69 and 24. Subsequently, Spanish was to take over the second place in British schools. The British were helped by the popularity of English in the EU. In 1991–2, 83 per cent of secondary-school pupils in the EU were learning English as a foreign language, followed by French at 32 per cent.

Economically and politically, an empire-shedding and post-imperial Britain identified more closely with the Continent in the second half of the century than in the first. The societies of western Europe felt threatened by Soviet power, while their economies were challenged by the staggering development of the 'dragon' countries of east Asia. Britain became more closely linked to Continental markets and suppliers than she had been in 1973, while her attraction for 'inward investment', especially from Japan, America and the other countries of the EEC, in part arose as a consequence of her access to that trading system. Yet, there were also important strains in the relationship.

SOCIAL CHANGE

The extent to which Britain was 'truly' part of Europe vexed commentators after the Second World War. In some respects, Britain, Ireland and the societies of western Europe became more similar. This was a consequence of broadly similar social trends, including secularisation, the emancipation of women and the move from the land. Sexual permissiveness, rising divorce rates, growing geographical mobility, the decline of traditional social distinctions, and the rise of youth culture, were all shared characteristics. Deference, aristocracies, and the rigidities of social stratification all declined, though differences in wealth, both capital and income, remained vast.

The decline of the role of the House of Lords was an important indication of a society that was less stratified, conservative and distinctive. In 1947, the Labour government was obstructed by the Lords in nationalising the steel industry. As a result, Attlee passed the Parliament Act (1949), which reduced the number of occasions on which the Lords could block legislation passed by the Commons before it became law from three to two, and reduced the delaying period of the Lords from two years to one. The aristocracy were also changed. The Life Peerages Act (1958) breached the hereditary principle of aristocratic status, by creating peerages that were not hereditary. The Peerage Act (1963) allowed peeresses to sit in their own right in the House of Lords, and permitted the disclaiming of hereditary peerages. Blair was to sweep most of the hereditary peers from the House of Lords.

The weakening of the Anglican Church in England, a process that really began with the Catholic Emancipation Act of 1829, gathered pace in the late twentieth century. The most influential clergyman of the inter-war years, William Temple, Archbishop of York 1929–42 and of Canterbury 1942–4, had sought to reverse the decline of organised religion, and to make England an Anglican nation again, and thus to justify the Church's claim to speak for it. But, although he strengthened the Church, Temple failed to give England a more clearly Christian character and his inspiration of the already developing role of the Church as a voice of social criticism and concern led to it being seen increasingly in a secular light. By the 1990s, only one in seven Britons was an active member of a Christian church, although over two-thirds claimed to be believers. Both for most believers and for the less or non-religious, faith became less important not only to the fabric of life but also to many of the turning points of individual lives, especially birth, marriage and death. Both the Church of England and the Scottish Episcopal Church were particularly badly hit. The position of the established churches in the British Isles, especially England, was also challenged by the rise of 'fundamentalist' Christianity, inspired from America, and also by 'new age' religions, while there was also an appreciable number of converts to Buddhism.

In Britain, Ireland and the Continent, social paternalism, patriarchal authority, respect for age and the nuclear family, and the stigma of illegitimacy, all declined in importance; while rights to divorce, abortion and contraception were established across most of western Europe (reducing the number of children available for adoption). In Britain, abortion was legalised in 1967 by the Abortion Act. Homosexual acts in private between consenting adults were decriminalised: in Britain by the Sexual Offences Act of 1967; although the Act was in part designed to control homosexuality, while the legislation was not extended to Scotland until 1981. As sexual freedom became more pronounced, the profile of avowed homosexuals and lesbians in society rose markedly. Co-habitation and one-parent families each became more common, while the number of lifetime celibates fell. About 31 per cent of live births in Scotland in 1994 were to unmarried mothers.

Throughout the British Isles, working hours and birth rates fell. Average rates of population growth in Britain as a whole were far lower in the inter-war period, when they fell to below replacement levels, than they had been in the nineteenth century. As a result, the number of children in an average family fell from three in 1910 to two in 1940. Despite a post-war birth-peak, or 'baby boom' in 1947, and another in 1962, population growth rates continued to decline in the 1950s and 1960s, to almost a standstill in the 1970s and early 1980s, before an upturn from

1982. However, after a stabilisation of the growth rate in the late 1980s and for most of the 1990s, it rose from the late 1990s, and greatly so in the 2000s. The distribution of the population also changed greatly. The population of suburban, commuter and southern England increased more rapidly than that of the north, London, and Scotland.

IMMIGRATION

In Britain, most of the immigration in the nineteenth and early twentieth centuries was from Europe: Irish after the potato famine of 1847–8; Russian and Polish Jews from the 1880s until the Aliens Act of 1905; and Poles and Ukrainians in the 1940s, after the Second World War; although there had also been substantial Chinese immigration at the end of the nineteenth and the start of the twentieth century, principally to sea-ports, such as London and Tyneside. There was a massive wave of Irish immigration during and after the Second World War. Successive waves of immigrants in the nineteenth and twentieth centuries faced poor housing and took on the less attractive jobs: the 'sweated' trades, such as tailoring, and casual labour in the docks and the building trade. Social position was crucial. Hannah Rothschild, from a wealthy Jewish banking family, could marry the future Liberal Prime Minister, Archibald, 5th Earl of Rosebery, in 1878 to the anger of a *Jewish Chronicle* opposed to mixed marriages. Herbert Samuel, also from a banking background, became, in 1909, the first practising Jew to sit in the British Cabinet, then a Liberal body; Disraeli was a convert to Christianity. However, most Jews faced much harsher conditions in the crowded conditions of the East End of London.

From the 1950s, there was large-scale immigration from the 'New Commonwealth', especially the West Indies and the Indian subcontinent. A temporary labour shortage in unattractive spheres of employment, such as transport, foundry work and nursing, led to an active sponsorship of immigration that accorded with Commonwealth idealism, but for which there was little popular support. Immigrants and other Black people encountered severe discrimination in the housing market as well as much personal hostility. The products of the 'imperial family' were not welcomed on the streets of Britain.

Concern about the scale of immigration and over growing racial tension, particularly over jobs and public housing, led to Immigration Acts (1962, 1968, 1971) that progressively reduced Commonwealth immigration. The Commonwealth Immigrants Act of 1968 deprived East African Asians with United Kingdom passports of the automatic right to entry.

Although racial discrimination was declared illegal in 1965, overt racism was a particular problem in the 1960s and early 1970s. In April 1968, a maverick Conservative MP, Enoch Powell, made a speech warning that immigration would lead to racial violence – 'rivers of blood' – and pressed for the limitation of immigration. A month later, a Gallup poll recorded that 74 per cent of Britons supported his views. In August 1972, the expulsion of 40,000 Ugandan Asians from Uganda and their admission into Britain fuelled fears of an immigration crisis. The racist National Front (NF) emerged in the years after 1970 as a potential force in British politics; although, due to the absence of proportional representation, no NF MP was elected.

The geographical impact of twentieth-century immigration varied greatly. West Indian, South Asian and African migrants concentrated in London, the west Midlands and south Yorkshire; relatively few went to Scotland, Wales, Ulster, rural or north-east England. In 1971, the percentage in Bradford was 7.1 and in Birmingham 6.7, but it was only 1.3 in Newcastle. Within individual cities, immigrants concentrated in particular areas, influenced by a mixture of opportunity and self-segregation. Few immigrants re-migrated. The overwhelming majority of the Caribbean immigrants who arrived in the 1950s and early 1960s planned to save money in order to buy land in the West Indies and return, but they only gained low-paid jobs and never earned enough: only a tenth of these immigrants returned in the 1980s.

Some immigrants sought assimilation. Thus the nineteenth-century Yiddish-speaking Jewish immigrants from eastern Europe were anglicised by the Jewish Board of Guardians and other institutions, so that their traditional language and culture were essentially lost. Many immigrant groups, however, strove to assert and/or retain a distinctive identity, as with the Notting Hill Carnival launched in 1964 as an attempt to celebrate Caribbean heritage in the face of much White discrimination. In certain cases, the assertion of a distinctive identity has been linked to a marked lack of sympathy for generally-accepted values, and over some issues, such as the mixed education of Asian Islamic women, this attitude created administrative and legal problems.

Britain has both 'multi-culturalism' and a degree of racial tension, and, though racial discrimination was illegal under the Race Relations Act (1977), racial violence played a role in the harassment of 'whites' and 'blacks'. For both, crime was a serious problem, with high rates of drug-dealing and muggings. Black hostility to what was seen as a discriminatory police force played a major role in the 1981 riots in south London and Liverpool and in subsequent violence. In October 1994, the 28,000-strong Metropolitan Police Force of London contained only 679 ethnic-minority officers; only one of the country's 384 chief superintendents then was from the same group. The situation subsequently improved, but there was another major upsurge of rioting in London in 2011. Although this rioting owed something to hostility to the police, the root cause was large-scale criminality by disaffected youths and a disproportionate percentage was Afro-Caribbean, although many were not.

While the effects of immigration became more of an issue in Britain, emigration fell; although it was still a major factor in the first quarter of the century, and net emigration, rather than net immigration, was the situation until the 1930s and then again in the 1950s.

BRITAIN AND THE EUROPEAN UNION

The expansion of the European Union led to a major rise in immigration in the 2000s, notably from Poland. Furthermore, the European Union proved far less amenable for the British economy than the empire had been, in large part because of the similarities between Britain and her neighbours, which made for a union of competitors rather than of partners. Britain ran a serious trade deficit with the rest of the EU from 1984 and this deficit dramatically increased from 2000 to reach £27,957 million in 2009.

There are also important political problems affecting the relationship. Scepticism about the notion of a European 'super state' and 'Euro-federalism' was widespread from the 1980s. Moreover, some of the apparent support for the European ideal in the 1980s was in fact tactical and opportunistic, and really designed to attack Mrs Thatcher. She signed the Single European Act in 1986 reducing national powers, but was not the most ardent admirer of European unity.

Two very different indicators were the scarcity of the European flag in Britain, and the markedly patriotic response of the British public to the Falklands Crisis of 1982, when British forces drove out invading Argentine troops. In contrast, it was difficult to note much of a willingness to kill or be killed for Europe, and there was little enthusiasm for the deployment of British forces in the Balkans in the 1990s. The divided EU was seen as irrelevant during the Gulf Wars of 1990–1 and 2003 in which Britain took a major role. Political identity was still clearly national, not international. By not joining the Euro, as Tony Blair had unsuccessfully sought to do in the late 1990s, Britain remained at a distance from the terrible fiscal crisis affecting the Eurozone in 2011–12.

DEMOCRATISATION

Across the British Isles in the twentieth century, there were powerful forces democratising society. The most important was the emancipation of women. At the same time, there was an ambivalence towards the democratisation of society. Hostility to democratic accountability was demonstrated, albeit in an implicit, not overt, manner, by the unwillingness of often self-defining elites, such as the judiciary or planners, to accept popular beliefs and pastimes as worthy of value and attention, and their conviction that they were best placed to manage society and define social values. Social and cultural condescension was linked to contempt for popular views on such matters as capital punishment or immigration. Most institutions resisted unwelcome pressures, while political parties tempered their desire for popular support with their wish to maintain their ideological inheritance. However, there was change. For example, in place of only MPs electing the leader of the Conservative Party, the final choice was transferred to all the members of the Party. In 1990, Douglas Hurd, one of the three candidates for the leadership of the Party, complained that his having been to Eton was counted against him. John Major, the least grand of the three, became leader, although his eventual successor as the next Conservative Prime Minister, David Cameron, was an old Etonian.

FEMALE EMANCIPATION

The legal and social position of women was limited at the beginning of the twentieth century, not least because most adult women did not have an independent income. In general, women lacked good jobs, and the employment rate among women with children was low, by modern standards. Over the twentieth century, however, the legal, economic and social dimensions of the situation were transformed.

Prior to the First World War, the suffragette movement won attention rather than support, as the Pankhursts, especially Emmeline Pankhurst, who founded the Women's Social and Political Union in 1903, urged their followers to acts of violence; but the war saw a substantial increase in the female workforce as society was mobilised for total war. Men had been conscripted into the military; and nearly 5 million women were in employment at the start of 1918, though their wages remained much lower than men's. That year, the vote was given to all men of 21 and over fulfilling a six-months residence qualification, and to women of 30 and over, although only as long as they were householders, wives of householders, occupants of property worth £5 annually, or graduates of British universities. A decade later, the voting age for women was dropped to 21, and the restrictions were removed.

Subsequent changes in the law removed the formal structure of discrimination. The Equal Pay Act (1970; implemented in 1975) was made more important by the major expansion of the female workforce from the 1940s. The expansion of the female workforce during the First World War had been partly reversed as men returned from the military and women turned to domesticity, but the expansion during the Second World War was not reversed to the same extent, although many women welcomed or at least accepted the post-war return to an emphasis on domesticity and motherhood.

The economic shift from manufacturing to service industries helped to create more opportunities for women workers. Whereas previously most women had given up work when they married, older married women, once their children had left school, entered the labour force as clerical workers in large numbers from the 1940s. Already, in 1935, the London County Council had ended the ban on married women teachers, a key measure of gender discrimination. Moreover, the number of married women entering the job market escalated from the 1960s. Clerical occupations became the largest single occupational category for women, but they were generally poorly paid and were particularly vulnerable to changes due to new office equipment and practices. Indeed, the banks, which employed many women, shed large numbers of staff in 1989–90, 1993–5 and the early 2010s. Furthermore, an increasing percentage of female employment was part-time and much was in low-skill and low-pay jobs. However, the male workforce was disproportionately hard hit by the decline in the industrial workforce.

Nevertheless, thanks to female employment (nearly 53 per cent of the workforce in 1994), the percentage of the population employed had increased since the 1920s; as, of course, had the possible number of unemployed. Rising female employment was also possibly responsible for the increase in school attainment among girls, which markedly rose at GCSE-level (examinations for 15–16-year-olds) from 1987, with the gap between male and female attainment also rising in the same period. Greater female participation in the workforce hit some voluntary activities, such as party political membership. It was also partly responsible for women postponing having children and having fewer children.

There was opposition to the expansion of opportunities for women. The National Association of Schoolmasters was founded in 1922 from a splinter group of male teachers opposed to the National Union of Teachers' support for equal pay, which was not achieved until after the Second World War. Its leaflets included such titles as 'Making our boys effeminate' (1927). The National Union of Foundry Workers only represented men during its history (1920–46), despite there being about 50,000 foundrywomen in the 1940s, a result of the entry of women into manufacturing during the war. More generally, the Labour Party and the trade union movement were reluctant to adopt issues pressed on them by female members, such as birth control and family allowances. In the 1920s, Labour had only a quarter of the Conservatives' female membership.

Changes in the position of women cannot be separated from other social questions. Class, for example, affected the recruitment of women for different tasks in both world wars. The mixture of the classes in munitions work during the first war, though stressed in propaganda, was limited. Similarly, in the Second World War, despite the propagandist suggestions of films, there was little mingling in the factories, and social distinctions were maintained. 'Positive discrimination' in favour of hiring and promoting women in the 1980s and 1990s worked most to the benefit of middle-class women; and the practice of endogamy (marriage within the clan, i.e. of members of similar social groups) may have ensured that social differences were reinforced.

As with other movements lacking a centralising structure, the 'women's liberation' movement of the 1960s and 1970s was a diverse one. It included pressure for changes in lifestyles and social arrangements that put women's needs and expectations in a more central position. The Abortion Act of 1967 was followed by a situation close to abortion on demand. Jobs and lifestyle became more important as aspirations for women, complementing rather than replacing home and family. The range of female activities expanded: the Women's Rugby Football Union was formed in 1983; the first Briton in space was Helen

Sharman; and, in 1987, Elizabeth II amended the statutes of the most distinguished of British chivalric orders, the Order of the Garter, to permit the admission of women on terms equal to those of the Knights Companion of the Order. After considerable controversy, the first women were ordained priests in the Church of England in 1994; the Church of Scotland had women ministers from the late 1960s. English Congregationalists ordained women from 1919 and, by the Second World War, Congregationalists were quite used to women ministers, though they were not numerous.

Although very atypical, the rise of Margaret Thatcher, the first British female party leader (1975) and Prime Minister (1979), was a demonstration of the increasing equality of British society and showed that there was no ceiling of opportunity for women. Her determination and success proved that a woman was easily capable of the job. Never rejected by the electorate, the confrontational Thatcher was, in 1990, when she was toppled by disaffection among her overwhelmingly male MPs fearing defeat in light of the government's unpopularity, the longest-serving prime minister of the century, and the prime minister with the longest consecutive period in office since Charles, Earl of Liverpool (1812–27). Nevertheless, only 9.2 per cent of MPs were women after the 1992 general election, and the percentage of women in the higher levels of the establishment was also low. In contrast, the Labour victory in the 1997 general election greatly increased the number of women MPs and the Conservatives made major efforts in the 2000s to follow suit.

Legal changes continued to be of importance for the position of women. Divorce became considerably easier as a result of the Matrimonial Causes Act (1923), the Divorce Act (1937), the Legal Aid Act (1949), and the Divorce Reform Act (1969). The number of divorces more than doubled in 1971–92 and by 1992 there was one divorce for every two marriages and this remained the ratio into the 2010s. The legislative tide included the Sex Discrimination Act of 1976, which had considerable impact in the treatment and employment of women. Equally, general social trends were important. Alongside the stress on an eroticised vision of marriage, which was encouraged by Marie Stopes's successful book *Married Love* (1918), there was an emphasis on the techniques of sexual pleasure and a rise in sex education. The former became a major sphere of commercial activity; the latter one of educational policy, contrasting greatly with the ignorance of many, particularly, but not only, women, earlier in the century.

SOCIAL SHIFTS

Capitalism was another force shaping the democratisation of society, for, at the same time that the differing wealth and income of individuals ensured that their purchasing power varied, each was a consumer able to make his or her own purchasing decisions. This element of choice, and the need to shape and cater to it, combined to ensure a whole range of social shifts, among which the most striking was the emergence, from the 1950s, of the youth consumer and the development of cultural and consumer fashions that reflected the dynamism and volatility of this section of the market. It is easy to focus on rock, pop and drug culture transmitted via the Beatles and the Sex Pistols, psychedelia and punk, but more significance can be attached to the wish and ability of youth first to create an adolescent identity – not to be younger copies of their elders – and secondly, and more specifically, to reject the opinions of their parents; pop culture was only one manifestation of this. The willingness to try different foods, to holiday in different places, to move away from parental religious preferences, to go on to higher education, or to purchase property, were as interesting and possibly more important. In 1968, the voting age was reduced to 18.

Certainly, the interrelationship between the aspirations of youth and socio-economic changes played a role in the major expansion of the middle class that was such a marked feature of the period, particularly from the 1960s. In 1900, 75 per cent of the labour force were manual workers, members of the working class. By 1974 the percentage had fallen to 47, and by 1991 to 36. The manufacturing base had declined, and the service sector had grown. White collar replaced blue collar (the fall in the working class hitting the traditional character of the Labour Party), and average incomes for those in work rose appreciably, so that real disposable income for the average household rose 46 per cent between 1971 and 1992. Tax rates, which under Harold Wilson rose to a maximum of 98 per cent, subsequently fell substantially: direct taxation grew considerably in the 1960s and 1970s, but, as a result of major cuts in income tax under Thatcher, there was a shift to indirect taxation in the 1980s.

The long-term impact of the social revolution of recent decades, crucial aspects of which were falling union membership (the Trades Union Congress had more than 13 million members in 1979, fewer than 8 million in 1992), and rising home ownership (three-quarters of trade unionists by the late 1980s), is still unclear. However, the basic lineaments of society at the close of the twentieth century (and for the foreseeable future), were of a capitalist, consumerist, individualist, mobile, predominantly secular and urban, property-owning democracy, with a substantial and embittered underclass. Indeed, large numbers of beggars appeared on the streets, especially in London, and cases of tuberculosis among the homeless rose. Over 20 per cent of 18–25-year-olds had not registered to vote in 1992. Rising house prices led to a marked increase in the average age of first-time buyers, to reach near 40 by 2011. More generally, affluence and social fluidity challenged notions of cohesion and collectivism that were often ambivalent about growth and opportunity.

'Who governs Britain?' was the slogan of the Heath government that, although it won more votes than Labour, was, nevertheless, defeated in February 1974. Thatcher's defeat of the coal miners' strike of 1984–5 appeared to answer the question, and was followed by several years of boom and optimism. The substantial increase in individual and corporate debt in the 1980s as a consequence of the liberalisation of the financial system and government encouragement of the widespread desire to own property, combined with structural economic problems, ensured, however, that many who were not in the underclass were in a vulnerable situation. Private household debt rose from £16 billion to £47 billion, and mortgages from £43 billion to £235 billion in 1980–9, as rising house prices and greater personal credit mutually interacted. By June 1992, repossessions of houses by creditors were at an annual rate of about 75,000, while 300,000 mortgage-holders were six months or more in arrears. These circumstances were to recur, notably in the late 2000s.

A more general problem was posed by rising crime figures, the related perception of a more disorderly and lawless, and less safe society, and the difficulties of policing. Between 1981 and 1993, the British Crime Survey showed a rise of 77 per cent in crime, with a 39 per cent rise in violent offences. A perception of growing crime tempered public civility and lessened confidence in the use of public space, for example parks. Authority was also challenged by the widespread antipathy to the Poll Tax, introduced by Thatcher. This antipathy indicated a willingness to oppose laws deemed unfair. The unpopularity of the tax, combined with a worsening economic situation, helped to bring about the crisis of confidence in her leadership in the parliamentary Conservative Party that led to her fall in November 1990.

Unlike during the late 1940s, however, there was, by the mid-1990s, relatively little confidence in central planning and limited support for state collectivism, with the important exception of the National Health

Service. In addition, more people preferred to shop than to go to church on Sundays, and fewer of the population expressed their religious faith through the established churches than ever before. Moreover, traditional geographical loyalties were shaken by the Local Government Act of 1972 which, in the cause of 'rationalisation', totally reorganised local government in England, greatly altering county boundaries, and abolishing several counties as well as the ridings of Yorkshire. The pattern of local government in Scotland and Wales was changed even more radically.

Social differences, however, remained strong, and more so than in most of Continental Europe. In Britain, the working class ate less well, and had poorer housing, more children, lower expectations, and less access to higher education, than the middle class. Indeed, class mortality differences widened from the late 1950s; 2010 figures indicated that children eligible for free school meals were four times more likely to receive a permanent exclusion from school. That year, nearly 900 pupils a day were permanently or temporarily excluded from school for abusing or assaulting staff or classmates.

There were also clear variations between, and within, regions in many fields, including political preference, crime patterns, nuptiality, fertility and house ownership. Nevertheless, these differences were less marked than in the past. National broadcasting, state education and employment, and nation-wide companies, unions, products and pastimes all brought a measure of convergence that could be seen in the decline of dialect and distinctive regional practices, as in cooking. This decline in England, however, has to be weighed against the rise of nationalism in Scotland and Wales, the lack of penetration of anglicisation in Northern Ireland, and the impact in England of sustained large-scale immigration.

9

The British Isles Today

Throughout this book, there has been stress on the importance of the physical environment, which, itself, has been greatly affected by human activity. Woods have been cleared, so that, outside the Forest of Bere in Hampshire, very little of the original virgin forest has survived. Indeed, since 1945, 45 per cent of the United Kingdom's remaining ancient semi-natural forest has been damaged or destroyed. Rivers have been deepened and straightened, coastlines altered. This has been a long process. The marshland of the Fens, for example, has been progressively drained from the Roman period to the present day, with particular activity in the seventeenth century and following the arrival of steam pumps from the 1820s.

Yet, at no stage, has there been such pressure on the environment as in modern Britain. Other creatures are decimated by human activities, between 3,000 and 5,000 barn owls being killed on UK roads each year. Pine martens, members of the weasel family, were reported in 1995 to have vanished from England in 1994 and to be on the brink of extinction in Wales. On the other hand, the Welsh red kite has been brought back from the brink of extinction, while fish have returned to previously-polluted rivers such as the Taff, Thames, Tyne, Wandle and Wear, as de-industrialisation and better management have greatly increased their cleanliness. There is a regional dimension, with animals doing least well in the crowded south of England.

In part thanks to fears about climate change, environmental concern is greater now than ever before. This has been institutionalised with the creation of national parks in England and Wales (1949), the designation of areas of outstanding natural beauty, and the foundation of the Countryside Commission in 1968. There are conservation areas in towns, listed buildings, scheduled ancient monuments and sites of special scientific interest. More money than ever before is now spent on maintaining environmental standards, most obviously with payments – about £900 million in 1994 – under the Wildlife and Countryside Act 1981 to farmers to 'set aside' land from farming or to adopt less intensive farming methods. However, some of the drive that was building up behind the environmental movement in the 1980s seems to have been diverted into more self-centred concerns like organic foods, based on concerns about personal health rather than sustainable farming and energy conservation.

Mainstream politics co-opted some of the language of the 'Greens', but was unwilling to take on, or incapable of taking on, society's unbounded sense of material entitlements, which are the main drivers of environmental crisis. For example, tax credits and benefit payments for children were not limited to the first two children.

The environment was also put under great pressure from the rising population. That of the United Kingdom rose from 56.4 million in 1981 to 62.3 million in June 2010, with the rate of population growth, in absolute and percentage terms, in 2009–10 being the highest since 1962. In 2011, it was predicted to reach 70 million by 2027. Much of this rise was due to large-scale immigration as the Labour governments of 1997–2010 lost control of the situation in part due to the consequences of movement within the European Union but also due to the rate of non-European immigration. In 1997–2007, the total net inflow of foreign citizens was three million, while illegal immigrants possibly comprised another 600,000. In the year to December 2010, provisional figures available in November 2011 suggest net migration of 239,000. The high level of immigration resulted in an increase in the number of women of childbearing age. In 2009–10 nearly one in four births were to mothers born outside the UK. In 2010, Polish women were the largest group of these mothers.

Growing life expectancy was also significant in the rise in population. It rose from 46 for men and 50 for women in the 1900s to 77.7 and 81.9 respectively by 2006–8. As a result, the number and percentage of pensioners rose. By 2001, 19.6 per cent of the Hertfordshire population were pensioners. The age of many pensioners also rose, with the number of centenarians increasing markedly. This increase is projected to escalate rapidly, causing serious problems for the NHS and social services.

The net effect of the rise of population was heavy pressure on institutions, infrastructure, social capital, living standards and the environment. Pressure on living standards was seen in the more cramped conditions of modern housing. As an instance of pressure on institutions and infrastructure, the government, in July 2011, projected a rise in the numbers of five- and six-year-old pupils of 10 per cent over the following four years. There were also more detailed consequences as these national trends played out through regional variations. The biggest percentage increases in population in England in 2009–10 were in East Anglia and the south-east, notably in Norwich; while the smallest increases were in the north, and some towns there, such as Burnley, saw a fall in population.

It is paradoxical that a fast-increasing population and the forces of untrammelled consumption and selfishness co-exist with a widespread cultural consensus that the environment is one of the central issues of our time. The Foot and Mouth crisis in 2001, in which nearly six million animals, about one in eight of the livestock in the country, were slaughtered, highlighted increasing concern about the environment, as did the controversy about GM (genetically modified) crops. Public controversy was stirred up in 2010–12 over plans to shoot badgers in order to stop the spread of bovine tuberculosis, which in 2010 was responsible for the slaughter of 25,000 cattle.

The susceptibility of the environment to human pressure is dramatically apparent. There have been improvements. The toxicity of rivers such as the Thames and the Tyne has decreased, especially due to falling concentrations of heavy metal pollutants. Yet, cities that enjoyed far more sunshine hours from the clearer atmosphere after the declaration of smokeless zones have now started to notice a decline due to greater emissions from car exhausts. Building on greenfield sites is still more common than urban renewal, although pressure on 'brownfield' sites is contributing greatly to the tense, crowded feel of much (but far from all) city life. Near where I live, supermarkets swallow up land and views, and distort traffic.

More generally, purchasing power impacts on the environment. In 1971, food took one-fifth of the average family budget; in 1993, one-ninth, freeing disposable income for other forms of expenditure. Increased use of water, thanks in part to machines such as dishwashers, put great pressure on water reserves, and led to the depletion of natural aquifers and to restrictions on water use, not least in Sussex where, ironically, 2000–1 saw terrible flooding. In 1990, hosepipe bans affected 20 million customers. Evidence of global warming in the 2000s was linked to concern about the availability of sufficient water, notably in 2006. More material goods tend to mean a greater use of energy, although reliability and energy efficiency have risen. In 1990, 158 million tons of carbon dioxide were dispersed into the environment above Britain. In 2010, 72 per cent of British electricity was generated from gas and coal. Pressure on energy supplies and infrastructure led to the need to replace and expand generating capacity and transmission, as with the contentious plans to improve the transmission line from the Highlands to the Central Belt of Scotland.

The use of machines still spreads. By 1991, 90 per cent of households had a telephone, compared with 42 per cent in 1972: for washing machines the percentages are 88 and 66. In turn, mobile telephone technology both raised the extent of use and diminished the prevalence of land-lines. Moreover, new problems were created, including the use of telephones by drivers, an illegal as well as dangerous practice the police were unable to stamp out. An addiction to telephones and to 'being in touch' was also seen in a society where work–leisure boundaries were eroded. By 2008, there were 480,000 flights over London a year, leaving a strong noise imprint.

The consumer society continues to produce massive quantities of rubbish and the animal world responds. Seagulls, foxes and other animals increasingly feed on human rubbish rather than their traditional targets in the animal world. Noise is another consequence of technological development, and the number of complaints about it rose by 390 per cent in 1978–92. Noise Abatement Orders were introduced.

Consumerism is also linked to the decline of the idea that large parts of life cannot or should not be interpreted through the rules of the market. In addition, more aspects of life have become commodities themselves. For example, 'private life' itself has become a commodity as the values of tabloid journalism have circulated throughout the media with public interest confused with public prurience, helping, in 2011, to create a political crisis linked to issues of privacy. The prevalent notion of lifestyle is about a life lived through commodities, or, at least, one lived with that flavour.

The deserted or converted church or meeting house in both rural and urban Britain, such as Methodist chapels in Cornwall, are apt symbols of the nature of changing values. Once crucial to a sense of community, order, hierarchy and place, churches were increasingly declared redundant or demolished from 1950 on. For example, in the Withern group of parishes in Lincolnshire there were thirteen parish churches in the Middle Ages, eleven in 1900 and only five in 1993.

Empty churches symbolise the move from rural to urban, a process, intensified by transport policies, that was also marked by the closure of rural schools, shops, pubs and post offices. By 2001, about 30 per cent of parishes had no shop, while agriculture's share of the economy had fallen to 1 per cent. The rural population has also altered. Commuters now dominate many villages, reflecting the appeal of an idealised image of the countryside, but also ensuring a shift in the nature of rural life and the effective erosion of any significant boundary between rural and urban society. Commuting into London increased by 7 per cent in 1981–91, when it also rose by 18 per cent into Birmingham and 29 per cent into Manchester.

A striking feature of contemporary Britain has been the changing role of major cities. Their industrial bases have been largely destroyed and, after a period of severe decay, many city centres are in the midst of renewal projects encouraging resettlement and tourism and attempting to renew civic pride. Glasgow was often seen as the quintessential insanitary and violent industrial city but has now, despite continuing high unemployment, established itself as a beautiful and dynamic European city.

Deserted churches also reflect the increasingly sceptical and secular nature of society, the last a development that also affects members of other religions, such as Jews, Muslims and Sikhs; although Islam has become more active thanks to immigration, which also helped cause a marked rise in Roman Catholicism in the 2000s. Secularism has taken many forms. For example, religious opposition, as well as public prejudice, delayed the development of cremation, a policy supported by some doctors and Nonconformists, as opposed to earth burial. The first crematorium opened at Woking in 1885, but, for long, cremation was a minority option. In Manchester, where the first cremation in Britain was in 1892, cremation only became more popular from the 1940s. Now, in Britain, it is the usual way of disposing of bodies. Noise-abatement orders are now served on some churches by local authorities at the behest of people no longer happy to listen to church bells.

A different shift in national traditions is suggested by diet. Since the 1960s this has been increasingly affected by new ingredients and dishes introduced from foreign countries. Chinese, Indian and Italian meals dominate the restaurant trade, but there has been further diversity in the 1990s and 2000s, notably with the rise of Thai, Japanese, Vietnamese and Moroccan restaurants.

Supermarkets increasingly stock foreign foods; in the 1990s, there was growing consumption of continental-style breads. There has also been a widening in the range of fruit available: avocados, passion fruit, star fruit, kiwi fruit and mangoes, largely unknown in Britain in the 1960s, are now widely available in supermarkets. The increased consumption of convenience foods, generally reheated rapidly by microwave cookers, has provided a major market for new dishes. Wine and foreign types and brands of beer have become much more important, a process that also, in part, reflects technological and retail shifts, most obviously the growing sale of canned beers and the development of supermarket sales of alcohol. These sales are linked to rising alcoholism. Supermarkets have also been responsible for the decline in independent retail activity. High streets have become more uniform and outlets are increasingly dependent on a relatively small number of suppliers. As a result, large supermarket distribution centres located near major roads dot the country.

Alongside national trends, regional differences, nevertheless, remain substantial. The wealthiest regions are those that grew fastest: in England in 1977–89, Greater London and much of southern England. Conversely, there were low levels of both GDP (gross domestic product) per head and of economic growth in Cleveland, Merseyside and South Yorkshire. The impact, in the 1980s and 1990s, of the Conservative policies of monetarism, deregulation, privatisation and an abandonment of the goal of full employment exacerbated regional economic differences. So also did greater regional specialisation in which management, research and development jobs were increasingly separate from production tasks: the former were becoming concentrated in south-east England. The recession of 1990–3 hit the south and East Anglia disproportionately hard, but economic growth subsequently was much faster in these regions. In 1994, the average weekly earnings of a working man were £419.40 in the south-east, £327.80 in the north and only £319.20 in Northern Ireland.

As consumer spending and borrowing were high, regional differences in income fed directly into the local economy. This pattern was maintained in the subsequent economic growth of the late 1990s and early 2000s when growth rates were higher than in Continental Europe. The role of London and the south-east in the economy grew as, after the deregulation or the Big Bang of 1986, London's global importance in finance and business services continued to rise in the 1990s and 2000s while other aspects of the national economy declined. In 2011, London was the world's foremost centre for international bank lending and marine insurance and was responsible for two-fifths of the global turnover in foreign exchange. As a result, the banking crisis of 2008 initially hit London hard. Nevertheless, it still did better than most of the country. The rate of unemployment in London rose to 4.2 per cent in June 2009, but the national rate was then 7.2 per cent. In 2000–10, London and the South-east were the only two regions whose gross value added per person was over £30,000.

London's financial role was linked not only to its relative prosperity but also to the extent to which employment was in the private sector. In contrast, the public sector was relatively more prominent in Scotland, Northern Ireland and northern England. As a result, these areas were particularly challenged in 2011 by public expenditure cuts. They were also more seriously affected by falls in house prices. There were, and are, significant contrasts within the regions. In the north, Newcastle, Preston, Manchester and Wakefield did better in the early 2010s than Sunderland, Blackburn, Burnley and Hull. The June 2009 unemployment rates in London varied from 1.8 per cent in Chelsea and Wimbledon to 7.4 per cent in Hackney South and Shoreditch. Nevertheless, the prime contrasts were between the regions, with living costs lower in the north and unemployment higher. Whereas Liverpool had employed rates in July 2009 to June 2010 of 62.7 per cent and Sunderland 64.9 per cent, those for Milton Keynes and Bristol were 72.5 and 74.2 per cent.

Regional differences are readily apparent in the case of accents. Regional accents usually have a long genesis, but there has also been a pattern of change, usually linked to migration. Thus, the distinctive 'Scouse' dialect of Merseyside owes much to the arrival of Irish, Scots and Welsh seeking work in the nineteenth century. In recent decades, the distinctive Estuarine Twang of London has become more insistent across the south-east of England as Londoners have moved out from the capital. In turn, a West Indian youth dialect has become more influential in much of London. At the same time, outside the cities, regional accents have risen at the expense of smaller local counterparts as part of a pattern of national life in which the local has struggled to maintain a distinctive identity. Administrative changes play a role, as in the replacement of local schooling by large sixth form colleges drawing on a wide catchment area.

Until the 1970s there was a strong labour market for skilled and semi-skilled jobs and many jobs for the unskilled, but extensive de-industrialisation since has reduced opportunities for unskilled labour. The bottom tenth of manual workers earned only 64 per cent of average income in 1991. Thus, the differentiation within the workforce related to skills has widened greatly and this has strong regional consequences. Differential opportunity also affects migration, leading people to move from the north to the south of England, although this process is hindered by inflexible public housing policies and a limited low-cost private rental sector. This movement has continued in the early 2010s.

De-industrialisation continues: the last British match factory closed in 1994 after it had been acquired by a Swedish company, while, by the start of 2002, only 13 coalmines remained. However, there are dynamic manufacturing sectors, notably pharmaceuticals. The economy is also affected by a poor transport and energy infrastructure. By 2011, Britain was importing 50 per cent of its gas needs.

Socio-economic change has created unease for the many who search for stability and comfort. Such defensiveness is difficult to manage given the impact of global economic and financial shifts, and the vulnerability of the social fabric to the consequences of economic downturn. However, there have also been important socio-economic benefits in that, as the workforce became more flexible and willing to adapt to new roles, so the deregulatory reforms of the Thatcher years came to fruition, to Blair's benefit, with a labour market that was more conducive to business, and thus investment, than those elsewhere in western Europe.

Social hierarchies have always been more fluid than might at first appear, tempered and complicated as they have been by mobility (both up and down), marriage and problems of classification. Hierarchies have become far more fluid in recent decades, not least because a society that was increasingly structured round liquid wealth has had to adapt to the volatility of the latter. A comprehensible way of talking about social and economic class in post-corporatist, post-industrial (in the sense of industry's more marginal position in the economy) Britain has not emerged. The term 'middle-class' is so vague and widely-encompassing as to be of scant value, but, paradoxically, it is still highly-meaningful to many people. There are persistent and structural inequalities in British society, but a waning of traditional class 'markers': everything from attitudes and allegiances to institutions. It seems that class no longer generates social and individual meanings in the way it used to, or it may take different forms of expression. The controversy over bankers' pay in the early 2010s, however, was redolent of hostility to the 'rich', suggesting that class still had meaning in that most diffuse of fashions.

Despite the refusal of much of its population to believe this, Britain continues to benefit from aspects of immigration – as has been the case throughout its history. Apart from the different native cultures of the British Isles, there is also a growing cultural diversity. A spectacular recent example is the East African Asian community which settled in the 1960s and 1970s. Multiple cultural identities are more common. As a result of mass immigration, Britishness has become a container for many nationalities: one can be British and Pakistani, Ghanaian and Greek, as well as English or Scottish, although many of the immigrants from Eastern Europe who arrived in the 2000s, notably the large number of Poles, only intended to stay for a short period, and the recession of the late 2000s led to large-scale re-emigration. By 2001, there were two million Muslims in Britain, the vast majority in England. Public discussion about racism cast in terms of 'black and white' addresses the issue of 'institutional' racism, but tends to posit a non-existent unitary 'black community' and a dubious notion of 'whiteness'. Instead, multi-cultural Britain sees a myriad of tensions and alliances in which place, ethnicity, religion, class and other factors (e.g. criminous Jamaican Yardies versus churchgoing Caribbean) co-exist. This was readily apparent during the riots in Bradford and Oldham in 2001, and in London in 2011. The shifting clustering and dispersal of interests in society poses problems for identity and governance.

Changes in attitude also affected government. For example, a stress on the importance of individual customers and consumers affected not only business but also administration in general with an emphasis on responsiveness to customers in both government and the public sector, for example in the NHS. This appearance of responsiveness was expressed in the 1990s in terms of 'charters', setting out the rights of patients, pupils, etc. and the responsibility of management. This process was linked to a so-called 'quality revolution' which claimed to produce an improvement in the management of both the public and the private sector, but often simply expanded the public sector. A major problem of the 1960s and 1970s, this was partly resolved by better training and education, but spectacular failures of planning and management continued, for example the Millennium Dome of 2000 and then delays in major rail and defence projects. Furthermore, by international standards, labour productivity and skills remained insufficient, in part due to inadequate training, hastened by Mrs Thatcher's abandonment of the Training Levy.

The older landed society, which, in fact, benefited from links with the more commercial aspects of society for centuries, saw some traditional means of classification decline. In 1958, the ritual presentation of debutantes (young unmarried aristocratic women) at Buckingham Palace was abolished. Presentations were the centrepiece of a London season that had already been sapped by the decline of landed wealth. In 2004, fox hunting was banned with the passage of the Hunting with Dogs Act. Opposition in the Lords was overcome by invoking the Parliament Act. Britain as a propertied society has long seen little need for the traditional possessors of much landed property, and the aristocracy is increasingly treated, like the monarch and established churches, as a form of heritage and tourism for the nation, and not as a power in the state. The legislation against fox hunting drew on a powerful antipathy to what was seen as social privilege.

The aristocracy, like the Crown and other traditional defenders and products of a hierarchical society, have been affected by a post-war decline in deference that began to gather force in the 1960s and became very prominent in the early 1990s with particular crises of confidence in the monarchy, the Church of England and the Conservative Party. In 2008–11, there was another bout of crises, hitting MPs, bankers and the popular press in succession. These specific issues have been matched by a sense of social change, if not crisis. The decline of marriage and the family ensured that an increasing percentage of children did not live with both their natural parents. As a very different aspect of change, but again hitting traditional patterns, the countryside and Rights of Way Act of 2000 provided access to large areas, compromising the rights of landowners. The rapid decline of deference has not been restricted to class deference but extends to all professionals, trade unionists and politicians. This decline weakened the case for professional self-regulation and made central government intervention easier to sell politically.

Spreading illegality is another product and cause of the decline of respect. The prohibition of drug consumption has not only failed to control drug use, but has critically undermined respect for the rule of law. In 2001, it was calculated that 44 per cent of 16- to 29-year-olds had smoked cannabis. Drug use also massively capitalised Britain's formerly modest organised criminal syndicates, as well as attracting new ones from abroad and linking the informed economy to international networks. These profits have been reinvested in other forms of crime, such as computer fraud and the smuggling in of illegal immigrants.

A combination of the collapse of the old industrial base with the continuing rise of consumerism and the decline in respect for the law has led to a ballooning of the 'hidden economy'. By 2001, 1 in 3 cigarettes sold in the United Kingdom were sold illegally, in pubs, clubs, markets, and openly on the streets, according to HM Customs. A substantial and increasing number of people no longer view activities such as buying stolen goods as illegal. The riots in August 2011 indicated the strength of criminality in particular groups and a willingness to resort to looting.

Although the riots led to an increase in the prison population to a record high of close to 87,000, the 'tough on crime' approach shared by all major political parties masks a near abandonment of tackling petty crime by the police in some areas. Their fatalism is shared by the public. Home Office statistics show crime falling in the late 1990s, but the British Crime Survey indicates that this is not the case, which suggests that non-reporting has increased. Of the 4.159 million offences recorded by police in England and Wales in the year ending April 2011, only 1.6 million were solved.

POLITICS

The general election held on 1 May 1997 led to a sweeping political transformation. Thanks to unpopularity and, partly, to tactical voting (which itself reflected unpopularity), the Conservatives lost heavily while, helped by a degree of enthusiasm, Labour, with 418 seats, won a big majority. It took seats not only in traditional areas but also in many parts of the more prosperous south of England. The victorious Tony Blair fought on the platform of 'New Labour', discarding socialism and state direction in order to create a social democratic system able to embrace aspects of Thatcherism, not least the marketplace, and modest rates of taxation, but not what was presented as a threat to social cohesion. This policy was presented as a 'third way' that was different from, but involved cooperation between, the state and the private sectors. In 1995, Clause Four of the Labour Party's 1918 constitution as amended in 1928 – its commitment to public ownership of the means of production, distribution, and exchange – was abandoned at Blair's instigation after a ballot of Party members. This was seen as the end of an era. Hugh Gaitskell had singularly failed to achieve the same goal when he tried to push it through in 1959.

There were still important differences, however, between Conservatism and New Labour and the charge of being a Thatcherite brought against Blair tells us more about tensions in the Labour Party than about Blair's ethos and policies. In practice, there was considerable continuity between the attitudes associated with Gaitskell and, in the 1960s, Tony Crossland, and those of Blair. The 1997 joke 'Did you know that Tony Blair MP is an anagram of 'I'm Tory Plan B'? made little sense in Scotland or Wales, where assemblies with legislative powers were created. Furthermore, the government in 1999 removed most of the hereditary peerage from the House of Lords as part of its policy of at once 'rebranding' Britain and securing Labour hegemony.

Thanks to Conservative unpopularity, Blair easily won the 2001 and 2005 elections, but confidence in Labour's intentions, integrity and competence was badly hit by their years in office. Image became all-important under Blair, as the name New Labour suggests, and 'spin doctors' and focus groups assumed centre stage. Taxation rose without any equivalent improvement in public services. Instead, there was increasing concern about the state of education, health and transport, and a growing sense that government could not solve these problems. This attitude created problems for the political process, and, in the 2001 election, turnout fell to 60 per cent, the lowest since 1918. This fall was a reflection of widespread dissatisfaction with politicians, not of confidence in the government, which indeed had seriously mishandled protests against taxes on petrol, briefly creating a crisis in governability. Blockades of oil refineries led to grave concern about public order. Moreover, the major extension of welfare benefits under Labour both placed a strain on public finances and was poorly focused. Incentives to work appeared compromised as many families came to lack the experience of work. Welfare dependency became more marked and was seen by critics as a sign of social breakdown alongside the large number of broken homes.

War in the Middle East, the decision to support the USA in the attack on Iraq in 2003, greatly compromised Blair's popularity. Alongside serious divisions within the government, this led to his resignation in 2007. Blair's lacklustre Labour replacement, Gordon Brown, proved an extraordinarily poor manager of the nation's finances. As Chancellor of the Exchequer in 1997–2007 and Prime Minister from 2007 to 2010, Brown's policies contributed greatly, despite his claims to the contrary, to Britain facing the worldwide fiscal crisis and economic recession of 2008–10 in a worse condition than other major countries. Indeed, the economy shrank by 6.4 per cent between the first quarter of 2008 and the fourth quarter of 2009. The expensive social democracy advocated by New Labour seemed unaffordable. Britain ended up with a large budget deficit, a large public debt that was growing at a fast rate, and a large private debt, as well as a weak economy and inflation that was over target.

In May 2010, the unpopular Brown lost the general election, winning 258 seats compared with 307 for the Conservatives and 57 for the Liberal Democrats. The latter formed a coalition, with the Conservative leader since 2006, David Cameron, becoming Prime Minister and the Liberal Democrat leader, Nick Clegg, Deputy Prime Minister. The parlous state of the nation's finances and the fact that government spent about half of the national income led Cameron to emphasise public expenditure cuts alongside his plans for a 'Big Society' in which public activism replaced or supplemented some of the social welfare functions of government. At the same time, the coalition government struggled with a range of problems, notably an over-ambitious and costly military intervention in Afghanistan and the difficulties of funding pensions in the public sector in the light of rising longevity.

Moreover, although Britain benefited greatly from not being in the Euro and from its currency's freedom to float, economic growth proved weak, and below levels in the USA, Germany and France. Expansion in the year to June 2011 was only 0.7 per cent, so that British GDP was still nearly 4 per cent lower than it had been three years earlier. This recovery was weaker than that after recessions since the 1930s. As an index of decline on the world scale, sterling by July 2011 had fallen by about a quarter from its 2007 peak, contributing to inflation not least by accentuating the problems of higher oil prices. Inflation was restrained more by the global recession than by the strengths of the British economy. Economic problems hit public finances, and in 2011 the budget deficit was about 8.8 per cent of GDP.

MODERN IRELAND

In the late 1980s and early 1990s it seemed apparent that the Anglo-Irish agreement of 1985 was not going to serve as the framework for a settlement in Northern Ireland. The political and security situation continued to deteriorate. Violence became increasingly an economic issue with, for example, the construction industry subject to threats. In addition to nationalist terrorism – by the Provisional IRA – 'loyalist' terrorism, by the Ulster Defence Force, the Ulster Freedom Fighters and similar bodies, increased. Alongside specific acts of directed terrorism, there were also 'tit for tat' killings: the random murder of members of the other denomination designed to instil terror. Indeed in 1992 more Catholics were killed than Protestants, though not all Catholics were killed by Protestants. At the same time, the bloody disintegration of Yugoslavia, and the development of 'ethnic cleansing' there, led to new fears about the future of Northern Ireland. Since the troubles began there had already been a process of ethnic concentration operating in Ulster, with Protestants moving to the east and Catholics to the west.

The peace process was carried forward from 1997 when the IRA declared a resumption of the 1994 ceasefire. Tony Blair was assisted by American pressure on Sinn Fein and, in 1998, the Good Friday Agreement was followed by the resumption of devolved government. A power-sharing agreement brought Nationalist and Unionist politicians together.

Meanwhile, broader trends have also transformed the situation. As elsewhere in the United Kingdom, de-industrialisation has been a major problem. This has affected both traditional heavy industries, such as shipbuilding and heavy engineering, and newer light industries. Thus, synthetic fibre plants established in the 1960s closed in the early 1980s. In the Republic of Ireland (Eire), in contrast, the economy boomed, benefiting from a number of factors including the impact of Ireland's entry into the European Union in 1973. Development aid played a major role in a substantial measure of industrialisation since the 1960s. Thanks to strong export expansion, the annual average growth rate in GDP in Ireland in 1990–4 was over 5 per cent, the highest in the EU: Britain's in contrast was only 0.7 per cent, the lowest apart from Sweden. This growth helped to cause serious inflationary pressures in Ireland, and a poorly-regulated asset bubble in the 2000s was followed by a collapse into grave indebtedness in the early 2010s.

The republic has also experienced a substantial measure of secular-isation. There have been legal and political battles over such issues as divorce, homosexuality, abortion and contraception, as the authority of the Church has been contested. Irish society is still more sectarian than that of England, but the declining role of the Church in Irish politics, society and culture is readily apparent. This decline has been linked to a measure of emancipation for women that culminated with the selection of Mary Robinson as President in 1990. In contrast, in Ulster neither the Unionist nor the Nationalist cause has had much time for feminism, although a number of active IRA members have been women, and there is a strong tradition of female involvement in Irish and Scottish nationalism.

In Ulster, it is unclear whether the legacy of the catastrophic dimen-sion of much Irish history – conquest, expropriation, colonisation, discrimination, poverty, myth-making and bitterness – can be lessened by economic growth, secularisation and social change. The recession of the early 2010s and the pressure on state expenditure in a regional economy heavily dependent on it were linked to a rise in sectarian tension. In terms of the political response to the recession, the situation in the republic was far more promising.

MODERN SCOTLAND

Over the last two decades, Scotland has substantially shared the same economic and social trends as the rest of Britain, but its political trajectory has been different, as has more generally been the case since 1959 with the decline of Scottish Conservatism, although it was only in 1965 that the party became Conservative. Before that it was Unionist only. This change of title has been seen as the Englishing of Scottish Unionism. As in England and Wales, there has been a decline in 'smoke-stack' industries, the traditional heavy manufacturing sector. The size and economic importance of the coal, heavy engineering, ship-building and steel industries have all declined and in Scotland there has been particular sensitivity about the fate of the Ravenscraig steelworks. The textile industry has also been badly hit. What was once the biggest linen damask factory in the world, that of Erskine, Beveridge and Co. in Dunfermline, closed, and was converted to flats in 1983–4. Economic decline has hit Strathclyde particularly badly, and the urban fabric there has been under considerable challenge, despite urban regeneration.

New technology has led to new industry and employment, for example in offshore oil fields, but the pattern of the workforce is very different from that in the nineteenth-century townscapes of industrial decline. Instead, much of the new work places little stress on manual strength or traditional skills, and in areas such as Glenrothes there are higher rates of female than male employment. The bitter dispute over attempts to introduce new working practices at the US-owned Timex plant at Dundee in 1993 indicated that economic change was not welcomed by all, but it also revealed the consequences of growing foreign ownership of Scottish concerns: the management decided to shut the plant. The continued success of the long-established financial services industry in Edinburgh and of service-industry employment in Glasgow, a European Union 'city of culture', have brought a measure of prosperity, but it is significant that Wales has been more attractive to foreign investors.

It is unclear whether independence would not create fresh economic problems; Scotland would be part of the EU, but very peripheral to its markets, and the crisis that affected Ireland in the early 2010s stilled talk of following the example of that 'Celtic Tiger'. The most recent prominent Scottish literary declaration of cultural self-determination, James Kelman's novel *How Late It Was, How Late* (1994), was published in London by an English publisher and won the Booker Prize, a national award. In the mid-1990s, 50 per cent of the Scottish sales of tabloid newspapers were of London titles and 75 per cent of those of the 'quality' press; 72 per cent of total tourism expenditure in Scotland in 1994 was by English tourists.

Socially, Scotland has experienced shifts similar to those in England. The role of the churches continued to decline, there has been a broadening out of the middle class, and the nuclear family is under strain. Rates of heart disease remain very high. Edinburgh has acquired a new reputation as a major centre of drug abuse and AIDS. Yet, there has also been a major contrast in that Scotland has not matched England's high rate of population growth. Emigration has long been important: in 1900–90, there was only one year (1932–3) in which Scotland gained from migration. Combined with declining birth rates, lower than those of England and Wales, this led to a fall in population: 152,000 people in 1976–86. There was no comparison to the large-scale immigration into England in the 2000s and 2010s, and this contrast was highly significant to the difference between the societies in the two countries, Scotland being far less diverse than England.

Meanwhile, the nature of the Scottish economy, with its limited opportunities, and the strength of the education system ensure that Scotland continues to export talent. In 1988–9, 30 per cent of Scottish graduates from Scottish universities got their first job in England and Wales, whereas only 0.3 per cent of English and Welsh graduates from English and Welsh universities gained their first post in Scotland. Within Scotland, there has been a substantial move from the urban areas of Strathclyde – 172,360 people in 1976–86 – and net gains in the Highlands and Islands, the Border region and south-western Scotland.

Politically, the late 1980s and early 1990s lent fresh impetus to the debate about the constitution. This had abated after the devolution referendum of 1979, but the unpopularity in Scotland of Mrs Thatcher's Conservative government (1979–90) and markedly contrasting electoral results in Scotland and England led to a revival in debate. The extent to which administrative responsibility for Scottish affairs was transferred from Whitehall to the Scottish Office in Edinburgh helped to encourage a sense of governmental autonomy and responsibility in Scotland, but there was little real element of democratic control over the Office. Scottish ministers effectively determined policy on the domestic front. In 1987 Labour won fifty of the seventy-two seats, the Conservatives only ten. The link between the Conservative party and working-class Protestant culture declined markedly: the only working-class Glasgow seat held after 1964 was Cathcart, held by Teddy Taylor to 1979. Hillhead, lost in 1982, was not working-class. In contrast, Labour's links with Irish Catholic Glasgow-Celtic nationalism were not weakened. In 1989 the introduction of the Poll Tax, a year ahead of England and Wales, was particularly unpopular.

The general election of 1997, in which Labour won power in Westminster and the Conservatives won no Scottish or Welsh seats, led to a new departure in policy. The Blair government had such a powerful position in Parliament that it had no need to consider nationalist moves, but Labour had decided to support devolution, as a means, it hoped, to assuage nationalist sentiment. Devolution also sat easily with New Labour's drive to create a new Britain with modernised institutions and to replace what was seen as the over-centralised character of the British constitution and government. Referenda in September 1997 resulted in the establishment in 1998 of an Assembly in Cardiff and a Parliament in Edinburgh, with the latter wielding powers of taxation. The outcome of the referenda revealed the different degrees of support which devolution continued to enjoy: whereas only 50.3 per cent of those who voted backed it in Wales, 74.9 per cent did so in Scotland.

It is unclear whether this will be a lasting solution, or a half-way house to the independence sought by nationalists. In May 2011, the SNP, which had run the Scottish administration since 2007, won a majority for the first time in the elections to the Scottish Parliament and they have promised a referendum on independence. Public opinion polls in Scotland that briefly gave a majority for such an option in 2008 returned this verdict anew in 2011. The referendum is anticipated for 2014.

Sovereignty is only a zero-sum game in nineteenth-century power politics, and an independent Scotland could seek to be like Ireland or Estonia. However constrained by the federalism of the EU and by multinationals, independence would represent a major change. An independent Scotland would not have to search for a sense of identity as the changes since the 1990s are very marked. Nevertheless, opposition both to England and to the notion of Britain would not prevent divisions within Scotland from being more apparent. Moreover, whilst aware of the extent and role of regional economic differences, many commentators fail to consider adequately the nature of the regional political and cultural experience. Alongside the vitality of Scotland and the Scots, there are also tremendous differences between Strathclyde and Shetland, or between Ayr and Aberdeen, although they are much less prevalent now than in the 1970s. Politicians and others will need to work with the nation's diversity in mapping out the future for Scotland, which increasingly seems like an independent country.

MODERN WALES

Wales has seen major social changes in recent decades, not least the growth of a white-collar workforce for whom traditional loyalties had scant interest. This was a workforce living not in the valleys but on the north and south coasts and in the Cardiff urban region. Expansion in service industries and, in particular, in administrative agencies based in Cardiff (declared capital of Wales by Parliament in 1955) created much new employment, as did investment, especially from Japan, in new industrial plants. These were concentrated in south Wales, the economic importance of which was boosted by a new proximity to markets, thanks to the opening of the Severn Bridge (which had been called for since the 1930s) and the extension of the M4 motorway into south Wales. A new geography of wealth and employment greatly favoured Cardiff and, to a lesser extent, Bridgend, Newport, Swansea and Wrexham. Conversely, coal and steel were badly hit. The expansion of the late 1940s, in particular in the Port Talbot steelworks opened in 1951, was succeeded by closures and massive layoffs. Despite the cushioning of social security, economic problems had a serious impact on the social framework.

The profound geographical differences that have always characterised Wales and that economic growth made even more central still have important cultural and political resonances. The creation of the Welsh Assembly provided a new occasion for the voicing of regional anxieties within Wales. However much lessened by all-Welsh preoccupations with Nonconformity and rugby football, such regional differences are particularly apparent in Wales because of the language issue and everything that that represents and can be made to symbolise. Thanks to language, some of the Welsh are, at least in this respect, far more distinct from the English than are the vast majority of Scots; but, equally, the Welsh as a whole are less interested in independence than are the Scots.

SUMMARY

Britain today experiences general world trends as well as those found in particular categories of countries. Under the first heading, the most prominent are environmental change and a rapid rise in population. Global warming is the most significant instance of the former and has been linked to alterations in the British climate in recent decades. These include hotter summers and more stormy winters. The population rise also impacts on the environment, notably with serious pressure on the availability of drinking water and with demands for energy, building land, and food. The net effects are the more intensive practice of use of existing resources, notably land, as well as related changes in land use. Population and resource pressure accentuates strain on facilities and institutions, and makes it harder to reconcile competing interests. The resulting problems for society and government are considerable, with the social fabric under strain.

Government faces the repeated unwillingness of many people to accept the constraints of living in a complex and volatile society where expectations of living standards and styles are often highly unrealistic. These are general problems, accentuated by a commitment in both law and popular perception to what are claimed to be Human Rights. The latter have been given legal form with the Human Rights Act of 1998 which incorporated the European Convention on Human Rights in domestic law. Britain also faces the particular problems stemming from industrial decline, the rise of powerful competitive economies, the legacy of past imperial activity, mass immigration, and the heavy governmental and individual indebtedness arising from the widespread failure to adopt prudent expenditure patterns and to manage borrowing. These problems are especially characteristic of western Europe, and here Britain is also confronted by the specific flaws of the European Union as well as by the mismatch between the federalist aspirations of the latter and the national, democratic assumptions of the bulk of the British population. Thus, to many, the European Union appears not only not the solution, but also part of the problem.

This response is an important instance of the extent to which there are more specific issues relating to Britain, not least the question of how it responds to problems also found elsewhere. The strains of the political system, notably the issue of relations within the British Isles, are significant. So also is the legacy of assumptions about how society should be organised. These assumptions focus on an unstable relationship between the rights and entitlements claimed by individuals and the belief that someone else should provide. This relationship has played a powerful part in the spending of the future that is central to borrowing patterns and the use of resources. In many spheres, this relationship compromises the possibility of a rational solution, or, looked at from a different angle, the rationality of any solution is expressed in contentious and divisive political platforms and social demands.

The difficulties of governance have also contributed to the sense of decline or at least uncertainty that is widely felt. This uncertainty was made more pressing by the large-scale rioting in England in August 2011. Confidence in cohesion and society was badly shaken, and the appearance of anarchy in London, Manchester, Birmingham and a number of other cities was driven home across the country by the sustained nature of television coverage. The resulting controversy over the causes of, and response to, the disturbances laid bare real anxieties over social trends, notably the extent, alienation and potential violence of what was seen as an underclass and its grounding in moral, social and cultural chaos.

More generally, over a longer time span, successive attempts from across the political spectrum to fire up confidence, if not enthusiasm, have had only limited success over the last quarter-century. The net impression is of an often fretful public in a somewhat tired country. This situation is a challenge, one of individual responsibility, public awareness and collective action, to which an understanding of our situation in the continuum of national history will contribute significantly.

10
. . . .
Conclusions

History is like travel. To go back in the past and then to return is to have seen different countries, other ways of doing things, various values. The traveller might not have the time or resources to appreciate fully what he or she is seeing, but is nevertheless made aware of variety and change. To travel today is to be made aware of some of the strengths and weaknesses of the British Isles and its inhabitants. Reviewing the history of the British Isles, it is possible to conclude by stressing continuity, and to emphasise a constant expression of a deep sense of history, an organic, close-knit society, capable of self-renewal, and the rooted strength of institutions and culture. The British certainly have a genius for the appearance of continuity, but the manufacture of traditions often masks shifts in the character of power.

It is also possible to stress the role of chance. The relative stability of Britain in the twentieth century was due not only to deep-lying forces and trends, but also to victory in both world wars. Most European countries were defeated and occupied, with the accompanying strains. Many right-wing political groupings were contaminated, or at least stained, by collaboration; their left-wing counterparts compromised, or at least affected, by the rise of Communism. In contrast, in Britain (with the exception of the Channel Islands in 1940–5), as in Ireland, there was no foreign invasion, and no seizure of power by undemocratic forces from left or right.

Similarly, in the longer term, it was far from inevitable that Britain would survive French invasion attempts in the eighteenth century and the Napoleonic period. There have also been domestic crises whose peaceful resolution was far from inevitable, as well as civil conflicts whose outcome was far from certain to contemporaries. The result of the conflicts involving John and Henry III, the mid-seventeenth-century civil wars, and the Jacobite rising in 1745–6 are obvious examples.

While stressing chance, it is also necessary to draw attention to those in the past who were unsuccessful. British society can be presented as both organic and divided. The Glorious Revolution of 1688, for example, plays a role in the British public myth, but many, particularly in Ireland, were not comprehended within the Whig consensus, and both the Revolution Settlement and the Hanoverian regime were only established by force. Moreover, for all their talk about being the natural party of government in Britain, only thrice in the twentieth century (the Conservatives and their allies in 1900, 1931, and 1935) did either the Labour or the Conservative Party gain more than 50 per cent of the popular vote, and the British political system does not favour one party gaining this figure. Conversely, the confused response after the election of 2010 to the Conservative–Liberal Democrat coalition government, which did have such a majority, reflected a degree of lack of understanding and support for such an outcome.

Aside from the variety of opinions that have been held in and about the past, deterministic approaches to the past are suspect, and it is necessary to qualify any emphasis on patterns, whether or not they are presented as inevitable, by stressing the role of chance and contingency. This emphasis is directly relevant today. It is unclear whether the changes currently discussed or in prospect mean the collapse of Britain, or whether the proposed reconfigurations within the British Isles and Europe amount to a necessary modernisation that is appropriate to the demands of the twentieth-first century and, specifically, to the challenges posed by Irish, Scottish and Welsh nationalism and by globalisation. Not only the sovereignty and cohesion of the United Kingdom, but also the character of England, are being recast – or is it destroyed? – in the name of modernity.

Readers will have their own views. This book has been all about change, but to claim that traditions have been, are, and can be moulded, even created, is not the same as suggesting that they are without value. Nor is it the case that this process of moulding and creation necessarily justifies the replacement of the existing practices and ideas that give people a sense of continuity, identity and value. Although Queen Victoria died in 1901, much of the Victorian world, not least many social assumptions, persisted, despite the impact of two world wars, as well as the Modernism of the early decades of the twentieth century, but it was blown apart in the social revolution of the 1960s. The consequences of this collapse are still being felt and come to terms with, and this situation accentuates the difficulties of searching for any widely held new (or old) basis for national identity. Although Britishness has continually been defined and redefined, the destruction, or weakening, from the 1970s, of traditional and, until then, still vital benchmarks of national identity – Parliamentary sovereignty, national independence, the monarchy, the established churches and, arguably, a culture of liberal viable alternatives to governmental control – have all made national identity less clear and more fragile. As a consequence, it became harder for politicians from across the spectrum at the British level to define and advance convincing accounts of the national interest.

To conclude on a note of uncertainty and dissolution is not to offer the 'upbeat' summary of national achievements and character that popular historical works frequently proffer. Such a conclusion, however, would be inappropriate, an insult to readers well aware that we are all in a period of unprecedented flux. An historian, moreover, can offer a warning. Any reading of the past leads to an understanding that change is unpredictable, the promises of politicians discarded, and the hopes of future benefit often facile. It is all too easy for the sake of alleged benefits to throw away our history, the sense of place and time that provides identity and helps maintain social values.

Selected Further Reading

The following is necessarily a selective list, concentrating on recent books. Other works and articles can be traced through the bibliographies in these books.

GENERAL WORKS

The Penguin Atlas of British and Irish History (2001).
T. Bartlett, *Ireland: A History* (2010).
T. M. Devine, *The Scottish Nation, 1700–2000* (1999).
B. J. Graham and L. J. Proudfoot, *Historical Geography of Ireland* (1993).
P. Jenkins, *A History of Modern Wales, 1536–1990* (1992).
H. Jewell, *The North–South Divide: The Origins of Northern Consciousness* (1994).
C. Jones (ed.), *A Short History of Parliament* (2009).
R. Kain and W. Ravenhill (eds), *The Historical Atlas of the South West* (1999).
H. Kearney, *The British Isles: A History of Four Nations* (1989).
M. Lynch, *Scotland: A New History* (1992).
M. Lynch (ed.), *The Oxford Companion to Scottish History* (2011).
N. J. G. Pounds, *The Culture of the English People* (1994).
F. Pryor, *The Birth of Modern Britain: A Journey into Britain's Archaeological Past, 1550 to the Present* (2011).
B. Short (ed.), *The English Rural Community* (1992).
D. Short (ed.), *An Historical Atlas of Hertfordshire* (2011).
I. G. Simmons, *An Environmental History of Great Britain* (2001).
T. C. Smout, *A History of the Scottish People, 1560–1830* (1990).
T. C. Smout, *Nature Contested: Environmental History in Scotland and Northern England since 1600* (2000).
K. Tiller and G. Darkes (eds), *An Historical Atlas of Oxfordshire* (2010).

BRITONS AND ROMANS

K. J. Edwards and I. B. M. Ralston (eds), *Scotland: Environment and Archaeology, 8000 BC–AD 1000* (1997).
B. Finlayson, *Wild Harvesters: The First People in Scotland* (1998).

R. Hingley, *Settlement and Sacrifice: The Later Prehistoric People of Scotland* (1998).

B. Jones and D. Mattingly, *An Atlas of Roman Britain* (1990).

G. Maxwell, *A Gathering of Eagles: Scenes from Roman Scotland* (1998).

P. Salway, *The Oxford Illustrated History of Roman Britain* (1993).

P. Ottaway, *Archaeology in British Towns: From the Emperor Claudius to the Black Death* (1992).

400–1066

E. Campbell, *Saints and Sea-Kings: The First Kingdom of the Scots* (1999).

S. Foot, *Aethelstan: The First King of England* (2011).

D. Griffiths, *Vikings of the Irish Sea* (2010).

H. Hamerow et al. (eds), *Oxford Handbook of Anglo-Saxon Archaeology* (2011).

D. Kirby, *The Earliest English Kings* (1990).

C. Lowe, *Angels, Fools and Tyrants: Britons and Anglo-Saxons in Southern Scotland* (1999).

O. Owen, *The Sea Road: A Viking Voyage through Scotland* (1999).

B. Smith (ed.), *Britain and Ireland, 900–1300: Insular Responses to Medieval European Change* (1999).

A. Woolf, *From Pictland to Alba* (2007).

MEDIEVAL BRITAIN

G. W. S. Barrow, *Robert Bruce and the Community of the Realm of Scotland* (1998).

R. H. Britnell, *The Commercialisation of English Society, 1000–1500* (1992).

A. D. Carr, *Medieval Wales* (1995).

E. J. Cowan and R. A. McDonald (eds), *Alba: Celtic Scotland in the Medieval Era* (2000).

A. Curry, *The Hundred Years War* (1993).

R. R. Davies, *The First English Empire: Power and Identities in the British Isles, 1093–1343* (1998).

C. Fletcher, *Richard II: Manhood, Youth and Politics, 1377–99* (2010).

B. Golding, *Conquest and Colonisation: The Normans in Britain, 1066–1100* (2nd edn, 2012).

M. Hicks, *The Wars of the Roses* (2010).

R. A. MacDonald, *The Kingdom of the Isles: Scotland's Western Seaboard, c. 1100–c. 1336* (1997).

W. M. Ormrod, *Political Life in Medieval England, 1300–1450* (1995).

M. Prestwich, *English Politics in the Thirteenth Century* (1990).

R. L. Storey, *The End of the House of Lancaster* (1999).

N. Vincent, *The Birth of the Nation: 1066–1485* (2012).

SIXTEENTH-CENTURY BRITAIN

G. Burgess, *British Political Thought, 1500–1660* (2009).

S. Doran, *England and Europe in the Sixteenth Century* (1998).

S. Gunn, *Early Tudor Government, 1485–1558* (1995).

R. Hutton, *The Rise and Fall of Merry England: The Ritual Year, 1400–1700* (1994).

R. Hutton, *The Tudor and Stuart Dynasties, 1485–1660* (2012).

S. Jack, *Towns in Tudor and Stuart Britain* (1996).

H. Jewell, *Education in Early Modern England* (1998).

J. G. Jones, *Early Modern Wales, c. 1525–1640* (1994).

D. Loades, *The Mid-Tudor Crisis, 1545–1565* (1992).

D. MacCulloch, *The Later Reformation in England, 1547–1603* (1990).

R. Rex, *Henry VIII and the English Reformation* (1992).

A. Walsham, *The Reformation of the Landscape: Religion, Identity and Memory in Early Modern Britain and Ireland* (2011).

I. Whyte, *Scotland's Scotland and Economy in Transition, c. 1500–c. 1760* (1997).

STUART AND INTERREGNUM BRITAIN

K. M. Brown, *Kingdom or Province? Scotland and the Regal Union, 1603–1715* (1992).

S. J. Connolly, *Divided Kingdom: Ireland, 1630–1800* (2010).

E. Cruickshanks, *The Glorious Revolution* (2000).

I. Gentles, *Oliver Cromwell* (2011).

A. Hughes, *The Causes of the English Civil War* (2nd edn, 1998).

R. Hutton, *The British Republic, 1649–1660* (2nd edn, 1999).

L. L. Knoppers (ed.), *The Cambridge Companion to Early Modern Women's Writing* (2009).

J. Raymond (ed.), *Cheap Print in Britain and Ireland to 1660* (2011).

J. Spurr, *English Puritanism, 1603–89* (1998).

M. Young, *Charles I* (1997).

1689–1815

J. Black, *Eighteenth-Century Britain* (2nd edn, 2008).

W. Gibson, *The Making of the Nation, 1660–1851* (2012).

R. Harding, *The Evolution of the Sailing Navy, 1509–1815* (1995).

R. A. Houston, *Social Change in the Age of Enlightenment: Edinburgh, 1660–1760* (1994).

J. Mokyr, *The Enlightened Economy: An Economic History of Britain, 1700–1850* (2009).

A. Murdoch, *British History, 1600–1832: National Identity and Local Culture* (1998).

M. Pittock, *Jacobitism* (1998).
C. A. Whatley, *Scottish Society, 1707–1830: Beyond Jacobitism, towards Industrialisation* (2000).

AGE OF REFORM AND EMPIRE, 1815–1914

R. Barker, *Politics, Peoples and Government: Themes in British Political Thought since the Nineteenth Century* (1994).
J. Belchem, *Popular Radicalism in Nineteenth-Century Britain* (1995).
E. Biagini, *Gladstone* (1999).
A. Bourke, *The Visitation of God? The Potato and the Great Irish Famine* (1993).
P. Buckner (ed.), *Canada and the British Empire* (2010).
J. Davis, *A History of Britain, 1885–1939* (1999).
S. Dentith, *Society and Cultural Forms in Nineteenth-Century England* (1999).
J. Garrard, *Democratisation in Britain: Elites, Civil Society and Reform since 1800* (2002).
T. A. Jenkins, *The Liberal Ascendancy, 1830–1886* (1994).
T. A. Jenkins, *Sir Robert Peel* (1999).
A. Kidd, *Society and the Poor in Nineteenth-Century England* (1999).
I. Machin, *The Rise of Democracy in Britain, 1830–1918* (2001).
J. McCaffrey, *Scotland in the Nineteenth Century* (1998).
A. McIvor, *A History of Work in Britain, 1880–1950* (2001).
H. McLeod, *Religion and Society in England, 1850–1914* (1996).
D. Schreuder and S. Ward (eds), *Australia's Empire* (2010).
G. R. Searle, *The Liberal Party: Triumph and Disintegration, 1886–1929* (1992).
W. D. Stephens, *Education in Britain, 1750–1914* (1999).
W. E. Vaughan (ed.), *Ireland Under the Union* (2011).

THE TWENTIETH CENTURY

C. J. Bartlett, *British Foreign Policy in the Twentieth Century* (1989).
J. Black, *Britain Since the Seventies* (2004).
D. G. Boyce, *The Irish Question and British Politics, 1868–1996* (2nd edn, 1996).
C. Brown, *Religion and Society in Twentieth-Century Britain* (2006).
S. Bruley, *Women in Britain since 1900* (1999).
D. Childs, *Britain since 1939* (2nd edn, 2002).
W. H. Fraser, *A History of British Trade Unionism, 1700–1998* (1999).
D. Gladstone, *The Twentieth-Century Welfare State* (1999).
H. Goulbourne, *Race Relations in Britain since 1945* (1998).
D. Harkness, *Ireland in the Twentieth Century* (1995).
B. Harrison, *Seeking a Role: The United Kingdom, 1951–1970* (2011).

B. Harrison, *Finding a Role? The United Kingdom, 1970–1990* (2011).

J. R. Hill (ed.), *Ireland, 1921–84* (2010).

D. Hirst, *Welfare and Society, 1832–1991* (1999).

I. G. C. Hutchison, *Scottish Politics in the Twentieth Century* (1999).

A. Jackson, *The Two Unions: Ireland, Scotland, and the Survival of the United Kingdom, 1707–2007* (2011).

K. Jefferys, *Retreat from New Jerusalem: British Politics, 1951–64* (1997).

R. McKibbin, *Parties and People: England, 1914–1951* (2011).

I. Packer, *Lloyd George* (1998).

M. Pittock, *The Road to Independence? Scotland Since the Sixties* (1986).

D. Powell, *The Edwardian Crisis: Britain, 1901–1914* (1996).

K. Robbins, *England, Ireland, Scotland, Wales: The Christian Church, 1900–2000* (2010).

N. Smart, *The National Government, 1931–40* (1999).

M. Thatcher, *The Downing Street Years* (1993).

A. Thorpe, *A History of the British Labour Party* (2nd edn, 2001).

N. L. Tranter, *British Population in the Twentieth Century* (1995).

I. Wood, *Churchill* (1999).

J. Young, *Britain and European Unity, 1945–1999* (2000).

Index

Note: Subheadings are usually arranged in chronological order.